WOMEN IN THE WESTERN

For my daughter Rebecca

WOMEN IN THE WESTERN

Edited by Sue Matheson

EDINBURGH
University Press

Edinburgh University Press is one of the leading university presses in the UK.
We publish academic books and journals in our selected subject areas across the
humanities and social sciences, combining cutting-edge scholarship with high editorial
and production values to produce academic works of lasting importance. For more
information visit our website: edinburghuniversitypress.com

© editorial matter and organization Sue Matheson, 2020, 2022
© the chapters their several authors, 2020, 2022

Edinburgh University Press Ltd
The Tun—Holyrood Road
12(2f) Jackson's Entry
Edinburgh EH8 8PJ

First published in hardback by Edinburgh University Press 2020

Typeset in 10/12.5 pt Sabon
by IDSUK (DataConnection) Ltd

A CIP record for this book is available from the British Library

ISBN 978 1 4744 4413 2 (hardback)
ISBN 978 1 4744 4414 9 (paperback)
ISBN 978 1 4744 4415 6 (webready PDF)
ISBN 978 1 4744 4416 3 (epub)

The right of Sue Matheson to be identifiedastheeditorofthisworkhasbeen
asserted in accordance with the Copyright, Designs and Patents Act 1988, and the
Copyright and Related Rights Regulations 2003 (SI No. 2498).

CONTENTS

Figures ix
Acknowledgments xi

    Introduction 1
    Sue Matheson

PART ONE   ROLES ON THE RANGE

1. Silent but Rowdy: Stuntwomen of the Early Frontier 11
   Cynthia J. Miller

2. Suffering Heroines on the Frontier—Melodrama and Pathos, 1914–39 27
   Sue Matheson

3. When East Goes West: The Loss of Dramatic Agency in DeMille's Western Women from the 1910s to the 1930s 45
   David Blanke

4. The Virginian and the Rose: Two Key Female Roles in Western Films and Comics 61
   David Huxley

5. Freud, "The Family on the Land," and the Feminine Turn in Post-war Westerns 75
   Gaylyn Studlar

6. Clytemnestra and Electra under Western Skies 91
   Martin M. Winkler

7. "Never seen a woman who was more of a man": Saloon Girls, Women Heroes, and Female Masculinity in the Western 107
   Christopher Minz

8. Gender Politics in the Revisionist Western: Interrogating the Perpetrator–Victim Binary in *The Missing* (Howard 2003) 121
   Fran Pheasant-Kelly

PART TWO WOMEN'S ISSUES IN POST-WAR, REVISIONIST, AND FEMINIST WESTERNS

9. Trading Places—Trading Races: The Cross-Cultural Assimilation of Women in *The Searchers* (1956) and *The Unforgiven* (1960) 141
   Kelly MacPhail

10. Western Nostalgia, Revisionism, and Native American Women in *Wind River* (2017) 159
    Robert Spindler

11. Mostly Whores with a (Very) Few Angels: Asian Women in the Western 173
    Vincent Piturro

12. "We been haunted a long time"—Raped Women in Westerns 187
    Maria Cecília de Miranda N. Coelho

13. "My body for a hand of poker": *The Belle Starr Story* in Its Contexts 201
    Erin Lee Mock

14. The Female Avenger in Post-9/11 Westerns 223
    Martin Holtz

15. You've Got Something: Female Agency in *Justified* 243
    Paul Zinder

16. Eastward the Women: Remapping Women's Journeys in Tommy Lee Jones's *The Homesman* (2014) 257
    J Paul Johnson

17. Women Gotta Gun? Iconography and Female Representation in *Godless* 271
    Stella Hockenhull

18. Wagon Mistress 287
    Andrew Patrick Nelson

PART THREE   FILMOGRAPHY AND BIBLIOGRAPHIES

19. Women in the Western Filmography and Bibliography 303
    Camille McCutcheon

Contributors 335
Index 341

FIGURES

1.1	Eileen Sedgwick as gun-slinging Nan Madden in *The Riddle Rider* (1924)	12
2.1	Lucy Mallory (Louise Platt) is unaware that she is being saved from a Fate Worse Than Death in *Stagecoach* (1939)	35
4.1	Fawcett Movie comic no. 17, 1952. A photo cover underlines the connection to the film	70
4.2	Fawcett Movie comic no. 17, 1952. Rose guns down her enemies	71
5.1	The realization of love in death throes: Pearl (Jennifer Jones) and Lewt (Gregory Peck) in *Duel in the Sun* (1946)	81
5.2	Learning she is disinherited, Vance Jeffords (Barbara Stanwyck) prepares to throw a pair of scissors at her father's fiancée (Judith Anderson) in *The Furies* (1950)	85
6.1	A furious Vance in *The Furies* (1950)	93
6.2	Hidden family dynamics are becoming clear in *The Violent Men* (1955)	96
9.1	The closing shot of *The Searchers* (1956) excludes Ethan from the domestic sphere and returns him to the rugged landscape where he belongs	143
9.2	During the climactic battle scene, Rachel faces a crisis of identity upon finally meeting Lost Bird, her presumptive brother in *The Unforgiven* (1960)	149
10.1	Celluloid princess or sexualized maiden? Kelsey Asbille as Natalie Hanson in *Wind River* (2017)	160

11.1 Thomas Hayden Church and Gwendoline Yeo in *Broken Trails*   178
13.1 Elsa Martinelli is Belle Starr in *The Belle Starr Story/Il mio corpo per un poker* (Lina Wertmüller, 1968)   209
15.1 Ava Crowder (Joelle Carter) alternates between an archetypical Western power figure and a stereotypical female submissive throughout the course of the series   249
16.1 Hilary Swank as Mary Bee Cuddy and Tommy Lee Jones as George Briggs form an unlikely bond in *The Homesman* (2014)   258
18.1 Mrs Tetherow (Michelle Williams) takes up arms against Stephen Meek (Bruce Greenwood) in *Meek's Cutoff* (2010)   292

ACKNOWLEDGMENTS

This collection is the work of many people interested in women and the Western. First, many, many thanks to the writers for their intellectual work, their perseverance, and their grit. This volume, *Women in the Western*, took more time than was expected. A huge thank you also goes out to Gillian Leslie for her enthusiasm and support of this project. I cannot thank Gillian and her colleagues Richard Strachan and Eliza Wright (from Edinburgh University Press) enough. It was a joy to work with them. I learned so much from their expert guidance, heartening encouragement, and endless patience.

I have a big shout-out of thanks for my Vice President Academic/Research at the University College of the North, Dan Smith, who gave me the time, encouragement, and support that I needed to get my work done, and for my Dean Harvey Briggs, who cleared the way so I could have the time (and materials) to edit this book.

As well, I am indebted to those interested in the Western, who encouraged my work and helped me retain my sense of humor. I also wish to thank Kathy Merlock-Jackson for her support and understanding of my work throughout this project and Ray Merlock and Gary Hoppenstand for their continued enthusiasm and encouragement regarding my writing.

I have yet another huge thank you for my son Stuart, whose insights and reactions while I was researching and writing about women and the Western have been invaluable, and for my daughter Rebecca, to whom this collection is dedicated. I could not have completed this project without them.

INTRODUCTION

Sue Matheson

She is essential: as Anthony Mann has pointed out, without a woman, a Western wouldn't work (Cook, in Kitses and Rickman 1998: 293). Since Edwin S. Porter's *The Great Train Robbery* (1902), women have populated the Western—among them, a telegraph operator's daughter and train passengers, sagehens and soiled doves, cowgirls and army wives, outlaw queens and school marms, ministers amd madams, cattle queens and saloon keepers, doctors and lawyers, mail-order brides and barmaids, nuns and temperance workers, homesteaders and Indian princesses, boarding house matrons and respectable "widders." Standout female characters in horse operas include Helen Holmes, Annie Oakley, Frenchy, Dallas, Lucy Mallory, Abbie Irving, Elizabeth Bacon, Clementine Carter, Tess Millay, Calamity Jane, Rio MacDonald, Oliva Dainridge, Abbie Allshard, Helen Ramirez, Amy Fowler Kane, Annie Greer, Denver, Sister Ledyard, Sierra Nevada Jones, Mrs. Jorgenson, Fifi Danon, Kathleen Yorke, Vienna, Pearl Chauvez, Vance Jeffords, Cat Ballou, Kitty Russell, Hannie Caulder, Mattie Ross, Constance Miller, Jill McBrain, Hallie Stoddard, Victoria Barkley, Belle Starr, Josephine Monaghan, Lorena Wood, Ada Munroe, Magdelena Gilkeson, Alma Garrett, Juliette Flowers, Mary Bee Cuddy, and Jane Hammond.

These women (like all women in Westerns) transmit complicated cultural coding about the nature of westward expansionism, heroism, family life, manliness, and femininity. To date, however, scholarship about the Western's gender relations (and expectations) has been primarily concerned with issues of masculinity, masculine desire, and masculine display. Oddly, when critical attention has been directed to issues of femininity, feminine desire, and feminine display, the conversation has usually returned to the topic of the Western hero. Consider John Cawelti's revealing remarks about the Western's approach to gender typing in *The Six-Gun Mystique Sequel*. Lamenting the limitations of the genre's gender roles, Cawelti remarks there are only two kinds of women in the Western—blondes and brunettes. According to Cawelti, these types reflect the dual nature of . . . the male hero (1999: 30). Symbolizing a more "full blooded, passionate and spontaneous nature" (1999: 31), "[t]he dark girl" is "a feminine embodiment of the hero's savage, spontaneous side. She understands [the hero's] . . . deep passions, his savage code of honor and his need to use personal violence." On the other hand, the [blonde] school marm, whom Cawelti says represents "genteel, pure femininity," functions like a superego in a Western psychomachea, rejecting the passionate urges and and the freedom and aggressiveness that mark this side of the hero's character: "[w]hen the hero becomes involved with her, the dark woman must be destroyed or abandoned" (1999: 31). For Cawelti, the Western is (among other things) a sexist epic (1999: 11), a male preserve: its hero archetype, the cowboy; its central group and vital relationships, male; its women, embodiments of the genre's masculine psychomachea.

Jane Tompkins also asserts the Western is "fare for men," because manhood in this genre is "*the* ideal, certainly the only one worth dying for" (1992: 17, 18). In *West of Everything*, she observes that Westerns carry "compacted worlds of meaning and value, codes of conduct, standards of judgment, and habits of perception that shape our sense of the world and govern our behavior" (1992: 6). "Women," she says "regularly identify across gender lines" when "engaged" by Westerns, and are forced to look at women from the point of view of men (1992: 17). "[S]imultaneously attracted and repelled by the power of Western heroes, the power that men in our society wield" (1992: 6), she finds that the Western transmits "[t]he whole soul of man." Then, astoundingly, thirteen pages later, she halts and asks the question "'Man?' What about woman?" (1992: 15).

It is an excellent question. To date, no collection of Western scholarship has been devoted exclusively to the nature and development of women characters in the Hollywood West. Consisting of eighteen articles, a selected filmography, and two selected bibliographies, *Women in the Western* offers a variety of approaches on selected topics and significant shifts in Hollywood's transmission of American gender values and expectations regarding under-studied aspects of women in the Western. Here it should be noted that the analyses found in *Women in the Western* divide themselves into two sections: "Roles on the Range" houses chapters that chart the increasing complexity of Western women as the Western develops as a genre; "Women's Issues in Post-war, Revisionist, and Feminist Westerns" contains chapters which investigate race and gender politics, matters of rape and revenge figures, and the ongoing problem of female agency in the Western. Each chapter demonstrates how women in Westerns refract changes for women that take place in the American zeitgeist of the twentieth and twenty-first centuries and considers the longevity of gender stereotypes as well as the assimilation of new ideas and ideologies into America's cultural mileu.

"Roles on the Range" begins with the daring roles that the early Western offered female actors. Cynthia J. Miller s "Silent but Rowdy: Stuntwomen of the Early Frontier" examines female characters, who laid claim to the skills and iconic qualities generally attributed to their male counterparts in silent-era serials and silent feature films. Miller's in-depth look at rowdy women during the birth of the Western establishes how the genre housed a broader and more complex range of roles for women than that found in many other genres during the silent era, and contributed to the "quiet revolution" that would change women's roles in society, as well as on screen, while setting the stage for the depth and diversity of genre's female characters in the mid-twentieth century. Sue Matheson's "Suffering Heroines on the Frontier—Melodrama and Pathos, 1914–39" returns the volume's discussion to roles considered conventional for the Western's leading ladies. In this chapter, Matheson looks at the Victorian constructions of women in the Western: the genre's suffering heroines, the indispensable pathos they generate, and their remarkable (and lasting) makeovers as working women in 1939. David Blanke's "When East Goes West: The Loss of Dramatic Agency in DeMille's Western Women from the 1910s to the 1930s" then examines the impact of strong women characters on the career of one of Hollywood's most influential women's directors. As Blanke points out, without the Western's women, Cecil B. DeMille would never have become "DeMille."[1] In this chapter, Blanke investigates the complexity of women's roles in the Western, demonstrating how the genre and strong female performances were critical to DeMille's initial success in the 1910s, and vital to the director's mid-career professional revival in the mid-1930s, during which the loss of dramatic agency in the representation of women took place. Bridging the gender gap between early and post-war Westerns, David Huxley's study, "The Virginian and the Rose: Two Key Female Roles in Western Films and Comics" also concentrates on the changing roles of women in the genre. He points out the ways in which female characters are not restricted to domestic roles in Owen Wister's 1903 *The Virginian* and its film adaptations and Harry Keller's *The Rose of Cimarron*, a 1952 Twentieth Century Fox production.

The next three chapters in "Roles on the Range" discuss the American Western's post-war engagement with the ideas of Sigmund Freud that helped generate psychologically complicated female characters in frontier melodramas. The oater's fusion with Freud created strong, sophisticated, and controversial leading ladies in "adult" Westerns in their treatments of the darker side of women's sexual desires and their family lives via *film noir*'s *femme fatale*. Considering *noir*-affiliated characterizations of women in King Vidor's *Duel in the Sun* (1946) and Raoul Walsh's *Pursued* (1947), Gaylyn Studlar's "Freud, 'The Family on the Land,' and the Feminine Turn in Postwar Westerns" demonstrates how family-on-the-land Westerns elevated the importance of women, emphasising the home as a site "of sexual secrets and emotional upheaval while offering "defiant daughters, delinquent sons, sexualized matriarchs and flawed, overreaching patriarchs involved in intergenerational conflict" (2020: 76). Next, Martin M. Winkler's "Clytemnestra and Electra under Western Skies" interrogates the function of revenge, the Electra Complex (as it is commonly understood), and complicated, conflicted portrayals of women in Anthony Mann's epic-tragic *noir* family drama, *The Furies* (1950). In "'Never seen a woman who was more of a man': Saloon Girls, Women Heroes, and Female Masculinity in the Western," Christopher Minz argues compellingly that the Western has never been specifically about men. Revisiting Nicholas Ray's cult classic *Johnny Guitar* (1956) and Roger Corman's *Gunslinger* (1956), Minz observes there has always been an unconscious masculinity in the aesthetic and narrative aspects of the genre, particularly in its portrayals of strong women. Then, Fran Pheasant-Kelly's "Gender Politics in the Revisionist Western: Interrogating the Perpetrator-Victim Binary in *The Missing* (Howard 2003)" considers how *The Missing*'s gender and racial coding reframes the classic Western's traditional model of the savage "Indian" and woman as helpless victim. Pheasant-Kelly observes that this twenty-first century feminist Western presents a more realistic representation of women than is usual for the genre.

Since the release of James Youngdeer's "White Fawn's Devotion: A Play Acted by a Tribe of Red Indians in America" (1910), miscegenation has been a controversial element of the American Western. The second section of *Women in the Western*, "Women's Issues in Post-war, Revisionist, and Feminist Westerns" begins with chapters that examine film narratives driven by race-mixing and racial stereotypes. Tracing racial and gender coding back to Cynthia Ann Parker's influential captivity narrative,[2] Kelly MacPhail's "Trading Places—Trading Races: The Cross-Cultural Assimilation of Women in *The Searchers* (1956) and *The Unforgiven* (1960)" considers the controversial subject of women assimilated across cultures and ethnic groups in the cinematic adaptations of Alan LeMay's *The Searchers* (1954) and *The Unforgiven* (1957). According to MacPhail, directors John Ford and John Huston challenge essentialist suppositions of gender and cultural identity, as well as notions of power based in ideas about racial superiority in these films. Robert Spindler's "Western Nostalgia, Revisionism, and Native American Women in *Wind River* (2017)" then considers prototypes of the Celluloid Indian Maiden before arguing that Taylor Sheridan's *Wind River* (2017) continues this design despite its revisionist stance.

After establishing the prominence of Asians in the historical West, Vincent Piturro's "Mostly Whores with a (Very) Few Angels: Asian Women in the Western" investigates the absence of roles for Asian women in Hollywood's West. Piturro first examines the singular representation of Chinese women as whores in the Western via Robert Altman's *McCabe and Mrs. Miller* (1971) and Walter Hill's *Broken Trail* (AMC, 2006), then compares these depictions with representations of women in Asian Westerns like Akira Kurosawa's *Yojimbo* (1961) and Takashi Miike's *Sukiyaki Western Django* (2007).

Remarkably, the Western was one of the first American film genres after the Second World War to probe the nature of rape culture. Maria Cecília de Miranda Nogueira Coelho's "'We been haunted a long time': Raped Women in Westerns" traces representations of rape in rape-revenge stories from the Greek classics and Shakespeare's *Titus Andronicus* to post-war Westerns via analyses of *Sergeant Rutledge* (Ford, 1960), *Duel in the Sun* (Vidor, 1946), *The Searchers* (Ford, 1956), *Man of West* (Mann, 1958), *The Bravados* (King, 1958), *For a Few Dollars More* (Leone, 1965), *Hang 'em High* (Post, 1968), *Cemetery Without Crosses* (Hossein, 1969) and *The Ballad of Little Jo* (Greenwald, 1993). Following Erin Lee Mock's "'My body for a hand of poker': *The Belle Starr Story* in Its Contexts" moves from cause to effect. Mock observes *The Belle Starr Story*, the only Spaghetti Western that features a female protagonist, borrows tropes from exploitation cinema to smuggle a "female rape-revenge" plot into the male-dominated subgenre. Contending that Lina Wertmüller's revision of the Western's traumatized gunfighter validates women's experiences of trauma in *The Belle Star Story*, Mock assesses radical revisions of female subjectivity, examining the bandit queen and Wertmüller's deviations from the heroine's historical and generic record. Next, in "The Female Avenger in Post-9/11 Westerns," Martin Holtz considers how rape-revenge and the figure of the female avenger act as ideological barometers in three post-9/11 Westerns: *The Missing* (2003), *Bandidas* (2006), and *True Grit* (2011).

Throughout the Western, the conflicted question of agency for women is often addressed but seldom resolved—even in revisionist and feminist Westerns. As Paul Zinder's "You've Got Something: Female Agency in *Justified*" demonstrates, the story arcs of powerful female criminal masterminds—Mags Bennett, Katherine Hale, Winona Givens, and Ava Crowder—support the efficacy of men in this popular televised series. Following this, J Paul Johnson's "Eastward the Women: Remapping Women's Journeys in Tommy Lee Jones's *The Homesman* (2014)" considers Tommy Lee Jones's feminist Western's attempts to revise traditional expectations of the genre by highlighting the frontier's debilitating conditions and emphasizing the resolute character and strength of its female lead, while rending mute the women to whom it aims to give voice. In "Women Gotta Gun? Iconography and Female Representation in *Godless*," Stella Hockenhull determines that, despite its masculinized female characters and the predominance of women, *Godless* (Netflix 2017) retains the tradition of a male hierarchical figure in which violence rules, and its women ultimately conform to being feminine stereotypes. Finally, Andrew Patrick Nelson's "Wagon Mistress" argues that Kelly Reichardt's feminist Western *Meek's Cutoff* (2010) does not simply revise its portrayal of Western women according to contemporary sensibilities, which is the usual approach for feminist Westerns. According to Nelson, Reichardt's film, which shows in detail "women's work" that is not seen in many Western narratives, aligns the audience's experience of the film's events with its three female characters. *Meek's Cutoff*, he says, is a feminist intervention into the Western, because the film is not only a matter of what we see, but also how we see it.

Women in the Western does not claim to be a comprehensive work on the subject of women in Westerns. Indeed, the scope of the critical work that remains outstanding on women in the Western is so immense that it could easily fill volume after collected volume. For example, for reasons of space, chapters dealing with portrayals of women in Westerns filmed to support the American war effort during the Second World War could not be housed here. In Raoul Walsh's well-regarded recruiting film, *They Died With Their Boots On* (1941), Libby Custer (Olivia de Havilland) courageously furthers her husband's army career and accepts his "sacrifice" at Little Big Horn. Female characters in B-Westerns also supported the war effort on America's home front. John English's *Raiders of Sunset Pass* (1943), S. Roy Luby's *Black Market Rustlers* (1943), Sam Newfield's *Wild Horse Rustlers* (1943), Benjamin Kline's *Sundown Valley* (1944), and Elmer Clifton's *Gangsters of the Frontier* (1944) all contain cowgirl versions of "Rosie the Riveter." As Phil Loy points out in "Soldiers in Stetsons: B-Westerns Go to War," these tough, competent female characters (and others like them in B-Westerns during the Second World War) call for more critical attention.

Like the women in the war-effort Westerns, women in Western comedies also call for their own volume (or volumes)—especially those appearing in films like George Sherman's *Feudin', Fussin and A-Fightin* (1948), Norman Z. Mcleod's *The Pale Face* (1948), Preston Sturges's *The Beautiful Blonde from Bashful Bend* (1949), Richard Sale's *A Ticket to Tomahawk* (1950), George Sidney's *Annie Get Your Gun* (1950), R. G. Springsteen's *Oklahoma Annie* (1952), David Butler's *Calamity Jane* (1953), Raoul Walsh's *The King and Four Queens* (1956), George Cukor's *Heller in Pink Tights* (1960), John Sturges's *The Hallelujah Trail* (1965), Elliot Silverstein's *Cat Ballou* (1965), William Graham's *Waterhole #3* (1967), Burt Kennedy's *Support Your Local Sheriff* (1969), Gene Kelly's *The Cheyenne Social Club* (1970), Anton Leader and Ranald MacDougall's *The Cockeyed Cowboys of Calico County* (1970), Paul Bartel's *Lust in the Dust* (1984), Richard Donner's *Maverick* (1994), Joachim Rønning and Espen Sandberg's *Banditas* (2006), William Phillips's

Gunless (2010), and Gore Verbinski's *Rango* (2011). As well, the diverse and powerful female characters of the professional Western deserve more critical attention than this collection is able to provide. From Chiquita (Claudia Cardinale) in Richard Brooks's *The Professionals* (1966) to Josephine MacDonald (Michele Carey) in Howard Hawks's *El Dorado* (1967) to Mattie Ross in Henry Hathaway's *True Grit* (1969) to Teresa (Sonia Amelio) in Sam Peckinpah's *The Wild Bunch* (1969) to Mrs. Lowe (Ann-Margaret) in Burt Kennedy's *The Train Robbers* (1973) to Jill McBain (Claudia Cardinale) in Sergio Leone's *Once Upon a Time in the West* (1968) to Jean-Claude La Marre's *Gang of Roses* (2003), portrayals of women in professional Westerns not only challenge women's advertised roles, they also challenge what the proponents of the second wave of American feminism have had to say about them.

In short, the largely unexamined roles of women in the overwhelming numbers of Westerns produced on film and television, before and after the Second World War and the appearance of the "feminist Western" offer new frontiers for the genre's scholars and general audiences. Designed to generate further discussion about women in the Western, *Women in the Western* concludes with Camille McCutcheon's Selective, Representative Filmography of Female-Led US Westerns; Selective, Representative Bibliography of Resources on Women in the Western; and Selective, Representative Bibliography of Resources on Women in the Nineteenth-Century US West. It is hoped that these excellent resources will encourage further viewing of women-led Westerns, more reading about women in Western films and the historical West, and more scholarship about women in the Western. To have been considered for inclusion in the filmography, films must have been set in the American West, have been included in the American Film Institute (AFI) Catalog of Feature Films, and feature female actor(s) in a prominent role or roles. As well, the principle female actor must have received first or second billing.

Because lingering Victorian stereotypes and twentieth-century gender politics make women in the Western reliable markers of cultural change in Amerca's gender politics, refracting our actual gender values rather than presenting them as how we wish them to be, I continue to ask (like Tompkins in 1992) when watching Westerns, what about women? Has the status of women in American culture really undergone change—or is the improved status of women in America a convenient fiction put forward that my daughter and her generation will have to debunk? It is my hope that *Women in the Western* will prompt others to ask, "What about women?" off screen, while acting as a staging point for travelers who wish to journey West. I look forward to the conversations that *Women in the Western* will generate and hope that opportunities for further study will continue as long as more Westerns are made.

Notes

1. For more on DeMille's extended career and reputation among Hollywood's classical era directors, see David Blanke's *Cecil B. DeMille, Classical Hollywood, and Modern American Mass Culture, 1910–1960* (New York: Palgrave Macmillan, 2018).
2. Arguably, the most famous Indian captive in American history, Cynthia Ann Parker was born in Illinois around 1827. She moved to Texas with her family in 1833. The Parkers helped build Fort Parker in what is now Limestone County. In 1836, the Comanche attacked the fort. At the age of nine, Parker was taken captive and spent the next twenty-four years with the Indians. She married Peta Nocona, with whom she had two sons and a daughter. In 1860, Texas Rangers and federal soldiers rescued her (and her infant daughter) during an attack on a Comanche encampment in north Texas. Reunited with her natural family whom she did not remember, she was unable to assimilate successfully a second time. She died in 1871 and was buried in Anderson County in East Texas. Her son, Quanah Parker, became the most important Comanche leader of his day, representing southwest indigenous Americans to the United States legislature.

Bibliography

Cawelti, John G. (1999) *The Six-Gun Mystique Sequel*. Bowling Green, OH: Popular Press.

Cook, Pam (1998) "Women in the Western," in Jim Kitses and Gregg Rickman (eds), *The Western Reader*. New York: Limelight, pp. 293–300.

Loy, Phil (2003) "Soldiers in Stetsons: B-Westerns Go to War," *Journal of Popular Film and Television*, 30, pp. 197–205.

Studlar, Gaylyn (2020) "Freud, 'the Family on the Land,' and the Feminine Turn in Postwar Westerns," in Sue Matheson (ed.), *Women in the Western*. Edinburgh: Edinburgh Press, pp. 75–89.

Tompkins, Jane (1992) *West of Everything: The Inner Life of Westerns*. Oxford: Oxford University Press.

PART ONE

ROLES ON THE RANGE

1. SILENT BUT ROWDY: STUNTWOMEN OF THE EARLY FRONTIER

Cynthia J. Miller

Our popular understandings of the women of the frontier are often one-part fact, two-parts myth, thanks to the romantic portrayals found in literature and film. Motion pictures, in particular, have conveyed vivid, engaging images of the women of the West that liberally intermingled fact and fiction as they wove tales of heroism and harmony. Archetypes such as the rancher's daughter, the schoolmarm, the soiled dove, and the female gunslinger filled the big screen for generations, each adding to the legend of the North American West—a legend that, despite decades of revisionist challenge, still retains a place in American national identity today.

Rowdy women of the silent West laid claim to the skills and iconic qualities generally attributed to their male counterparts, while retaining the emotional range of roles written for women. This, however, may not be the most significant contribution made by the stuntwomen of early Westerns. The presence (and proliferation) of stars like Helen Gibson, Helen Holmes, Fay Tincher, and Texas Guinan signaled an expansion of character types offered to women, creating a broader and more complex range of roles than could be found in many other genres during the silent era—and with that expansion, greater employment opportunities for female actors who may not have been considered otherwise appropriate for featured roles.

While much has been written about portrayals of frontier women in film from the 1930s onward, women of the silent film era have received less consideration. Although, as Ron Lackmann notes, the majority of women featured

Figure 1.1   Eileen Sedgwick as gun-slinging Nan Madden in *The Riddle Rider* (1924).

in silent-era Westerns portrayed "respectable, and hard-working citizens" who carried out their designated gender roles with glamour and grace, a closer look at silent Westerns complicates this picture (1997: 147). Unconventional female characters were the subject of many silent-era serials, such as *What Happened to Mary* (1914) and *The Vanishing Rider* (1928), as well as early silent feature films such as *Rowdy Ann* (1919). These characters rode, raced, roped, and wrassled in the same cinematic contexts as their more domestic counterparts, challenging traditional binaries typically attributed to gender roles on the frontier. Ron Lackmann, in fact, identifies some sixty silent Western films, produced between 1909 and 1929, in which women held key roles, and many of those featured women who displayed not only courage and "pluck" but frontier skills ordinarily attributed to men (Lackmann 1997: 151–2). Rowdy women of the silent West laid claim to the skills and iconic qualities generally attributed to their male counterparts, while retaining the emotional range of roles written for women. This, however, may not be the most significant contribution made by the stuntwomen of early Westerns. The presence (and proliferation) of stars like Helen Gibson, Helen Holmes, Fay Tincher, and Texas Guinan signaled an expansion of character types offered to women, creating a broader and more complex range of roles than could be found in many other genres during the silent era—and with that expansion, greater employment opportunities for female actors who may not have been considered otherwise appropriate for featured roles.

This essay, then, will take an in-depth look at these stuntwomen of the silent-era Westerns—their films and contributions—as well as the ways in which their roles dovetailed with and participated in a "quiet revolution" that would change women's roles in society, as well as on screen, setting the stage for the genre's female characters of the mid-twentieth century, whose depth and diversity would be rivaled only by those of *film noir*.

Girls of the Golden West

In 1905, a charming saloon owner named Minnie provided comfort and a moral compass to Gold Rush-era California miners, only to fall hopelessly in love with an outlaw hiding his true identity but destined to perish for his crimes, in David Belasco's *Girl of the Golden West*. Unaware of his true identity, Minnie, who has never been kissed, gives her heart to a stranger, but upon finding out the truth, she sends him away, and he is captured. Just as her renegade lover is about to be hung, however, Minnie arrives on the scene, brandishing a gun, and frees him, ending the melodramatic tale on a note of "happily ever after." In Minnie, American author Belasco created an iconic character that would form the basis for an opera, a novel, four films and an off-Broadway musical of the same title, along with countless character adaptations in both silent and sound Westerns. More significantly, The Girl—the product of a West that never was—became a powerful part of the gendered myth of the frontier, both constructing and complicating binary opposites acted out in classic stories of good and evil.

Theater, art, popular literature, political tracts, newspapers, letters, and diaries were all key in disseminating and perpetuating the myths surrounding the American West, and all influenced silent film. With its ability to give form to larger-than-life images on screen, early film was a particularly powerful means of conveying the mythical qualities of the Old West. Early silent Westerns took the form of cinematic chapter plays, owing much to their predecessor, the dime novel, and offered movie house audiences weekly cliffhangers that showcased the adventure, danger, and romance of the frontier. In a 1919 editorial in *Photoplay* magazine, Frederick Barner argued that "Serials are the Modern Dime Novels! They supply the demand that was once filled by those bloodcurdling thrillers. Melodrama! Of course, it's melodrama" (in Singer 1996: 177). Women's roles were, of course, a key factor in the narrative arcs of those serials. Strong heroines appeared in dime novels as early as 1845, and Western heroines appeared as a distinct character type by 1860. Shortly after the turn of the century, motion picture shorts followed their lead. The women in these Western films owed equally as much to their real-life, high-profile popular culture predecessors: Annie Oakley, Belle Star, Lucille Mulhall, and the popular female performers in Wild West shows who roped, rode, and used firearms as well as their male counterparts. Like the women featured in these spectacular live attractions, the heroines of early silent Westerns "handled horses and guns with skill and confidence" (Smith 2003: 28).

In 1906, the Vitagraph Company adapted this robust female hero in *The Prospectors: A Romance of the Gold Fields*, and the following year, Gilbert M. "Bronco Billy" Anderson integrated the character into a narrative short that combined physical prowess, Wild West riding stunts, and marksmanship in *The Girl from Montana*. Anderson was no stranger to using women in non-traditional roles, and was noted for casting "rough-and-tumble looking girls"—who were generally more reliable and less inclined to drink—dressed as men to round out his films' Western posses (G. M. Anderson, n.d.: 13–17).

The film opens with a close-up of local Denver "society-girl"-turned-actress Pansy Perry and her horse, identifying her as not only a central character, but an action figure. When a working cowboy and a wealthy Easterner vie for her attention, she rejects the latter, despite his riches, in favor of his humble frontier rival. The easterner retaliates by framing the cowboy for horse thievery and, following the narrative arc of *Girl of the Golden West*, the girl rides to his rescue, and saves him at the last minute by shooting the rope and holding the mob at bay with her gun while he makes his escape. The Selig Company advertised the girl's ride to save her lover as "one of the most thrilling and exciting scenes which has ever been produced in a moving picture" (Selig Polyscope 1907: 44). Anderson's next film, *Western Justice*, featured another female hero: the daughter of a murdered marshal, she leads a posse in a thrilling chase to capture her father's killer. *Moving Picture World* describes the scene:

> A rocky and precipitous trail presenting some of the wildest and most beautiful scenery that can be found in the foothill country gives an opportunity for a marvelously sensational and stirring chase; the riders are men who have practically lived in the saddle for years and to whom every trick of horsemanship is an open book. The most difficult and dangerous passes are negotiated with masterful ease and through all, the girl herself, who inspired the chase, keeps well in the forefront and gives an exhibition of horsemanship which words cannot fairly portray. (*Moving Picture World* 1907: 268)

This legacy of *The Girl of the Golden West*—the beautiful girl who excels at valued aspects of both male and female gender roles—is a thread that weaves in and out of Westerns, both silent and sound, creating a "new" heroine for a new era. At the same time, that iconic image shines a spotlight on the changing world of Western audiences of the silent era, where the "new" woman of the twentieth century was beginning to emerge. As feminist anthropologist Elsie Clews Parsons elaborated: "the woman not yet classified, perhaps not classifiable, the woman *new* not only to men, but to herself" (in Rosenberg 1982: 172). These new women pushed the boundaries of the "possible," in both the Eastern and Western United States, altering and expanding notions of what women could and should do. Pioneer Martha Jane Chappell wrote of her journey West: "Nobody told us how. We set ourselves a job, then we did it. We used common sense. We helped one another. We didn't whine" (in Warren 2003: 4). As production of silent shorts and serials featuring the daring exploits of stuntwomen and female action stars increased, Westerns—and the West provided romanticized images of this "new" independent, capable American woman, while at the same time, opening up very real possibilities for aspiring women to step into lives previously unimagined, through careers on the silver screen, and live out their own adaptation of that iconic role.

Of Madonnas and Daredevils

As Andrew Brodie Smith observes, these films responded to, and were an integral part of, changing social conditions in America. Across classes and backgrounds, young women were becoming more independent and increasingly mobile, moving to cities and taking their place in the workforce. Movies became a force for social change in the wider society, combined with other popular culture forms such as newspapers and Wild West shows, reflecting the interests and concerns of their growing female audiences—suffrage chief among them—and for many, portrayals of frontier life offered the agency they sought.

> Like their real-life counterparts, the early Western-film heroines challenged Victorian notions of decorum. These characters were not homebound upholders of traditional moral values that would appear in later Westerns but were women who did the things men did and who took action in the public realm. (Smith 2003: 29)

As opportunities for teaching, along with factory work and other semi-skilled labor grew, young, single women transitioned from the domestic to the public sphere, beginning a trend that would amplify when the US entered World War I in 1917. As they increasingly worked outside the home, young women found themselves with disposable income, which granted them access to a range of public entertainment, from ice cream socials to dime museums to vaudeville theaters to movie houses. Female heroes of Western films spoke to the members of this shifting demographic among American women in the East and urban areas, providing them role models and proxies for their independence, as well as offering them a sense of ownership in the segment of national identity that finds its roots in the conquest of the frontier and the myth of the American West.

For some women, though, the images of Western heroines excelling at skills like riding, roping, and shooting were simply glamorized versions of taken-for-granted everyday life. Most Western women traveled to the frontier in covered wagons with their families, beginning in the 1840s, but these women did not conform to W. H. D. Koener's nineteenth-century portrait of the "ideal" pioneer woman, *The Madonna of the Prairie*:

> In this work, a beautiful young woman with clear eyes and rouged cheeks, seated on a covered wagon, stares past the viewer into the land beyond. The canvas of the wagon forms a halo around her head... She holds the heavy black reins in delicate hands. (Bush 1987: 22)

This highly romanticized image of the iconic woman of the frontier is a far cry from the lived realities of the actual women who migrated to the American West. As Ronald Lackmann reminds us, "The everyday lives of pioneer women left them little time to 'gaze fondly' at the pastoral splendor of their habitats, though there is no question that these women loved their new homes, or they would have headed straight back East" (1997: 106).

For nearly thirty years, the largest migration in US history took place—a migration in which women were significantly represented. For most of the nineteenth century, no woman in the United States could vote, run for public office, or own property, but that began to change in the West before anywhere else in the country. In 1869, women were granted the right to vote and hold public office in Wyoming, which declared that "every woman of the age of twenty-one years, residing in this territory, may at every election to be holden under the laws thereof, cast her vote, and her rights to the elective franchise and to hold office shall be the same under the laws of the territory, as those of the electors" (Report of the Governor of Wyoming Territory 1878: 53). Other Western states and territories, including Utah, Colorado, Idaho, Washington, and California, followed Wyoming's example, often with an eye toward increasing their female population. A few years prior, the Homestead Act of 1860 guaranteed that 160 acres could be claimed in the West by women, as well as men, if they were twenty-one and unmarried, and while men far outnumbered women, as Holly George Warren notes, there were 172,000 women over the age of twenty out West by 1870 (2003: 5). Many, as Warren relates, believed that "the new country offered greater personal liberty than the old" (2003: 5).

> While back east most women lived within society's traditional rules, pioneer women had to adapt to survive the harsh circumstances of their journey and new surroundings. Many began to take on chores formerly done only by men... Some of these women homesteaders learned to

master the skills of riding horses, roping cattle and other animals, and shooting a gun when necessary. (Warren 2003: 5)

Many thrived on these shifts in, and expansions of, their gender roles: Sally Skull, known as "Mustang Jane," was one of the first women in Texas to own her own ranch. Her life was commemorated by a marker stating that "she was a sure shot with the rifle she carried on her saddle or the two pistols strapped to her waist" (Warren 2003: 9). Sarah "Sadie" Creech Orchard, who operated the Mountain Pride Stagecoach Line, wrote: "I always thought the drive through the beautifully wild Black Range Country exciting and challenging. I never felt terribly in danger, although sometimes I could sense there were Indians and bandits lurking about" (Warren 2003: 9). And while Ella Watson, known as Cattle Kate, was accused of cattle rustling and murder, a reporter for the *Cheyenne Daily Leader* painted a picture of the bold young woman that inspired awe, as well as disdain:

> Of robust physique, she was a daredevil in the saddle, handy with a six-shooter and adept with the lariat and branding iron. Where she came from, no one seems to know, but that she was a holy terror, all agreed. She rode straddle, always had a vicious bronco for a mount, and seemed never to tire of dashing across the range. (Bommersbach 2014: 248)

The zealous reporter conveyed a romanticized image of a daring and feisty cowgirl who applied "every imaginable opprobrious epithet to the lynchers, [cursing] everything and everybody" and then summoned her own horse to carry her to the gallows, vaulting to its back from the ground (Bommersbach 2014: 248).

Frontier women such as these—pioneers, homesteaders, cowgirls, and bad girls—bartered hardships and hard work for the freedoms and opportunities that the West had to offer. They owned and worked on ranches, drove freight wagons and stage coaches, broke horses, cleaned dishes, worked the land, tended the sick, and buried the dead. The renditions of those lives that reached the East, however, and the silver screen wrapped those realities in a veil of adventure, melodrama, and intrigue.

Stuntwomen on the Silver Screen

> She can ride her horse like a cattleman,
> She can handle a rope or gun,
> And my heart beats now in a rat-a-plan
> When I think of the risks she's run.
>
> (Sumner 1912: 112)

Silent films and radio helped to popularize romantic notions of Western cowgirls and heroines. Selig, Essanay, and Bison studios were all early entries into the popular "cowboy girl" subgenre, and in 1912, Vitagraph also gained attention with its *A Girl of the West*, which featured a plucky cowgirl who does her own horseback riding as she single-handedly foils a rustler's plot. The *Mirror* praised the daring, expert skills of Kalem Company's cowgirl "beauties," and just a few months later, the *Morning Telegraph* applauded the stuntwomen of *Bronco Billy's Narrow Escape* (1912), in which a rancher's daughter "makes a hard ride" to prevent the lynching of a ranch hand falsely accused of stealing her father's horse.

As Molly Gregory relates, "Silent movie actresses like Helen Gibson were the first stuntwomen. They were actresses who could ride horses, drive cars, and do high dives" proving that the "weaker sex" could perform surprising feats (Gregory 2015a: n.p.). Phoebe Moses, better known as Annie Oakley, starred in a 21-second Edison Kinetoscope, "Little Sure Shot of the Wild West," an exhibition of sharpshooting filmed in Edison's Black Maria Studio in 1894. In this brief predecessor to commercial silent film, Oakley fired her rifle at not only stationary targets, but at glass balls tossed in the air by her male assistant (most probably her husband, Frank Butler). In the decades to come, Oakley, along with other Wild West stars such as Calamity Jane and Belle Starr, was featured in numerous film productions. In fact, as Anthony Slide's research suggests, "The simple fact that all the major serial stars were female demonstrates the prominence of women at this time, as opposed to the sound period when serial stars were men, and women were reduced to simpering and generally incompetent supporting roles." According to Slide, more than half of the top 500 silent film actors were women (1984: 13).

But it was not only the "big name" Wild West stars who moved from trick riding in arenas to stuntwork in films. Del Jones was one of the first cowgirls to be featured as a stunt rider in films. As a young girl, Jones (born Odelle Osborne) would sneak into nearby farm fields and use fences to climb up on the horses and ride bareback (Colker 1993: n.p.). At thirteen, she ran away from her home in Philadelphia and made her way to Madison Square Garden to audition for the 101 Ranch Real Wild West Show. She was hired that day, and rode in the grand entry parade, along with other riding segments of the show. After her marriage to cowboy Buck Jones, the pair traveled around the country with Ringling Bros. Circus, and later to Los Angeles where she did day work as a stunt double in films for actresses who could not ride. In an interview with the *Los Angeles Times*, she recalled that she even doubled for Douglas Fairbanks when his regular stunt double was injured. Unable to remember the name of the movie, she confessed: "Most times I never knew which movie I was working on," she said. "I just showed up and did the ride" (Colker 1993: n.p.).

Film historian Kevin Brownlow relates that "Stunting in the silent days meant walking on tigers" tails. It was an occupation with few veterans. Whatever your qualifications ... you faced fresh challenges and unknown hazards at every call" (Brownlow 1976: 27). Mollie Gregory elaborates, noting that a report on injuries among thirty-seven movie companies from 1918 to 1919 stated that: "Temporary injuries amounted to 1,052. Permanent ones totaled eighteen. There were three fatal injuries." This was deemed "a surprisingly low rate of accidents, considering the risk" (Gregory 2015a: 14–15). A significant percentage of those injuries were incurred by women, many of whom had no training or experience in risky physical stunts. In an attempt to capitalize on audience thrills, Louis Gasnier of Pathé Studios advised his writers, "Put the girl in danger." They fulfilled that mission with vigor (Gregory 2015b: 15).

While largely uncredited, records of the careers and escapades of several notable stuntwomen remain. Serial queen Ruth Roland, "one of the nerviest girls in pictures," came to the silents from vaudeville in 1908, working first for Kalem Studios, then Balboa Films and Pathé, as well as her own production company, Ruth Roland Serials. Her riding skills landed her the lead in the serial *Ruth of the Range* (1923) and several other Westerns, and she went on to star in eleven serials, producing six of them. Director George Marshall recalled, "She did everything herself. I remember I used to shoot at her feet with real bullets. Didn't bother her none. Sometimes I wonder what would happen today if actresses had to do what she did" (Gregory 2015b: 20).

Films such as *The Lone Hand* (1922), *40-Horse Hawkins,* (1924), and *The Riddle Rider* (1924) all starred another stuntwoman of the frontier, Helen Holmes. Playing an independent, quick-thinking, and inventive heroine, Helen's exploits included leaping onto runaway trains and treacherous horseback chases after villains. As Molly Gregory notes, while plots occasionally called for Helen to be rescued by a handsome male hero, in most episodes it was the dauntless Helen herself who found an ingenious way out of her dire predicament and single-handedly collared the bad guys, bringing them to justice (2015b: 21).

Holmes typically did her own stunts, but was sometimes doubled by another Helen: Helen Gibson, who was, quite possibly, the first stuntwoman to double a female action star. In 1909, she and a friend went to a Wild West show and were "enraptured" by the frontier action. When they inquired about jobs they were advised that the Miller Brothers' 101 Ranch in Ponca City, Oklahoma, "wanted girls who were willing to learn to ride horses" (Gregory 2015b: 21). As Gregory relates:

> Gibson made the cut, and in 1910, at age eighteen, she not only learned to ride a horse, but also mastered the trick of "picking up a handkerchief from the ground" at a full gallop. When veteran riders warned her that she might get kicked in the head, she didn't believe it would happen to her—a confidence that stunt women have shared for decades. (Gregory 2015b: 21–2)

In 1911, Gibson augmented her Wild West income by working as an extra in films, and in 1912 she received her first billed role as Ruth Roland's sister in *Ranch Girls on a Rampage*, the story of a group of rough-and-tumble California ranch girls on a day of rowdy antics at Venice, the Coney Island of the West. The film showcased the actresses' daring, but drew criticism from one reviewer, who claimed that the film's "beauties" played characters no better than "hoodlums" (Abel 2006: 74). Gibson went on to star in sixty-nine episodes of *The Hazards of Helen* (replacing Helen Holmes when she left to form her own production company), where, in addition to starring, she wrote episodes and developed action stunts, before moving to Universal and finally creating Helen Gibson Productions in 1920.

Western comedies sometimes required just as much daring as the genre's adventure serials. Al Christie Productions cast actress Fay Tincher as a wild, Western (often crossdressing) cowgirl, in the popular *Rowdy Ann* (1919), as well as *Go West Young Woman* (1919), *Wild and Western* (1919), and *Dangerous Nan McGrew* (1919). As a comic actress, Tincher reveled in roles that asked her to perform athletically and to face down danger for a laugh. *Rowdy Ann*, Tincher's only extant film, has been described by Andrew Grossman, as "one of the first American films, comic or otherwise, to legitimately address the social psychology of gender construction" (2002: n.p.).

> Clad in a plaid shirt, floppy hat, and oversized, fur-lined chaps, Tincher's cowgirl "Ann" is not so much cross-dressed as she is ambiguously butch. She lassoes her misbehaving, alcoholic father, brawls with villains who make unwanted romantic overtures, rescues from a bully a kindly but ineffectually effeminate cowboy who shows her meek affections, and trigger-happily shoots up saloons, trains, and anywhere else she pleases. Never in film history, before or since, has a woman wielded a gun so wantonly, recklessly, and joyously, and her violent slapstick frenzies remain startling even today. (Grossman 2002: n.p.)

Also standing out from the crowd, despite her five-foot stature, diminutive Winnie Brown was "the best stunt rider and broncobuster and horse wrangler ever to wear chaps. The 'idol of real cowboys,'" according to an article in *Photoplay*. Transitioning into films from a career in the army and a stint as the only female in the Mexican Border Patrol, Brown did 100-foot falls over cliffs on horseback for $5 a fall, advising a reporter for *Picture Play* that "If you fall limber, you can't get hurt" (Gregory 2015b: 26). She appeared as a rider and stuntwoman in films such as *Campaigning with Custer* (1913), *Trail of the Lonesome Mine* (1913), *Captain Courtesy* (1915), *Prairie Trails* (1920), and *The Iron Trail* (1921), and was a member, along with Harry Carey and other notable Western actors and riders, of filmmaker John Ford's silent-era "Wild Bunch" at Universal Studios.

Stars and Social Change

Gibson, Roland, and Brown, along with other stuntwomen and female action actors, became part of a "star discourse" that emerged around 1912—"up close and personal" newspaper articles focused on screen personalities from comedy, melodrama, and of course Westerns. Richard Abel observes that nearly two-thirds of these were devoted to female actors—young, active, and independent—seen in Westerns and adventure films, and celebrated for their daring and horsemanship.

> Among them one can count the "regal-looking Miriam Nesbitt," who, supposedly "bored by the world," turned to the movies and "likes rough and ready parts." Or Jesslyn Von Trump "a capital rider" at American, who "likes herself in a cowgirl costume very much, Indeed" ... Or "dainty, daring" Clara Williams, Lubin's "leading lady," "who can beat the boys at anything on a horse." Or Leona Hutton, who finds that "being 'almost killed' 365 days in the year is only a hum drum regularity" in her busy life at Kay-Bee. (Abel 2006: 243)

These articles appeared in "small, cheap" newspapers that targeted working-class audiences ("the ninety-five percent of the population that were not rich and powerful") and were aimed at a particular readership: women (Abel 2006: 243). Increasingly, newspapers, such as those owned by the Midwest's Scripps-McRae syndicate where many such articles were published, were acutely aware of the undercurrent of change in the social climate, and made a particular effort to "provide content of interest to working class women,"[1] and those women formed a rapidly growing audience for movie house fare. Newspapers such as these, then, highlighted the confluence of socio-economics, dramatic changes in young women's ambitions and identities, and motion pictures. Stuntwomen and cowgirls of the silent Westerns spoke to all of these, providing positive, capable images of the "possible."

Many of these popular, influential figures were also, predictably, part of a growing movement advocating for women's suffrage. Pauline Bush, star of numerous American Film silent Western shorts between 1911 and 1917, was applauded as an "ardent suffragette" by the *Des Moines News*. Similarly, the cowgirls of the 101 Wild West show—training ground for many motion picture cowgirls and stuntwomen—were also celebrated for their ties to the suffrage movement ("Western Girl You Love in the Movies is a Sure Enough Suffrager" 1913: 3; "Girls With Wild West Show to Help Women Gain Equal Suffrage" 1912: 7).

Silent-era stuntwomen and female action stars thus linked the West with a sense of agency for women that was clearly present in reality—in both lifestyles and civic life—but not on screen, embracing risk and muddying the gendered waters of the frontier. Susan Armitage argues that "most histories of the American West are heroic tales—stories of adventure, exploration, and conflict—and that while these are fine stories, with narrative drive and drama, their coherence is achieved by a narrowing of focus" (Armitage 1987: 10). In these stories, particularly in motion pictures, pioneering women's roles are limited to but a few: respectable women, such as school marms and missionaries; entertainers who toured or settled in the Western territories; helpmates, such as army wives, and those of ranchers and farmers; and bad girls—outlaws, prostitutes, and madams. In each case, the role portrays a woman who is shaped by, rather than shaping, the frontier:

> The lady ... is defined by being too genteel for the rough and ready West. She is either uncomfortable, unhappy, or is driven literally crazy by the frontier. Apparently the only way she can prove her gentility is to become a victim. On the other hand, the strong and uncomplaining helpmate adapts to the West, but in the process, becomes a work-worn superwoman, losing all her individuality. The bad woman has glamour and power, but she loses them along with her life as she comes rapidly to her appropriate end—a bad one. (Armitage 1987: 12)

As we look at both the real lives and on-screen images of silent-era stunt women and female action stars, however, this picture becomes deeper and more complex. While still wildly romanticized, these women and the roles they play encompass, but extend, the simple, often binary, categorizations that have characterized Western women—and women, in general—in the late-nineteenth and early-twentieth centuries. They were alternately (and sometimes, simultaneously) helpmates, action heroes, bad girls, entertainers, entrepreneurs, and even ladies, both on and off screen. Ranchers' daughters were avenging angels, moral beacons freed outlaws, and soiled doves came to the rescue of lawmen. These women and the roles they played were both agents and artifacts of a historical moment of great possibility, where a woman could learn to ride, master a firearm, see her image projected in a movie house, open a production company, star in her own films, marry, and still not reach the end of the opportunities available for the taking. Silent Western films, in conjunction with Wild West shows, vaudeville, stage plays, and other forms of popular entertainment, helped to change the image and direction of women on screen and in society at large.

As talking pictures increased production in the late 1920s, the wild exuberance of the silent era vanished, and the rowdy, risky frontier filmmaking that had offered unprecedented opportunities for women vanished with it. Movie audiences changed, and so did the tales of the silver screen. But, as Mollie Gregory assures, "the story of stuntwomen was just beginning, and like the plot of a great movie, it had everything: humiliation, injustice, injury, death, determination, courage, excitement, and finally, hard-fought success" (Gregory 2015b: 24).

Note

1. By 1920, Scripps-McRae delivered content to roughly 400 newspapers, with offices in Cleveland, Chicago, and San Francisco.

Filmography

40-Horse Hawkins, director Edward Sedgwick, featuring Hoot Gibson, Anne Cornwall, Richard Tucker (Universal, 1924).
A Girl of the West, featuring Tom Powers, Helen Case, Lillian Christy (Vitagraph, 1912).
Bronco Billy's Narrow Escape, director Gilbert M. "Broncho Billy" Anderson, featuring Gilbert M. "Broncho Billy" Anderson, Vedah Bertram, Arthur Mackley (Essanay Film Manufacturing, 1912).
Campaigning with Custer, director Henry McRae, featuring William Clifford, Sherman Bainbridge, Val Paul (Bison, 1913).
Captain Courtesy, directors Phillips Smalley and Lois Weber, featuring Dustan Farnum, Winifred Kingston, Courtenay Foote (Hobart Bosworth, 1915).
Dangerous Nan McGrew, director Scott Sidney, featuring Fay Tincher, Earle Rodney, Eddie Barry (Christie Film, 1919).
Go West Young Woman, directors Al E. Christie and Sidney Scott, featuring Fay Tincher, Neal Burns, Helen Darling (Christie Film, 1919).
"Little Sure Shot of the Wild West," featuring Annie Oakley (Black Maria Studio, 1894).
Prairie Trails, director George Marshall, featuring Tom Mix, Charles K. French, Kathleen O'Connor (Fox, 1920).
Ranch Girls on a Rampage, director Pat Hartigen, featuring Edward Coxen, Ruth Roland, Marshall Neilan (Kalem, 1912).
Rowdy Ann, director Al E. Christie, featuring Fay Tincher, Eddie Barrie, Katherine Lewis (Christie Film, 1919).
Ruth of the Range, director Ernest C. Warde, featuring Ruth Roland, Bruce Gordon, Lorimer Johnson (Ruth Roland Serials, 1923).
The Girl from Montana, director Gilbert M. "Broncho Billy" Anderson, featuring Pansy Perry (Selig Polyscope, 1907).
The Hazards of Helen, directors James Davis, J. P. McGowan, Robert G. Vignola, featuring Helen Holmes, Helen Gibson, J. P. McGowan (Kalem, 1914).
The Iron Trail, director Roy William Neill, featuring Wyndham Standing, Thurston Hall, Reginald Denny (United Artists, 1921).
The Lone Hand, director B. Reeves Eason, featuring Hoot Gibson, Marjorie Daw, Helen Holmes (Universal, 1922).
The Prospectors: A Romance of the Gold Fields (Vitagraph, 1906).
The Riddle Rider, director William James Craft, featuring William Desmond, Eileen Sedgwick, Helen Holmes (Universal, 1924).
The Vanishing Rider, director Ray Taylor, featuring William Desmond, Ethlyne Clair, Nelson McDowell (Universal, 1928).
Trail of the Lonesome Mine, featuring Jack Conway, Lucille Young, Paul Machette (Nestor Film, 1913).

What Happened to Mary, director Charles Brabin, featuring Mary Fuller, Marc McDermott, Charles Ogle (McClure Publishing and Edison, 1914).

Wild and Western, director Al E. Christie, featuring Fay Tincher, Earle Rodney, Neal Burns (Christie Film, 1919).

Bibliography

Abel, Richard (2006) *Americanizing the Movies and "Movie-Mad" Audiences, 1910–1914*. Berkeley, CA: University of California Press.

Armitage, Susan (1987) "Through Women's Eyes: A New View of the West," in Susan Armitage and Elizabeth Jameson (eds), *The Women's West*. Norman, OK: University of Oklahoma Press, pp. 9–18.

Bommersbach, Jana (2014) *Cattle Kate*. Scottsdale, AZ: Poisoned Pen Press.

Brownlow, Kevin (1976) *The Parade's Gone By*. Berkeley, CA: University of California Press.

Bush, Corlann Gee (1987) "The Way We Weren't: Images of Women and Men in Cowboy Art," in Susan Armitage and Elizabeth Jameson (eds), *The Women's West*. Norman, OK: University of Oklahoma Press, pp. 19–24.

Colker, David (1993) "Life of a Saddle Champ: Del Jones Has Donated Memorabilia from Her Never-Dull Past to the Gene Autry Museum," *Los Angeles Times*, 3 March <http://articles.latimes.com/1993-03-05/news/va-286_1_del-jones>.

"Complete Catalog," Selig Polyscope, Selig Polyscope Collection, Margaret Herrick Library, Los Angeles, CA, 1907.

"G. M. Anderson," Oral History Transcript, pp. 13–17.

"Girls With Wild West Show to Help Women Gain Equal Suffrage," in *Toledo Blade*, 17 August 1912, p. 7.

Gregory, Mollie (2015a) "Put the Girl in Danger!" in *The New Republic*, 3 December <https://newrepublic.com/article/124981/put-girl-danger>.

Gregory, Mollie (2015b) *Stuntwomen: The Untold Hollywood Story*. Lexington, KY: University Press of Kentucky.

Grossman, Andrew (2002) "FayTincher," <http://sensesofcinema.com/2002/23/symposium3/#tincher>.

Lackmann, Ronald W. (1997) *Women of the Western Frontier*. Jefferson, NC: McFarland, 1997.

Moving Picture World, 29 June 1907, p. 268.

"Report of the Governor of Wyoming Territory," US Government Printing Office, 1878.

Rosenberg, Rosalind (1982) *Beyond Separate Spheres: Intellectual Roots of Modern Feminism*. New Haven, CT: Yale University Press.

Singer, Ben (1996) "Female Power in the Serial-Queen Melodrama: The Etiology of an Anomaly," in Richard Abel (ed.), *Silent Film*. New Brunswick, NJ: Rutgers University Press, pp. 163–93.

Slide, Anthony (1984) *Early Women Directors*. New York: Da Capo Press.

Smith, Andrew Brodie (2003) *Shooting Cowboys and Indians*. Boulder, CO: University Press of Colorado.

Sumner, John (1912) *Motion Picture Story Magazine*, June.

Warren, Holly George (2003) *The Cowgirl Way: Hats Off to America's Women of the West*. Boston: Houghton Mifflin Harcourt.

"Western Girl You Love in the Movies is a Sure Enough Suffrager," in *Des Moines News*, 11 February 1913, p. 3.

Western Justice, Selig Polyscope Supplement 57, June 1907, Selig Polyscope Collection, Margaret Herrick Library, Los Angeles, CA.

2. SUFFERING HEROINES ON THE FRONTIER—MELODRAMA AND PATHOS, 1914–39

Sue Matheson

Jane Tompkins ably points out in *West of Everything: The Inner Life of Westerns* that Westerns "carry within them compacted worlds of meaning and value, codes of conduct, standards of judgment, and habits of perception that shape our sense of the world and govern our behavior" (1992: 6). She also notes that freed from "domestic dramas" and "the whole women's culture of the nineteenth century," the cowboy became "a model for men who came of age in the twentieth century" (1992: 17). A stylized masculine ideal, the cowboy has commanded the lion's share of the critical attention concerning the Western. To date, issues of masculinity, masculine display, and masculine desire are considered essential components of the frontier melodrama even though changing expectations and notions of feminine identity on the frontier are as important. Women, playing vulnerable innocents at risk, are an essential element of the Western's excessive drama, emotion, and audience identification. As Anthony Mann remarked, "without a woman the Western wouldn't work" (see Cook, in Kitses and Rickman 1998: 293). Lee Clark Mitchell, for example, argues successfully in *Westerns: Making the Man in Fiction and Film* that the Western, shaped by the gender politics of late nineteenth- and twentieth-century America, is "a complex reaction to new feminist upsurges, particularly those associated with the 'new Woman' ideal and the movement for women's suffrage" (1996: 152). It, however, must be noted that this reaction is heavily mediated by genre considerations. Deeply embedded in melodrama, the Western's highly exaggerated stock characters reflect clearly defined, socially constructed gender roles. Thus Mitchell's comment immediately brings to mind Rooster Cogburn (John Wayne), a confirmed, aging bachelor, who considers the determined Mattie Ross to be "a lot of work" in Henry Hathaway's *True Grit* (1969) and points out in Stuart Millar's *Rooster Cogburn* (1975) that the indomitable Eula Goodnight (Katherine Hepburn) is "frightening ... She's something ... If we ever give them the vote, God help us." Informed by melodrama, Rooster's arm's-length relationships with women are a familiar staple of the Western, being at first antagonistic, before proving themselves complementary, enhancing and emphasizing the gendered value of the women in his care. Examining the importance of the melodramatic heroine in the Western, this chapter considers the genre's suffering heroines, those women who fuel plots and subplots by being embroiled in sensational crises involving love and murder and recovery and loss. Their generic roots, the importance of their pathos, and three of their remarkable (and lasting) makeovers as working women in 1939, Hollywood's Year of the Western, will be discussed.

Borrowed from Victorian melodrama, the early Western's innocent (and beautiful) heroine generally plays a supporting role. Her vulnerability, helplessness, and distress heighten her audience's emotions and further her film narrative's dramatic tension. Informing social and political issues, her romance with the cowboy also acts as a nexus for the Western's gender-coded antimonies of East and West, town and wilderness, and civilization and savagery. Edward Buscombe points out, "[t]hose who assume that the Western hero traditionally preferred horses to women may be unprepared for the frequency with which romantic love turns the mechanism of the plot in these early films' (1998: 26). Expressing expectations of femininity and cultural coding concerning heroism and manliness, cowboys rescued and married their sweethearts in silent Westerns. As Virginia Wright Wexman remarks, the central role played by the romantic couple in silent Westerns creates the Western's ideological meaning, and "forms the cornerstone of the genre's image of the family on the land" (1996: 142).

Because pain (produced by sensational action) renders the melodrama's protagonists morally superior, suffering, which evokes pathos, also signifies virtue in the early Western (Lusted 1996: 65). Goodness therefore is a salient characteristic of the early Western's leading lady, even Anne Larson (Clara Williams), the tormented heroine of Tom Chatterton's *His Hour of Manhood* (1914) despite her story's shocking (and outrageous) plot twists. In *His Hour of Manhood*, Anne leaves Pete Larson (William S. Hart), her brutal husband, and goes home to her father. When her father dies, she decides to live in the South. While traveling, she runs short of provisions and is rescued by Jim Dawson (Tom Chatterton). Dawson takes the passive Anne home to his mother who cares for her. He falls in love with the woman he has rescued and proposes marriage; believing her husband dead, she accepts his offer. Larson, however, reappears after Anne has married again and blackmails her. As long as she supplies him with the money he needs, he keeps his identity secret, and her secret is safe from Dawson. When the intoxicated Larson kills a man, the long-suffering Anne even shelters him in her new husband's home to protect her marriage. Anne is finally rewarded for her misery in this moral tale. A posse catches and kills Larson, his secret dies with him, and Dawson never knows that his virtuous wife was a polyandrist.

Much of the early Western's melodramatic pathos was also generated by the Victorian chestnut that good women have the power (in supporting roles) to rehabilitate men—through love and marriage. In *The Bargain* (1914), William S. Hart plays Jim Stokes, the first of his many "good badmen" reformed by good women. In *The Bargain*, after Stokes, a bandit, robs a stagecoach, he is wounded. While recuperating at a ranch, he falls in love with and marries the rancher's daughter, Nell Brent (Clara Williams). Attempting to redeem himself, he tries to return the stolen money but is recognized and captured. When the Sheriff loses the recovered money at a crooked roulette table, he and Stokes strike a bargain. Stokes recovers the money, is freed, returns to Nell, is forgiven, and the lovers cross the state line to live happily ever after, far from the long arm of the Law.

Like William S. Hart's heroes, Harry Carey Sr's Cheyenne Harry is also an ambivalent protagonist, a "sort of a bum . . . instead of a great bold gun-fighting hero" (Bogdanovich 1978: 40), who is first supported and then redeemed by the women with whom he falls in love. In *Straight Shooting*, the story of a one-sided range war, Cheyenne Harry (Harry Carey Sr) defends the Sims, an honest and penniless farming family, from a ruthless and powerful rancher, Thunder Flint (Duke R. Lee). The grateful Sim (George Berrell) tries to adopt Harry as his son, but the cowboy, who has fallen in love with Sims's virtuous Joan (Molly Malone), declares that he cannot be a farmer. We never learn as the movie concludes whether Harry rides off into the sunset or changes his mind and becomes Sims's son-in-law—another good-bad man domesticated and rehabilitated by marriage.

The frequency of the Victorian melodrama's feminine ideal driving the Western's narrative cannot go unnoticed. In *Bucking Broadway*, for instance, Cheyenne Harry's girlfriend and his boss's daughter, the irresistible Helen Clayton (Molly Malone) is swept off her feet by Eugene Thornton (Vester Pegg), a wealthy, smooth-talking city slicker who convinces her to break her promise to marry Harry, and run away with him to New York, where he proves himself to be a cad and a bounder. Harry saves his beloved (and her father) from social disgrace after receiving her cry for help. He finds his sweetheart in the big city and rescues her during a showdown between Thornton's friends and her father's ranch hands on the terrace of the Columbia Hotel. The sensational action of *Hell Bent*'s romance and its happy ending also demonstrate the early Western's melodramatic linking of pathos, romantic success, and social rehabilitation. In *Hellbent*, Mary Thurston (Neva Gerber) is forced by her shiftless brother to work as a saloon girl until Cheyenne Harry rescues her from this

Fate Worse Than Death. Harry then falls in love with Mary, but because he is a drifter, he is unfit for polite society. Socializing her admirer, Mary teaches him how to drink tea, but their budding romance is interrupted when she is kidnapped by the outlaw leader, Beau Ross (Joe Harris). Harry recovers her and the stolen gold. Redeemed by love, he proposes to Mary, but the movie ends before she answers his question.

As Marcia Landy observes in *Imitations of Life: A Reader on Film and Television Melodrama*, "the melodramatic vision of the early twentieth century with its concern for the regeneration of traditions in the midst of a changing conception of society and sexuality was made to order for the western setting" (1991: 43). Throughout the 1920s, the suffering heroine of the low-budget Western remained a site of moral and social regeneration. Accordingly, Fox Film Corporation's "good" cowboy, Tom Mix, dressed in sparkling white, thwarted black-hatted villains in over 700 frontier melodramas, surpassing Williams S. Hart in popularity, as he and Tony the Wonder Horse rescued innocent, helpless (and sometimes seduced) heroines, generally played by Colleen Moore, Esther Ralston, Laura La Plant, Billie Dove, and Clara Bow. Big-budget Westerns which expressed America's nation-building also offered their viewers angelic leading ladies. Paramount struck box office gold with James Cruz's *The Covered Wagon* (1923),[1] the first Western epic to chart the adventures of a group of pioneers traveling from Kansas to Oregon.[2] The movie's romantic subplot features a melodramatic love triangle: its pretty protagonist, Molly Wingate (Lois Wilson) is forced to choose between Sam Woodhull (Alan Hale), the melodrama's requisite villain, and Will Banion (J. Warren Kerrigan), the handsome captain of the other wagon train. Predictably, the villain is defeated, and Will wins Molly's heart.

Wishing to copy Paramount's success, Fox immediately assigned John Ford to a similar project. Released in 1924, *The Iron Horse* (1924) charted the story of western expansion via the building of the transcontinental railroad. Ford's epic, like Cruze's, rests heavily on its romantic subplot which enriches Abraham Lincoln's dream of linking the civilized East with the untamed West. The joining of the tracks belonging to the Central Pacific and Union Pacific locomotives, "Juniper" and "116," is not only an apt metaphor for America's nationhood as Leland Stanford (uncredited), president of the Central Pacific, and Thomas C. Durant (Jack Ganzhorn), president of the Union Pacific pound in the railway's last golden spike; this coupling of the rails also expresses Dave Brandon (George O'Brien) and Miriam Marsh's (Madge Bellamy) love for one another, adding psychological and emotional depths to Ford's rendering of American history. As the tracks are wedded, Dave's misery vanishes, and the couple's individual differences are dissolved in the collective identity of their marriage.

Christine Gledhill remarks that melodrama speaks in any discourse "that demarcates the desirable from the taboo," its primary drive being the identification of moral polarities (in Byars 1991: 11). Notably, the moral polarities of

Ford's nation-building epic are most evident when one compares Miriam with *The Iron Horse*'s fallen woman, Ruby (Gladys Hulette). Ford's presentation of Ruby, which lacks moral and psychological complexity, borrows from nineteenth-century melodrama's tradition of the fallen woman. Intelligent and immoral, this soiled dove, the "bright—but not too particular—star of the 'Arabian Nights' dance tent," lacks Miriam's idealized loving nature. Indeed, Ruby, who appears to suffer little, proves to be the heroine's moral opposite. Beautiful and debased, the soiled dove is a seductress, a prostitute, and a murderess. A saloon girl, she embodies the harlot's vices, and the unsavory company she keeps are her masculine counterparts, the happy-go-lucky Judge Haller, who dispenses "likker" and justice indiscriminately, and the ruthless Deroux, a cut-throat capitalist cut from the same cloth as Thunder Flint in *Straight Shooting* and Eugene Thornton in *Bucking Broadway*.

Seen as slow to respond to social change, the Western and its old-fashioned heroines lost ground with Hollywood's A-list audiences throughout the 1930s. Tellingly, the first movie to be shot in 70mm, Raoul Walsh's *The Big Trail* (1930), budgeted at $1.25 million ("Fox Expected . . ." 1930: 99), grossed a disappointing $2.9 million at the domestic box office.[3] The following year, Wesley Ruggles's *Cimarron* (1931), which duplicated *The Covered Wagon*'s epic formula, grossed $3.6 million domestically. However, *Cimarron*'s success at the box office, its Oscar for Best Picture of 1931, the NBR Award in 1931, and *Photoplay*'s Medal of Honor in 1932 can be attributed to its marketing as a culturally relevant drama, *not* as a Western. Notably, the *New York Times* reviewer Mordaunt Hall found *Cimarron*'s long-suffering, working wife, who runs her husband's business, the film's most memorable asset. Hall admires "the indomitable Sabra (Irene Rich), Cravat's sterling wife, who sticks to the newspaper that he starts in the early days to the last." According to the reviewer, "[n]o matter how gallant Cravat may be during certain interludes, it is invariably his wife who enlists one's sympathy." He goes on to say, "Imagine a husband who has deserted his wife and children to go to the Cherokee strip, returning five years later and asking his wife whether she missed him!" (1931: n.p.).

Generally associated with the B-list and serials during the Depression, Westerns climbed back onto the Hollywood A-list in 1939, when Cecil B. DeMille's Western epic, *Union Pacific* (1939) and Henry King's *Jesse James* (1939) became smashes at the box office.[4] John Ford's *Stagecoach* (1939), George Marshall's *Destry Rides Again* (1939), and Michael Curtiz's *Dodge City* (1939) were also top-money pictures.[5] Tellingly, the suffering heroines of these films are working women, written to appeal to female audiences at a time when more women were working outside the home to support their families and husbands and prostitution was also on the rise. Remarkable for their romantic, culturally relevant subplots, *Stagecoach*, *Destry Rides Again*, and *Dodge City* offer their audiences sympathetic prostitutes, "domestic angels" whose behavior is less than ideal, and last, but not least, a spunky journalist, paving the way for later women-led psychological, professional, and revisionist Westerns.

STAGECOACH

An important forerunner of the classic Western,[6] *Stagecoach* radically revises the early Western's feminine gender ideals and complicates its heroines' pathos. As Michael Mok notes in his 1939 interview with John Ford and Dudley Nichols, their unusual approach to the Western was part of an effort on their behalf to revolutionize the film industry and end "elaborate insipid screen slush" (2001: 21). Speaking to Mok, Dudley emphasizes that the leading woman is a prostitute (2001: 22). Indeed, the plight of the fallen woman, in this case a saloon girl, helps to begin the film's narrative, which goes to great lengths to establish polite society as its villain. Creating sympathy for the socially marginalized, the good doctor (who is also an unabashed alcoholic) escorts Dallas (Claire Trevor) to her "tumbril," announcing that he and she are the victims of "a foul disease called social prejudice."

Generally, melodrama idealizes the audience's moral view and defines evil as alien to the social order (Vicinus 1981: 140), but *Stagecoach*'s moral representatives, Mrs Gatewood, the banker's wife, and her colleagues, hideous in their ugly bonnets and high necklines, are comic Victorian caricatures of social and sexual repression. The ugliness of those who lack Christian charity immediately establishes the viciousness of their social Othering. A victim of Tonto's social savagery, Dallas comments, there are "things worse than Apache." Yet, however unpleasant these respectable women appear and act, at the beginning of *Stagecoach*, it is apparent that the stage contains the town's social pariahs. As Ford himself says, "[t]here's not a single respectable character in the cast" (Mok 2001: 22). With the exception of Gatewood, the banker, the male travelers are good badmen. Each epitomizes an unresolved social problem—the doctor is an addict; the devoted family man, a whisky drummer; the banker, a thief; the gentleman, a coward, a murderer and a gambler; the cowhand, a murderer and an escaped convict. The female characters in *Stagecoach*'s ship-of-fools story are far more complicated (and, arguably, more interesting) than their male counterparts.

In melodrama, Virtue can hold no intercourse with Vice, and at first this seems to be the case. As Dallas is summarily loaded into the stagecoach, there is no doubt about her degraded nature. The showy, plaid dress that she wears calls attention to her décolletage, its taffeta apron pulled back to reveal her underbodice. Living in a time when it was deemed inappropriate for women to flaunt their bosoms and even the legs of wooden tables were modestly covered (because they resembled female appendages), Dallas signals her calling as a common whore. She lifts her skirts to climb into the stagecoach and shows off her gaudily striped stockings. As she flaunts her calves and ankles for the gawking men who watch her depart, her behavior is not only bold, it is also shocking. Lucy's wardrobe, on the other hand, is what one would expect a lady of her social standing to wear. Tasteful and demure, she is covered fully, from head to toe, in dark, subdued colors. Her traveling cloak prohibits any hint of décolletage. Because of her cloak and her bustle, her form is not visible. It is therefore surprising that she has been traveling while heavily pregnant even though references are made during the journey that she is not feeling well and should be attended by a doctor. Unlike Dallas's bawdy, blonde curls which escape from her frowsy hat, Lucy's hair is restrained and hidden by her understated bonnet.

To be effective, melodrama cannot run counter to the cherished beliefs of its audience, which, of course, include ideas of female purity (Vicinus 1981: 141). It is not surprising that Mrs Gatewood, the leader of the Law and Order League asks Lucy, the Southern aristocrat and devoted wife, if she should be traveling in close quarters with "that creature." It is indeed unusual that Lucy risks social *and* physical contamination by sitting in close quarters with Dallas on the stage. In the nineteenth and the first part of the twentieth century, prostitutes were thought to spread disease in ways other than sexual intercourse. Audiences in the 1930s believed that syphilis could spread through abrasions in the skin or mucous ducts. In 1930, Marion Potter, for instance, wrote that nurses and physicians often were infected via abrasions on their hands being in contact with syphilitic chancres (Potter 1930: 157). Aptly, Hatfield, the male representative of antebellum norms and forms, makes the danger of contagion obvious, by giving Ringo the canteen filled with water, but not offering Dallas the silver cup from which Lucy has drank. Given the risks of encountering "creatures" like Dallas in the West, one must wonder what catastrophe could have prompted Lucy, about give birth, to abandon the safety of hearth and home to join her husband in Lordsburg.

It is completely understandable therefore that Lucy, in her "delicate" condition, is outraged when Ringo invites Dallas to eat at the table with the other passengers while the horses are being changed. Both Lucy and Dallas are keenly aware that the women should not be seated together. Unable to return Lucy's angry gaze, Dallas accepts and internalizes society's image of her as the Great Social Evil of her time despite her protests to Doc Boone on the streets of Tonto that she too has a right to live. Again, it is Hatfield, who, protecting the lady, asks Mrs Mallory if she would like to sit beside the window where it is cooler. Ironically, Ringo believes that it is he who has "the plague," but keenly aware of her pollution, Dallas acknowledges that she is a social pariah and physical degenerate. She tells Ringo that the reason the other passengers have moved down the table to avoid eating with them is not because he is an ex-con but because of her contagion.

As Hatfield notes, Lucy begins her journey being "an angel in a very dangerous jungle." The birth of her daughter, however, changes her (and the audience's) notions of social propriety. During and after the baby's birth, Dallas and Lucy both perform the nineteenth-century women's "sacred duties" (Studlar 2001: 49), upholding the traditional "feminine" values of altruistic self-sacrifice, home and family, and the institutions of marriage and parenthood. When circumstances force Dallas to assume the role of nurse for Lucy's baby, born during the journey, she is socially purified and reclaimed. Bedridden after the birth of her child, Lucy, whom one would expect to be the melodrama's primary heroine, becomes a secondary figure. As Gaylyn Studlar points out, the madonnaesque image of Dallas showing off the newborn in her arms solidifies Ringo's romantic response, and even though she is a fallen woman, she becomes "the kind of girl a man wants to marry"—and more important, the film confirms Ringo's judgment of her rather than society's (2001: 53). Lucy herself acknowledges Dallas's self-sacrificing nature, telling Doc Boone that her attendant stayed up all night with the baby while she herself slept.

Treated with considerable sympathy when she takes on the primary heroine's role, Dallas is one of the first good-bad girls in the Western A-list—part of the new pattern of the romantic heroine that accommodated changing conceptions of the female character in melodrama and relations between the sexes during the Depression. A favorite film stereotype of the 1930s and 1940s, "'the bad-good girl' [is] a heroine who appears at the beginning of the story to be wild and even immoral but who is eventually revealed to be a truly chaste and loving woman" (Landry 1991: 43). In Indian Territory, Dallas becomes a sympathetic rendering of this new type of woman, but when the stagecoach finishes its journey, Lordsburg's social dictums prove to be Tonto's—the prostitute once again finds herself placed beyond the social pale. As Lucy is taken away to begin her lying-in, she realizes the pathos of their situation: she cannot repay Dallas's kindness with kindness. Indeed, she endangers the privileges of her womanhood by even stopping to thank her. Ironically, it is the wife and mother, not the prostitute, who is shown to be society's prisoner at the film's end. On every level of her existence, Lucy's life is determined by the men and women with whom she lives. Even in Indian Territory, she is not free—as Hatfield demonstrates when all hope seems to be lost in the stagecoach during the film's dramatic chase scene, decisions regarding Lucy's life (and death) lie in the hands of others. Ford arrests the action of the pursuit as Lucy, huddled against the wall of the stagecoach and unaware that Hatfield is about to save her from A Fate Worse than Death, prays. At this moment, Peter Brooks would agree, "symbolic action entirely replaces words" (1976: 61). Ford heightens the moment's pathos and spotlights important cultural concerns about miscengenation via *tableau*, a melodramatic staple that presents a fixed and emotionally loaded pictoral scene. Breaking the frame, Hatfield's forearm aiming a derringer at Lucy becomes a stunning expression of masculine power. As Martha Vicinus claims, melodrama manifests "primal fears clothed in everyday dress" (1981: 128). As this "sensation scene" demonstrates, shooting Lucy is not an act of mercy but of socially sanctioned murder. Uninvited, Hatfield's hand and pistol are contained in the medium shot. The weapon points towards Lucy's head, but she does not glance at Hatfield. After Hatfield's hand drops and the pistol dangles, Ford cuts to Lucy, who has remained unaware of what was transpiring beside her. Emphasizing that Hatfield's intervention in this situation was undesired, unrequested, and finally unnecessary, Lucy exclaims, "Can you hear it? They're blowing the charge."

Stagecoach's negotiation with melodrama's pathos continues in Lordsburg, where, surprisingly, the tragic fate of the fallen woman does not catch up with Dallas. As Studlar remarks, "Ford's sympathy is with outcasts, no matter what their gender and *Stagecoach* is not the first or the last Ford Western to accord that sympathy to women who because of their lack of 'sexual purity' are judged harshly by other characters" (2001: 53). Overturning the conventions of melodrama, Ringo does not abandon Dallas when he discovers she is a streetwalker. Instead, he offers to marry her, and instead of dying or returning to a life of prostitution, Dallas is rewarded for her suffering. Improbably, at the movie's

Figure 2.1 Lucy Mallory (Louise Platt) is unaware that she is being saved from a Fate Worse Than Death in *Stagecoach* (1939).

end, she is morally rehabilitated and escapes "the blessings of civilization"—driving away with her lover to marry him in Mexico, beyond the constraints and social violence that women experience in the American West.

DESTRY RIDES AGAIN

The plight of the fallen woman is also an important subplot in George Marshall's *Destry Rides Again*, the story of Bottleneck, a lawless frontier town run by a corrupt judge, a crooked gambler, and a dishonest saloon girl played by Marlene Dietrich. As Florence Jacobwitz points out in "The Dietrich Westerns: *Destry Rides Again* and *Rancho Notorious*," Dietrich's appeal was directed largely towards a female audience—in part because the on-screen persona that she developed while working with Joseph von Sternberg challenged "the inevitability of women's oppression, manifested in the requisite social trajectory of self-sacrifice" (Jacobwitz 1996: 88).[7] Remarkably, the role of Frenchy, which revitalized Dietrich's sagging persona as a modern woman, also satisfies the requirements of the Western's melodrama. Having what the boys in the backroom have, this romantic heroine expresses the individual's right to first satisfy her own desires. After meeting Tom Destry (Jimmy Stuart), Frenchy also conforms to melodrama's demands of resolution and narrative closure at the film's end.

Generally, the situation of the fallen woman in melodrama conveys a critique of the lack Christian charity (on screen and in the audience), but, unlike Dallas in *Stagecoach*, Frenchy is not the victim of a witch hunt. She is instead what the Victorians would have deemed a necessary Social Evil. Accordingly, the tea-drinking women of Bottleneck, who do not approve of her, tolerate her presence. Treated with sympathy and understanding by the men around her, Frenchy begins as the film's primary heroine, appearing to be a carnival queen. Upending society's dictums, her transgressive behavior, associated with fun and freedom, not only defies moral authority, it also appropriates masculine traits and their attendant privileges. She drinks with boys. She rolls her own cigarettes and smokes with the boys. She plays cards with the boys. She even acquires men's clothes. Besting Callahan (Misha Auer) at poker, she insists on claiming his pants—and does.

When Callahan's outraged wife (played by Una Merkel) storms into the bar to reclaim her husband's trousers, a showdown between the film's fallen woman and its devoted wife takes place. The *New York Times* reviewer, Frank S. Nugent, remarks that this scene "really counts," "[f]or the real thing, with no holds barred and full access to chairs, tables, glasses, bottles, waterbuckets and as much hair as may be conveniently snatched from the opponent's scalp, we give you not 'The Women,' but the two women who fight it out in the Bloody Gulch over a pair of Mischa Auer's pants" (1939a: n.p.). After

Respectability in the form of a dripping Mrs Callahan flees the bar, Frenchy also chases Destry, the other representative of Social Order, from the saloon. The bar crowd buys the dance hall entertainer a drink to celebrate her victory, and Washington Dimsdale (Charles Winninger) hails Frenchy "the real boss of Bottleneck." As the film's primary heroine, she is "hard and tough and painted to the margins of the palette" (Nugent 1939a: n.p.) swaggering about the bar like Lola Lola in von Sternberg's *Der Blaue Engel* (1930). When not carousing with her customers, Frenchy works in the saloon's backroom with her lover Kent (Brian Donlevy), spilling coffee on the gullible, poker-playing locals and fleecing them of their farms.

Destry, the film's ethical center, attempts to rehabilitate the saloon worker. "I bet you've a lovely face under all that paint," he tells her, "Why don't you wipe it off some day and have a good look. Figure out how you can live up to it." But, by the time Destry collects a posse to arrest Kent and his gang, it is evident that he will have to jail Frenchy as well. After all, she is an accessory to murder and guilty of criminal theft. The demands of melodrama, however, neatly resolve Destry's romantic dilemma. As long as it seems love can rehabilitate Frenchy, she is the film's primary heroine. However, when it is clear that she cannot be rehabilitated, she becomes a secondary heroine. As Jacobwitz remarks, Frency's role at the film's end is "one of self-abrogation and self-effacement" (1996: 92–3). After gathering the townswomen together to halt the violence that erupts, she redeems herself by saving Destry's life. Shielding the deputy sheriff and taking Kent's bullet, Frenchy dies heroically, like one of the boys in the backroom, fulfilling the melodramatic convention of self-sacrifice. Finally, fully Americanized, the soiled dove's pathos overwhelms the narrative, as Jacobwitz points out, and Destry acknowledges the profound impact of the saloon girl's loss in the film's final moments (1996: 91–3). In the end, the melodrama's demand of individuals to sublimate themselves for the greater good of the community results in order, stability, and patriarchy. Even the Callahans' marriage is saved, as his domineering wife finally respects the "new regime" that he institutes after the barroom brawl. She promises to call him by his own name, Boris, at the film's end.

Dodge City

Four weeks after John Ford's *Stagecoach* was released, Michael Curtiz's epic Western *Dodge City* opened on 7 April 1939, starring Olivia de Havilland and Errol Flynn. Shot over a 48-day period from November 1938 to January 1939 on the Warner lot and on location in nearby Modestoat at the cost of $910,000, *Dodge City* was Warner Brothers' second biggest money-maker in 1939, bringing in $2.5 million at the box office (William Shaefer Ledger 1995: 20). In *Dodge City*, Wade Hatton (Errol Flynn) is a Texas cattle agent turned town sheriff who cleans up the "Longhorn center of the world and wide-open Babylon of the American frontier" run by a crooked saloon owner, Jeff Surrett (Bruce Cabot). As he does, Hatton also wins the heart of Abbie Irving (Olivia de Havilland), Dodge City's first female newspaper reporter. The story ends with the newly-wed couple in their covered wagon, traveling to Virginia City, another frontier town in need of Law and Order.

According to the *New York Times* reviewer, Frank S. Nugent, *Dodge City* is "an exciting thriller for the kiddies, or for grown folk with an appetite for the wild and woolly" (1939b: n.p.). Deeming *Dodge City* a film made for men, Nugent comments that:

> With or without his six-gun, Marshal Hatton is a match for any three of Surrett's backroom gang. He stalks among them single-handed and comes away with the man they were going to lynch. He doesn't waste lead: with bullets flying all around, he wades in with his bare knuckles and a confident smile. Men are clubbed, slugged or plugged on all sides; the Marshal marches on. (1939b: n.p.)

Charles Barr, however, finds *Dodge City* "more sophisticated, more knowing, in its treatment of gender issues than might at first appear" (1996: 188). A young middle-class woman, Abbie Irving (Olivia de Havilland), the film's primary heroine and Hatton's romantic interest, is a New Woman of the 1880s, that feminist ideal which emerged in the late nineteenth century, and enabled well-educated women to become lawyers, doctors, professors, and journalists, and retain their social respectability.[8]

In *Dodge City*, Hatton, is surprised to find Abbie employed as a journalist, writing copy in the newspaper office. He immediately objects to her working. "Of course you realize that people in general are inclined to think that a newspaper office is an odd place for a charming young lady like you to be working don't you?" Challenging Hatton's objection to her agency, Abbie snaps, "What's wrong my working here?" "Well it's undignified," he replies, taken aback, "It's unladylike." Then he points out that her proper place is at "home doing needlework." The New Woman snorts at and dismisses Hatton's chauvinism. "Sewing buttons on for some man I suppose . . . That's a fine career for an intelligent woman," she scoffs. Generally, Othering like Hatton's implies social hierarchy and keeps power where it already lies, but in *Dodge City*, Irving continues to work, maintaining her social respectability (and dignity) while exercising her autonomy. Ironically, at *The Star, quod licet Iovi, non licet bovi*.[9] Hatton finds himself utterly unable to explain the difference between a cow and a steer to Abbie when her story about livestock sales requires editing. The *Star's* editor, Joe Clemens, who is also too embarrassed to discuss intimate details of male physiology with the New Woman, decides that he will write the stockyard reports himself. Privileged by her gender, Abbie continues to be the paper's society columnist, producing copy about "what other women are wearing, how to make Lady Baltimore Cake with two eggs, who invited the minister to tea, and whose baby is going to be born and when."

Remarkably, Curtiz's taming of the West is accomplished by the town's sheriff *and* its recipe-writing reporter. As a journalist, Abbie helps Hatton and Clemens with their investigation of Surrett's criminal activities before she becomes a valuable witness who must be protected. Then, when she learns of Colonel Dodge's offer to Hatton to tame Virginia City, she asks him; "When do we start?" Given Abbie's earlier unwillingness to work in the home, her decision to forgo a honeymoon in the East and a home just outside Dodge City with Hatton is much more than a melodramatic act of self-sacrifice or subordination to the Western hero's desires. She is next seen sitting beside her husband on a horse-drawn wagon on the trail to Virginia City to help him tame the West. Ironically, as the Hattons achieve their melodrama's demands by marrying, the Western's gender relations are significantly revised in this film. Antimony becomes matrimony, as Hatton holds the reins and his wife holds his arm. They drive off into the glowing sunset creating a wonderfully over-the-top image, "with matching music," embodying what Barr notes is the film's effective pathos, a "peculiarly satisfying tension" (1996: 188).

At the conclusion of *Dodge City*, the reconciliation and marriage of the hero and heroine not only purges frontier society of its evils; it also demonstrates the increasingly dynamic nature of the Western's leading lady and opens the door for the good bad-girl—the woman who could work in a saloon, handle a gun, and still be marriageable like Tess Millay (Joanne Dru) in Howard Hawks's *Red River* (1947). Modifying the early Western's melodramatic ur-text in 1939, *Stagecoach*, *Destry Rides Again*, and *Dodge City* helped make possible the hard-working, guntoting heroines found in *The Furies* (1950), *Calamity Jane* (1953), *The Cattle Queen of Montana* (1954), *Johnny Guitar* (1954), *The Maverick Queen* (1956), *Forty Guns* (1957), *Cat Ballou* (1965), and *The Belle Starr Story* (1968). Complicating the dynamics of the Western's suffering heroine, *Stagecoach*, *Destry Rides Again*, and *Dodge City* embraced America's changing gender ideologies. However, these films' makeovers of the Western's early heroine also demonstrate the resistance of melodramatic stereotypes to change. *Stagecoach*, *Destry Rides Again*, and *Dodge City* continue to transmit Victorian expectations of American family life and femininity and convey the nineteenth century's cultural coding about heroism and manliness while their heroines offered the "modern" pathos of the working woman to Hollywood A-list audiences. Remarkably, *Stagecoach*, *Destry Rides Again*, and *Dodge City* were among the first A-list Westerns to showcase that all too-familiar double standard—the complex blending of Victorian mores and modern conduct by which American women have been judged throughout the twentieth and twenty-first centuries ... however much social order in the United States has been said to have changed.

Notes

1. Budgeted at an estimated $782,000, *The Covered Wagon* grossed $7,630,000 at the domestic box office. For more information see box office for *The Covered Wagon* at *IMDb*, <https://www.imdb.com/title/tt0013951/?ref_=fn_al_tt_1>.
2. Jesse L. Laskey, Jr remarks in the documentary, *Hollywood: A Celebration of American Silent Cinema* that James Cruze when making *The Covered Wagon* attempted "to elevate the Western, which had always been a sort of potboiler kind of film, to the status of an epic."
3. See *Ultimate Movie Rankings 1930* at <https://www.ultimatemovierankings.com/1930-top-grossing-movies/>.
4. According to *Ultimate Movie Rankings 1939*, *Union Pacific* grossed $3.2 million at the domestic box office; *Jesse James* grossed $9.5 million.
5. According to *Ultimate Movie Rankings 1939*, *Stagecoach* grossed $5 million; at the domestic box office, George Marshall's *Destry Rides Again* grossed $2.9 million, and Michael Curtiz's *Dodge City* $6.8 million.
6. Grossing over $5 million (<https://www.ultimatemovierankings.com/top-grossing-movies-of-1939/>), *Stagecoach* received seven Oscar nominations, including one for Best Picture.
7. Dietrich was billed in the advertisement for Josef von Sternberg's *Morocco* (1930) as "Marlene Dietrich: the woman all women want to see."
8. In *Notes on the New Woman*, Catherine Lavender points out that education and employment opportunities for women increased in the late nineteenth and early twentieth centuries as western countries became more urban and industrialized. More women won the right to attend university and college, obtain professional educations and then work as professionals. According to Lavender, "[t]he 'pink-collar' workforce gave women a foothold in the business and institutional sphere. In 1870, women in the professions comprised only 6.4 percent of the United States' non-agricultural workforce; by 1910, that figure had risen to 10 percent, then to 13.3 percent in 1920" (2014: n.p.).
9. Indicating the existence of a double standard, the Latin phrase, *quod licet Iovi, non licet bovi* literally means "What is permissible for Jove is not permissible for a bull."

Filmography

Bucking Broadway, director Jack Ford, featuring Harry Carey, Molly Malone, L. M. Wells (Universal, 1917).
Calamity Jane, director David Butler, featuring Doris Day, Howard Keel, Allyn Ann McLerie (Warner Bros., 1953).
Cat Ballou, director Elliot Silverstein, featuring Jane Fonda, Lee Marvin, Michael Callan (Columbia, 1965).

Cimarron, director Wesley Ruggles, featuring Richard Dix, Irene Dunne, Estelle Taylor (RKO Radio, 1931).

Destry Rides Again, director George Marshall, featuring Marlene Dietrich, James Stewart, Mischa Auer (Universal, 1939).

Dodge City, director Michael Curtiz, featuring Errol Flynn, Olivia de Havilland, Ann Sheridan (Warner Bros., 1939).

Forty Guns, director Samuel Fuller, featuring Barbara Stanwyck, Barry Sullivan, Dean Jagger (20th Century Fox, 1957).

Hell Bent, director Jack Ford, featuring Harry Carey, Duke R. Lee, Neva Gerber (Universal, 1918).

His Hour of Manhood, director Tom Chatterton, featuring William S. Hart, Clara Williams, Tom Chatterton (Domino, 1914).

Hollywood: A Celebration of American Silent Cinema, producers Kevin Brownlow and David Gill, Thames Television, 8 January—1 April 1980.

Jesse James, director Henry King, featuring Tyrone Power, Henry Fonda, Nancy Kelly (20th Century Fox, 1939).

Johnny Guitar, director Nicholas Ray, featuring Joan Crawford, Sterling Hayden, Mercedes McCambridge (Republic, 1954).

Stagecoach, director John Ford, featuring John Wayne, Claire Trevor, Andy Devine (Walter Wanger, 1939).

Straight Shooting, director Jack Ford, featuring Harry Carey, Duke R. Lee, George Berrell (Universal, 1917).

The Bargain, director Reginald Barker, featuring William S. Hart, J. Frank Burke, Clara Williams (New York Motion Picture, 1914).

The Belle Starr Story, director Lina Wertmüller, featuring Elsa Martinelli, Robert Woods, George Eastman (Eureka, 1968).

The Big Trail, director Raoul Walsh, featuring John Wayne, Marguerite Churchill, El Brendel (Fox, 1930).

The Cattle Queen of Montana, director Allan Dwan, featuring Barbara Stanwyck, Ronald Reagan, Gene Evans (Benedict Bogeaus, 1954).

The Covered Wagon, director James Cruze, featuring J. Warren Kerrigan, Lois Wilson, Alan Hale (Paramount, 1923).

The Furies, director Anthony Mann, featuring Barbara Stanwyck, Wendell Corey, Walter Huston (Wallis-Hazen, 1950).

The Iron Horse, director John Ford, featuring George O'Brien, Madge Bellamy, Charles Edward Bull (Fox, 1924).

The Maverick Queen, director Joseph Kane, featuring Barbara Stanwyck, Barry Sullivan, Scott Brady (Republic, 1956).

Union Pacific, director Cecil B. DeMille, featuring Barbara Stanwyck, Joel McCrea, Akim Tamiroff (Paramount, 1939).

Bibliography

Appendix 1 (1995) *Historical Journal of Film, Radio and Television*, 15: supl, pp. 1–31. Cited parenthetically as William Shaefer Ledger.

Barr, Charles (1996) "Dodge City," in Ian Cameron and Douglas Pye (eds), *The Movie Book of the Western*. London: Studio Vista, pp. 181–8.
Bogdanovich, Peter (1978) *John Ford*. Berkeley, CA: University of California Press.
"Box Office," *The Covered Wagon*, IMDb <https://www.imdb.com/title/tt0013951/?ref_=fn_al_tt_1>.
Brooks, Peter (1976 [1995]) *The Melodramatic Imagination: Balzac, Henry James, Melodrama, and the Mode of Excess*. New Haven, CT: Yale University Press <https://www.erudit.org/en/journals/ravon/2012-n62-ravon01483/1025999ar/>.
Buscombe, Edward (ed.) (1998) *The BFI Companion to the Western*. London: André Deutsch/British Film Institute.
Byars, Jackie (1991) *All That Hollywood Allows: Re-reading Gender in 1950s Melodrama*. Chapel Hill, NC: University of North Carolina Press.
Cook, Pam (1998) "Women and the Western," in Jim Kitses and Gregg Rickman (eds), *The Western Reader*. New York: Limelight Editions, pp. 293–300.
"Fox Expected to Make Films Abroad; Coast Convention Set; 48 in Line Up," in *Motion Picture News*, 24 May 1930, p. 99.
Hall, Mordaunt (1931) "THE SCREEN," *New York Times*, 27 January <https://www.nytimes.com/1931/01/27/archives/the-screen.html>.
Jacobwitz, Florence (1996) "The Dietrich Westerns: *Destry Rides Again* and *Rancho Notorious*," in Ian Cameron and Douglas Pye (eds), *The Movie Book of The Western*. London: Studio Vista, pp. 88–98.
Landy, Marcia (1991) *Imitations of Life: A Reader on Film and Television Melodrama*. Detroit, MI: Wayne State University Press.
Lavender, Catherine (2014) *Notes on New Womanhood* (PDF), The College of Staten Island/CUNY <https://csivc.csi.cuny.edu/history/files/lavender/386/newwoman.pdf> (27 October 2014).
Lusted, David (1996) "Social Class and the Western as Male Melodrama," in Ian Cameron and Douglas Pye (eds), *The Movie Book of the Western*. London: Studio Vista, pp. 63–74.
Mitchell, Lee Clark (1996) *Westerns: Making the Man in Fiction and Film*. Chicago: University of Chicago Press.
Mok, Michael (2001) "The Rebels, If They Stay Up This Time, Won't Be Sorry for Hollywood's Trouble," in Gerald Peary (ed.), *John Ford: Interviews*, Jackson, MS: University Press of Mississippi, pp. 21–3.
Nugent, Frank S. (1939a) "THE SCREEN IN REVIEW; Errol Flynn Restores Law and Order to 'Dodge City,' the Wild and Woolly Horse Opera at the Strand—Four Foreign Films Also Open Here At the Modern Playhouse At the 86th St. Garden Theatre At the 86th Street Casino At the 96th Street Theatre," *New York Times*, 8 April <https://www.nytimes.com/1939/04/08/archives/the-screen-in-review-errol-flynn-restores-law-and-order-to-dodge.html>.
Nugent, Frank S. (1939b) "THE SCREEN IN REVIEW; Marlene Dietrich Reaches a High in Horse Opera With 'Destry Rides Again,' at the Rivoli—'That's Right, You're Wrong' Shown at Criterion," *New York Times*, 30 November <https://www.nytimes.com/1939/11/30/archives/the-screen-in-review-marlene-dietrich-reaches-a-high-in-horse-opera.html>.

Potter, Marion Craig (1930) "Venereal Diseases: Part I: Syphilis," *American Journal of Nursing*, 30 (2), pp. 155–9.

Schatz, Thomas (2003) "Stagecoach and Hollywood's A-Western Renaissance," in Barry Keith Grant (ed.), *John Ford's Stagecoach*. Cambridge: Cambridge University Press, p. 32.

Studlar, Gaylyn (2001) "Sacred Duties, Poetic Passions," in Gaylyn Studlar and Matthew Bernstein (eds), *John Ford Made Westerns: Filming the Legend in the Sound Era*. Bloomington, IN: Indiana University Press, pp. 43–74.

Tompkins, Jane (1992) *West of Everything: The Inner Life of Westerns*. Oxford: Oxford University Press.

Ultimate Movie Rankings 1930 < https://www.ultimatemovierankings.com/1930-top-grossing-movies/>.

Ultimate Movie Rankings 1931 <https://www.ultimatemovierankings.com/1931-top-box-office-movies/>.

Ultimate Movie Rankings 1939 <https://www.ultimatemovierankings.com/top-grossing-movies-of-1939/>.

Vicinus, Martha (1981) "'Helpless and Unfriended': Nineteenth Century Domestic Melodrama," *New Literary History*, 13 (1), pp. 127–43.

Wexman, Virginia Wright (1996) "The Family on the Land," in Daniel Bernardi (ed.), *The Birth of Whiteness*. New Brunswick, NJ: Rutgers University Press.

3. WHEN EAST GOES WEST: THE LOSS OF DRAMATIC AGENCY IN DEMILLE'S WESTERN WOMEN FROM THE 1910s TO THE 1930s

David Blanke

The name Cecil B. DeMille rarely springs to mind when considering the performance of women in Westerns. This is understandable, for the director first made a name for himself producing modern marriage dramas—resplendent with alluring consumer goods and a loose Jazz Age morality—and concluded his career with one of the most successful and iconic Biblical epics ever produced. But both the Western genre and strong female performances were critical to DeMille's initial success in the 1910s, and perhaps even more vital to the director's mid-career professional revival in the mid-1930s. Without Western women, DeMille would never have become "DeMille."[1]

The changing cinematic expression of American Westerns certainly plays a prominent role in this oversight. While many assume that the genre retained a stable core of representative forms and signification—particularly its focus on white male fantasy fulfillment and a destined, glorified tale of national progress—in fact, as scholars have now long argued, the Western has displayed significant variation over time. Summarizing this research, Steve Neale admits that while nearly all Westerns are presented as "the meeting point between Anglo-Americans and their culture and nature and the culture of others," their dramas range widely across the ambiguities found between "opportunity and danger, hardship and bounty, adventure and violence" (2000: 134). Apropos to DeMille's work, David Lusted adds that while the symbolic relations found in early Westerns certainly featured traditional male heroes and villains, these characters existed within recognizable social hierarchies that spoke in tones that resonated with contemporary issues. Arguing for a stronger reading of class opposition and anti-authoritarianism in 1930s Westerns, for example, Lusted writes that these historical filters "can be unacknowledged or refused, but their material effects are always felt in conditions of labour" 1996: 63). Finally, and of particular importance to Westerns released at the dawn of the studio era, the genre's aesthetic mode trended far more consistently towards melodrama than what might otherwise be assumed in male-centered narratives. Linked to social problems that are again familiar to audience members, melodrama tends to linger over the moral conundrums exposed by contingent events. Victoria Lamont shows that these early works also allowed for much stronger and more nuanced female performances, in terms of both their narrative structure and the subjective positioning of the actors, than in any other genre of the era. In Westerns, gender functioned not merely as a form of voyeuristic pleasure but discursively as a cultural construct rooted in the audience's identification. Lamont writes that these early stage works, like Owen Wister's *The Virginian* (1889), explored "female domestic authority" in ways that resonated with the shifting social and cultural conditions of the modern urban audience (2016: 33).

Accordingly, DeMille's career offers an ideal test case to differentiate gendered representations between two critical phases of the Western genre. In the early period, spanning 1914 to 1917, the director experimented with profitable feature films and the ways these might exploit the existing taste hierarchies of the theater. Trained by David Belasco to consider the popular stage as a mixture of highbrow melodrama and spectacle, the Western proved a natural for him and a staple in his studio's early portfolio. Borrowing from the same stage performances explored by Lamont, DeMille released seven Westerns, including *The Squaw Man* (1914), *The Virginian* (1914), *The Call of the North* (1914), *The Rose of the Rancho* (1914), *The Girl of the Golden West* (1915), *The Trail of the Lonesome Pine* (1916), and *A Romance of the Redwoods* (1917). His second run of Westerns, from 1937 to 1947, re-established his tarnished reputation as a profitable director still capable of divining the public mood. These works, which included *The Plainsman* (1937), *The Buccaneer* (1938), *Union Pacific* (1939), *North West Mounted Police* (1940), and *Unconquered* (1947), fully conformed to the conventions of classical Hollywood cinema rather than the stage, and exhibited the male-dominated tropes that defined the genre throughout much of the second half of the twentieth century. Through DeMille's films, it is clear that a profoundly negative shift had occurred in the representation of Western women.

The historical context of DeMille's two Western film series is meaningful and helped shape the content and performance of his work. In the early years, commercial producers aped the aesthetic sensibilities of the "legitimate theater" to overcome cultural prejudice directed at the new media. DeMille, the son and brother to well-known Broadway playwrights with close ties to David Belasco, became the marketable brand upon which Jesse Lasky and Sam Goldwyn built their fledgling studio. Their early triumph with *The Squaw Man* (1914), a successful stage production fronted by a popular star, provided the firm with the liquidity to acquire additional "Famous Plays" directly from Belasco, which DeMille then brought to the screen. The visual elements added by DeMille conserved Belasco's penchant for spectacle but were decidedly "filmic" in their use of lighting (such as the impressionistic campfire scene in *The Virginian*), atmosphere (such as a functioning train depot in *The Squaw Man*), and nature (such as the forest scenes of *A Romance of the Redwoods*). In many ways, the security offered by the "legitimate theater" allowed DeMille room to experiment with novel narration and film performances. His West proved less a faithful representation of actual conditions on the frontier and more of a mythic simulacra envisioned by his Eastern patrons (Blanke 2018: 173–83).

By 1937, commercial cinema was now operated by the efficient economic and aesthetic imperatives of the studio system. DeMille's failed effort at independent production (from 1925 to 1928), history of bad-tempered relations with management, and profligate spending made him a risky investment during the Great Depression. The director's ability to return to the fold, rejoining Paramount in 1932, and nimble response to his managers' demands for cost-effective historical melodramas led him to drop highbrow European settings for the more readily available locales of the American West. The public's preference for cinematic realism was now well established, leading the now chastened, middle-aged director to follow the conventions of narration and performance defining the classical style (Blanke 2018: 183–96).

Notably, both phases witnessed destabilizing external conditions. Both were buffeted by war, economic upheaval, and radically new ideologies. In both, the role of women within the public sphere remained an open debate, from the demands of the "New Woman" and suffragists of the 1910s to the displaced Depression-era migrants and emerging "We Can Do It" determination of female laborers during World War II.

Yet the "apparatus" of American commercial cinema does not fully explain the content of DeMille's films from either period, particularly in terms of his representation of women. Even the director's staunchest critics admitted his profound respect for active, intelligent, and determined women in both his personal and professional life. J. E. Smyth's recent study, *Nobody's Girl Friday: The Women Who Ran Hollywood*, notes how the core of DeMille's most trusted colleagues and collaborators were all female, including Jeanie Macpherson, Gladys Rosson, and Anne Bauchens (2018: 1). While never considered a "woman's director," like Ernst Lubitsch or George Cukor, DeMille discovered a talent for dramatizing strong women characters. Jesse Lasky recalled how, before 1915 "I happened to pick plays with male stars, and we made fourteen pictures before we bought one that called for a female lead" (Lasky and Weldon 1957: 102). Once this changed, however, DeMille's work came to be dominated by female actors—from Geraldine Farrar and Mary Pickford to Julia Faye and Gloria Swanson—exploring both the traditional and revolutionary potential of gender. During these years, William de Mille wrote how his brother "delighted in dealing with *various* forms of feminine lure, with which the ladies of the audience fondly identified themselves" (1939: 239).

While sexism and patriarchy were core components of everyday life, the director explicitly rejected gender as a meaningful distinction of public morality. DeMille's (in)famous cinematic portrayals of infidelity, divorce, and lush consumerism carried no gender-specific stigma. In response to Adolph Zukor, who initially sought to censor DeMille's depiction of women's sexuality in *Old Wives for New*, the director argued, "If a woman has made a false step, as it is called, I don't see anything to agonize over. She has had an experience, and if she only knows how to profit from her misstep, she will become all the better." Unwilling to assign a scarlet letter, he thought "the best thing for her to do, in my opinion, is to forget it. Everyone else should forget it too. The 'ruined woman' is out of style; as out of style as the woman of the Victorian era who used to faint at every little alarm" (MSS 1400 LTPSC, Bx 315, Folder 4; Louvish, 2007: xvi). Accordingly, while the economic and aesthetic context of the times certainly influenced DeMille as he constructed his works for public consumption, the argument that these films represent a pure distillation of the paternal economic structure of his industry appear overwrought.

Moreover, DeMille was particularly comfortable with competent and strong-willed female actors. In this early phase, Winifred Kingston starred in the director's first three Westerns. A veteran actor, Kingston earned her fame on Broadway, co-starring with Dustin Farnum in *Soldiers of Fortune*, before appearing on DeMille's set. Red Wing (aka Lillian St Cyr), who plays Nat-U-Rich in *The Squaw Man*, began acting with Kalem Company in 1908, and appeared regularly for the New York Motion Picture Company and Pathé Frères. Finally, Mary Pickford, who starred in two DeMille productions, not only controlled her own production studio but was perhaps the single best-known motion picture actor of the 1910s (Birchard 2004: 5, 7).[2]

The plots of DeMille's earliest Westerns relied upon simple and direct narrative threads. In *The Squaw Man* (1914), English aristocrat James Wynnegate (Dustin Farnum) accepts the blame for a scandal perpetrated by his cousin, Sir Henry (Monroe Salisbury), and flees to the American West to preserve the family's name and shield Henry's wife, Lady Diana (Winifred Kingston), from disgrace. Wynnegate quickly displays the fortitude and honesty needed to thrive as a rancher. A smitten Native American woman, Nat-U-Rich (Red Wing, a Winnebago Indian), saves Wynnegate from both a murderous wrangler, Cash Hawkins (Billy Elmer), and the brutal natural environment. The two fall in love, conceive a child, and when Sir Henry's deathbed confession exonerates

Wynnegate—and elevates his child to heir of the family estate—Nat-U-Rich commits suicide to free Wynnegate to return "home" to Lady Diana and forestall an Indian uprising.

The Virginian (1914) shows the rapid development of DeMille's cinematic talents—featuring much more textured visual compositions and an effective use of parallel editing—and takes advantage of Wister's uncluttered melodramatic plot (reducing Native Americans merely to a threatening other in order to focus on the travails of the white colonists). The Virginian (Farnum) and his friend Steve (J. W. Johnston) move to the western cattle country, experiencing the hard life of saloons, roundups, and frontier banditry. The Virginian concentrates his time and attention on the new schoolteacher, Molly (again played by Kingston), thereby neglecting Steve who, now lacking his fun-loving playmate, falls in with the outlaw Trampas (Billy Elmer). Steve is hanged for his crimes and the Virginian, risking the love of Molly, pursues and kills Trampas to reap both justice and personal vengeance. While Molly's role remains muted, her character sets the narrative conditions through which the men must pass: demanding that the stage driver abstain from liquor, offering cowhands the promise of upward mobility through education, and later by threatening to leave Steve for his pursuit of vengeance.

The melodramatic elements of both pictures resonate with those of the popular stage, but DeMille accentuates this linkage through his use of well-known actors, like Farnum and Kingston (adding the intertextual dynamic of casting his wife as a dramatic love interest), and reliance upon stock company conventions (the familiar Billy Elmer plays the "heavy" in both films). These and other qualities—such as his reliance upon the dramatic "reversal of fortune" and interludes of pure spectacle—became the defining qualities of an emerging DeMille brand, ones he retained throughout his long career (Blanke 2018: 45–89).

But *A Romance of the Redwoods* (1917) shows that the director was also learning to take greater advantage of the more subtle storytelling qualities that film held over the stage. The narrative (a reworking of Belasco's *The Girl of the Golden West*) follows the travails of the orphaned Jenny Lawrence (Mary Pickford), who elects to travel west to live with her uncle John. Unknown to Jenny, John Lawrence is killed by Indians and his identity stolen by the rakish outlaw "Black" Brown (Elliot Dexter). Learning the harsh realities of both life in a frontier town and Brown's duplicity, Jenny endeavors to adjust to her new world. The two fall in love. When Brown is finally apprehended for a stagecoach robbery—committed in violation of his vow to Jenny to go clean, yet intended to stake them for a move further west—Jenny saves him from the hangman's noose by claiming that she is pregnant and that Brown is the father of her child. Unbelievably, the posse releases Brown and the couple are free to restart their lives on the frontier.

Assessing the films collectively, it is clear that DeMille's early Western women are all active protagonists that drive the narrative of the genre. Indeed, aside from several unrealistic twists of fate—including a poisonous geyser, a mountaineering accident, and a western vacation that brings the English aristocrats to the same isolated outpost where Wynnegate settled—the entirety of the Western portion of *The Squaw Man* is driven by Nat-U-Rich's decisions to murder Hawkins, rescue Wynngate, and take her own life. *The Virginian*'s Molly actively chooses to relocate to the frontier—to which her mother remarks, "I am so glad you are accepting the opportunity to go to the great west"—while Jenny, perhaps ignorant of the realities she faces, endures the trials of both an arduous journey and her chaotic arrival with steely determination. Thrown into the bawdy world of a Western saloon—where drunken, mixed-race groups of men mash with violent and opportunistic prostitutes—Jenny soon learns that the rules of female domesticity will not save her. Forced by Brown to validate his false identity, Jenny learns that she is the author of her own Western identity (a realization that later leads to her ingenious solution to Brown's hanging). For each, to "go to the great west" and persevere as free agents is not only a sign of their strength of character but, arguably, the narrative purpose of all three films. Unlike his later works, DeMille's West acts as a proving ground for all—women as well as men.

These films also introduce an essential theme to DeMille's Westerns—the dialectical relationship between East and West—that changes radically between the two phases. In the early works, the director presents Eastern society to his audience in familiar terms, featuring its restrictive, structured, static, and largely corrupted nature. Here civilization is regulated by arbitrary rules of behavior that define one's worth materially—through wealth, technology, and social standing—rather than through innate character and fortitude. This world is clearly negative in terms of women's volition, women who are seen as passive and asked to do little more than ornament a male-dominated society. This influence is shown subtly in *Redwoods* when "Black" Brown validates his purloined identity through the letters he receives from his eastern "relations." But when Jenny is faced with her chaotic new life with Brown and his henchmen—in a cabin riven with rats, dirt, and garbage—she doesn't pine for the lost creature comforts that once defined her gender but rather begins re-fashioning her home with what she finds at hand.

Of equal importance, given the shifts seen later, this portrayal of the East forcefully undermines the logic of cultural assimilation. If the old is a place of repression and conformity, then the new offers an unstructured and open proving ground for the expression of innate character. Accordingly, the West in DeMille's early pictures exists to *reveal* the authenticity and agency of characters who learn to abandon the questionable structures of a falsely ordered world. The narrative pleasures emerge as the audience sorts through the imposters, offering a refreshingly novel reading to the hackneyed trope of "the innocent Easterner."

Physical goods—always attractive to the lens of DeMille—play an important symbolic role in this dynamic between East and West. While muted in *The Squaw Man*, both Molly and Jenny arrive West laden with numerous hatboxes, birdcages, and fancy clothing. Jenny's repurposing of a set of doll's clothes—purchased by Brown as a symbol of Eastern-gendered domesticity—to exonerate (or, at least, to deflect the charges against) the outlaw reveals how intelligent women could now *use* material possessions *in situ*, rather than passively consume products and conform to the expectations of others. Jenny's small Eastern gun—which initially elicits laughter from hardened Westerners—may not be capable of intimidating criminals but she uses it later to shoot Brown, a disguised highwayman, to inflict an injury that then identifies him to the local constables. Repurposed for their new environment, possessions grant Western women the opportunity to demonstrate their own legitimacy, repurposed in a foreign, hostile, and unregulated terrain.

Not only does DeMille give Western women the ability to prove their social worth, but, in all three films, it is women who finally endorse the male characters' legitimacy. Collectively, these works introduce the audience to a Western world without rules and driven by crime, violence, drinking, and prostitution. In *The Virginian*, Steve's benevolent nature is revealed (and his tragic fall to a life of crime heightened) by the harmless pranks he and the Virginian play on the settlers. But without the guiding hand of an intelligent woman to aid him, Steve falls prey to Western vice and his own downfall. By contrast, Molly redeems the Virginian through education while Jenny converts Brown to an appreciation of hard work, convincing him to pan for gold rather than accept the ill-gotten gains of robbery. Even the illogical conclusion to *Redwoods*, where the posse frees Brown from the noose due to Jenny's "pregnancy," validates the role of active women in absolving men of their sins. In the closing scene, the sheriff agrees, "We're going to let you marry that cuss—and give you a chance to make him straight." Collectively, the narrative arc of all three films peaks when a Western woman validates the man's growth and change.

Significantly, children and family play only minor roles in the performance of the leading women. While Wynnegate's child and Jenny's pregnancy serve important narrative functions, there is little concern that both conceptions occur out of wedlock. Children are not pictured in the Eastern scenes, but what little is shown in the West suggests almost no gendered responsibilities for women alone. Passages depicting the baby-swapping prank and, more chillingly, older children role-playing a public lynching in *The Virginian* elicit no maternal instincts in Molly and exist solely as narrative threats posed to both women and men. Only the awkward pathos of *The Squaw Man*, where a Native American woman's love and heroic sacrifice is blithely used to justify the reunification of two English aristocrats, does DeMille even hint that domesticity factors into the lives of his Western women. Perhaps somewhat ironically, then, the film concludes with the discovery of Nat-U-Rich's suicide and the anemic pity offered by the marshal in closing: "Poor little mother."

In sum, the early phase of DeMille's Western cycle exhibited a set of shared narrative and performance qualities concerning gender. In each film, the leading female characters are all strong women, possessing volition and agency that mark them as narratively independent of their male counterparts. The East is presented as a place of structured conformity heightened by the unpredictable freedoms now available on the frontier. There is no sense that Eastern values could or even should stand as a test of Western character. DeMille's Western women embrace the opportunities offered in the West, repurposing their skills and possessions to meet the contingencies of their new lives. Finally, none are defined by "home" or "childrearing." While these aspects are present, the romantic union that results from the various plot twists leave notions of family unresolved. Both Molly and the Virginian and Jenny and Brown depart as couples to uncertain fates. Rather, it is the way that Western women actualize the potential of the leading male characters that completes the melodrama.

During his second phase of Western film production, DeMille benefitted from the more polished narrative techniques established by the Hollywood studios. Better film technologies and the growing demand for realism helped producers to reinvigorate a genre that, by the late 1920s, appeared stale and uninteresting. These narratives turned more violent, more male, and their messages more proscriptive than the female-centered melodramas of the 1910s. The development of new Western stars—such as Gary Cooper, Joel McRae, and John Wayne –solidified this shift in tone and refashioned the narratives ascribed to Western women.

DeMille's first contribution to this renaissance was *The Plainsman* (1937). Loosely based on the lives of "Wild Bill" Hickok (Gary Cooper), "Calamity Jane" Canary (Jean Arthur), and "Buffalo Bill" Cody (James Ellison), the complex narrative tracks their efforts to prevent John Lattimer (Charles Bickford), a corrupt, post-Civil War gunrunner, from arming hostile Native Americans. The characters are humanized by an ill-fated love interest, between Hickok and Canary, and the contrast between the rugged individualism of Hickok and the sudden domesticity of his best friend, the newly married Cody. The action follows their passage West, Hickok's efforts to pacify the hostile Indians, his torture—when Canary, in an effort to save her lover, provides Yellow Hand (Paul Harvey) the location to a small team of military scouts—and Hickok's efforts to undo the effects of her betrayal and bring Lattimer to frontier justice. While these events are purely fictionalized—although Hickok, of course, dies from treachery after being dealt the "dead man's hand" of black aces and eights—DeMille peppers the staging with convincing historical cameos of Abraham Lincoln, members of his Cabinet, and George Armstrong Custer (who dies with guns a-blazing).

Two years later, DeMille released *Union Pacific* (1939), an adaptation of John Ford's *The Iron Horse* (1924). Again, corrupt capitalists provide the dramatic tension to the tale of completing the transcontinental railroad. Here Sid Campeau (Brian Donlevy) is charged by deep-pocketed stock speculators to delay construction of the line by any means necessary. Civil War hero and sharpshooter Jeff Butler (Joel McCrae) is hired to thwart Campeau and his henchmen, including Butler's fun-loving wartime buddy Dick Allen (Robert Preston). Jeff must also negotiate through an awkward love triangle between himself, Allen, and the irascibly spunky Mollie Monahan (Barbara Stanwyk), an Irish immigrant, daughter to the train's engineer, and postmistress for the railroad. Indians again serve a menacing role—yet notably, as in *The Plainsman*, DeMille presents them as tragic and generally honorable figures, the unintended victims of unscrupulous capitalists—just as the director again relies on numerous historical figures to legitimize the tale.

Notably, the erosion of social agency expressed by DeMille's Western women stands in stark contrast to the strong performances given by his lead female actors: Jean Arthur and Barbara Stanwyck. While initially offering the role of Mollie Monahan to Claudette Colbert (a veteran DeMille performer), the director later admitted he never witnessed "a better workman, to use my term of highest compliment, than Barbara Stanwyck." Indeed, the strength of personality displayed by both Arthur and Stanwyck only accentuates their characters' indecisiveness and subjectivity (Hayne 1959: 364–5).

Both films were box-office hits, are visually attractive, and remain strangely engaging today. Admitting to the racial othering of Native Americans—so prevalent in the genre—should not overshadow the lengths to which DeMille went to humanize non-whites and immigrants in both productions. Again, while the assimilation model is correctly seen today as a form of cultural imperialism, the director generally absolves the guilt of indigenous people as the product of white greed. Black, Mexican (Akin Tamiroff plays "Fiesta" in *Union Pacific*), and a host of white ethnic characters are also given the space to make a legitimate claim on their American Dream.

The greatest tonal shift in addressing gender flows from the director's new handling of the cultural dynamic between East and West. Whereas in his earlier treatments the East was presented as a dramatically deadened place of structured conformity, in these more recent films the East now serves as a moral compass, an unerring North Star to guide male progress across the plains. DeMille begins both films with extended prologues set in Washington. Containing sophisticated facsimiles (relying on dense *mise-en-scène* compositions and multiple tracking shots) of Congressional debates, Cabinet meetings, and boardroom politics, their openings lead to the assassination of Lincoln and vows by somber idealists to see his democratic vision for the West fulfilled. With male (save for Mary Todd Lincoln, no women appear in either prologue) greed creating the dramatic tension, the West is not set up as an open proving ground to *reveal* character but rather as a test of one's fidelity to the higher ideals already established and validated by "great men" in the East.

In two pivotal scenes, Hickok announces his role as herald and male defender of these truths. Explaining to Louisa Cody (Helen Burgess) why her husband must leave their home and return to the dangers of the wilderness, he patiently reminds her of their civic obligation to national development:

> *Hickok*: There are things that have to be done, ma'am. You know, Lincoln set a goal that we have to work toward. He said the frontier must be made safe.
> *Louisa*: Oh, but Lincoln's dead. What right have the dead to tell the living what to do?
> *Hickok*: His words are alive. Bill Cody knows that as well as I do.

Later, when addressing a mob riled by the Indian ambush, Hickok reprises this same theme. Delivered as if quoting scripture, Cooper lectures the mewling townsfolk: "Lincoln said this country's got to be made safe. Those are his words." Two years later, DeMille works the same ideas into the male characters in *Union Pacific*. Railroad contractors should not allow western contingencies to cloud eastern certainties. "I promised Mr. Lincoln," one engineer intones soon after the assassination, and "my promise to him is not dead."

This pronounced reversal in the positive values ascribed to East and West produce a profoundly negative effect on the performance of Western women. Arriving with a firm vision of an ideal society fully formed, Western men no longer needed women to validate their actions or to forgive their violent sins (as witnessed in the earlier trilogy). Indeed, women's individualism now appeared to be a negative consequence of the emotions unleashed by their westering experience. In *The Plainsman*, Calamity struggles to justify her Western sexual freedoms to a Hickok enthralled by Eastern domesticity and order. At their initial reintroduction, on the busy river landing of Leavenworth, Canary questions why he never wrote. Ironically, the exchange directly contrasts comments delivered earlier on women's sexual freedom:

> *Hickok*: A woman who has a fellow at every stage station and a beau in every cavalry troop west of the Missouri—that woman doesn't need any letters from me.
> *Canary*: Those fellows don't mean nothing to me.
> *Hickok*: Well, they did to me.
> *Canary*: Aww, let's forget it. Maybe I did make a mistake.
> *Hickok*: Well, you won't get a chance to make that mistake again.

Hickok dismisses the unruly Calamity to help the overwhelmed Mrs Cody load her many goods onto the stage. Canary uses her whip to snatch the hat off Hickok's head as he walks away, demanding he "tip your hat when you speak to a lady," to which he replies, "I will, when I speak to a lady." Similarly, when Jeff and Dick struggle to deal with Mollie's rambunctious Western spirit Dick reminds his friend that "You can't fight Mollie and live." Unlike girls back East, Mollie is not only a free spirit but torn by her public obligation. She is no Eastern debutante but "the postmistress at End of Track," Dick explains, "The eyes and tongue of a thousand men . . . She belongs to the railroad, although you'd think the railroad belonged to her."

Failing the test of Eastern civility, both Calamity Jane and Mollie Monahan are essentially flawed and incomplete characters corrupted by the West. Both are freed by the looser social restrictions on the frontier (handled flawlessly by the remarkable talents of Arthur and Stanwyck), but for both these liberties turn them away from the higher principles of the East. Both are denied the agency and moral fortitude that motivated characters like Nat-U-Rich or Jenny Lawrence. Mollie admits she's become "an outrageous flirt" while working on the tracks, but we see that her behavior is merely an extension of the unhealthy liberties afforded by her Western lifestyle. As she explains to Jeff (intoned with an Irish brogue), in the West she can play the role of an emotional gunslinger.

> But did you never know that flirting gets into a woman's blood like fighting gets into a man's? Now a girl begins coquetting to discover if she has the power. Then she goes looking, like a fighter after a bully, for the hardest man to conquer. But this is never the man she wants, 'tis the pleasure of bringing him to her feet.

With these inherent flaws, the Western women now serve largely as distractions from the real business at hand. A recurring visual device employed by DeMille in *The Plainsman* is for Calamity unexpectedly to kiss Hickok, only to have the scout purposefully wipe his lips as if removing the residue of emotions that might cloud his judgment. In later scenes, a wounded Hickok seeks temporary refuge in the home of Louisa Cody. Pregnant and desperate to keep her husband at home, she becomes hysterical when Bill demands they treat the wounds Hickok received during a recent shoot-out.

> You brought this man to our house, a murderer! When is this going to stop?! This killing and killing! Why don't they [Army] kill him too? And then you can be the next, and then me, and then . . . [looking to her own midriff and the unborn baby]

Calmly explaining his battles as part of a larger ideological fight, Hickok corrects the sobbing woman by noting that he requires no forgiveness from her.

His violence was justified, he concludes, "I was never a murderer. I never did fight unless [his ideals were] put upon."

Given the relative scarcity of male violence depicted in his earlier series, the repeated reliance upon physical confrontation is quite stark. Undeniably, DeMille's early films displayed shoot-outs, ambushes, and threats of mob justice. Yet these typically served as simple narrative devices that resulted in a new dramatic problem for the characters to solve: an orphaned Jenny or a charge of murder leveled against Nat-U-Rich. By contrast, in the more recent works violence or the threat of violence served as critical indicators of male characters acting on principles established either before their appearance in the West or off camera entirely. The audience, not Western women, were now tasked with forgiving their sins. The repeated use of knives and whips, displayed by Hickok or Fiesta for example, suggests how these behaviors serve as legitimate tools for principled men to resolve conflict. The humanizing interplay between Hickok and a Tom Sawyer-like boy at the St Louis River dock ends when Hickok throws his eight-inch hunting knife from the departing boat, embedding it in a beam mere inches from the boy's head! Coming on the heels of their male bonding—with Hickok imparting fatherly wisdom about girls, bison, and Indians—the scene reinforces the idea that violence acts as a necessary extension to ideological certainty. One could never be a "murderer" if the killing served one of these higher ends. Viewing the film years after its initial release, it remains stunning how seamlessly DeMille's depiction of Hickok's smoldering rage—where he is willing to kill his best friend to achieve what he considers justice—anticipates that of John Ford's Ethan Edwards in *The Searchers* (1956), just as Cooper's confrontation with the mob's bloodlust and cowardice hints at his Award-winning performance in *High Noon* (1952).

Finally, the presentation of goods further reveals this shift in gendered perspectives. In the earlier films, material possessions from the East—like hatboxes or a doll's clothes—provided opportunities for characters to reimagine and repurpose their new lives on the frontier. The later films, by contrast, suggest that women in particular, and non-whites in general, were unable to avoid the egocentric lures of consumerism. Calamity Jane—presented initially as a free-spirited and unburdened product of the West—is entranced by the fine clothing offered to her by Louisa Cody, thereby allowing a group of hostile Indians to enter their cabin and take them hostage. In both *The Plainsman* and *Union Pacific*, Native Americans are rendered passive by alluring merchandise while white ethnics prove themselves to be easy victims to alcohol and the consumed vice at the "End of Line" saloon. Notably, DeMille first introduces the audience to Buffalo Bill as a newly married frontiersman. Unlike the functional garb of Hickok—who still donned his Union Army uniform—Cody is dandified and clumsily greets his friend through armloads of hatboxes and a birdcage (nearly the exact same goods carried by Molly in *The Virginian* and Jenny in *A Romance of the Redwoods*).

Hickok: I see a good fighting man who's been fool enough to get himself married. I see she hasn't cut your hair yet.
Cody: I don't know what you mean, Bill.
Hickok: You know what happened to Samson when Delilah opened her barbershop. Has she tamed you yet?
Cody: That ain't fair. She's different.
Hickok: You're different.

These goods distract Cody, preventing him from observing an incident revealing the presence of gunrunners, a fact noticed by the unburdened Hickok. It is not until Cody spends six weeks in the wilderness—tracking Hickok for the murder of three corrupt soldiers—away from the pleasures of both his wife and the creature comforts of their home that Cody regains his ideological purpose.

By contrast, the single male heroes all prove immune to these material distractions. Jeff Butler appears wholly uninterested in gambling or the degenerate lures of the rail towns (although he uses both to fool workers to do his bidding). While Hickok is enamored of a musical watch—containing an endearing picture of himself with Calamity—he recognizes that the product is meaningful merely for its use value in the West: as a bet in a high-stakes poker game or as a ruse to entice the Native warriors to arrange a meeting with their chief. As before, the ennobling actions, once open to all, including a female character like Jenny in *A Romance of the Redwoods*, has shifted to become an exclusively gendered quality of a Western *Übermensch* like Hickok.

Drawing lessons from the shifting representation of DeMille's Western women demands acknowledging the various levels of analysis open to film scholars. On the one hand, the conventions of cinematic genre need to be recognized as permeable boundaries open to highly subjective interpretations. While the functional properties of genre—its semantics and syntax—remain stable, the line separating the performance of women as symbols of the Western homestead versus their ability to act upon the individual freedoms offered by the frontier are clearly buffeted by historical context, audience expectations, and commercial needs. DeMille plainly presents, in all of the films reviewed, women as active narrative agents essential to the plot's final resolution. Yet, just as obviously, the performance of these characters shifted from neutral representations of gender (that is, as women reacting to the same challenges and opportunities as men) to symbolic characters placed within the story to resolve male-centered plots (where women themselves present threats or distractions to male objectives). The shift from domestic melodrama to historical melodrama, ironically, relegated Western women's agency from the public, as witnessed in the films of the 1910s, now to the private sphere.

In his early years—before the studio system gained control over his film production—DeMille's Western women served as capable individuals eager to meet the emotional challenges posed by melodrama. Reflecting the director's own biases, those of the female audience he sought to entertain, and perhaps drawing upon the zeitgeist of first-wave feminism, these early films looked beyond the limits posed by sexism in the East to the opportunities afforded by new frontiers. They argued that female protagonists like Natu-U-Rich, Molly, and Jenny not only could overcome these obstacles but that the West's fluid and unstable social structure presented the very conditions whereby these women's strengths could finally be realized. Notably, the broader syntax of these early Westerns presented the East (not women) as the "problem," a static and highly structured social arrangement that was antithetical to individual freedom.

By contrast, DeMille's later films earned the full support of the studio system and epitomized Paramount's Depression-era marketing of commercial film. Here, the syntax of the Western turned towards a national self-examination. While glorifying populist elements common to the era, these works also subsumed the quest for individual freedom on the frontier for plots that reassured citizens of their country's collective progress past difficult obstacles. This distinction was made most evident through DeMille's semantic use of goods. Where once these items offered creative women tools to rework their new environment, now they represented alluring traps (offering comfort and pleasure) to those too weak or too privileged to maintain the rugged discipline that Western expansion demanded (Altman 1984: 6–18; Neale 2000: 2, 18).

The intensifying depiction (and acceptance) of male violence further distanced female characters from bridging this increasingly gendered divide. Serving little role in the syntax of his early Westerns—violence was typically used to establish a sense of immaturity and social irresponsibility in a character—women like Nat-U-Rich and Jenny could, as with Eastern goods, use violence selectively to further the narrative aims of the picture. By the 1930s and the revival of the Motion Picture Production Code, however, violence was not only an exclusively male quality but was both misunderstood and feared by the female characters. Hickok's sociopathic bent—willing to kill anyone, including his closest friends, who threatened his fundamental reading of "His words"—made his actions appear illogical, even sociopathic to these Western women (whose moral reasoning was largely neutralized by the Code), yet he was a hero to his audience.

In many ways, the most insidious effect of this shift was to neutralize the moral reasoning of both the leading female characters and the audience. In its earliest guise, DeMille's Western women performed as active, free spirits capable of evaluating the merit of one's character based on behavior (and often playing critical narrative roles in the absolution of male guilt, as was the case for Wynnegate, the Virginian, and "Black" Brown). By 1937, however, the women DeMille depicted had lost this capacity. They evaluated society based on personal notions of happiness, security, and fear. The lessons drawn by an audience were cautionary tales of gender uncontained by the dire conditions found in the West.

While it is tempting to look to the apparatus of commercial film production and the unfettered sexism that ran through the leading institutions of Hollywood, it remains the shifting goals to which DeMille and others now set the Western. When fixed to examine the function of gender within a society that had yet to establish clear rules and power structures, DeMille's early films offered women opportunities that find modern similarities within the plot lines of HBO's *Westworld*. Yet when set to examine national exceptionalism during years of growing anxiety, women's contribution to this self-examination was increasingly ignored. Perhaps, then, it should come as no surprise that Cooper's performance, in 1937, presaged the Western male ideal of Cold War-era Westerns like *High Noon* or *The Searchers*. The syntactical gymnastics largely completed, Hollywood now shifted the "threat" to male independence (morphing "others" from hostile Indians and the environment to emotional women and ideological collaborators) and assertively ignored the need to explore the performances of their female cast members.

Notes

1. For more on DeMille's extended career and historical reputation among the Classical era directors, see David Blanke, *Cecil B. DeMille, Classical Hollywood, and Modern American Mass Culture, 1910–1960* (New York: Palgrave Macmillan, 2018).
2. Pickford's interactions with DeMille were complicated in 1917 by her weakening position within Famous Players-Lasky Company. See Blanke, *DeMille, Classical Hollywood, and Modern American Mass Culture*, pp. 73–7.

Filmography

A Romance of the Redwoods, director Cecil B. DeMille, featuring Mary Pickford, Elliott Dexter, Tully Marshall (Artcraft Pictures and Paramount Pictures, 1917).

High Noon, director Fred Zinnemann, featuring Gary Cooper, Grace Kelly, Thomas Mitchell (Stanley Kramer Productions, 1952).

North West Mounted Police, director Cecil B. DeMille, featuring Gary Cooper, Madeleine Carroll, Paulette Goddard (Paramount, 1940).

Old Wives for New, director Cecil B. DeMille, featuring Elliott Dexter, Florence Vidor, Sylvia Ashton (Artcraft Pictures, 1918).

The Buccaneer, director Cecil B. DeMille, featuring Frederic March, Franciska Gaal, Akim Tamiroff (Paramount, 1938).

The Call of the North, director Oscar Apfel and Cecil B. DeMille, featuring Robert Edeson, Theodore Roberts, Winifred Kingston (Jesse L. Lasky Feature Play, 1914).

The Girl of the Golden West, director Cecil B. DeMille, featuring Mabel Van Buren, Theodore Roberts, House Peters (Jesse L. Lasky Feature Play, 1915).

The Iron Horse, director John Ford, featuring George O'Brien, Madge Bellamy, Charles Edward Bull (Fox, 1924).

The Plainsman, director Cecil B. DeMille, featuring Gary Cooper, Jane Arthur, James Ellison (Paramount, 1937).

The Rose of the Rancho, director Cecil B. DeMille, featuring Bessie Barriscale, Jane Darwell, Dick La Reno (Jesse L. Lasky Feature Play, 1914).

The Searchers, director John Ford, featuring John Wayne, Jeffrey Hunter, Vera Miles (C. V. Witney Pictures, 1956).

The Squaw Man, directors Oscar Apfel and Cecil B. DeMille, featuring Dustin Farnum, Monroe Salisbury, Winifred Kingston (Jesse L. Lasky Feature Play, 1914).

The Trail of the Lonesome Pine, director Cecil B. DeMille, featuring Charlotte Walker, Thomas Meighan, Earle Foxe (Jesse L. Lasky Feature Play, 1916).

The Virginian, director Cecil B. DeMille, featuring Dustin Farnum, Jack W. Johnston, Sydney Deane (Jesse L. Lasky Feature Play, 1914).

Unconquered, director Cecil B. DeMille, featuring Gary Cooper, Paulette Goddard, Howard Da Silva (Paramount, 1947).

Union Pacific, director Cecil B. DeMille, featuring Barbara Stanwyck, Joel McCrea, Akim Tamiroff (Paramount, 1939).

Westworld (HBO), featuring Evan Rachel Wood, Jeffrey Wright, Ed Harris (Bad Robot, Jeffrey Weintraub, Kilter Films, 2016).

Bibliography

Altman, Rick (1984) "A Semantic/Syntactic Approach to Film Genre," *Cinema Journal*, 23 (3), pp. 6–18.

Blanke, David (2018) *Cecil B. DeMille, Classical Hollywood, and Modern American Mass Culture, 1910–1960*. New York: Palgrave Macmillan.

Birchard, Robert S. (2004) *Cecil B. DeMille's Hollywood*. Lexington, KY: University Press of Kentucky.

DeMille, William C. (1939) *Hollywood Saga*. New York: E. P. Dutton.

Hayne, Donald (ed.) (1959) *The Autobiography of Cecil B. DeMille*. Englewood Cliffs, NJ: Prentice-Hall.

Lamont, Victoria (2016) *Westerns: A Women's History*. Lincoln, NE: University Press of Nebraska, 2016.

Lasky, Jesse L. and Weldon, Don (1957) *I Blow My Own Horn*. New York: Doubleday.

Louvish, Simon (2007) *Cecil B. DeMille: A Life in Art*. New York: Thomas Dunne Books.

Lusted, David (1996) "Social Class and the Western as Male Melodrama," in Ian Cameron and Douglas Pye (eds), *The Movie Book of the Western*. London: Studio Vista, pp. 63–74.

MSS 1400, The Cecil B. DeMille Archives; Film/Music Archives; L. Tom Perry Special Collections, Harold B. Lee Library, Brigham Young University.

Neale, Steve (2000) *Genre and Hollywood*. New York: Routledge.

Smyth, J. E. (2018) *Nobody's Girl Friday: The Women Who Ran Hollywood*. New York: Oxford University Press.

4. THE VIRGINIAN AND THE ROSE: TWO KEY FEMALE ROLES IN WESTERN FILMS AND COMICS

David Huxley

INTRODUCTION

This chapter will concentrate on two very different Western texts and look at the ways in which they do not restrict women to the home and domesticity. The first text is Owen Wister's 1903 *The Virginian*, which is one of the most famous of Western novels and has been adapted into different media on many occasions. The second is a much more obscure 1950s film and its comic book adaptation, *The Rose of Cimarron*. What links the two is their portrayal of women, the latter with a central heroine and the former with, in some versions at least, a perhaps surprisingly powerful female presence. For many Western directors the role of women is summed up by Budd Boetticher, "What counts is what the heroine provokes, or rather what she represents. She is the one . . .who makes him act the way he does. In herself the woman has not the slightest importance" (quoted in Buscombe 1993: 241). Although this may be something of a truism for many mainstream Hollywood Westerns, it is by no means ubiquitous. Historically, Western texts, which feature a strong central female figure as opposed to important, or even peripheral, love interest, are rare. Not surprisingly when these do occur at any time in the so-called classic period of Hollywood, they have received a lot of critical attention—a major example of this phenomenon is Nicholas Ray's 1954 Western, *Johnny Guitar*.[1] I do not intend to add to any of this specific literature here, but rather will concentrate on *The Rose of Cimarron*, a 1952 Twentieth Century Fox production directed by Harry Keller and written by Maurice Geragthy. First, however, I will look at the changing role of women in various versions of Owen Wister's classic novel *The Virginian* and its precursors. Although *The Virginian* might appear to be a text which features a classic and essentially inactive heroine as love interest, in some versions women are able to make a key contribution to the plot. Arguably, the original novel is closer to the ideas of Theodore Roosevelt (to whom the book is dedicated); "The man must be glad to do a man's work, to dare and to endure and to labor; and to keep those dependant on him. The woman must be the housewife, the helpmate of the homemaker, the wise and fearless mother of many children . . ." (quoted in Slotkin 1993: 52).

The Dime Novel

Owen Wister's novel, *The Virginian*, is rightly acknowledged as a key book in the development of the Western *mythos*, and in particular the distillation of the image of the cowboy as hero. However, any sense of seeing the book as a starting point is to ignore a vast amount of cheap dime novel material produced well before that book. The quality of this material is highly variable, and often very poor, but the sheer quantity that was produced in the forty years before the novel was published demonstrates that the Western story was well established as the events that they fictionalized were still taking place. Although melodramatic in tone, and normally populated with women who require rescuing by the hero, there are exceptions. In *The Rover of the Forest, or the Warrior's Last War-Whoop*, an anonymous 1865 entry in Munro's Ten Cent Series, the heroine, though she is destined to undergo various tribulations and eventually marry the hero, is introduced thus: "Mary was a beauty, delicate and fair, and seemed better fitted to adorn a drawing room than to figure as the heroine of a backwoods tale. And yet, though fair, she was possessed of both nerve and vigor, and could handle a rifle or wield an axe with wonderful precision and ease" (quoted in American Antiquarian Society, available at <http://americanantiquarian.org/dimenovelwomen/exhibits/show/the-women/mollie-hanley> [last accessed 3 July 2018]). In among the many stereotypes in so many dime novels, it is encouraging, and perhaps surprising, to see this tribute not only to her shooting ability but also her slightly worrying "precision" in axe work. At the same time there were, of course, also plays and shows that contributed to the dissemination of the myth, in particular *Buffalo Bill's* Wild West and *Congress* of Rough Riders of the World, which (in various forms) performed its version of the West all over the world from 1883 to well into the twentieth century. Buffalo Bill Cody's star performer (and most proficient shot in his entire company) for much of this time was, of course, "Little Miss Sureshot," Annie Oakley.

The Virginian; A Horseman of the Plains: The Novel, 1902

The novel was hugely successful, with its strong, heroic central character and its romanticized portrayal of the hardships and dangers of the American West. There are many twists and turns in the plot, but two of its central themes are the Virginian's rivalry with the villainous cowboy Trampas, and his reluctant duty in hanging his friend turned cattle rustler, Steve. The latter event is pivotal to the narrative, and leads to a key disagreement between the Virginian and his love interest, the innocent Eastern schoolteacher, Molly. This is the point when Molly has to realize that the law of the West is different to her concept of justice in the East that leads to a hugely important conversation that undergoes interesting changes in different versions of the text.

In the novel, the lynching has to be explained to Molly by Judge Henry, although he does do it at the behest of his wife. First, he realizes that it will not be easy to explain himself. He muses that, "He was well aware that if he was to touch at all upon this subject with the New England girl, he could not put her off with mere platitudes and humdrum formulas; not, at least, if he expected to do any good. She was far too intelligent, and he was really anxious to do good" (Wister 1902: n.p.).

His argument is that, in a lawless land, it is up to the inhabitants to try and impose a rule of law for themselves:

> "Judge Henry," said Molly Wood, also coming straight to the point, "have you come to tell me that you think well of lynching?"
>
> He met her. "Of burning Southern negroes in public, no. Of hanging Wyoming cattle thieves in private, yes. You perceive there's a difference, don't you?"
>
> "Not in principle," said the girl, dry and short. (Wister 1902)

This debate, as Wister would have been aware, was very much a live issue in the West. In *A Lady's Life in the Rocky Mountains*, English traveler Isabella Bird commented, "At Alma and Fairplay vigilance committees have been lately formed, and when men act outrageously and make themselves generally obnoxious they receive a letter with a drawing of a tree, a man hanging from it, and a coffin below, on which is written, Forewarned" (1982 [1879]: 209). She goes on to recount the tale of a subsequent hanging, and although at one level, she is repulsed by violence, she nevertheless sees this as a necessary system for the West. For Molly, however, it is much more difficult to accept this violent lynch law. She finally relents, to an extent, when the judge is able to argue that citizens, who elect delegates, who then make laws, have the right to establish their own laws in the absence of formal legal apparatus.

Despite her intelligence and strength, Molly in the end succumbs to the Virginian, and she forgives not only the hanging incident, but also the killing of Trampas (which she begs him not to do), and she marries him. Jane Tompkins argues that "... Wister sees the relationship between men and women as a version of the East–West, parlor–mesa, word–deed opposition" (Tompkins 1992: 63). This dichotomy, for Molly, or rather Wister, can only be resolved by her succumbing to the Virginian's worldview.

This conversation, important as it is, has perhaps been overshadowed by the most famous line in the novel. This is the Virginian's response, when he is called a "son of a –" by the villain Trampas, and he replies, "When you call me that, SMILE!" The full version of the villain's oath is not given in any of the versions under consideration here, but the response encapsulates the hero's *sangfroid* in the face of provocation and underlines the sense that he is more than merely a figure who depends on brute strength. Nevertheless, it is the conversation about the hanging that is at the moral core of the novel, and in this original version it is, as Tompkins suggests, about the contrast between East and West, and perhaps it is also about a female/male dichotomy when hard decisions have to be made in the West.

The Virginian films (Cecil B. DeMille 1914; Victor Fleming, 1929; Stuart Gilmore, 1946)

In Cecil B. DeMille's 1914 version there is clearly not the space to rehearse a complex argument through the intertitles, and when Molly is about to leave she simply finds an injured Virginian and forgives him. With the advent of sound in the 1929 version, directed by Victor Fleming, this central moral debate could be reintroduced. The crucial difference here is that the explanation of the nature of the West and lawkeeping is delivered not by the judge, but by Mrs Henry. It is very difficult to establish exactly who was responsible for the changes in the script, as the screenplay is credited to five different writers: Kirk LaShelle, Grover Jones, Howard Estabrook, Keene Thompson and Edward E Paramore Jr. LaShelle is credited as he had collaborated with Wister on the stage adaptation of the novel in 1905. Paramore was very new to screenwriting, so it is unlikely that he wrote such an important scene. It is tempting to see Estabrook as the key author. He was the most distinguished of the screenwriters, and two years later he won the Academy Award for his adapted screenplay of Edna Ferber's 1929 novel *Cimarron*. Both the novel and the film also feature a major strong female character, Sabra (played by Irene Dunne in the film) who at one point has to run her absent husband's newspaper and then becomes the first congresswoman in Oklahoma. Whoever wrote this particular passage changed the whole dynamic of the interchange, which is still about the contrast between the East and the West, but now also has a new element. Instead of a mature male explaining the issues to a younger woman, it is now a mature woman who imparts her wisdom.

In the 1929 film both Mrs Henry and Molly rehearse the arguments around the hanging, but they also explicitly reference the role of women. The conversation between the two women is worth examining in detail. The exchange begins when Molly asks for confirmation that the Virginian was involved in the hanging:

Molly: Did he do it?
Mrs Henry: Somebody had to do it! He was in charge and it had to be done! That's our kind of law!
Molly: Don't you realize that's murder!
Mrs Henry: No use talking about it. Crimes are ranked different in different countries. Out here, stealing's the meanest, lowest thing a man can do!
Molly: That doesn't justify killing! And Steve was his friend . . .
Mrs Henry: It ain't a question of friends or enemies, it's a question of right and wrong! If we didn't hold a rope and a gun over them outlaws, you couldn't teach at all! Our lives wouldn't be worth nothing!
Molly: Do you think I'll teach my children that? Teach a new generation to approve of murder?
Mrs Henry: Where you come from they have policemen and courts and jails to enforce the law. Here, we got nothing. So when we have to we do things our own way!

This is very similar to the novel's version of the debate, but at the end the discussion moves quite specifically on to the role of women in this harsh environment:

Mrs Henry: You don't belong here! We don't want your kind! Go on back East where the living is soft and easy! Sit on silk cushions and get hired girls to wait on you and drink your pink tea! Why when I married Taylor I drove an ox team 1,000 miles to this very spot! I fought Indians with my father's rifle and him lying dead across my knee! I killed a Sioux squaw with her own axe! And you were talking . . . This is a new country we're building up here, and there ain't no room for weaklings! Men or women! Go on back East! And I will say, Good Riddance!
Molly: Now you listen to me! My people built a country in New England too. And they fought and died just as bravely as you Westerners! Do you think you're the only people who ever fought Indians? Did you ever hear of the Cherry Valley

> Massacre? Well my Grandfather Stark was killed in the blockhouse at Cherry Valley! And my Grandmother walked 90 miles on foot to get help to save the survivors! Don't tell me I can't do anything when it's got to be done! I can stand anything you can and more! I'm not going away! I'm going to stay here and look after him![2]

There are several things happening here. First, Molly is equating the experiences of the pioneers in the eighteenth century with the Western experience in the nineteenth century. Thus the founding and the expansion of America are seen as being part of the same narrative and part of the same struggle. Second, both women are emphasizing their right, as women, to be an equal and significant part of this narrative. Third, although the significant enemies of the novel and films are white criminals, they both posit the idea that it was the struggle against the indigenous tribes that legitimized their place in this society. Finally, it is also made clear that the women—Mrs Henry and Molly's grandmother in particular—are able to indulge in desperate violence or extreme physical hardship to overcome the obstacles in their way.

A complex legal argument also becomes a more straightforward plea for strength for both woman and men. Mrs Henry demonstrates that she belongs fully in the Western milieu, not just in the domestic sphere. Molly's spirited response, in this version at least, shows that she too can make the adjustment from Eastern comfort to Western hardship.

The 1946 version of the film, the first adaptation in color, stars the versatile Joel McCrea as the Virginian. It is virtually a remake, so the conversation remains broadly similar, and thus both Mrs Henry and Molly make the same pleas for female strength. The only major difference between the two films is the staging. In the 1929 version, Molly is physically much more hesitant. She pauses, and almost stops, before she delivers the final part of the speech given above. In the 1946 version, Molly, played by Barbara Britton, stands her ground, confident throughout. In each of these versions, both Molly and Mrs Henry demonstrate their importance. For the matriarchal Mrs Henry in particular, this is an unusual opportunity. As Jenni Calder comments, "The ordinary pioneer woman is elusive on screen. The glimpses that we do catch are most often of a hatchet-faced caricature" (Calder 1976: 158). It is rare that such an important message is given to a female voice, much less a mature matriarchal figure like Mrs Henry.

THE VIRGINIAN: CLASSICS ILLUSTRATED COMIC (GILBERTON, 1965)

Classics Illustrated comics was a series created in 1941 by Albert Kanter, originally under the title Classic Comics, with sometimes fairly loose adaptations of out-of-copyright stories into a comic book format. The comics became more faithful to their original stories, and in 1947 the title of the series was changed to Classics Illustrated. They were keen to stress their educational value in the face of growing criticism of the comics medium, and eventually began to add the following message at the end of each adaptation: "Now that you have read the Classics Illustrated edition, don't miss the added enjoyment of reading the original, obtainable at your school or public library."[3] Inevitably, the comic must make shortcuts and various changes. In deference to the potential age of their audience and the censorship restrictions of the 1954 comics code, the famous insult that Trampas throws at the Virginian becomes, "You son of a gun." Their version of the Virginian was first produced in 1959, drawn by experienced artist Norman Nodel. Once again, just as with silent film, the format of a comic book does not allow for a lengthy text discussion. There are certain strengths that the comic book format can bring to the adaptation of a written text. The drawing style, design of pages and the juxtaposition of images can add layers of meaning, but the representation of a complex, verbose exchange is more of a problem. As Gilberton were, by this period, keen to produce a faithful version of an original book, they return to the version of this conversation in the novel, but they are restricted to a single page with four panels. The judge explains, "The hanging may seem to you to defy law and order. Actually, it asserts it. You see, here in Wyoming, those who should enforce the law do not do so. For years they have been letting cattle thieves go. This means we must somehow enforce the law ourselves until civilization reaches us." Molly is reduced to commenting how awful it all is, and there is no sense of the complex argument from earlier versions. By the next page they are off to be married. The comic is much more effective in other areas. The Virginian himself, allowed a convincing period moustache that Hollywood eschewed, makes a convincing, idealized hero, and looks not unlike Charles Russell's 1911 illustrations of the character. The scenes of action cannot rival the animation of the filmic versions, but the shooting of Trampas is portrayed in a large panel where the static falling figure of the villain dominates the frame. The portrayal of action in comics, despite its obvious limitations, can be both dramatic and elegant.

ROSE OF CIMARRON (20TH CENTURY FOX, 1952)

I have written elsewhere about the perhaps surprising nature of strong decisive women in popular cultural artifacts featuring a Western setting in the 1950s.[4] Dell produced a comic book series based on the television series Annie Oakley, where the titular character, although not really related to the historical figure, was nevertheless a brilliant shot who was able to intervene and capture villains through her own prowess. The B-picture was also an area where small budgets and comparative independence could lead to more experimental and challenging themes. The picture was produced by Edward L. Alperson, directed by Harry Keller and written by Maurice Geragthy. All three had been involved in many B-picture productions, but Geragthy, in particular, was an interesting character. His father was a prolific screenwriter and his sister, Carmelita, was a successful film star in the silent period. Before *Rose of Cimarron* he had already written over twenty screenplays, often Westerns and always B-pictures. He was essentially a jobbing writer, but he clearly had a deep interest in Western female characters, as demonstrated in two of his earlier films: *Calamity Jane and Sam Bass* (1949) and *Dakota Lil* (1950). He went on to write further films, and then Western television shows, many of which he directed. This screenplay draws on some of the well-known Western tropes with which Geragthy would have been familiar. A Comanche attack on a wagon train leaves only one survivor, a baby, who is brought up by a Comanche. The key differences to more common versions of this story is that the baby is a girl, and the Comanche is not one of the war party, but a non-combatant who takes the child to his parents who own a farm. Thus the girl is brought up by Comanches, but her family live partially in the white world. Although she is destined to meet a traditional happy ending, falling in love with the local sheriff, her journey to that point is then very different to the usual one for a Western heroine. I will examine this journey through the comic book adaptation of the film, which, despite some changes, is very faithful to the script.

Rose of Cimarron: Fawcett Movie Comic, 1952

The adaptation of film titles into comic book format was an important part of the marketing of the Hollywood product to a younger audience, particularly in the late 1950s and early 1960s. In an age before various media recording systems, it also allowed the younger reader to return again and again to a favorite story that was not available in any other way. The major player in this field was Dell comics, publisher of Disney comic stories, and they produced literally hundreds of titles adapting film titles and television series. Fawcett was a more minor publisher in the comics field, but they also produced a short-lived series, mainly based on Western films. A key element in both series was the use of full color photographic covers which underlined the "authenticity" of the titles. Thus the *Rose of Cimarron* comic has a photographic montage of the central characters, played by Mala Powers and Jack Beutel, and a street scene where they stand among two (presumably) dead bodies. Inside the front cover there are two further photographs which act as a buffer between the "real" characters on the cover and the drawn versions that follow. The comic ends in the same way with the end of the story being followed by two more black and white photographs inside the back cover, and a further color photograph on the back cover itself, easing the reader back into the "veracity" of the film version. As the comics took the relevant film script as a starting point, they sometimes contain some more mature themes, particularly if produced before the imposition of the draconian Comics Code in 1954. The *Rose of Cimarron* comic opens with a "splash" (full page) panel in which we see Rose, dressed in a fetching buckskin dress, with two pistols shooting down two men in the street. There is no introduction (except for the previous two unrelated pages on the film details and the song lyrics from the film). We simply see the opening of the story with Rose gunning down the two armed men, but her drastic action is juxtaposed with her comparatively traditional feminine garb. This is somewhat different, even to later films, where the positive actions of a female heroine make her image problematic. Philip Green explains that even in *The Ballad of Little Joe* made in 1993, ". . . an independently produced Western, the most masculine of genres of all has been given a female protagonist who masquerades as a man throughout the movie, without betraying her femaleness or recuperating maleness in the manner of Tootsie and Mrs Doubtfire" (Green 1998: 163). Rose, by contrast, in a minor picture of the 1950s, does not need to appear, in visual terms, in any way ambiguous. She is taking drastic and violent action, but she is, visually, clearly female. Even when a female character is strong enough to take decisive action, as A. P. Nelson points out in relation to some Barbara Stanwyk roles from this period, they also tend to dress like men, "These ladies both dress and act like men—indeed, dressing and acting like a man go hand-in-hand" (Nelson 2013: 72).

We are still left with no obvious motivation for her actions, even the text panel only adds the information that "Men called her Rose—a wildflower of the prairie, blooming in beauty! But her heart was a seething cauldron of hate and her blood throbbed only to the call of vengeance . . . a six-gun vengeance that knew no mercy, knew no law!" The next two pages begin to relate the origin story as delineated in the film, so this means that the opening scene of violence remains uncontextualized, for the moment. We only know that Rose is "a cauldron of hate" and "knew no mercy," but we also know that she shoots men to death for some currently unknown reason. It is then made clear in the introductory section that she is a highly accomplished hunter—returning from a hunt having only killed one cougar is described as a "poor hunt." The artwork in the comic is highly effective, with a clear attempt to maintain likenesses of the key characters. While she is away from the ranch, the reason for her vengeance becomes clear when three white outlaws kill her adoptive parents in cold blood. Rose knows she can recognize the men by their stolen horses, and on page thirteen we get to the incident from the opening of the comic, where she outdraws and kills two of the men. This is structurally different to the film, where the opening titles appear over arrows flying into a wagon, and then the attack that orphans Rose follows immediately. Thus both versions

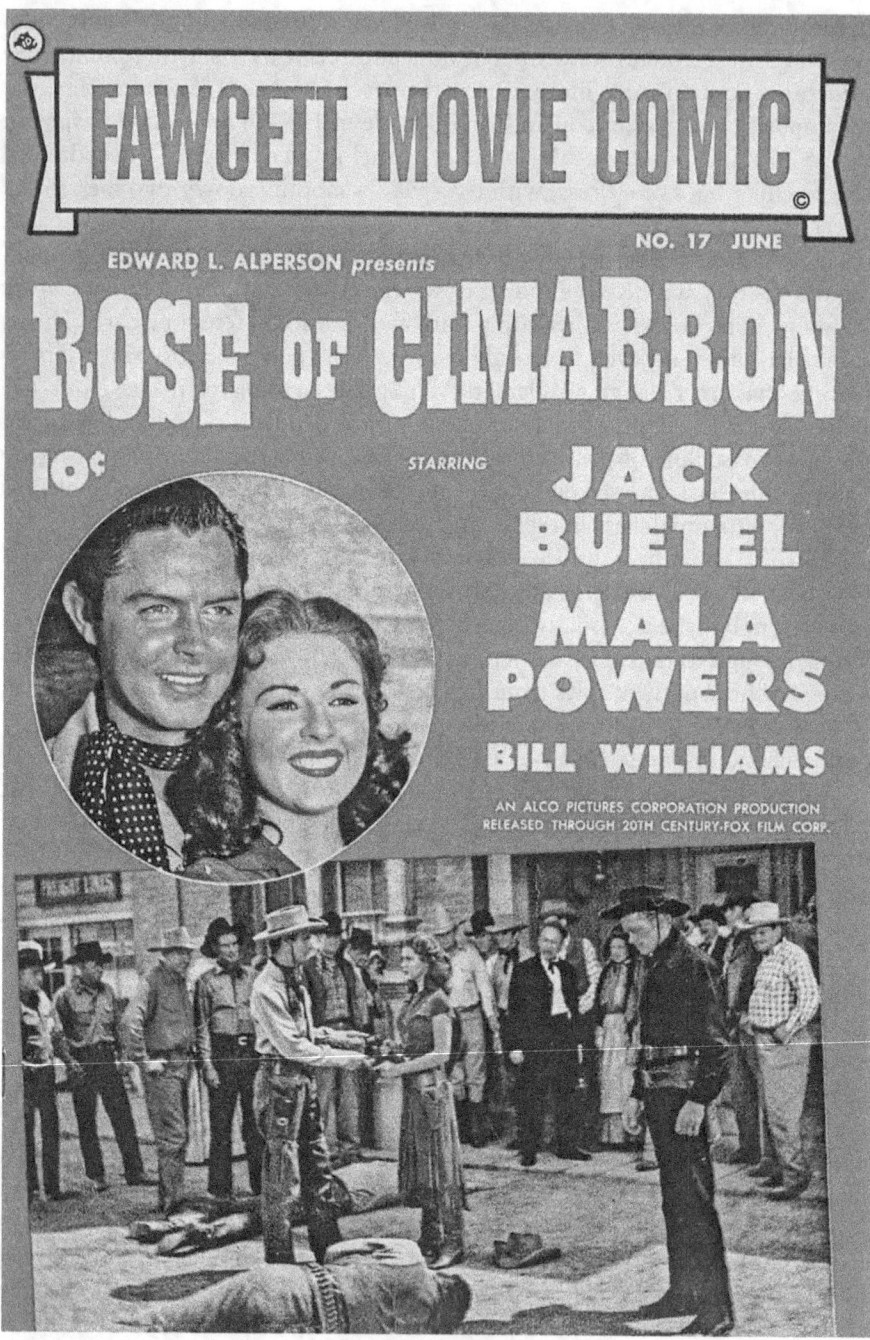

Figure 4.1   Fawcett Movie comic no. 17, 1952. A photo cover underlines the connection to the film.

TWO KEY FEMALE ROLES IN WESTERN FILMS AND COMICS

Figure 4.2   Fawcett Movie comic no. 17, 1952. Rose guns down her enemies.

open with a violent event, but the comic foregrounds female power in the large panel which is a "flash forward," out of chronological sequence. But in the film and the comic, the actions of Rose are different to the stereotypical active female as described by Pam Cook: "Over and over again, the woman relinquishes her desire to be active and independent, ceding power to the hero and accepting secondary status as mother figure, educator, and social mediator. If she is allowed to be active, it is in the hero's cause rather than her own" (Cook 1998: 294). Rose is, by contrast, acting purely in her own vengeful cause.

Conclusion

The two very different texts under consideration have very different reputations—indeed *Rose of Cimarron* has virtually no reputation and is largely forgotten. Although *The Virginian* may be read less frequently, it lives on in various filmic versions (and a largely unrelated television series) and is widely acknowledged to be a "classic." It continues to be adapted into film. Interestingly, in a 2000 television film, directed by, and starring, Bill Pullman, the words of the key justification for the hanging are put in the mouth of the Virginian himself. The debate is curtailed, and the Virginian persuades Molly with a few simple statements, concluding, "I punished men that crossed the line—It might not be the best thing to be done, but it's the only thing to be done."

So, in the hundred years since the publication of the book, the 1929 and 1946 film versions of *The Virginian* stand alone in regard to how the West must address lawbreaking to female dissenting voices. It is tempting, given the date of the film, to attribute this to the changing position of women in the inter-war years and in post-war America. In the 1950s, it appeared that a strong, active central female character would still only appear in B-Westerns. The advantage of cheaper or "poverty row" productions at this period was that there was more freedom from the constrictions of mainstream Hollywood conventions. Indeed there would be a temptation to look for novelty in these kinds of productions—anything to try and rival the more lavish and star studded mainstream Hollywood fare. *Rose of Cimarron*, whatever its faults, in both the filmic and comic book versions is a clear attempt to provide a meaty role for its titular female character. What links the key scene in the 1946 *Virginian* film and *Rose of Cimarron* is that their interesting take on women in the West has remained somewhat neglected. The former has been swamped by other male-dominated versions, and *Rose of Cimarron* has suffered the neglect typical of minor Westerns of the period. It would seem almost inevitable that if other B-Western films and neglected Western comics are investigated some will reveal further surprises with their sympathetic and adventurous portrayals of women.

Notes

1. There are several other 1950s films where the main female character, whether or not she also performs the function of love interest, has to take up arms and fend for herself. These include *Montana* (Raoul Walsh, 1950), *Ramrod* (André D. Toth, 1947), *Rawhide* (Henry Hathaway, 1951), and *Forty Guns* (Sam Fuller, 1957).
2. The Cherry Valley Massacre was a real event. In 1778, a group of various tribes and loyalists attacked this village near New York and killed many non-combatants.
3. A long campaign against comics in America culminated in the publication of Dr Fredric Wertham's *Seduction of the Innocent* in 1954. Wertham described the pernicious influence of all kinds of comics. Ironically, one of the specific titles selected for disapprobation by another campaigner, Geoffrey Wagner, was the Classics Illustrated adaptation of Dostoevsky's *Crime and Punishment*.
4. Both strong female and indigenous characters feature in some comics of the period, and some are discussed in Huxley (2018).

Filmography

Calamity Jane and Sam Bass, director George Sherman, featuring Yvonne De Carlo, Howard Duff, Dorothy Hart (Universal, 1949).
Dakota Lil, director Lesley Selander, featuring George Montgomery, Rod Cameron, Marie Windsor (Edward L. Alperson Productions, 1950).
Forty Guns, director Sam Fuller, featuring Barbara Stanwyck, Barry Sullivan, Dean Jagger (20th Century Fox, 1957).
Johnny Guitar, director Nicholas Ray, featuring Joan Crawford, Sterling Hayden, Mercedes McCambridge (Republic, 1954).
Montana, director Ray Enright, Raoul Walsh [uncredited], featuring Errol Flynn, Alexis Smith, S. Z. Sakall (Warner Bros., 1950).
Ramrod, director André D. Toth, featuring Joel McCrea, Veronica Lake, Don DeFore (Enterprise Productions, 1947).
Rawhide, director Henry Hathaway, featuring Tyrone Power, Susan Hayward, Hugh Marlowe (20th Century Fox, 1951).
Rose of Cimarron, director Harry Keller, featuring Jack Buetel, Mala Powers, Bill Williams (20th Century Fox, 1952).
The Ballad of Little Joe, director Maggie Greenwald, featuring Suzy Amis, Bo Hopkins, Ian McKellen (Joco, 1993).
The Virginian, director Bill Pullman, featuring Bill Pullman, Diane Lane, John Savage (TNT, 2000).
The Virginian, director Cecil B. DeMille, featuring Dustin Farnam, Jack W. Johnston, Sydney Deane (Jesse L. Lasky Feature Play, 1914).
The Virginian, director Stuart Gilmore, featuring Joel McCrea, Brian Donlevy, Sonny Tufts (Paramount, 1946).
The Virginian, director Victor Fleming, featuring Gary Cooper, Walter Huston, Mary Brian (Paramount, 1929).

Bibliography

American Antiquarian Society, *Women and the World of Dime Novels* <http://americanantiquarian.org/dimenovelwomen/exhibits/show/the-women/mollie-hanley> (last accessed 3 July 2018).

Anon. (1865) *The Rover of the Forest, or the Warrior's Last War-Whoop*. New York: George Munro.

Bird, Isabella (1879, 1982) *A Lady's Life in the Rocky Mountains*. London: Virago Press.

Buscombe, Edward (1993) *The BFI Companion to the Western*. London: André Deutsch.

Calder, Jenni (1976) *There Must be a Lone Ranger*. London: Sphere Books.

Cook, Pam (1998) "Women and the Western," in Jim Kitses (ed.), *The Western Reader*. New York: Limelight Editions, pp. 293–300.

Green, Philip (1998) *Cracks in the Pedestal*. Amherst, MA: University of Massachusetts Press.

Huxley, D. (2018) *Lone Heroes: The Myth of the American West in Comic Books 1945–1962*. New York: Palgrave.

Madsen, Leah (2014) *Maverick Queens: Women in Western Film, 1947–1953* <https://centerofthewest.org/2014/09/17/maverick-queens-women-western-films-1947-1953/> (last accessed 22 June 2018).

Nelson, A. P. (2013) "Only a Woman After All? Gender Dynamics in the Westerns of Barbara Stanwyk," in Sue Matheson (ed.), *Love in Western Film and Television: Lonely Hearts and Happy Trails*. New York: Palgrave.

Savage, Candace (1996) *Cowgirls*. London: Bloomsbury.

Slotkin, Richard (1993) *Gunfighter Nation*. New York: Harper Collins.

Tompkins, Jane (1992) *West of Everything: The Inner Life of Westerns*. New York: Oxford University Press.

Wister, Owen (1902) *The Virginian* <https://www.gutenberg.org/files/1298/1298-h/1298-h.htm> (last accessed 22 June 2018).

5. FREUD, "THE FAMILY ON THE LAND," AND THE FEMININE TURN IN POST-WAR WESTERNS

Gaylyn Studlar

It is widely recognized that in the years following World War II, the American Western evidenced a number of significant changes. For A-budget features, these included increased use of color film stock, adoption of widescreen or 3-D technology, multi-star casts, and a return to location shooting. All these moves reflected broader film industry responses to post-war economic challenges. Industry and popular press commentators noticed other emergent changes in post-war Westerns impacting character motivation, narrative structure, themes, visual style, and worldview. There was a new emphasis on talk instead of action, psychological complexity rather than traditional stereotyping, sex instead of sexlessness (Spinrad 1947: X4). There was also more moral ambiguity and pessimism attached to the mythic story of nation building that secured the western frontier for US Manifest Destiny. A darker view of the motivations and actions of white American pioneers also came to be inscribed in personal terms, in the representation of heterosexual desire and of family life that necessitated the presence of women in a genre often regarded as overwhelmingly male-centric.

This set of emerging characteristics in the post-war Western complicates the conclusions Jane Tompkins reaches in *West of Everything*; she argues that Westerns strive to create a womanless milieu so that male protagonists can achieve the freedom, independence, and isolation that an imaginary West offers as appealing alternatives to heterosexual domesticity (Tompkins 1992: 127). More recent scholarship reconceptualizes the importance of women to the genre as both literature and film, leading to a questioning, directly or implicitly, of ahistorical generalizations like those of Tompkins.[1] Responding to widespread scholarly emphasis on the Western hero as a nomadic and often solitary male, Matthew Carter and Marek Paryz asserted in 2018: "The family is crucial for both the narrative strategies and ideological concerns of the Western genre" (2018: 3).

This reconceptualization recalls the analysis of Virginia Wright Wexman, who argued in 1993 that "the family on the land" was a central trope of the genre, leading to "nostalgia for the dynastic model of marriage . . . the object of which is to make use of land to build a patrimony for future generations" (Wexman 1993: 81). In the post-World War II era of American feature filmmaking, a raft of films including *Duel in the Sun* (1947), *Ramrod* (1947), *Pursued* (1947), *The Sea of Grass* (1947), *The Furies* (1950), *The Violent Men* (1954), and *The Big Country* (1958), among others, centralized "the family on the land" trope and the acquisition or consolidation of property in the form of land and cattle. Many post-war "family on the land" Westerns successfully exploited movies' technological advancements in their depiction of epic conflicts such as range wars in which "cattle barons" (male or female) opposed farmers, small cattle ranchers, sheepmen or the unwelcome intrusions of government, bankers, land speculators, or the railroad.

Paradoxically "family on the land" films simultaneously elevated the importance of women in stories that focused on the most intimate of relationships and the home, the traditional domain of women. Those films branded as "adult" or "new school" often represented the family as charged by aggression, ambivalence, and transgressive desire rather than as cohesive, loving, and nostalgically revered as "normal" (Spinrad 1947: X4). In this mode, "family on the land" films often became the site of sexual secrets and emotional upheaval, racked by intra- as well as inter-family rivalries leading to violence. Unlike wartime morale-building melodramas in which tribulation brought families closer together, post-World War II "family on the land" films presented defiant daughters, delinquent sons, sexualized matriarchs, and flawed, overreaching patriarchs involved in intergenerational conflict. Milking the melodramatic potential of these fictional old West families was not difficult, for as Geoffrey Nowell-Smith has suggested, melodramas generally are concerned with the bourgeois family under patriarchy so that the dynamic of power and powerlessness in families is often associated with the acquisition or loss of private property and thus with questions of inheritance (Nowell-Smith 1985: 191). Representations of women played a crucial role in the changes associated with this type of Western. The appearance in post-war Westerns of top women stars in important female roles was recognized as a "new movie trend" even as it was occurring. In February 1947, a photographic layout in *The New York Times* featured six major female stars then currently cast in A-level Westerns: Barbara Stanwyck, Linda Darnell, Jennifer Jones, Teresa Wright, Katharine Hepburn, and Veronica Lake ("Leading Ladies Take to the Great Outdoors in a New Movie Trend" 1947: X5).[2]

In the late 1940s, roles for women in Westerns spun out of the conventional orbit of generic stereotypes, to the shock of some commentators. In summer 1947, a *New York Times* review of *Ramrod* by A. Weiler opened with this observation: "Time was when the ladies of Western movies were demure damsels who came on the scene perhaps to pour a cup of coffee, teach school or to ride off into a pristine sunset with an equally pristine hero. But things, as has become only too apparent, have changed" (Weiler 1947: 25). A trade paper response to *Ramrod*'s perceived excesses could have served equally well for other "adult" Westerns: ". . . the western scene is the stage for a drama of violent passions, frustration boiling to violence, inter-family strife, bestiality, brutality, bloodshedding and a variety of love that is unusual. Here the treatment is different. Difference has always been a factor in luring an audience" ("Reviews of New Films: 'Ramrod'" 1947: 9).

Seeking difference, central female characters, including middle-class mothers and daughters, were inscribed in unsympathetic ways evoking the *femmes fatales* or good bad women of the psychologically and visually dark crime films we now call *film noir*. Actresses like Barbara Stanwyck, Joan Crawford, Judith Anderson, Virginia Mayo, and Veronica Lake transferred qualities associated with their *noir*-affiliated screen personas into post-war Westerns. One reviewer referred to Connie Dickason (Veronica Lake) in *Ramrod* as a "beautiful but flinty blond dame" (Weiler 1947: 25). *Variety* noted of the film: "The femme angles give more than ordinary substance to this western"; while "predatory" [Connie] "dares to challenge the marauding cattlemen" (Abel 1947: 10). Another review called Connie "both heroine and villainess" of the film (Scott "'Ramrod' Super Western" 1947: 7). Connie is the headstrong daughter of a wealthy rancher. She rejects her father's choice of husband for her, his middle-age ally, Frank Ivey (Preston Foster). A ruthless cattle baron, Ivey displays a penchant for sexual masochism. When Connie slaps him over and over in response to his torture of one of her ranch hands, he smiles and declares with some satisfaction, "Thanks, Connie, that's the first time you've ever touched me." Attractive but rebellious females were frequently shown as being contained by the end of films by matrimony or death, but Connie faces a different fate, one that precludes the triumphant formation of a "family on the land." After winning a range war to secure her own land and cattle, she runs to her foreman, Dave (Joel McCrea), whom she professes to love. He has just bested Ivey in a gunfight. Dave confronts her with his newly acquired knowledge of her deceitful machinations. Her actions have led to the deaths of many men, including his best friend. Connie responds: "Would it make a difference if I said I'm sorry, terribly sorry? . . . But what counts is our happiness, our freedom, the way we want to live." Dave responds, "Not *we*, Connie, just *you*—alone," and he walks away from her. In spite of conventionally moral endings that condemn and punish women like Connie Dickason in most Westerns of the period, the storylines that precede these resolutions often show rebellious women challenging individual men as well as the male power structures that oppressed them, whether in the public or private realm.

Because of cultural as well as industrial reasons, the post-war Western was altered along the lines of gender that defied its reputation as the genre most resistant to change (Spinrad 1947: X4). However, this was by no means the first time that gendered changes had occurred in the Western as a form of storytelling. In his classic study, *The Virgin Land*, Henry Nash Smith noted that US Western pulp fiction in the late nineteenth century transferred "the skills and functions of the Wild Western hero to a woman, [with] the use of the theme of revenge to motivate violence, and the promotion of the Amazon to full status as a heroine" (Smith 1950: 116). Expanding upon Richard Abel's discussion of "cowboy girl" Westerns in *The Red Rooster Scare* (Abel 1999: 171–2), Laura Horak argues for the importance of cross-dressing cowgirls in action-centered transitional era movie Westerns as an example of generic evolution and how women might embody "a national fantasy of spatial mastery" on screen (Horak 2014: 87). By way of contrast, in the early sound era, women were made thoroughly dispensable to the genre as the Hollywood industry largely abandoned A-Westerns and B-films were aimed at boys and working-class men who avoided love stories (Stanfield 2001: 122–33). Peter Stanfield remarks on how "precarious" the heterosexual couple was in 1930s Westerns until the comeback of A-budget films in 1939–40, in a strategy that exploited the casting of handsome male stars who might attract female viewers and created a few interesting roles for women stars (Stanfield 2001: 191). Such roles can be located in *Union Pacific* (1939), *Destry Rides Again* (1939), *Arizona* (1940), and *Belle Starr* (1941).

During World War II, rationing and other wartime strictures radically depressed the production of A-Westerns even as US female audiences enjoyed the so-called "women's films" featuring female stars as protagonists in narratives usually revolving around romantic problems or the family. Dominating the box office with men away at war, female audiences were credited with raising to box-office success a wide variety of woman-centered films. One rare, largely interior bound Western, *The Great Man's Lady* (1942), was part of this phenomenon and took in over a million dollars for Paramount ("101 Pix Gross in millions" 1943: 58). More typically, women's films were contemporary love stories, some with psychologically fragile heroines like those in *Now, Voyager* (1942) and *Love Letters* (1945); others paid tribute to the resilience of females on the home-front, as in MGM's *Mrs. Miniver* (1942) and David O. Selznick's independently produced *Since You Went Away* (1945).

In the second half of the 1940s, a feminine turn in Hollywood Westerns was inspired by the tremendous box-office success of *Duel in the Sun* (1946), a film that was built on producer Selznick's established track record of making woman-centered melodramas. After a long and troubled production, *Duel in the Sun* went into general release in 1947. Hedda Hopper declared it was, "sex rampant . . . lusty, lush and lascivious" even as rival gossip columnist Louella O. Parsons declared: "There's never been a more out-and-out melodrama" (Weaver, 11 January 1947: 22). The film was nicknamed "Lust in the Dust" by the popular press but its sexual content was taken more seriously by others. It was denounced by Lloyd T. Binford, the chief censor of Memphis, Tennessee, as a "lecherous depiction of sexual abnormality and brutality [that] would be contributing to the delinquency of minors" (Binford 1947: n.p.). His expression of outrage was joined by that of religious leaders and civic organizations even as audiences flocked to the film, encouraged by an unprecedented $2 million advertising campaign and saturation booking of theaters. In spite of lackluster reviews, the film was the second biggest domestic box-office success of 1947, with a take of $11 million (Golden 1948: 3). It would ultimately be identified as one of the highest box-office earners in the history of the genre (Studlar 2013: 279).

A "family on the land" melodrama set in 1880s Texas, *Duel in the Sun* established a commercial model for the American film industry to present women in A-Westerns as more central, psychologically complex, and sexually bold characters. Sex was an angle Westerns had largely avoided before independent producer Howard Hughes made *The Outlaw*, which faced stiff opposition from the US film industry to its exhibition in 1943 and again in 1946. As George N. Fenin and William K. Everson noted in their classic study of the genre, in the postwar era "sex was the first element to establish itself obviously because there had been precedents, and it seemed safe to tamper with the ironclad Western tradition when the new product would sell so well" (Fenin and Everson 1973: 266). Selznick's stated reason for turning to a genre he previously had disdained corroborates Fenin and Everson's view of the situation: "Seeing how profitable westerns always were, I decided that if I could create one that had more spectacle than had ever been seen in a western and combine it with a violent love story, then the two elements would give me a great success" (quoted in Haver 1985: 353). Selznick also sought a star vehicle for his lover and protégé, actress Jennifer Jones, that would eclipse the success of his production of *Gone with the Wind* (1939). Selznick wanted to make a film that would sex-up Jones's image and prove her versatility as an actress. He worried that Jones, known primarily for her Academy Award winning performance in *The Song of Bernadette* (1943) as an awkward adolescent who achieves sainthood, would be typecast as a character actress.

In advancing his plan, Selznick bought from RKO the rights to a 1944 novel, *Duel in the Sun*, by Niven Busch as well as Busch's screenplay drafts. Busch's novel focused on Pearl Chavez, who, at the beginning of his story, is a twelve-year-old. She is a "half-breed." Her dissolute white father meets a violent end; her mestizo mother does not want her second marriage to be burdened by the twelve-year-old child from her first, so she sends Pearl to live with her dead husband's second cousin and former lover, Laura Belle McCanles. Laura Belle shares an enormous Texas ranch with her husband and four sons. From the first day of her life at Spanish Bit, Pearl has to fight off one son, Lewt, who ultimately sexually assaults Pearl and coerces her into joining him in outlawry. Mrs McCanles declares that no one of Pearl's racial heritage can ever marry one of her sons, but Pearl promises to marry Jesse, another McCanles son who loves her. As her lawyer, he defends Pearl when she is put on trial for aiding and abetting Lewt's crimes (Busch 1944: 49). Pearl is found innocent and then tracks Lewt down. With cold calculation, she shoots him to death because she knows Lewt will never let her and Jesse live in peace. Leaving Spanish Bit, Pearl and Jesse stake a homestead claim in the Cherokee land rush and spend their first night as newlyweds on their land as they look forward to the promise of the future.

On the release of Selznick's $6 million film, *Variety* concluded, "The book and the picture differ radically, but that is the way Selznick wanted it" (Grant 1946: 3). There was little doubt that the changes Selznick and his co-screenwriter Oliver Garrett made to Busch's story made Pearl a more psychologically and socially fragile heroine and intensified the Freudian implications and melodramatic potential of Busch's novel. As I have discussed at length elsewhere, these changes leave the impression that Pearl is a hysteric with an unresolved Oedipal conflict that traps her in contrary gender identifications and binds the woman's sexual display to anxiety and torment (Studlar 2013: 192–4). Freudian implications are immediately ratchetted up by Selznick's addition of a night scene that shows Pearl's catch as catch can upbringing in a Texas–Mexico border town. She is older than in the book, a teenager whose innocence is conveyed by her jaunty dancing for an audience of Latino children. This occurs in the street, outside a spectacular gambling casino/bar. Inside the casino, her mixed race (Indian-Mexican) mother (in stereotyped Indian costume) engages in a spectacularly sexualized dance atop a bar. Her dance ends with her kissing her lover (Sidney Blackmer) in a close-up. He accosted Pearl on his way in, caressing her bare arm and telling her: "Like mother like daughter . . . I'm commencing to think I prefer the daughter." The film then calls attention to Pearl's uncomfortably close physical relationship with her father, Scott Chavez (Herbert Marshall), a gentleman gambler. Pearl tries but cannot prevent her father from shooting dead her mother and the mother's lover. Selznick and Garrett also added a highly emotional scene in which Pearl visits her father in jail before he is hanged for the killings. Their embraces suggest the physicality of lovers rather than of father and daughter. Scott Chavez praises Pearl's strength and sends her to live with his former flame Laura Belle McCanles, because, he says, Laura Belle was the "wonderful girl . . . who might have been your mother."

When the orphaned Pearl arrives at Spanish Bit, Laura Belle's husband, Senator McCanles (Lionel Barrymore), attacks her with racial slurs. Mrs McCanles is cowed by her bitter husband who is confined to a wheelchair, crippled by a riding accident that occurred when he was pursuing his wife on the belief that she was leaving him for Pearl's father. The family is riven by factions: husband vs. wife, son vs. son. Senator McCanles's only pleasure is in spoiling his handsome but amoral younger son, Lewt (Gregory Peck). Laura Belle (Lillian Gish) is devoted to older son Jesse (Joseph Cotten), a mild-mannered lawyer who challenges his father's desire to fight the arrival of the railroad. Jesse too long delays in telling Pearl of his love for her. When he does, Pearl has already been raped by Lewt, and Jesse misunderstands Pearl's feelings toward Lewt. He leaves the ranch and finds love with a railroad tycoon's beautiful daughter. Lewt refuses to marry Pearl because marrying her would endanger his inheritance: his father has warned him that the ranch should never become "an Indian reservation." Pearl decides to marry an older man but Lewt murders him on the eve of the wedding. Lewt becomes a wanted man, but he returns to make love to Pearl, who cannot resist him. He then shoots down an unarmed Jesse in the street, prompting Pearl to embark on a plan to kill Lewt before he can finish his brother off. She finds him hiding in wild country, at Squaw's Head Rock. She shoots him, and he returns fire, wounding her. Realizing that she loves him, Pearl crawls up the mountain. She and Lewt die in each other's arms.

Figure 5.1 The realization of love in death throes: Pearl (Jennifer Jones) and Lewt (Gregory Peck) in *Duel in the Sun* (1946).

Selznick not only changed the ending of the novel, but he had to vigorously fight the industry's moral regulator, the Production Code Administration, to keep his *liebstod* version. Nathan Platte sees in this ending Selznick's "desire to reapply psychoanalytic explanations from *Spellbound* to the wild west" with Pearl trapped by "impulses born of trauma" (Platte 2018: 267). Selznick had more than a passing interest in psychoanalysis. Two of his previously produced films, *Spellbound* (1945) and *Since You Went Away*, directly referenced psychoanalysis and included psychiatrists. In fact, a female psychoanalyst (Ingrid Bergman) is the protagonist of *Spellbound*; she works to cure the amnesia of her love interest, who may be a murderer. *I'll Be Seeing You* (1944), another film made by Selznick International, included a soldier (Joseph Cotten) suffering from psychoneurosis instigated by combat. Moreover, Selznick's artistic and commercial exploitation of the subject had a personal connection. In the early 1940s, Selznick was in therapy with a woman psychoanalyst, Dr May Romm, who served as a consultant on *Spellbound* (Selznick, 1983: 235–6).

Selznick's personal and professional interest in psychoanalysis was by no means unusual for Hollywood folk or among the general public in the 1940s. Freudian theories of psychological and sexual disturbance broadly impacted US culture in the 1940s through commentary in the press as well as by practical use (as in the diagnosis of soldiers' war neurosis). Freudianism was incorporated into a number of Hollywood features with psychoanalytic terminology and theory referenced in everything from musicals to crime dramas, gothic melodramas to Westerns (Krutnik 1991: 45–55).

Contrary to Busch's novel, a happy ending is not possible in Selznick's film because of (1) its investment in the Freudian psychodynamics of sexuality that originates within the Oedipalized family, and (2) its emphasis on Pearl as the classic victim in a melodramatic structuring of experience. On the one hand, Freudian theory was often accused in the 1940s of being pessimistic. On the other, *Duel in the Sun* reflects Nowell-Smith's view that melodrama cannot resolve the contradictions it raises. It fails ideologically and "cannot accommodate its problem either in a real present or in an ideal future" (Nowell-Smith 1985: 194). This is certainly true of *Duel in the Sun*. Arguing for the film as one of the genre's strongest critiques of patriarchal structures and white privilege, Robin Wood notes that Pearl is "destroyed by conflicts that are as much ideological as personal, [which] can find no reconciliation in life" (Wood 1996: 194). *Duel in the Sun*, unlike many of the "family on the land" Westerns that followed like *The Violent Men*, *The Furies*, and *Forty Guns*, did not try to reassure audiences with a happy ending pulled out of the wreckage of its characters' lives.[3]

Thus the film version of *Duel in the Sun* modeled what David Lusted says became typical of a number of A-Westerns in the 1950s. Lusted says these films were characterized by a shift from a structure of action to melodrama with psychoanalytic implications: "A central trope of melodrama is the dramatic connection between social and psychic repression, leading to an excess of misery in the central protagonist and matched by emotion tension in the audience" (Lusted 1992: 65). *Duel in the Sun* led the way to the post-war Western's deracination of the home as a site of safety and stability and to a transformation of the cinematic image of women and the family in the genre. It also problematized the myths and masculine ideals of a genre that traditionally confirmed the value of the American West as a crucible for US national identity. In reference to this, Robin Wood states that *Duel in the Sun* deserves to be recognized "as the Hollywood cinema's most challenging and subversive statement about American civilization" (192). Demythification through an emphasis on psychological instabilities and ideological contradictions impacted male as well as female characters. Reacting negatively, Lindsay Anderson drew attention to such changes in his review of what has become the most famous Western from the 1950s, John Ford's *The Searchers* (1956). Lindsay called Ethan Edwards (John Wayne), the ostensible hero of the film, "an unmistakable neurotic" and asked, "Now what is Ford, of all directors, to do with a hero like this?" (Anderson 1960: 95).[4]

Ethan Edwards was by no means the first neurotic post-war "hero" of a "family on the land" film whose psychological problems are related to home, family, and a woman forbidden to him by taboo (married to his brother). A *Film Daily* review credited *Pursued* (1947) with "introducing the neurotic to the Western movie" and went on to call it "an adult tale of twisted personalities, ulterior motives and lurking threat of death arising from dishonored families" ("Reviews: 'Pursued,'" 1947: 7). The original screenplay for *Pursued* was written by Niven Busch. Like his script drafts for *Duel in the Sun*, *Pursued* was conceived as a starring vehicle for his wife, Teresa Wright, but *Pursued*'s neurotic protagonist is not a woman but a man, Jeb Rand (Robert Mitchum). Like Pearl, he is an orphan and an outsider. His family is massacred as revenge for his father's adulterous relationship with "Ma" Callum (Judith Anderson), who adopts him and clearly favors Jeb over her own son Adam (John Rodney). In his film review, Edwin Schallert called the mother, played by Anderson, "the key figure in the strangely sinister plot" (Schallert 1947: A5). Ma is a formidable figure, but in spite of her best efforts to forge a loving family, her home becomes uncanny, a place where the familiar is made strange, literally and figuratively a dark space torn apart by jealousy and violence. Through lighting, set design, and camera work, it harbors a repressed menace.

This menace that haunts Jeb's dreams acquires real-world embodiment in a murderous father figure, Grant Callum (Dean Jagger), Ma's brother-in-law, who contaminates her family with hate. Like Satan whispering in the ear of the vulnerable sinner, Callum feeds Adam's long-standing jealousy of his adopted brother; he uses Adam and every other means he can muster to kill Jeb as the last of the Rands.[5] He is free to do so because Ma refuses to tell Jeb that it was her sexual relationship with his father that motivated the destruction of his birth family and the continuing pursuit of Grant Callum. Unable to access the past except in frightening dreams related to the night his family was killed, Jeb begins to believe that somehow he is responsible for the hatred and violence that follow him. Only through Ma's intervention and Jeb's retrieval of repressed memories can a happy ending be achieved.

In "Busch" influenced Westerns like *Duel in the Sun* and *Pursued*, the woman and her presumptive domain, the home, can become uncanny, creating a forcefield of desire that differs significantly from most pre-war Westerns' articulation of woman and home-centered domesticity in the genre. In 1950, following the release of another film based on a Busch novel, *The Furies*, a review suggested of its heroine, "Vance could probably use some psychiatric advice about father complexes" ("Movies" 1950: 71). In her dead mother's bedroom, Vance attempts to kill her father's fiance, who threatens her inheritance of the vast ranch promised to her by her beloved father. Three years earlier, in the *New York Times*, Leonard Spinrad outlined the "changing styles" of movie Westerns and observed that the emergent "new style" Western had already been nicknamed after Busch. Spinrad attempted to capture the essence of the difference in these films: "The 'burning Busch' Western, which attempts to tell an adult story of the development of characters, is based on the idea that a clash of guns is not necessarily a replacement for a clash of emotions" (Spinrad 1947: X4).

The psychoanalytic approach to the family favored by "burning Busch" Westerns and the female-centered melodramatic excess that Selznick embraced with *Duel in the Sun* became twin pillars of the "adult" trend that dominated post-World War II A-Westerns, especially those in "family on the land" mode. The refiguration of women in many of these films presented an opportunity to bring the psychical and social contradictions long the subject of melodrama more forcefully to the foreground in a genre already informed by violence. At the same time, these films complicated American myths, whether by calling subtle attention to contradictions in them, or through more overt questioning of assumptions about gender and sexuality as well as race and class. The post-war turn in "family on the land" films that were "adult" Westerns embraced difference that altered the psychological and emotional terrain of the genre. This was not an insignificant occurrence or an isolated one. Such strategies would also be evident in important and popular melodramas of the 1950s associated with directors like Douglas Sirk (*Imitation of Life*), Nicholas Ray (*Rebel Without a Cause*), and Vincente Minnelli (*Some Came Running*). Framing the post-war Western within industry trends of production and reception as well as demonstrating how the genre is related to periodized cultural influences is a large enterprise, but every step we make towards incorporating this approach will enhance our understanding of the genre in all its complexity and give us a more precise view of how it represented women in more dramatically complex and often startlingly unexpected ways.

FREUD AND THE FEMININE TURN IN POST-WAR WESTERNS

Figure 5.2 Learning she is disinherited, Vance Jeffords (Barbara Stanwyck) prepares to throw scissors at her father's fiancée (Judith Anderson) in *The Furies* (1950).

Notes

1. A corrective to Tompkins's discussion of Western literature and its male writers may be found in Victoria Lamont, *Westerns: A Women's History*. Mark E. Wildermuth argues for the pro-feminism of movie Westerns in which "women function as agents in both the private and public realms" in his *Feminism and the Western in Film and Television*.
2. Of this group of stars, only Stanwyck was regularly cast in Westerns, appearing in four in the 1940s and eight in the 1950s. She would anchor a Western television series, *The Big Valley*, originally broadcast 1965–69. In 1973, she was inducted into the National Cowboy and Western Heritage Museum's Hall of Fame of Great Western Performers.
3. Samuel Fuller did not want a happy ending for *Forty Guns*, but he says it was forced on him by the marketing department of Fox. See Fuller, *A Third Face* (2002: 357–8).
4. The film wordlessly reveals the repressed desire between Ethan Edwards and his brother's wife when she retrieves Ethan's coat. This is relayed to the film viewer by the look (and then averted eyes of) the Reverend Captain Clayton (Ward Bond). Illustrating the symbolic importance of inheritance in the "family on the land" trope, Ethan disinherits his niece Debbie because "she's been living with a buck" as a captive of

the Comanche. For an analysis of how Ford's film can be read as advancing a counter discourse of female-centered values in contrast to the death dealing ones of Ethan and other whites, see Studlar, "What Would Martha Want?" (Studlar 2004: 171–95).
5. Grant not only tries to kill Jeb himself several times, but schemes to get Jeb sent to the Spanish-American war, tries to get him convicted as Adam's murderer when Jeb shoots Adam in self-defense, and bullies a hapless suitor of Jeb's adopted sister, Thor, into trying to shoot Jeb for "insulting" Thor at a dance. For a consideration of trauma in relation to Oedipality and the film's presentation of Grant Callum as a father figure, see Janet Walker, "Captive Images," especially pp. 229–35.

Filmography

Arizona, director Wesley Ruggles, featuring Jean Arthur, William Holden, Warren William (Columbia, 1940).

Belle Starr, director Irving Cummings, featuring Randolph Scott, Gene Tierney, Dana Andrews (20th Century Fox, 1941).

Destry Rides Again, director George Marshall, featuring Marlene Dietrich, James Stewart, Mischa Auer (Universal, 1939).

Duel in the Sun, director King Vidor, featuring Jennifer Jones, Joseph Cotten, Gregory Peck (Selznick International, 1947).

Forty Guns, director Samuel Fuller, featuring Barbara Stanwyck, Barry Sullivan, Dean Jagger (20th Century Fox, 1957).

Gone with the Wind, director Victor Fleming, featuring Clark Gable, Vivien Leigh, Thomas Mitchell (Warner Bros., 1939).

I'll Be Seeing You, director William Dieterlie, featuring Ginger Rogers, Joseph Cotten, Shirley Temple (Selznick International, 1944).

Imitation of Life, director Douglas Sirk, featuring Lana Turner, John Gavin, Sandra Dee (Universal, 1959).

Love Letters, director William Dieterlie, featuring Jennifer Jones, Joseph Cotten, Ann Richards (Hal Wallis Productions, 1945).

Mrs Miniver, director William Wyler, featuring Greer Garson, Walter Pidgeon, Theresa Wright (MGM, 1942).

Now, Voyager, director Irving Rapper, featuring Bette Davis, Paul Henreid, Claude Rains (Warner Bros., 1942).

Pursued, director Raoul Walsh, featuring Teresa Wright, Robert Mitchum, Judith Anderson (United State Pictures and Warner Bros., 1947).

Ramrod, director André de Toth, featuring Joel McCrea, Veronica Lake, Don DeFore (Enterprise Productions, 1947).

Rebel without a Cause, director Nicholas Ray, featuring James Dean, Natalie Wood, Sal Mineo (Warner Bros., 1955).

Since You Went Away, director John Cromwell, featuring Claudette Colbert, Jennifer Jones, Joseph Cotton (Selznick International, 1944).

Some Came Running, director Vincente Minnelli, featuring Frank Sinatra, Dean Martin, Shirley MacLaine (MGM, 1958).

Spellbound, director Alfred Hitchcock, featuring Ingrid Bergman, Gregory Peck, Michael Chekhov (Selznick International, 1945).
The Big Country, director William Wyler, featuring Gregory Peck, Jean Simmons, Carroll Baker (Anthony Productions, 1958).
The Big Valley (ABC), creators A. I. Bezzarides and Louis F. Edelman, featuring Richard Long, Peter Breck, Lee Majors (Levee-Gardner-Laven Productions, 1965–9).
The Furies, director Anthony Mann, featuring Barbara Stanwyck, Wendell Corey, Walter Huston (Wallis-Hazen, 1950).
The Great Man's Lady, director William A. Wellman, featuring Barbara Stanwyck, Joel McCrea, Brian Donlevy (Paramount, 1942).
The Outlaw, director Howard Hughes, featuring Jack Buetel, Thomas Mitchell, Jane Russell (Howard Hughes Productions, 1943).
The Sea of Grass, director Elia Kazan, featuring Katherine Hepburn, Spencer Tracy, Robert Walker (MGM, 1947).
The Song of Bernadette, director, Henry King, featuring Jennifer Jones, Charles Bickford, William Eythe (20th Century Fox, 1943).
The Violent Men, director Rudolph Maté, featuring Glenn Ford, Barbara Stanwyck, Edward G. Robinson (Columbia, 1954).
Union Pacific, director Cecil B. DeMille, featuring Barbara Stanwyck, Joel McCrea, Akim Tamiroff (Paramount, 1939).

Bibliography

"101 Pic Gross in Millions," *Variety*, 6 January 1943, pp. 3, 58.
Abel [Green, Abel], "Ramrod," *Variety*, 26 February 1947, p. 10.
Abel, Richard (1999) *The Red Rooster Scare: Making Cinema American, 1900–1910*. Berkeley, CA: University of California Press.
Anderson, Lindsay (1960) "Film Reviews: *The Searchers*," *Monthly Film Bulletin*, 26 (2), pp. 94–5.
Anon. (1947) "Reviews of New Films: 'Ramrod,'" *Film Daily*, 25 February, p. 9.
Binford, Lloyd T. (ca. 1947) Letter to David O. Selznick (no date, ca. 1947), *Duel in the Sun* Production Code File, Academy of Motion Picture Arts and Sciences Special Collections.
Busch, Niven (1973 [1944]) *Duel in the Sun*. New York: Popular Library.
Carter, Matthew and Paryz, Marek (2018) "The Visual Language of Gender and Family in the Western: Introduction," *Papers on Language and Literature*, 54 (1), pp. 4–6.
Fearing, Franklin (1946) "The Screen Discovers Psychiatry," *Hollywood Quarterly*, 1 (2), pp. 154–8.
Fenin, George N. and Everson, William K. (1973) *The Western from Silents to the Seventies*, revised edn. Harmondsworth: Penguin Books.
Fuller, Samuel (2002) *A Third Face: My Tale of Writing, Fighting, and Filmmaking*. New York: Alfred A. Knopf.
Golden, Herb (1948) "Top 'Golden Circle,'" *Variety*, 1 January 1948, p. 3.
Grant, Jack D. (1946) "Selznick's 'Duel in the Sun' Truly Magnificent Smash," *Hollywood Reporter*, 31 December, p. 3.

Haver, Ronald (1985) *David O. Selznick's Hollywood*. New York: Bonanza Books.
Horak, Laura (2014) "Landscape, Vitality, and Desire: Cross-Dressed Frontier Girls in Transitional-Era American Cinema," *Cinema Journal*, 52 (1), pp. 74–98.
Krutnik, Frank (1991) *In a Lonely Street: Film Noir, Genre, Masculinity*. London and New York: Routledge.
Lamont, Victoria (2016) *Westerns: A Woman's History*. Lincoln, NE and London: University of Nebraska Press.
"Leading Ladies Take to the Great Outdoors in a New Movie Trend," *New York Times*, 9 February 1947, p. X5.
Lusted, David (1996) "Social Class and the Western as Male Melodrama," in Ian Cameron and Douglas Pye (eds), *The Book of Westerns*. New York: Continuum Press, pp. 63–74.
Monticone, Paul (2014) "The Noir Western: Genre Theory and the Problem of the Anomalous Hybrid," *Quarterly Review of Film and Video*, 31 (4), pp. 336–49.
"Movies," *Newsweek*, 4 September 1950, p. 71.
Nowell-Smith, Geoffrey (1985) "Minelli and Melodrama," in Bill Nichols (eds.), *Movies and Methods Vol II: An Anthology*. Berkeley, CA: University of California Press, pp. 190–4.
Platte, Nathan (2018) *Making Music in Selznick's Hollywood*. Oxford: Oxford University Press.
"Reviews: 'Pursued,'" *Film Daily*, 21 February 1947, p. 7.
"Reviews of New Films: 'Ramrod,'" *Film Daily*, 25 February 1947, p. 9.
Schallert, Edwin (1947) "Adult Western Subject Complex," *Los Angeles Times*, 15 March, p. A5.
Scott, John L. (1947) "'Ramrod' Super Western," *Los Angeles Times*, 31 May, p. 7.
Selznick, Irene (1983) *A Private View*. New York: Alfred A. Knopf.
Smith, Henry Nash (1950) *Virgin Land: The American West as Symbol and Myth*. Cambridge, MA and London: Harvard University Press.
Spinrad, Leonard (1947) "Boots and Saddles," *New York Times*, 8 June, p. X4.
Stanfield, Peter (2001) *Hollywood, Westerns and the 1930s: The Lost Trail*. Exeter: University of Exeter Press.
Studlar, Gaylyn (2004) "What Would Martha Want? Captivity, Purity, and Feminine Values in *The Searchers*," in Arthur M. Eckstein and Peter Lehman (eds), *The Searchers: Essays and Reflections on John Ford's Classic Western*. Detroit, MI: Wayne State University Press, pp. 171–95.
Studlar, Gaylyn (2013) *Precocious Charms: Stars Performing Girlhood in Classical Hollywood Cinema*. Berkeley, CA: University of California Press.
Tompkins, Jane (1992) *West of Everything: The Inner Life of Westerns*. New York and Oxford: Oxford University Press.
Walker, Janet (2001) "Captive Images in the Traumatic Western," in Janet Walker (ed.), *Westerns: Films Through History*. New York: Routledge, pp. 219–51.
Weaver, William R. (1947) "Coast Reviewers React to 'Duel,'" *Motion Picture Herald*, 11 January, p. 47.
Weiler, A. (1947) "The Screen in Review: 'Ramrod,'" *New York Times*, 30 June, p. 25.

Wexman, Virginia Wright (1993) *Creating the Couple: Love, Marriage, and Hollywood Performance*. Princeton, NJ: Princeton University Press.
Wildermuth, Mark E. (2018) *Feminism and the Western in Film and Television*. Cham, Switzerland: Palgrave Macmillan.
Wood, Robin (1996) "*Duel in the Sun*: The Destruction of an Ideological System," in Ian Cameron and Douglas Pye (eds), *The Book of Westerns*. New York: Continuum Press, pp. 189–95.

6. CLYTEMNESTRA AND ELECTRA UNDER WESTERN SKIES

Martin M. Winkler

Revenge is the fundamental narrative impulse in Western literature.[1] The plot of our earliest work, Homer's *Iliad*, is set in motion when Achilles, the greatest of the Greek heroes in the Trojan War, foregoes immediate revenge for an insult received by Agamemnon. Achilles' suppressed impulse leads to the death of his close friend Patroclus, which Achilles then avenges in a horrendous killing spree against the Trojans, culminating in his pitiless duel with Hector, Patroclus' killer. While Achilles may be the most famous avenger in classical mythology, female avengers play their devastating parts as well, whether they are connected to the Trojan War and its aftermath or not. The best known example of the latter is the Medea of Euripides, with virtually all later retellings of her story. The best known example of the former is Clytemnestra, wife of Agamemnon. Almost as well known, Agamemnon and Clytemnestra's daughter Electra comes to hate her mother and patiently waits for the return of her younger brother Orestes as avenger. Orestes then kills Clytemnestra. Electra, too, is responsible for this matricide.[2]

While the tale of Medea has been told and retold in a variety of media, the myth of Clytemnestra,[3] Electra, and Orestes has received comparatively less attention, not least in the cinema. Best known is Michael Cacoyannis's film *Electra* (1962), with a young Irene Papas in the title part. In this chapter, I examine traces of this complex Greek myth in a screen genre that may not be considered likely to contain any version of it, although American and, in their wake, European Westerns have always shown close affinities to archetypes of classical myth.[4] Three remarkable Western films have transposed Clytemnestra and Electra archetypes to the screen. One of them has what may be the genre's best demonstration of the Electra complex as it is commonly understood.[5] This film is *The Furies* (1950), directed by Anthony Mann from a screenplay by Charles Schnee.[6] He was involved with two highly Freudian Westerns: the epic *Duel in the Sun* (1946) was based on his novel, while *Pursued* (1947), virtually a *film noir*, was derived from his original script. Director Mann had a distinguished record of *noir* films before embarking on a series of classic Westerns full of dark and serious overtones during the 1950s. These are his greatest achievements. As a result, *The Furies* is an epic-tragic *noir* family drama.

The Furies is the name of widowed T. C. Jeffords's cattle empire. T. C., as he is generally called, has a weak son but a strong-willed daughter, Vance, to whom he intends to leave The Furies. Vance is played by Barbara Stanwyck. The bond between father and daughter is so close as to border on the incestuous, a remarkable feature if we consider the time of the film's production (and a miracle to have passed the censors). Father and daughter see much of themselves in each other and much of each other in themselves. This parallels the statement by Sophocles' Electra about her dead father: "I was of the same nature" (Sophocles, *Electra* 1,023). The fact that the daughter's first name is Vance rather than something more feminine-sounding is one indication of this. "I like being T. C.'s daughter," Vance comments at one time. A Mexican childhood friend of hers will later say: "You look like T. C., standing there ordering us." Father and daughter often test each other's will; she always holds her own. Their closeness extends to her love life, which has been virginal so far. When they are discussing a potential husband for her, Vance tells T. C.: "You sound like you'd rather I *never* married." His answer is telling: "You won't have it easy finding a man. I've spoiled most of 'em for you." This is clearly the case. Then he adds: "You want a man like me." One of the most revealing close-ups in the film, which must have been daring for its time, drives home the point visually. The profiles of father and daughter fill the screen; they look like a couple passionately in love. In any other context, filmgoers would expect such a moment to lead to a kiss. Here we find one of the subliminally most erotic shots in the history of the Western: the Electra Complex in full force.

But this is Hollywood, and what must not be will not be. The plot takes a different but predictable turn. T. C. introduces Vance to Mrs Florence Burnett, a self-assured but impoverished middle-aged widow from the East with useful political connections and a measure of class. T. C. intends to marry her. Mrs Burnett describes herself as an "adventuress" and freely admits that she is mainly marrying for the security that comes with money. Even before finding this out, Vance dislikes her on sight: a clear case of sexual rivalry and jealousy. The situation becomes a kind of love triangle, in which the women are stronger than the man. Vance is becoming aware that now she runs the risk of being bested after all. The women's antagonism starts on an outwardly polite level. Mrs Burnett is all proper manners even though Vance may glower at her. The tension between them increases to a stage of verbal sparring and clever repartee, as in this exchange:

Mrs. Burnett: My dear, I had a wonderful notion –
Vance, interrupting: I had a notion you'd have a wonderful notion.

The older woman turns politely haughty ("You're such a brave creature") and proposes to pack Vance off on a Grand Tour to Europe. Vance, already being eclipsed in her father's affection, now also has to be concerned about being summarily dismissed and having a stranger take over The Furies. Mrs Burnett meddles in Vance's bookkeeping and even proposes to redecorate her mother's bedroom, which has been kept unchanged as a kind of sanctuary. "There'll always be room for you at The Furies," Mrs Burnett tells Vance with astonishing condescension. To someone who expects to be the sole heir of the entire estate, such words must be dismaying and infuriating. To someone with Vance's temperament, fury is likely to eclipse dismay, even if she is nonplussed for the time being. "I just don't know how to fight her," she admits. Her brother knows the reason: "You're fighting a woman."

Their fight erupts into violence, with unexpected suddenness and ferocity, in T. C.'s presence. Irate, Vance throws a pair of scissors at Mrs Burnett and horribly disfigures her face (Figure 6.1). An extraordinary moment in purest *noir* style immediately afterwards makes clear, wordlessly, that we are dealing with a volatile woman who is imprisoned, as it were, by her inner demons. Vance's

Figure 6.1 A furious Vance in *The Furies* (1950).

explosive eruption takes care of her rival, but her father throws her out. "She's your own flesh and blood," he is told but only responds brutally: "She's a canker to be cut out." The evident if unacknowledged love between father and daughter has turned into equally deep hatred, the other side of the emotional coin. "You've found a new love in your life, haven't you, Vance?" she will be told later. "You're in love with hate." When T. C. has Vance's Mexican friend hanged, she erupts at him menacingly:

> You're old, you're getting foolish, and you've made a mistake. It's *me* you should have hung! Because now I hate you in a way I didn't know a human *could* hate! . . . You won't see me again until the day I take your world away from you.

Vance does just that. She succeeds in ruining her father, turning bitter in the process. But such revenge is anything but sweet: "You thought that when you'd licked T. C. and finally gotten your revenge," she is told, "it would be the greatest moment in your life." That it certainly is not. Vance has The Furies back, but it is unlikely that she will be entirely rid of the Furies inside her. Although the plot contrives finally to reconcile Vance and T.C., there is no happy reunion and certainly no Hollywood ending. T. C. dies, shot by the mother of the Mexican he had hanged.[7]

In terms of plot, the intensity of the near-incestuous nature of Vance's love for her father and any impossibility of its consummation make the arrival of a rival for his affections virtually inevitable. If Vance is an Electra out West, T. C. is her living Agamemnon, and Mrs Burnett should be a Clytemnestra. But such is hardly the case. T. C. is not murdered by a family member, and the widow, Vance's antagonist, is by no means murderous. Nor is she killed. Nor is there any kind of blood revenge within the family. Vance herself may show some of Clytemnestra's nature, even though her act of violence is unpremeditated. The film's parallels to Greek myth and literature are therefore not as clearly delineated as one might expect. Director Mann himself saw in *The Furies* a version of Dostoevsky's *The Idiot*, while critic Robin Wood considered it a reworking of Shakespeare's *King Lear*.[8] Both were correct. But there is one other consideration, which tilts the emphasis back to classical roots. Why are novel and film called *The Furies*? It seems unlikely that any nineteenth-century cattle baron should have called his ranch by such a name. Clearly it must have a significance different from realism or history. If seen in this light, T. C.'s words after one particular exchange with Vance ("Can't I never get the best of you? Never?"—"Never!") are decisive. He concludes: "You've got The Furies in you all right." T. C. means primarily that Vance embodies the spiritedness, energy, and willpower that had enabled him to become an empire builder and ruler over as vast an estate as The Furies. But he will find out that she also has got the Furies in her very psyche: "As its title indicates, Greek mythology underpins *The Furies*, mainly through the Electra myth" (Coelho 2017: 115). In this regard, the casting of Barbara Stanwyck, who received first billing, was just right. She was "virtually without peer in the portrayal of tough, fearsome women of the West" (Stanfield 1998: 385). Although in her early forties at the time and too old to play a woman in her late teens or early twenties, Stanwyck perfectly conveys the streak of destruction latent in Vance. Although often a brunette, as in some of her famous incarnations as heroine in screwball comedies such as Preston Sturges's *The Lady Eve* and Howard Hawks's *Ball of Fire* (both 1941), here she is a blonde. Stanwyck had been a predatory blonde in the pre-code *Baby Face* (1933) and a murderous blonde as her most famous *femme fatale*, the adulteress in Billy Wilder's *noir* classic *Double Indemnity* (1944). Gentlemen may prefer blondes, but blondes can be deadly, as Euripides' Clytemnestra already exemplified (Euripides, *Electra*: 1,071).

Overtones of the Clytemnestra/Electra myth appear where spectators least expect them. Rudolph Maté's *The Violent Men* (1955), one of the earliest CinemaScope releases and filmed in color on attractive locations, is more of a tragic than merely a spectacular tale. *The Violent Men* illustrates the ease with which archetypal characters or plot elements can be transposed to different times and places, even without any conscious awareness on their makers' part. The story is taken from a novel by Donald Hamilton, better known for the source novel of William Wyler's epic Western *The Big Country* (1958) and best known as the creator of suave secret agent Matt Helm. First-time viewers of *The Violent Men* who are unfamiliar with Greek tragedy or myth may be surprised when they find out that the daughter of an aging and crippled rancher hates her mother. In a clever and understated way, Maté has alerted them to the emotional undercurrent linking the two. At one early point the daughter, while speaking to the film's hero, seems to interrupt herself in mid-sentence without any reason. A moment later we see whom she has just seen off screen: her mother. We now also begin to realize that the daughter has been egging the hero on to fight—not her father, as the rancher-vs.-settlers plot has seemed to indicate, but her mother. Now viewers who know their mythology can predict the entire family dynamic. It is evident that her mother has no love for her much older husband and is involved with her younger and virile brother-in-law; both are scheming against the husband. The wife will eventually avail herself of a chance to kill him. A revealing moment shows us the daughter on the top of the screen, watching from a staircase—she has been "keeping to herself," her father says—both her parents and her uncle below (Figure 6.2). Forming the apex of a triangle, as it were, she appears exactly in the middle between her father and mother, while the mother is placed between husband and lover, a little closer to the latter and slightly turning back at the former. Her husband, on crutches, is the most powerless figure among them all.

Figure 6.2 Hidden family dynamics are becoming clear in *The Violent Men* (1955).

Unlike the myth, the father survives against all odds; as in the myth, the adulterers do not. As in the myth and especially in Aeschylus' *Agamemnon*, the adulterous wife is harsh and strong. "You don't need anybody; you never have, you never will," she is told by her lover toward the end. And she is utterly ruthless. She throws away her helpless husband's crutches while he is trying to get out of their burning house. As with *The Furies*, various plot details do not conform to classical narrative, but such is to be expected. Rather unexpected is the cast who plays the family: Edward G. Robinson as the father and Brian Keith as the duplicitous adulterer. Barbara Stanwyck this time around is the Clytemnestra figure. And she is blond again. The daughter, played by a pretty but bland Dianne Foster, is no match for her. Accordingly, her confrontations with her mother are kept brief, although not lacking a measure of tension. And they do not resolve anything.

Ferdinando Baldi's *The Forgotten Pistolero* (*Il pistolero dell'Ave Maria*, 1969) is clearly based on Greek tragedy. Published plot summaries are often too brief to show this film's debt to classical literature.[9] Around 1867, a Mexican general returns victoriously from his campaign, only to be murdered by his wife Anna (or, in Spanish, Ana) and her lover Tomás. The general's two little children, Isabella and Sebastian, are saved by their nanny, together with their playmate Rafael. Isabella had witnessed her father's death, while Sebastian rather implausibly had slept through it and the accompanying massacre of his father's soldiers. Equally implausibly, he then grew up believing his nanny to be his mother. Years later Rafael, pursued by Tomás's gunmen, meets Sebastian and informs him about his mother's true identity and his father's death. The two decide on revenge. Rafael corresponds to Orestes' companion Pylades, but unlike Pylades he had previously run afoul of Tomás's henchmen and had been castrated (off-screen, fortunately). Isabella the eyewitness has been married off to a meek storekeeper. He loves her but does not touch her because he knows that she does not love him. Rafael and Isabella had been childhood sweethearts. Isabella's marriage conforms to Electra's marriage to a well-meaning peasant; he, too, does not touch her.[10] In Euripides, Electra remains virginal until Orestes eventually gives her to Pylades for his wife (Euripides, *Electra*, 43–6).[11]

We first see the adult Isabella as she kneels and prays at her father's grave, a scene modeled on Electra's entrance in Aeschylus' *The Libation Bearers*. (The title refers to the serving women who accompany her to pour libations at Agamemnon's grave, a common ancient rite.) Upon her reunion with Sebastian Isabella tells him: "You will help me to catch his murderess . . . Revenge must be taken." This, too, conforms to the classical pattern.[12] As was Electra, so Isabella is the driving force. And now Sebastian finds out that his mother had been in on the assassination. "Swear you'll kill them," Isabella tells him.

The climactic confrontation of Isabella, Sebastian, and Rafael with Anna and Tomás partly adheres to and partly deviates from the model of classical tragedy. Sebastian at first pretends not to be Anna's son, but she recognizes him. Faced with the children's accusation of killing their father, Anna blames it all on Tomás although we know that she had used Tomás to kill her husband. She had first made the general easily vulnerable to Tomás' dagger, then finished him off by repeatedly shooting him in the back, adding: "Everything went as we had planned it." So it is not surprising that now Tomás feels betrayed by his lover, who had earlier tried to get rid of him by bribing him to depart. He shoots Anna. This is the first major plot twist. Sebastian feels pity for his dying mother and wants to go to her, but Isabella denounces her the more. At first, she is as fierce as Electra had been. Then she breaks down.

Now comes the greatest twist. Anna asks the children's forgiveness, but Tomás reveals to them the truth that has been buried all these years: not Anna but a servant woman who died in childbirth was their mother. This is undeniably a shock to viewers, especially to those who are aware of the classical background to the film. This change seriously weakens the entire revenge plot. Tomás shoots and wounds Rafael and is in turn shot and killed by Sebastian. Meanwhile their hacienda is engulfed in flames. Isabella, driven out of her mind, appears to be burning to death. In Greek myth and literature, madness affects Orestes, the actual killer of Clytemnestra, not Electra. The final scene shows brother, sister, and Rafael riding off. Rafael is holding Isabella in his arms on his horse.

All this is astonishing to friends of Aeschylus, but it will be less so to friends of the arcana of Greek myth. That his nurse saves Sebastian from certain death after his father's assassination parallels the versions mentioned by Pindar and the tragedians.[13] When Sebastian tells Anna that he is not who he is, this echoes the elaborate deception used by Electra and Orestes in Sophocles.[14] Orestes tells Clytemnestra that he is someone else and that Orestes is dead. The ostensible proof is an urn that is said to contain his bones. The revelation that Anna is not the mother of Sebastian and Isabella has its ancient precursor as well, if only indirectly. Clytemnestra's revenge against Agamemnon is chiefly over the sacrifice of their daughter Iphigenia, which had become necessary for the Trojan War to be able to take place. This is the subject of Euripides' *Iphigenia in Aulis*. But the second-century AD grammarian Antoninus Liberalis summarizes an account by Nicander, in which Iphigenia was not the daughter of Agamemnon and Clytemnestra but of the latter's sister Helen, future wife of Menelaus and cause of the Trojan War, and the hero Theseus. Theseus had abducted Helen as a young girl and made her pregnant; Clytemnestra then took the baby and passed it off on an unsuspecting Agamemnon as her own. Thus she saved her sister's reputation, for Helen had maintained that she had returned from Theseus as a virgin (Antoninus Liberalis, *Metamorphoses*, 27). This different parentage of Iphigenia undermines Clytemnestra's revenge on Agamemnon, which in turn precipitates Orestes' and Electra's revenge on Clytemnestra. The chain of cause and effect in these acts of revenge is, if not broken, then significantly changed.

The director Baldi is best known internationally for Westerns and other action films. Versatile as many Italian filmmakers had to be in the 1950s and 1960s, he also made a number of films set in ancient Rome. His nickname was *il professore*, so we need not be surprised that he infused classical plot elements into as archetypal a genre as the Western. At the time when *The Forgotten Pistolero* was made, the Italian Western had already begun its decline, notwithstanding the huge international success of Italian comedy and parody Westerns. (Hence the film's title, copied, as it were, from religious terminology in the Italian and foreign-release titles of contemporary Westerns such as the *Trinity* and *Alleluja* films.) *The Forgotten Pistolero* may be regarded as an attempt to keep the dark, serious, and politically conscious Italian Western, the "opera of violence," as it has been called, alive a little longer.[15] The dark look of much of the film and, to its detriment, Baldi's visual style is due to hectic camera moves, rapid zooms into and out of faces, fast cutting to express emotional intensity, and extreme close-ups. All this makes the film look dated. It compares unfavorably with Baldi's *Texas, Adios* (1966), which profits from greater stylistic restraint. This film's plot is similar to that of the later film. A Texas sheriff and his younger brother travel to Mexico to avenge the death of their father on a rich landowner. A major twist reveals that the killer is also the young brother's father. In flashback the sheriff remembers watching his father being shot and his mother coming out of the house after being raped. The general's assassination and the ensuing massacre in *The Forgotten Pistolero* also occur in flashback.

With the *Oresteia* by Aeschylus as its direct model, the mother–daughter conflict in *The Forgotten Pistolero* is much more pronounced than it was in *The Violent Men*. Anna is played by Luciana Paoluzzi, best known as the SPECTRE assassin in the James Bond film *Thunderball* (1965). Anna can be beautiful and seductive. In the flashback to the general's return, and more emphatically than later in the film, her hair is a prominent, and doubtless symbolic, red. A Meander decoration on her dress may be intended to indicate that a family tragedy in a Greek key is about to be re-enacted. Using an extreme close-up on her eyes during husband and wife's first embrace, Baldi hints to viewers that she is up to no good. Isabella watches her in a tight embrace with Tomás after her father's murder, but we learn later that Anna will take several other lovers. The adult Isabella comments: "My mother has no virtue. She has become addicted to her desires." Although Anna saves Rafael's life ("I couldn't stand any more bloodshed in the house") and turns to a priest to enlist his help when she knows that Sebastian is about to return, Tomás will later tell her that she is incapable of remorse.

Isabella can be almost as ruthless.[18] Played by a young Pilar Velázquez in her first major dramatic appearance on the big screen, Isabella holds her own against her mother much more than the daughter had managed to do in *The Violent Men*. Tomás has her kidnapped and brought to his place.[17] Anna comes to take her back. Isabella now pretends to be Tomás's lover. She approaches him seductively (the top of her blouse is off her shoulders), embraces him, smiling, kisses him on the cheek, and sweet-talks him. She intends to make Anna suspicious and jealous. This works. "It isn't what you think," Tomás can only tell her. Viewers are meant to recognize the clichéd defense. Tomás is telling the truth, but Anna does not believe him. Here Baldi rises to the occasion, because his shot counter shot of tight close-ups on the women's faces fully express their hidden antagonism. There is a hint of a contemptuous smile on Isabella looking at Anna, consternation on Anna's face before she turns away and leaves. This round goes to Isabella. In another close-up, she hitches her blouse up and over her shoulders, a sign that she knows she has won. Earlier, Isabella had watched Anna driving past her in a buggy in the town square; this was the first scene in which an adult Isabella was seeing her mother again.[18] Similar but longer crosscutting in that scene had visually placed the women in conflict with each other and prepared viewers for their shorter but more intense confrontation later. Viewers conversant with Greek tragedy will recognize that brief moment as an extreme condensation of the long verbal arguments between Electra and Clytemnestra in Sophocles and Euripides.[19] Cacoyannis, in his *Electra*, had already provided the visual model.

The Forgotten Pistolero is anything but a milestone of cinema or of adaptations of classical myth and literature to modern popular culture, but it is not as casual about its sources as a cursory viewing might lead some viewers to believe. As mentioned earlier, the Western has always shown its awareness of classical archetypes, so director Anthony Mann was correct in saying: "You can take any of the great dramas; doesn't matter whether it's

Shakespeare, whether it's Greek plays, or what: you can always lay them in the West. They somehow become alive" (in Mayersberg 2008: n.p.).[20] A comment by Barbara Stanwyck about the Western may be adduced in this context. She put the matter simply and nobly: "That's our royalty, our aristocracy" (quoted in Drew 1981: 45).[21] Female figures resembling archetypes from classical and medieval myth and literature, however, have appeared in the Western much less frequently than male ones. Mann once observed that the Western, essentially a male-dominated genre, does not readily provide women with decisive parts (Bitsch and Chabrol 2008: 22). In this, too, he was correct. But, alongside the ultra-Freudian *Johnny Guitar* (1954), *The Furies* is an exception, at least as far as Westerns made during the studio era are concerned. It is fitting that the main character of *The Furies* is, if not an outright Electra, then at least a powerful illustration of her complexities.[22] And the Clytemnestra of Greek tragedy can hold her own alongside any male Western villain. As Sophocles' Orestes observes, the spirit of Ares the war god exists in women, too (Sophocles, *Electra*, 1,243–4). He means Clytemnestra, but, if we take the intention for the deed, this statement applies equally to Electra. Like mother, like daughter. Aeschylus' Electra already said as much, referring to Orestes and herself: "We are bloody-minded like a wolf; / our spirit comes from a savage mother" (Aeschylus, *The Libation Bearers*, 421–2).

So we may conclude: *Westward the women!* But also: *Westward the* Greek *women!*

Notes

1. Elisabeth Frenzel, *Motive der Weltliteratur: Ein Lexikon dichtungsgeschichtlicher Längsschnitte*, 6th edn (Stuttgart: Kröner, 2008), pp. 63–78 (s.v. "Blutrache"), provides a first orientation, with additional references. The history of tragic drama offers particularly fertile examples, with Elizabethan and Jacobean tragedies among the most familiar. For classical drama and its legacy see especially Anne Pippin Burnett, *Revenge in Attic and Later Tragedy* (Berkeley, CA: University of California Press, 1998), and John Kerrigan, *Revenge Tragedy: Aeschylus to Armageddon* (Oxford: Clarendon Press, 1996; rpt. 2001). Will Wright, *Sixguns and Society: A Structural Study of the Western* (Berkeley, CA: University of California Press, 1975; rpt. 1977), pp. 59–74 and 154–63, has a useful introduction to the revenge topic in the Western.
2. On this see, for example, Jill Scott, *Electra After Freud: Myth and Culture* (Ithaca, NY: Cornell University Press, 2005), especially pp. 6–11 and 170–2; and Hendrika C. Freud, *Electra vs Oedipus: The Drama of the Mother–Daughter Relationship*, trans. Marjolijn de Jager (London and New York: Routledge, 2011), especially pp. 63–82 and 179–81 (notes; chapter titled "Electra versus Oedipus"). Both contain further references, especially to sources (Jung, Freud). Scholarship on psychoanalysis and antiquity is extensive; the following provide useful introductions (and

more) in English: Richard H. Armstrong, *A Compulsion for Antiquity: Freud and the Ancient World* (Ithaca, NY: Cornell University Press, 2005; rpt. 2006); Rachel Bowlby, *Freudian Mythologies: Greek Tragedy and Modern Identities* (Oxford: Oxford University Press, 2007; rpt. 2009); Vanda Zajko and Ellen O'Gorman (eds), *Classical Myth and Psychoanalysis: Ancient and Modern Stories of the Self* (Oxford: Oxford University Press, 2013).

3. The myth of the House of Atreus, as it is often summarily if not quite correctly called, evinces intra-familial revenge killings (and worse) over five generations:

Tantalus
Pelops
Atreus, Thyestes
Agamemnon, Menelaus, Aegisthus
Orestes

Aeschylus' *Oresteia*, our only surviving tragic trilogy consisting of *Agamemnon*, *The Libation Bearers*, and *The Eumenides*; plays titled *Electra* by both Sophocles and Euripides; Euripides' *Iphigenia in Aulis*, *Orestes*, and *Iphigenia in Tauris*; centuries later, Seneca's *Thyestes* and *Agamemnon*—these are the most important surviving plays about the House of Tantalus, as we might prefer to call this dysfunctional and violent dynasty. Only divine absolution eventually clears Orestes from pollution as matricide and ends the intra-familial bloodshed in the clan's history.

4. See, for example, Martin M. Winkler, "Classical Mythology and the Western Film," *Comparative Literature Studies*, 22 (1985), pp. 516–40, and "Homeric *kleos* and the Western Film," *Syllecta Classica*, 7 (1996), pp. 43–54.

5. Psychoanalysis is rather vague on the concept: "The greatest cultural myth surrounding Electra is that there is no Electra complex per se. Jung made only fleeting reference to the complex without ever fully defining or describing it" (quoted in Scott 2005: 8). Even so, the Electra Complex is worth taking seriously.

6. Charles Schnee which in turn was based on the 1948 novel by Niven Busch. Schnee had previously written the epic Western *Red River* (1948), the *film noir* classics *I Walk Alone* (1947) and *They Live by Night* (1948); in 1951 came *Westward the Women*. Busch had co-written *The Westerner* (1940) and *The Postman Always Rings Twice* (1946).

7. The ending is the film's greatest weakness. Robin Wood, in "Mann of the Western" (an essay written for the booklet accompanying the 2008 Criterion Collection DVD of the film), pp. 7–14, observes: "Vance is softened and sweetened." This contrasts with, but fortunately cannot negate, "the film's earlier energy, complexity, and audacity." Both quotations are from Wood, "Mann of the Western," p. 14.

8. Wood, "Mann of the Western," pp. 9–10 and 12–13; Charles Bitsch and Claude Chabrol, "Interview with Anthony Mann." trans. Alison Dundy (Criterion Collection booklet; excerpts), pp. 17–32, at p. 30. The original: Charles Bitsch and Claude Chabrol, "Entretiens avec Anthony Mann," *Cahiers du cinéma*, 69 (1957), pp. 2–15.

9. And they may be incorrect, as is, for example, the entry in Thomas Weisser, *Spaghetti Westerns—the Good, the Bad and the Violent: A Comprehensive,*

Illustrated Filmography of 558 Eurowesterns and Their Personnel, 1961–1977 (Jefferson, NC: McFarland, 1992; rpt. 2005), p. 121.
10. Electra is without a husband in Aeschylus' *Libation Bearers* and Euripides' *Orestes*.
11. Euripides, *Electra*, 247–62 and 1,249; *Orestes*, 1,658–9. One ancient explanation of the name *Elektra* is based on its closeness to *alektra* ("woman without [marriage] bed") and expresses her long-lasting virginity (Aelian, *Historical Miscellany*, 4.26). *Electra* is thus a nickname; her original name was Laodice. On the latter, which occurs in Homer, *Iliad*, 9.145 and 287, see the note by Bryan Hainsworth, *The Iliad: A Commentary*, vol. III: *Books 9–12* (Cambridge: Cambridge University Press, 1993; rpt. 2010), p. 77. Electra meets Pylades only when he arrives with Orestes for revenge.
12. Cf. Euripides, *Electra*, 647, 967–87, and 1,224–5. Sophocles' Clytemnestra thinks Electra is more dangerous than Orestes (*Electra*, 783–7); his Electra urges her sister Chrysothemis to kill Aegisthus and, when the latter demurs, proposes to do so herself (461–3, 947–89, 1,019–20). In Euripides' *Orestes* it is Electra who devises a trap to capture and, if necessary, kill Hermione.
13. At Pindar, *Pythian Odes*, 11.17–19, Orestes' nurse is called Arsinoa. Aeschylus, *The Libation Bearers*, 749–62, has his nurse Cilissa report that she had received him from Agamemnon and looked after him as a baby. In Sophocles, an old male servant and Electra together save Orestes (*Electra*, 11–14 and 1,130–5). At Euripides, *Electra*, 16–18, the savior is an old male servant, who had been Agamemnon's tutor (487–8, 505–7, and 555–7).
14. Sophocles, *Electra*, 47–8, 673–763, and 1,110–18. At the beginning of this play Orestes had already proposed such a ruse to his tutor (44–66). Aeschylus, *The Libation Bearers*, 674–90, is a shorter and simpler version. Hyginus, *Fabulae*, 119, is a later mythographer's summary of this part of the revenge plot.
15. I allude to Laurence Staig and Tony Williams, *Italian Western: The Opera of Violence* (London: Lorrimer/Odeon, 1975). This book deals chiefly with musical scores.
16. The mythical Electra could be so even more. Hyginus, *Fabulae*, 122, reports that Electra was ready to kill Iphigenia at Delphi for Iphigenia's sacrifice of Orestes in the land of the Taurians but was at the last moment prevented by Orestes himself. Iphigenia as a priestess presiding over human sacrifices is the subject of Euripides' *Iphigenia in Tauris*. In this version, the sacrifice of Iphigenia at Aulis was averted at the last moment by divine intervention.
17. Aegisthus threatens Electra with imprisonment in the final moments of Seneca, *Agamemnon* (988–1,000). There is no reason to assume that he will not make good on this threat after play's end.
18. At that time she was carrying a bucket of water to her husband's store. This parallels Electra's action in Euripides, *Electra*, 56.
19. Sophocles, *Electra* 516–33; Euripides, *Electra*, 998–1,146.
20. Also quoted from excerpts contained in the Criterion Collection issue of *The Furies*. Mann was at that time directing his last film; he died during its production.

21. This sounds more medieval than classical, but that difference is not decisive. On medievalism in the Western see Martin M. Winkler (1988), "Mythologische Motive im amerikanischen Western-Film," in Jürgen Kühnel et al. (eds), *Mittelalter-Rezeption III: Mittelalter, Massenmedien, Neue Mythen*. Göppingen: Kümmerle, pp. 563–78, and (2003) "Fritz Lang's Epic Medievalism: From *Die Nibelungen* to the American West," *Mosaic*, 36 (1), pp. 135–46. On medieval myth in Mann's *oeuvre* and its connections to his Westerns, see Martin M. Winkler (1993) "Mythical and Cinematic Traditions in Anthony Mann's *El Cid*," *Mosaic*, 26 (3), pp. 89–111.
22. If *The Furies* is Mann's Electra Western, *The Man from Laramie* (1955) could rightly be considered his Oedipus Western. On this film see, for example, Jean-Loup Bourget (2005) "L'Homme de la plaine: Œdipe à Santa Fe," *Positif*, 527, pp. 101–3.

Filmography

Baby Face, director Alfred E. Green, featuring Barbara Stanwyck, George Brent, Donald Cook (Warner Bros., 1933).
Ball of Fire, director Howard Hawks, featuring Gary Cooper, Barbara Stanwyck, Oskar Homolka (Samuel Goldwyn, 1941).
Duel in the Sun, director King Vidor, featuring Jennifer Jones, Joseph Cotton, Gregory Peck (Selznick International, 1946).
Electra, director Michael Cacoyannis, featuring Irene Papas, Giannis Fertis, Aleka Katselli (Finos Film, 1962).
I Walk Alone, director Byron Haskin, featuring Burt Lancaster, Lizabeth Scott, Kirk Douglas (Hal Wallace Productions, 1947).
Johnny Guitar, director Nicholas Ray, featuring Joan Crawford, Sterling Hayden, Mercedes McCambridge (Republic, 1954).
Pursued, director Raoul Walsh, featuring Teresa Wright, Robert Mitchum, Judith Anderson (United States Pictures and Warner Bros., 1947).
Texas, Adios / Texas, Addio, director Ferdinando Baldi, featuring Franco Nero, Alberto Dell'Acqua, Elisa Montés (B. R. C. Produzione, 1966).
The Big Country, director William Wyler, featuring Gregory Peck, Jean Simmons, Carroll Baker (Anthony Productions, 1958).
The Forgotten Pistolero / Il pistolero dell'Ave Maria, director Ferdinando Baldi, featuring Leonard Mann, Luciana Paluzzi, Pietro Martellanza (B.R.C. Produzione, 1969).
The Furies, director Anthony Mann, featuring Barbara Stanwyck, Wendell Corey, Walter Huston (Wallis-Hazen, 1950).
The Lady Eve, director Preston Sturges, featuring Barbara Stanwyck, Henry Fonda, Charles Coburn (Paramount, 1941).
The Man from Laramie, director Anthony Mann, featuring James Stewart, Arthur Kennedy, Donald Crisp (Columbia, 1955).
The Postman Always Rings Twice, director Tay Garnett, featuring Lana Turner, John Garfield, Cecil Kellaway (MGM, 1946).

The Return of Ringo / Il ritorno di Ringo, director Duccio Tessari, featuring Giuliano Gemma, Fernando Sancho, Lorella De Luca (Produzioni Cinematografiche Mediterranee, 1965).
The Violent Men, director Rudolph Maté, featuring Glenn Ford, Barbara Stanwyck, Edward G. Robinson (Columbia, 1955).
The Westerner, director William Wyler, featuring Gary Cooper, Walter Brennan, Doris Davenport (Samuel Goldwyn, 1940).
They Live by Night, director Nicholas Ray, featuring Cathy O'Donnell, Farley Granger, Howard Da Silva (RKO Radio Pictures, 1948).
Thunderball, director Terence Young, featuring Sean Connery, Claudine Auger, Adolfo Celi (Eon Productions, 1965).
Westward the Women, director William A. Wellman, featuring Robert Taylor, Denise Darcel, Hope Emerson (MGM, 1951).

Bibliography

Armstrong, Richard H. (2006 [2005]) *A Compulsion for Antiquity: Freud and the Ancient World*. Ithaca, NY: Cornell University Press.
Bitsch, Charles and Chabrol, Claude (1957) "Entretiens avec Anthony Mann," *Cahiers du cinéma*, 69, pp. 2–15.
Bitsch, Charles, and Chabrol, Claude (2008) "Interview with Anthony Mann," in Alison Dundy (tr.), excerpted in booklet of Criterion Collection DVD of *The Furies*, pp. 17–32.
Bourget, Jean-Loup (2005) "L'Homme de la plaine: Œdipe à Santa Fe," *Positif*, 527, pp. 101–3.
Bowlby, Rachel (2009 [2007]) *Freudian Mythologies: Greek Tragedy and Modern Identities*. Oxford: Oxford University Press.
Burnett, Anne Pippin (1998) *Revenge in Attic and Later Tragedy*. Berkeley, CA: University of California Press.
Coelho, Maria Cecília de Miranda N. (2017) "Horses for Ladies, High-Ridin' Women and Whores," in Sue Matheson (ed.), *A Fistful of Icons: Essays on Frontier Fixtures of the American Western*. Jefferson: McFarland, pp. 113–23.
Drew, Bernard (1981) "Stanwyck Speaks," *Film Comment*, 17 (2), pp. 43–6.
Frenzel, Elisabeth (2008) *Motive der Weltliteratur: Ein Lexikon dichtungsgeschichtlicher Längsschnitte*, 6th edn. Stuttgart: Kröner.
Freud, Hendrika C. (2011) Marjolijn de Jager (trans.), *Electra vs Oedipus: The Drama of the Mother–Daughter Relationship*. London and New York: Routledge.
Hainsworth, Bryan (2010 [1993]) *The Iliad: A Commentary, Vol. III: Books 9–12*. Cambridge: Cambridge University Press.
Hughes, Howard (2004 [2006]) *Once Upon a Time in the Italian West: The Filmgoers' Guide to Spaghetti Westerns*. London: Tauris.
Kerrigan, John (2001 [1996]) *Revenge Tragedy: Aeschylus to Armageddon*. Oxford: Clarendon Press.

Mayersberg, Paul (2008) "Action Speaks Louder Than Words: The Films of Anthony Mann," 1967 BBC television interview, excerpted on Criterion Collection DVD of *The Furies*.
Scott, Jill (2005) *Electra After Freud: Myth and Culture*. Ithaca, NY: Cornell University Press.
Staig, Laurence, and Williams, Tony (1975) *Italian Western: The Opera of Violence*. London: Lorrimer/Odeon.
Stanfield, Peter (1998) "Stanwyck, Barbara," in Edward Buscombe (ed.), *The BFI Companion to the Western*. New York: Da Capo.
Weisser, Thomas (2005 [1992]) *Spaghetti Westerns—the Good, the Bad and the Violent: A Comprehensive, Illustrated Filmography of 558 Eurowesterns and Their Personnel, 1961–1977*. Jefferson, NC: McFarland.
Winkler, Martin M. (1985) "Classical Mythology and the Western Film," *Comparative Literature Studies*, 22, pp. 516–540.
Winkler, Martin M. (1988) "Mythologische Motive im amerikanischen Western-Film," in Jürgen Kühnel et al. (eds), *Mittelalter-Rezeption III: Mittelalter, Massenmedien, Neue Mythen*. Göppingen: Kümmerle, pp. 563–78.
Winkler, Martin M. (1993) "Mythical and Cinematic Traditions in Anthony Mann's *El Cid*," *Mosaic*, 26 (3), pp. 89–111.
Winkler, Martin M. (1996) "Homeric *kleos* and the Western Film," *Syllecta Classica*, 7, pp. 43–54.
Winkler, Martin M. (2001) "Tragic Features in John Ford's *The Searchers*," in Martin M. Winkler (ed.), *Classical Myth and Culture in the Cinema*. New York: Oxford University Press, pp. 118–47.
Winkler, Martin M. (2003) "Fritz Lang's Epic Medievalism: From *Die Nibelungen* to the American West," *Mosaic*, 36 (1), pp. 135–46.
Winkler, Martin M. (2004) "Homer's *Iliad* and John Ford's *The Searchers*," in Arthur M. Eckstein and Peter Lehman (eds), *The Searchers: Essays and Reflections on John Ford's Classic Western*. Detroit, MI: Wayne State University Press, pp. 145–70.
Wood, Robin (2008) "Mann of the Western," Booklet of Criterion Collection DVD of *The Furies*, pp. 7–14.
Wright, Will (1977 [1975]) *Sixguns and Society: A Structural Study of the Western*. Berkeley, CA: University of California Press.
Zajko, Vanda and O'Gorman, Ellen (eds) (2013) *Classical Myth and Psychoanalysis: Ancient and Modern Stories of the Self*. Oxford: Oxford University Press.

7. "NEVER SEEN A WOMAN WHO WAS MORE OF A MAN": SALOON GIRLS, WOMEN HEROES, AND FEMALE MASCULINITY IN THE WESTERN

Christopher Minz

With few critical deviations, the American Western has been considered the space of a deeply masculinist project. Jim Kitses, in the introduction to *The Western Reader*, argues that it is "the most male-oriented of the genres" (Gledhill 2012: 1–11). Many of the iconic images of the West that we recognize—gunslingers, riding off into the sunset, bandits and outlaws, and good-natured sheriffs—all seemingly come to us in our collective imaginations as male, or at the very least primarily so. Yet in my opening sentence I specifically mobilize the term masculine, rather than the biological term male, and I do so for a specific reason. While the Western has certainly seen far more males riding the range and shooting down outlaws at high noon, the Western has never been specifically about men in its mythological structure. Moreover, the Western has never been the consistent, solidified genre that it has so often been taken to be. In that introduction Kitses again directly refers to this myopic critical eye saying, "a major problem bedeviling discussion of the genre . . . has been the persistent and narrow identification of the Western with its traditional model, as if it were a monolith" (Gledhill 2012: 17). For the most part, I would concur and argue further that even that very traditional model is not nearly so illustrative of a coherent generic monolith as it would seem. While we can easily point to the lone male hero of the traditional Western (and frankly often in the revisionist and further postmodern Westerns), rarely is that figure what he is, on the surface, perceived to be. Christine Gledhill argues that much criticism has "assumed that 'men' in movies . . . function like—men. But if we understand gender as generic, and 'woman' as a symbolic as well as referential figure, and if we dissolve gender-to-gender identification, then exploration of the aesthetic effects, affective appeals, and significations of genrified masculinity becomes possible" (Gledhill 2012: 6). The focus of this essay is to look at what erupts from the unconscious of the Western, and to suggest that while the Western is a generally masculinist genre, it is not, and never has been, a distinctly male one, and to show how prevalent, and indeed vital, a non-male masculinity has been.

Utilizing the works of Kaja Silverman and J. Halberstam and their divergent surrounding theoretical models, this essay contends to examine, however briefly, the concept of masculinity as it applies to certain females in the American Western. I use the biological here to distinguish that I am not exploring the wealth of fluid and myriad forms that masculinity can take *en masse*, but specifically how masculinity manifests in the women in a cross-section of Westerns. This approach also does not negate the various feminine traits that are present in any example to varying degrees. Often, indeed, it is the very tension between the masculine and feminine elements of the character's personality that creates the most interest, both visually and narratively. There have been, recently, attempts to redress the Western's form and to directly rewrite the mythological scope, giving women, queers, African-Americans, and Natives their historical significance in the genre that is wholly deserved and quite frankly necessary to keep the mythology thriving. While these films are often fascinating and excellent, I turn my focus to that supposed monolith of the traditional Western to show that even in that, there has always been an unconscious masculinity in the aesthetic and narrative aspects of the genre, that rode clinging to the underbelly of the covered wagon, and often sealed the gaps that the overt masculine project had left in its traumatic wake. A masculine female presence has always had what Yvonne Tasker refers to as a "peculiar position of marginal Centrality" (1998: 51) in the Western. I will begin by looking back at the prevalence of the saloon girl and what I see as a certain phallic quality associated with them, before revisiting Nicholas Ray's *Johnny Guitar* (1956) and determining how this movie positions a certain butchness among its dueling women. I will also spend considerable time examining the butch in Roger Corman's *Gunslinger* (1956), a film, custom-tailored for Mystery Science Theatre 3000, that has received very little comment save derision.

Why we attach masculinity so readily to the male body and therefore assign it to the male hero traditionally in the Western may be traced to what is a hegemonic understanding of its function. Kaja Silverman posits that there is what she refers to as "the Dominant fiction." Following Jacques Lacan's theory of the phallic signifier, Silverman argues that we have unconsciously agreed to the equation of the phallus with the biological penis. This equation privileges males and "functions to construct and sustain sexual difference" (Silverman 1992: 8). In Silverman's formulation, Hollywood has a noted investment in this process, and often calls on women to "disavow the male subject's castration and—by looking at him with her 'imagination' rather than her eyes—to confer on him phallic sufficiency" (1992: 8). As Silverman points out, phallic sufficiency is something through which all humans essentially structure their psyches. Thus men fear castration, but their anxiety is ultimately a phantasmatic one. For Silverman there are varying ways to deviate from the dominant fiction, although most of them continue/remain biologically male focused, discovering marginal and subaltern male subjectivities that resist the dominant fiction of phallus = penis. In this essay I will argue that masculine women have always provided a fecund space in which to challenge the Dominant Fiction, especially in the Western.[1]

Two Rubys in the Rough

It is not uncommon in the traditional Western for a woman to be placed in such a situation that she is forced to pick up a gun and use it to defend herself or those around her. We may forgive a certain degree of amateur psychoanalysis in suggesting that in picking up the gun, the woman is adorning herself in the phallic trappings of the men surrounding her. By lifting the long rifle, she appropriates the masculine and makes use of it for the violence and protective nature associated with the masculine. There is something nearly universal about the women who do ultimately join in the phallic display, and that is their implied or sometimes explicit profession: they are Saloon Girls. This Western archetype is discussed in the earliest critical works on the Western, most notably by Robert Warshow, who remarks "those women in Western movies who share the hero's understanding of life are prostitutes . . . [they know that] love can be an irrelevance" (2001: 108). According to Warshow, a woman who engages in the phallic game must be one who, like the Western hero, is untethered by love. Thus, when the Western hero chooses the "good girl," he is rejecting a way of life, turning from the very thing that makes him the archetype in the first place. Warshow says that which defines the prostitute is "her quasi-masculine independence: nobody owns her, nothing has to be explained to her, and she is not . . . a 'value' that demands to be protected" (2001: 108). However, there is nothing "quasi" about the Saloon Girl's masculinity, at least symbolically. She is a type that has existed in all her masculine qualities since the earliest days of the Western. John Ford's *The Iron Horse* (1924) has the first of the two Rubys I will discuss. Though not an elaborate character, Ruby (Gladys Hulette) is a saloon girl (and comfort woman for the railway workers) and does not portray the meek sobriety (both of drink and morality) of Miriam (Madge Bellamy). There is a sinister quality to Ruby, and John Ford uses his exquisite lighting to portray this. Sue Matheson points out that "the absence of light associated with Ruby is a significant element in Ford's characterization of amoral characters" (2016: 46–7).[2] Moreover, Ruby's slippage between the worlds of the civilizing railroad and the villains lends more impetus to the plot of the film than Miriam. It is Ruby's seductive powers that facilitate the crisis that threatens to throw a wrench in the works of the oncoming railroad, while Miriam seems to exist almost entirely as an exemplar of an "idealized, loving nature" that is paralleled symbolically by the transcontinental railway's golden spike that unites the coasts of the United State (Matheson 2016: 46).

This incongruity that Ruby displays is a fairly common element in the Western and provides men with a scale on which to measure their own masculine efficacy. Yvonne Tasker argues that "discourses of masculinity in the Western are defined in relation to female figures, such as the showgirl, and a structuring opposition between wives and whores" (1998: 51). As Warshow would agree, we can see how the male has to decide on which path to take, and through that his masculinity is decided upon. Rejecting the saloon girl, the man rejects a part of his own identity, revealing how tenuous any position on that spectrum may be. In fact, his masculinity can only be defined via its relation to the non-male body and character. J. Halberstam argues in *Female Masculinity* that "far from being an imitation of maleness, female masculinity actually affords us a glimpse of how masculinity is constructed as masculinity . . . what we understand as heroic masculinity has been produced by and across male and female bodies" (1998: 1–2). Ruby does not simply take on the qualities of masculinity in a temporary sense. As a Saloon Girl, she is inherently and defiantly masculine in her interiority, if not in her exterior expression. In the final climactic shootout in *The Iron Horse*, Ruby, who has been portrayed as rather conniving and self-preserving (the latter a trait rarely seen as wholly negative in men), redeems herself in a way that demands a solidification of her masculine gendered position. She picks up a rifle and begins to fight for the protagonist and the cause of the railroad. Her gender insistence here is ultimately what the social order cannot abide, and therefore she is, expectedly, killed. Her death affords the gender conforming characters to lament her, all the while celebrating the driving of the golden spike, itself a quilting point for an ideological position. The male protagonist, David Brandon (George O'Brien), regains his own masculinity after avenging his father's death, but also through the sacrifice of the deviant avatar of female masculinity. He is only truly masculine after this fact, showing what Halberstam calls "the absolute dependence of dominant masculinities on minority masculinities" (1998: 4) which again shows the fragility of what Kaja Silverman terms the "delusory" nature of conventional masculinity (1998: 43).

The second Ruby I will discuss appears in a rather different context, particularly because she comes out of the films of Budd Boetticher Jr, a man not known for a complex view of the women in his films. He says, "What counts is what the heroine provokes . . . In herself, the woman has not the slightest importance" (Russell 1998: 200). For the most part he holds staunchly to his position. Even the heroines of his film are often not suitable for the protagonist, who is frequently portrayed as beyond the pale of needing companionship. Thus, in Boetticher's films, the traditional roles afforded to women are generally rendered null. However, in *Decision at Sundown* (1956), a masculine woman proves to be an exception to this rule, disrupting the gendered directives of the male characters and the Western narrative's traditional ending. As I have argued elsewhere, Ruby (Valerie French) is the one female character in Boetticher's Westerns who defies the logic he sets up. She is there to be "more than the crowd in a bullfight. She actively intervenes . . . ultimately she saves the day" (Minz 2017: 186). Deviating from her traditionally gendered role, Ruby refuses to stay upstairs above the saloon, and continues to ply her trade. Even though her lover dominates, often cutting her off so that only her eyes show on the screen, she refuses to be penned in. Despite his demand that she not be present when he marries the town's wealthiest young woman, she makes her face and her body present in the front row of the church. Ruby's nonconformity is a marker of her masculine nature. As Halberstam points out, "heterosexual female masculinity menaces gender conformity in its own way . . . all too often it represents an acceptable degree of female masculinity as compared to the excessive masculinity of the dyke" (1998: 28).[3] In the Western, the saloon girls portray an excess of femininity that abstracts into pure performance, if not entirely drag. Thus when they pick up the rifle, and don the phallic device, showing themselves as masculine and capable as any male, they are brought into even further relief. They become a fluid representation of the affectations of gender, and often floating quite freely between them, being sensuous and objectified as sexual capital, while always bearing the dangers of violence are the desert rose and its thorn.

The final shootout of *Decision at Sundown* itself undermines the masculinity of the men involved and gives agency to Ruby. Randolph Scott's Bart Allison injured and broken staggers out to fight Ruby's lover Tate Kimbrough (John Carroll). Kimbrough is a manipulating force with the unarmed townsmen, slick and oily with his charm, which barely conceals his menace. The dandy aristocratic demeanor begins to slough off as he walks out to meet Allison. The two men meet in the street and before either can shoot a shot rings out. Kimbrough falls to the ground as it is revealed that it was Ruby who shot him in the arm. Trying to maintain the moral high ground awarded to him by his position, Allison demands that Kimbrough stand so he can be shot dead. Ruby, however, has the last word. She reveals the truth—that Allison's wife is not worth avenging and that his whole quest was based on a fiction he created. Ruby rides off with Kimbrough, his arm in a sling, at the end of the film, upending the classic Western's trope of the reformed prostitute. This in itself is an inversion of the classical trope of the reformed prostitute. In its usual formation, the hero chooses the prostitute because of qualities in her that he sees as being malleable into the feminine that complements his own masculinity. The only way this woman can be a non-Other, and thus an acceptable partner, is if she returns to a gender conformity. Those who do not, end up all too often like the Ruby in *The Iron Horse* who gives up nothing but ends up dead. In *Decision at Sundown*, Boetticher's Ruby is defiant, and her reformation comes from asserting her phallic status and reclaiming her position as Kimbrough's partner. She is not his. Weakened and defeated, he is hers. Although both characters appear in the trappings of gendered norms, her excessiveness and use of a rifle and his notable dandyism (itself a form of masculine appropriation of feminine gender expression while still maintaining male authority) reflect something that cannot be fitted easily into the Western's social construct: a regendered dynamic of the sexually differentiated couple, all while showing how much the phallus is desired by each member to be or to possess.

Big Gun, Little Gun

Although Nicholas Ray's *Johnny Guitar* explicitly posits female masculinity in the Western, critical responses to the film often ignore this structural dynamic of gender inversion at the narrative level. Notably, Will Wright is loathe to recognize Joan Crawford's Vienna as the primary protagonist of the film and only afford Vienna co-hero status. Other critics have offered a far more nuanced account of the film,[4] and the majority of these accounts focus to varying degrees on how the film mobilizes gender critiques and stereotypes to make a broader discussion of the Hollywood blacklist and hysteria.

The saloon girl in the above discussion provides a fine transition to discuss Vienna in *Johnny Guitar*. While Vienna is not presented as a prostitute like the saloon girls, she is coded as part of that world. Yvonne Tasker suggests that by virtue of Vienna's sexual past and her ownership of the saloon that "her success in business marks her as 'working girl' in both sexual and economic senses" (1992: 51–2). Vienna has built a successful saloon and has a solid lead on land purchase allying with the incoming railroad to ensure her economic future. Her business saavy is undercut in the eyes of the town by the fact that she may or may not have used sexual wiles to secure status. All this notwithstanding, Crawford's Vienna is aesthetically upright and demands a sense of respect, even among those who are opposed to her (all except Mercedes McCambridge's Emma Small) and her railroad ties. Joan Crawford has always been a star who could demand a certain butchness, even in roles that were distinctly female. Crawford's is a demanding and curated toughness that often comes across as harsh, and yet never seems to diminish her sympathetic posture. Even in *Mildred Pierce* there is a coding of masculine attribution to her, if only in the wide-padded shoulders of her costuming.[5]

In *Johnny Guitar*, Tasker says, "Like Joan Crawford's star image, Vienna's costumes and costume changes (first butch, then femme, then butch again) suggest her mobility in terms of gendered signifiers" (Tasker 1992: 52).

Tasker spends her entire consideraton of the film discussing Vienna, with only a passing mention of Emma Small. This seems a particularly egregious method of exploring the film. Emma functions as the primary antagonist to Crawford's Vienna. It is Emma's authority that appears to be the structuring factor in the town's anti-Vienna caucus. When Vienna is confronted by the town, demanding she give up the location of the Dancing Kid, a suspected outlaw, it is Emma, rather than Ward Bond's McIvers, who is most forthright and demanding, despite McIvers being ostensibly the higher authority. It is Emma who shoots dead the Dancing Kid, the potential heterosexual threat between the two women, and Emma with whom Vienna shares the final climactic gunfight. Emma is a near total phallic woman, and this becomes abundantly clear when she engages in the final shootout, after the men refuse to fight, their own phallic symbolization becoming flaccid in the visible field. She is not the fluid Saloon Girl that can ease her way between conservative gendered roles. Vienna's masculinity is much more the Saloon Girl template, and is tempered by her ability to dazzle the men in her eye-piercingly white dress, itself a seeming signifier of feminine excess, "exuding placid feminine righteousness" (Peterson 1996: 11). Earlier in the film when Emma claims that Vienna has big talk for such a small gun, it is only in relation to Emma's big gun that it matters. The phallus rests easily in Emma's domain.

Jennifer Peterson also spends more time with Vienna, although for different reasons. For Peterson, what is vital about discussions of the film are recognitions of the tensions that it provides, specifically on gendered lines, that she rightly sees as multiple discourses of gender occurring. "A responsible reading of the film must recognize these oppositions, for this very polyvalency is its key" (Peterson 1996: 4). What Peterson sees as a conflict in the film is the difference between the competing genders of Emma and Vienna. Moreover, while Vienna has a fluidity to her gender signification, Emma is reified in her masculine position; "while Emma's problem is her rigidly pathological identity, Vienna's strength is in her gender mobility" (Peterson 1996: 10). Within the confines of the film's narrative this is certainly true. Vienna's masculinity is seemingly not whole, "she has it all, both breasts and a gun, and remains intact even after her saloon has burned down" (Peterson 1996: 12). This is in opposition to Emma whose masculinity is much more rigid, and this is, within the social structure of the Western, the ultimate cause of Emma being fatally excised from the social order. However, as Peterson points out, even this dichotomy is conflicted and challenging, especially in regard to Vienna "such vehement validation of a female character in fact verges on grotesque parody" and "the film's camp can be read as either containing or liberating, depending on one's attitude toward gender play and strategic misreadings" (1996: 12). In short, Peterson warms to the idea that the film presents an intricate and multi-layered knot of meaning and discourse that cannot be easily solved by saying that the gender dynamics of the film are either progressive or regressive.

Emma is a difficult character to work around in the film because, if anything, she is a problem point in the film's attempts at a progressive ideology of resistance to mob order, as well as its attempt to defy gender roles. An icon of female masculinity, she is portrayed in a wholly negative light. Unlike Vienna who can be a sexual object/subject, Emma is so deeply into her masculinity that sexuality is inconceivable. According to Peterson, "she is a truly hysterical subject . . . not exactly an asexual character but rather a classical depiction of the pathological lesbian" (1996: 8). Halberstam asks, "What if the tomboy grew up with her masculinity intact?" and goes on to argue that Emma Small is "the grown tomboy" (1998: 191). While it is easy, and perhaps correct to map lesbianism on Emma's butchness, her sexual orientation and desire is of little consequence to the film. However, her ascendency as a tomboy demands her removal or intense correction. Halberstam points out that the tomboyishness of young girls is acceptable as long as its trappings of masculinity are shed as they become adolescents. In fact, "tomboyism may even be encouraged to the extent that it remains comfortably linked to a stable sense of girl identity. Tomboyism is punished . . . when it threatens to extend beyond childhood and into adolescence" (Halberstam 1998: 6). The Western is chock full of precocious tomboys, most notably Mattie in the two adaptations of *True Grit*. As Halberstam would agree, these are acceptable because she is a child, and it is understood that eventually she will adhere to feminine constructs. As Tasker points out, "the Western then, offers a (limited) textual space for tomboys/cowgirls to flourish" (1996: 53). Emma Small, however, is set in her masculine, phallic identity, and, like the saloon girl who becomes phallic in the traditional Western, is sacrificed to the genre's symbolic order. Halberstam remarks, "the death of Emma signifies the death of a female masculinity unmoored from male companionship and uncompromised by the marks of femininity" (1998: 195). In the end of the film, Emma's big gun becomes exposed through the gunfight and proves, much as the phallus always does, once visible, to be insufficient. It is though Emma has acceded to the Dominant Fiction's demand, and once doing so, becomes unable to exist as a phallic woman, lacking the Phallus = Penis fantasy position. Vienna's not quite phallic slippage is more amenable to existing in the symbolic order, and she displaces phallic sufficiency to a proxy: the otherwise relatively effeminate Johnny Guitar.[6]

BUTCH TAKES THE DAY: BUT WHAT DOES SHE WIN?

Roger Corman's ultra-B *Gunslinger* (1956) owes an obvious debt to *Johnny Guitar*, but rather than aspire to what Jennifer Peterson calls "a thick veil of campy self-consciousness" (1996: 4), the film appears to take itself seriously.[7] *Gunslinger* is the story of a woman, Rose Hood (Beverly Garland), who takes on the role of Marshal in the town of Oracle after her husband is killed. Knowing she will be led to the owner of the town's saloon, Erica Page (Allison Hayes), Rose hunts down and kills those who committed the crime. The plot is complicated by Erica hiring a noted gunman, Cane Miro (John Ireland), to kill Rose. Miro unexpectedly develops romantic feelings for his target. *Gunslinger* not only re-enacts the conflict of Johnny Guitar, but seems to push even further the narrative into a conflict between women, making the men in the film barely registered. There are four men in the film who bear note via their failed masculinity. The mayor of the town is an ineffectual leader who attempts to hide his uselessness in practical matters by bragging about his prowess fighting Yankees. Because of Cane Miro's intervention it is revealed that he is in fact a coward who leads his men to slaughter. The deputy is a kind and protective man, but he admits immediately that he is not capable of taking on the Marshal's role: he is a born follower. Erica has a man who works in her saloon, who is consistently emasculated, and referred to by both women in the film as "little man." Finally, Cane Miro himself, haunted by the trauma of the civil war, is passed between the women, as much sexual capital as any saloon girl. Emblematic of a fractured masculinity, he is unable to wield his gun as demanded.[8] The one male in this film who might seem untarnished or rather sure of his position is Rose's husband, the Marshal at the beginning of the film, but he is killed at the outset, leaving Rose to take the Marshal's badge after the deputy refuses it.

Neither Rose nor Erica are presented as being particularly butch in this film. In fact, Erica is depicted as being excessively feminine and adheres to a certain pernicious stereotype of sinister sexually manipulative womanhood. Erica plays out much like the *femme fatale* of *film noir*, almost aggressively feminine, yet able to fluidly cross into the masculine world of crime. When the mayor of Oracle questions her on her wide land holdings, which she is buying up in order to make money off of a possible railroad coming through, she answers suggestively, "I get around." Much like Vienna in *Johnny Guitar*, Erica is not said to be a madam or prostitute, but her ownership of the saloon and status as "working woman" tethers her to that identity. Erica's dress is sensual and sexually evocative, low cut and meant to invite the gaze. Again she is the *femme fatale* of *film noir*, yet to look and accept the invitation is to invite one's own demise. For the men who fraternize with her, however marginally, this is the case. Erica is seen only twice in more plain clothes, at the Marshal's funeral and when she murders a post carrier to hide her other crimes, yet even in these moments her dress is feminine. Erica is phallic in her signification as a dominant woman, but outwardly and in her gendered visuality she is abundantly *femme*.

Rose is far more masculine than Erica, only appearing in feminine clothing twice in the opening scenes of the film. She wears a white dress as the film opens and she brings breakfast to her husband. After he is murdered, she grabs a rifle without hesitation, kills one of the two assassins, and manages to fire off a shot at the other who flees. Her readiness to fight defies her assigned gender role. In the following scene, she appears in a dress, but the austere black and white of funeral garb, while feminine, also assigns a stoic symbolism that marks her character throughout the film. During the funeral, in a delightful scene as cold-blooded and steady as any male depiction of violence, Rose, about to toss the first dirt on her husband's grave, hurls the soil into the face of the other assassin who has been at the funeral as well and then shoots him. Under her dress she is already carrying a pistol, a phallus kept incognito by the masquerade of the feminine. Directly after shooting her husband's assassin, she takes the marshal's star from her husband's grave and is made sheriff until the new sheriff arrives. After she becomes the town's sheriff, Rose is seen in pants and a buttoned-up blouse tucked in. A red scarf is ever-present around her neck. Her deputy comments that people in the town might not think it proper for a widow to go around in pants "even if they are black," but Rose has little time for worrying about the town's gender concerns—there is law to be upheld. This costume that Rose continues to wear throughout the film—black pants, white blouse, and her gun belt—render her resistant to any simple codification along gender lines. While she is subject to the traditionally feminine concerns, she is not beholden to them. After all, someone has to be the man in this town. Watching Rose move so fluidly in her cowboy trappings demonstrates the flexibility of Western iconography. Discussing a postmodern revision of the Western *The Quick and the Dead* (Sam Raimi, 1995) and its heroine played by Sharon Stone, Patricia Mellencamp says "her movements reveal how sensual the costume and gesture of the Western male hero have been all these years. The hetero-codes of the old West barely disguise the homoeroticism and narcissism" (1995: 118).

At the end of *Gunslinger*, the butch wins. Unlike *Johnny Guitar*, there is no coupling, even a coupling that maintains a masculine female in a dominant role. The *femme*, Erica, is removed by the man, Miro, who is a diminished (thus unacceptable) phallic presence. Subsequently, Miro and his phallic masculinity (fractured though it is) is removed by the clearly phallic Rose who, though fostering a romantic inclination toward Miro, rejects its consummation and romantic positioning repeatedly. Rose refuses to be recapitulated into her traditionally prescribed feminine role as wife and lover, and while her inability to conform transmits her toughness and confirms her masculinity, like so many Western heroes she rides out of the chaos of Oracle as the new sheriff, promising law and order, rides in. Alone and sullen, Rose enacts the Western marker of masculine self-reproach: the ride into the sunset. Generally, women who become phallic—who challenge and break the Dominant Fiction—are subject to the cruelest frustration and virulent demands from the social order that she be divested of its phallic position. The issue at hand is that the phallus is desired by all, in a sense both to possess it and to be it. Lacan remarks, at least, "in order to be the phallus ... a woman rejects an essential part of femininity, namely, all its attributes, in the masquerade"—and when that masquerade is dropped, and she becomes literally (or at least apparently) phallic, "the organ that is endowed with this signifying function takes on the value of a fetish thereby" (2006: 583). Notably, it seems here that Lacan is hinting at the fact that by the very idea that a woman can become phallic, the Dominant Fiction is exposed as entirely fantastical and reveals "the delusory nature of conventional masculinity—its reliance upon anatomy as a safeguard against castration" (in Silverman 1992: 43). Most often the phallic woman is killed like Ruby in *The Iron Horse* and Emma Small in *Johnny Guitar*. Rose, however, is not killed for her transgression, and she shows us how that unconscious female masculinity rode clinging to the underbelly of the covered wagon, and often sealed the gaps that the overt masculine project had left in its traumatic wake. Hers is the cruelest punishment, far worse than the noble death, which created Ruby's redemption or Emma's comeuppance for her transgressions. Rose is sentenced to live with the fracture and the tragedy that masculinity generates—she ends a Western hero, perpetually melancholy in a state of decline.

Notes

1. As Silverman puts it, our belief in "normative identity ... depends upon a kind of collective make-believe in the commensurability of penis and phallus." According to Silverman, "our dominant fiction calls upon the male subject to see himself, and the female subject to recognize and desire him, only through the mediation of unimpaired masculinity. It urges both male and female subject ... to [believe] the commensurability of penis and phallus" (Silverman 1992: 42). Calvin Thomas points out that "males accede to the dominant fiction and identify with normative masculinity and its fictions of dominance by learning how to assuage this anxiety" and further that "the mechanisms of this assuagement are ideologically embedded in the cultural modes of representational containment that govern and restrict the visibility of male bodies and male bodily production" (Thomas 1996: 3).

    It also bears pointing out that Jacques Lacan in his theorizing about the phallus as a signifier and indeed the structuring factor in the symbolic order makes clear that one should not make that equation. "The phallus is not a fantasy ... nor is it an object ... still less is it the organ ... penis or clitoris—that it symbolizes" (Lacan 2006: 579). This is because for Lacan, the Phallus is something that cannot be revealed without dire consequences, or at the very least a dramatic shift in desire. Desire must be maintained and channeled via fantasy in order for the symbolic order to exist fluently. It must not achieve its goal. Thus for the phallus to be the biological penis is a tempting but also fraudulent idea in that it places the phallus at the site of something that can be exposed. Slavoj Žižek explains that "what Lacan calls 'phallic identification' is, on the contrary, the exact opposite of this 'revelation of the phallus': it is the identification with the phallus qua signifier of desire ... the

paradox of identification with nonidentity, with the gap which maintains desire" (Žižek 1992: 128). This hinges close to what Calvin Thomas was arguing above about the restricted visibility of male bodies. In a society that is governed by the Dominant Fiction, the penis must be kept hidden, lest it be revealed as little more than a fleshy facsimile of the phallus. It becomes something akin to the face of the phantom of the opera, and once revealed creates horror or revulsion, where once there was mystery and intrigue. Calvin Thomas writes that "the unveiling of the phallus constitutes its shame" (1996: 50).
2. Matheson's account of how Ford used lighting to express morality and amorality is concise and eloquent.
3. Furthermore "when and where female masculinity conjoins with possibly queer identities, it is far less likely to meet with approval" (Halberstam 1998: 28). I agree with this fully, and I admit to betraying Halberstam's intent slightly here by focusing on figures that are ostensibly heterosexual, and in this case not visually butch (we will get to that momentarily). However, I find that applying it to these saloon girls, as they already do not conform to social standards, is an honest application of the theoretical and methodological avenues that Halberstam pursues. Although they are presumably heterosexual, they are both women who exist outside the realm of normative coupling in their profession.
4. Most notably Jennifer Peterson (1996).
5. For a thorough and fascinating discussion of Crawford's clothing see: Charlotte Cornelia Herzog and Jane M. Gaines (1991), "Puffed Sleeves Before Tea-Time: Joan Crawford, Adrian, and Women Audiences."
6. It should not ignored that while Johnny is the bearer of the phallus at the end of the film, he is consistently shown to be lacking. While he is a quick-draw with his pistols, it is the more effeminate, musical quality that defines him. The guitar becomes his phallic substitute rather than weapons.
7. It is generally accepted that the 1971 film *Hannie Caulder* is a loose remake of *Gunslinger*. The later film though only draws out the woman's (Raquel Welch) ability via rape and further she does not fluidly take up arms and has to be taught by a man, as opposed to Rose who seems to need no instruction. *Hannie Caulder* is, interestingly enough, directed by Burt Kennedy, most notable for being the scriptwriter for Budd Boetticher whose attitudes about women were mentioned above. Kennedy did not write the script for *Decision at Sundown*.
8. It is interesting that Miro is played by John Ireland, most recognized as the deliciously sinister Cherry Valance in *Red River*. Ireland's body and presence irrevocably calls up a sensuous homoeroticism, most clearly on display in the Howard Hawks film caressing pistols and evidently flirting with Montgomery Clift.

Filmography

Decision at Sundown, director Budd Boetticher, featuring Randolph Scott, John Carroll, Karen Steele (Columbia, 1957).
Gunslinger, director Roger Corman, featuring John Ireland, Beverly Garland, Allison Hayes (Roger Corman Productions, 1956).

Hannie Caulder, director Burt Kennedy, featuring Raquel Welch, Robert Culp, Ernest Borgnine (Tigon British Film Productions, 1971).
Johnny Guitar, director Nicholas Ray, featuring Joan Crawford, Sterling Hayden, Mercedes McCambridge (Republic, 1954).
Mildred Pierce, director Michael Curtiz, featuring Joan Crawford, Jack Carson, Zachary Scott (Warner Bros., 1945).
Red River, director Howard Hawks, featuring John Wayne, Montgomery Clift, Joanne Dru (Monterey Productions, 1948).
The Iron Horse, director John Ford, featuring George O'Brien, Madge Bellamy, Charles Edward Bull (Fox, 1924).
The Quick and the Dead, director Sam Raimi, featuring Sharon Stone, Gene Hackman, Russell Crowe (TriStar, 1995).
True Grit, director Henry Hathaway, featuring John Wayne, Kim Darby, Glen Campbell (Wallis-Hazen, 1969).
True Grit, directors Ethan Coen and Joel Coen, featuring Jeff Bridges, Matt Damon, Hailee Steinfeld (Paramount, 2010).

Bibliography

Gledhill, Christine (2012) "Introduction," in Christine Gledhill (ed.), *Gender Meets Genre in Postwar Cinemas*. Urbana and Chicago: Illinois University Press, pp. 1–11.
Halberstam, J. (1998) *Female Masculinity*. Durham, NC and London: Duke University Press.
Herzog, Charlotte Cornelia and Jane M. Gaines (1991) "Puffed Sleeves Before Tea-Time: Joan Crawford, Adrian, and Women Audiences," in Christine Gledhill (ed.), *Stardom*. London and New York, pp. 74–91.
Kitses, Jim (1998) "Introduction: Post-modernism and the Western," in Jim Kitses and Gregg Rickman (eds), *The Western Reader*. New York: Limelight Editions, pp. 15–31.
Lacan, Jacques (2006) "The Signification of the Phallus," *Ecrits*, trans. Bruce Fink. New York: Norton, pp. 575–84.
Matheson, Sue (2016) *The Westerns and War Films of John Ford*. Lanham, MD and London: Rowan & Littlefield.
Mellencamp, Patricia (1995) *A Fine Romance: Five Ages of Film Feminism*. Philadelphia: Temple University Press.
Minz, Christopher (2017) "You Were Married But You Never Had a Wife: The Use of Space in the Westerns of Budd Boetticher," in Gary Rhodes and Robert Singer (eds), *The Films of Budd Boetticher*. Edinburgh: Edinburgh University Press, pp. 167–87.
Peterson, Jennifer (1996) "The Competing Tunes of 'Johnny Guitar': Liberalism, Sexuality, Masquerade," *Cinema Journal*, 35 (3), pp. 3–18.
Russell, Lee (1998) "Budd Boetticher," in Jim Kitses and Gregg Rickman (eds), *The Western Reader*. New York: Limelight Editions, pp. 195–200.
Silverman, Kaja (1992) *Male Subjectivity at the Margins*. New York & London: Routledge.
Tasker, Yvonne (1998) *Working Girls: Gender and Sexuality in Popular Cinema*. London and New York: Routledge.

Thomas, Calvin (1996) *Male Matters*. Urbana, IL and Chicago: University of Illinois Press.
Warshow, Robert (2001) *The Immediate Experience*. Cambridge, MA and London: Harvard University Press.
Wright, Will (1975) *Sixguns and Society: A Structural Study of the Western*. Berkeley, CA and Los Angeles: University of California Press.
Žižek, Slavoj (1992) *Enjoy Your Symptom! Jacques Lacan in Hollywood and Out*. New York and London: Routledge.

8. GENDER POLITICS IN THE REVISIONIST WESTERN: INTERROGATING THE PERPETRATOR–VICTIM BINARY IN *THE MISSING* (HOWARD 2003)

Fran Pheasant-Kelly

Introduction

At the core of the classic Western exists a mythology founded on convictions of American exceptionalism and white racial superiority. As Steve Neale notes, this mythology is "grounded in the notion (itself as imaginative as it is real) that there existed a moving western frontier in the US between the seventeenth and late nineteenth centuries. One of its basic tenets is that this frontier served to distinguish and to mark the meeting point between Anglo-Americans and their culture and nature and the cultures of others" (2000: 134). For John Cawelti, this juncture is one occurring "between civilization and savagery" (1999: 20). Bound up with its capacity to mediate a complex range of ideological issues, the Western also has a fundamental relationship to the construction of masculinity. In this respect, Cawelti defines three character types typical of the genre: "the townspeople or agents of civilization, the savages or outlaws who threaten this first group, and the heroes who are above all 'men in the middle,' possessing many qualities and skills of the savages but fundamentally committed to the townspeople" (1999: 29). Certainly, many Westerns have traditionally revolved around a male hero, with film narratives generally driven by the actions of the male character, and, as Martin Pumphrey notes, "[o]n the surface Westerns seem to give, in the unassailable masculinity of their heroes, a wholly unambiguous statement of what men should and should not do" (1990: 181). Invariably, this involves bridging the gap between savagery and civilization. In this respect, Cawelti explains that those townspeople protected by the male hero are "dominated by women. This sexual division frequently embodies the antithesis of civilization and savagery since women are primary symbols of civilization in the Western [. . .] There is also implicit in the presence of women the sexual fascination and fear associated with the rape of white women by savages" (1999: 30).

However, recent literature reveals that a significant number of both classical and revisionist Westerns challenge the position of men and the concept of an unassailable masculinity. They also reframe the traditional model of the savage "Indian" and of the woman as a helpless victim. *The Missing* not only provides a key example of this reworked gender and racial coding but is also progressive in its use of the Apache language as well as in its focus on a group of women. Engaging theoretically with scholars of the Western who focus on gender, including Pam Cook (1988), Peter Evans (1996), and Douglas Pye (1996), as well as historical experiences of women in the Old West (Myres 1982), this chapter analyzes the film *The Missing* and contextualizes its revisionist politics in relation to the film's post-9/11 milieu. Focusing on its portrayal of a group of women in relation to conventional Western representations of femininity as well as accounts of real-world westering women, it argues that the film not only subverts generic conventions of masculinity and confounds the cultural boundary between white and Native Americans, but also presents a more realistic representation of women than is usual for the Western, in terms of individual characterization as well as in the fact that the narrative is led and driven by a group of women.

Westering Women

In her study of westering women, Sandra Myres examined over four hundred library and historical collections of diaries, journals and letters written by frontierswomen (1982: xvii). This contrasts with previous studies which, as she explains, were not based on sound research, and prompted "accounts written by men rather than examining what women themselves had to say about their frontier experiences" (1982: xv). Formulating the results of this study as a book, she not only elucidates the role that women played in the Old West but also gives an account of their interactions with Native Americans, aspects relevant to an analysis of *The Missing* in which white women and Native Americans help and support each other. As she notes, "[l]ess well known than the always popular stories of Indian raids are the peaceful and often helpful encounters between women and Indians [. . .] Just as immigrants and Indians worked out mutually beneficial relationships along the overland trails, so, too, did settlers and Indians find ways of assisting each other" (1982: 62). Myres also describes the independence of women whereby "[w]idowed ranchwomen, like widowed farm women, often took over management of the ranch and herds after their husband's death" (1982: 260). At the same time, she notes that girls were self-reliant and involved in external pursuits: "[girls] were even more likely than their mothers to learn riding and roping skills, participate in ranch work, and understand business operations" (1982: 261). While Myres indicates that it remains unclear exactly to what extent the frontier provided opportunities for women, she concludes that

> women on the frontier modified existing norms and adopted flexible attitudes and experimental behavior patterns [. . .] What has perhaps confused the various interpretations of woman's place and the westering experience is that the *reality* of women's lives changed dramatically while the public *image* remained relatively static. Image, myth, and stereotype were contrary to what women were actually experiencing and doing [original emphasis]. (Myres 1982: 269)

Whereas Myres's study tends to centre on "ordinary" women, Ron Lackmann focuses on legendary women of the western frontier, and their subsequent representation in fiction and film. Like Myres, Lackman notes how these women, despite their contributions to the development of the American West, remained relatively obscure until the Women's West Conference, held in Idaho in 1983, brought together historians, academics, and authors to recognize the contribution that these frontier women had made (1997: 149).

Women, Westerns and the American Frontier

In tandem with this omission in historical accounts of women of the Old West, many academic studies of women in Westerns also fail to fully acknowledge their prominence, with limited but growing scholarship on the historical role of women at the Western frontier (Calder 1977; Lackmann 1997; Myres 1982; Prescott 2007), as well as on their depiction in Western literature and film (Peterson 1996). However, while there has been a feminist reclaiming of unacknowledged women Western writers (Lamont 2016; Modleski 1999), the academic study of the Western film has tended to center on biased representations of women, identifying roles that typically range from schoolteacher and conventional wife to prostitute and which are secondary to a male protagonist. In this respect, Douglas Pye notes that "it is generally accepted that the Western's representation of women is [. . .] massively skewed" (1996: 13). Pye goes on to state that "the whole history of the Western is therefore, at one level, inescapably bound up with reducing Native Americans and women to functions in a symbolic world centring on White male characters" (1996: 13) while Jenni Calder notes that "[t]he ordinary pioneer woman is elusive on the screen" (1977: 158).

Pam Cook (1988: 240) too acknowledges the marginalization of women in both history and film and suggests that "[i]t's tempting to put this down [...] to the male oedipal bias of the Western, a narrative based on a masculine quest for sexual and national identity which marginalizes women" (1988: 241). Cook further suggests that "[t]he search for realism is perhaps rather self-defeating in a genre which is more concerned with myth than historical accuracy" (1988: 241). Similar to usual analyses of women in Westerns, she observes that "[o]ver and over again, the woman relinquishes her desire to be active and independent, ceding power to the hero and accepting secondary status as mother figure, educator and social mediator" (1988: 241). In relation to the perpetrator–victim binary, she also remarks that "[t]he Western is haunted by the fear of miscegenation, the myth of the rapacious Indian bent on capturing and breeding with white women" (1988: 242). While Cook's comments are relevant to many classic Westerns, they are less so to certain revisionist films made since.

Although there is no doubt that historically, numerous Westerns do project a limited and stereotyped image of women, there is a significant number that are led by female protagonists and deviate from the aforementioned formulaic roles. These roles correspond with Myres's account which states that

> westering women came from different backgrounds, had different experiences, and responded to frontier conditions in different ways [...] The drudge and the brave pioneer mother were stereotypes but not myths. That both existed is evident from the literature. So did the soiled doves and the bad girls, but they were the exception. Their stories stood out because they differed from the lives of most pioneer women. (Myres 1982: 11)

Indeed, certain actresses, such as Barbara Stanwyck, are renowned for subverting such stereotypes. As Andrew Nelson observes of the Western roles that Stanwyck undertook: "many of these women defy the genre's conventional wife/whore dichotomy" (2013: 21). He further notes that, "Stanwyck's heroines, even after choosing love (dependence) over money and power (independence), always remain the agitating force that drives the narrative forward and brings about resolution" (2013: 25). Joan Crawford is equally well-known for her profile in the genre, with *Johnny Guitar* (Ray, 1954) being an iconic example. In a corresponding vein, Ron Lackmann (1997) ascertains that a number of silent Westerns as well as an extensive list of sound films afford women a primary function. Overall, such productions usually focus on a single female protagonist and are often based on real-life prominent women who were outlaws, entertainers, wives of well-known gunslingers, or who themselves were sharpshooters. The most familiar of these include Belle Starr, Calamity Jane, Etta Place, and Annie Oakley, all of whom have become represented in high-profile Western films. As Calder remarks, however, "Where they do occur they are generally comic or caricatured, like the numerous Calamity Janes. Most of these are glamorous, jolly, guntoting females without the remotest suggestion of the original. Calamity Jane was in fact a repulsive creature" (1977: 160).

More recently, the roles of women in Western films identified by Lackmann are achieving more balanced scholarly attention. For example, Mark Wildermuth (2018) gives a comprehensive account of feminism and the Western, and in response to commentaries that indicate that "the western and feminism seem to be contradictory terms" (Thumin, in Wildermuth 2018: 1), he observes that "to make such arguments [. . .] is to desert a comprehensive description of the genre, especially in film and television, where exceptions like *Dr Quinn*, *Westward the Women*, and *The Ballad of Little Jo* exist in far greater numbers than these authors suggest" (2018: 1). Indeed, he notes that there is an "increasingly radical postmodern feminist stance in films after the Cold War" (2018: 11).

Wildermuth traces the role of women in Westerns from the 1930s through to the immediate post-9/11 period, identifying a number of films where women dominate the narrative and deviate from commonly described stereotypes. While his study does not extend to include post-9/11 films, he highlights observations made by Lynn Spigel (2004: 146) regarding distinctions between the male hero and female victim that arose in television culture following 9/11. Wildermuth refers to this in relation to the fact that "[s]ince 2001, no Western series have appeared with women protagonists primarily in the lead" (2018: 147), suggesting that gender representations in the Western have been affected in the aftermath of 9/11. As Spigel notes, "The need to make American audiences feel that they were in the moral position ran through a number of television's 'reality' genres. One of the central ways that this moral position was promoted was through the depiction of women victims" (2004: 246). Spigel further notes that "[d]espite the fact that there were thirty-three women firefighters and rescue workers on duty on 11 September, the media portraits of heroism were mainly of men" (2004: 246) and that "[o]n television, these myths of gender were often connected to age-old Western fantasies of the East in which 'Oriental' men assault (and even rape) Western women and, more symbolically, the West itself" (2004: 246). In summarizing the claims of Spigel in relation to the Western, Wildermuth refers to "the rise of a culture of masculine protectionism in America post-9/11 culture where men are seen as protectors and women as helpless victims in the face of threat to the American security state posed by international terrorism" (2018: 46). In a similar vein, Susan Faludi discerns a "women as victim" trope in the immediate post-9/11 climate and relates this to the cowboy rhetoric of George W. Bush, suggesting that:

> The attack on home soil triggered a search for the guardian of the homestead, a manly man, to be sure, but one particularly suited to protecting

and providing for the isolated American family in perilous situations. He was less Batman than Daniel Boone, a frontiersman whose proofs of eligibility were the hatchet and the gun—and a bloody willingness to wield them. (Faludi 2007: 148)

Released in the immediate post-9/11 period, *The Missing* not only counters such contemporaneous perceptions of women and children as victims in the face of threat but affords its female protagonists a realistic frontier representation corresponding to the time period in which the film is set, and arguably contributes to the feminist reclaiming of the Western promoted by Wildermuth.

To Wildermuth's list, which is based on analysis of film and television up to and including the immediate post-9/11 period, one can also add prominent female characters of the latest revisionist films of the genre, including *True Grit* (Coen Brothers, 2010), *Meek's Cutoff* (Reichardt, 2010) and *Jane Got a Gun* (O'Connor, 2015). In short, women have long played and continue to play central roles in Westerns, but these have often been overlooked. Nonetheless, even though Westerns that are dominated by women persist and are increasing in output, and a growing number of authors acknowledge their roles, such films still tend to feature a single female lead. To date, while groups of "ordinary women" not subject to Western stereotypes are discernible in a limited number of films, such as Delmer Daves's *3:10 to Yuma* (Pheasant-Kelly 2016: 160), few productions feature a group of women as central to the narrative. One exception is highlighted by Peter Evans (1996) who observes that the film *Westward the Women* (Wellman, 1951) is distinctive, not only because it is led by women, but also because it focuses on a group of women rather than one or two female protagonists. This chapter locates a similar pattern in *The Missing*, and observes that it not only centers on a group of frontier females rather than a single female or group of men but also reverses the Native-American-as-perpetrator/white-woman-as-victim binary that has historically characterized the genre. Even though earlier post-war films such as *Fort Apache* (Ford, 1948) and *Broken Arrow* (Daves, 1950) were pivotal in rethinking representations of Native Americans, and provided more sympathetic and realistic portrayals than had previously been the case (for example, as Kim Newman notes, *Broken Arrow* "gives the Apache way of life some respect, and corrects some myths—'it is well known that Apaches do not take scalps'" [1990: 70]), *The Missing* is even more progressive. This is because many of its characters, including one of its protagonists, Samuel Jones (Tommy Lee Jones), speak Apache (Benke 2003), contrasting with earlier depictions in *Broken Arrow* in which, as Nelson notes, "[t]he Apache characters [. . .] speak in standard (if formal) English, a significant change from Indians speaking in broken, pidgin English, as was conventional at the time" (2016: 49). Moreover, its female protagonists deviate from any of the aforementioned stereotypes, instead promoting a perspective on westering women that more closely coincides with Sandra Myres's (1982) account of real frontier experience.

The Missing

The Missing is set in New Mexico 1885, and tells the story of a resourceful widow, Magdalena Gilkeson (Cate Blanchett), whose subsequent partner is killed in a horrific Apache massacre, and who goes in search of her kidnapped daughter, because the US cavalry refuse to deploy troops to help. Aided instead by her formerly estranged father, himself a convert to the Apache way of life, she tracks her daughter to a band of rogue Apaches led by Pesh Chidin (Eric Schweig). Several white men are also involved in the abduction, and while initially she has the help of her father, Samuel Jones (Tommy Lee Jones), he too falls victim to Chidin. Throughout the film, white male characters are therefore depicted either as villainous, corrupt, or ineffectual, or otherwise as fearless men who are nonetheless despatched by the band of Apache kidnappers. If, as Pumphrey states, "[c]haracteristically what defines [masculinity], puts it beyond question, is not sexual prowess or brute strength, good looks or smooth talk, but the ability to be 'tough'" (1990: 181), then most white male characters in *The Missing* are inevitably emasculated and feminized. In sum, their masculinity is constantly in question. The girls whom they capture are at first their terrified victims, but Magdalena and the captive girls turn on their abductors. Dottie (Jenna Boyd), Magdalena's youngest daughter, also proves to be an example of how revised gender politics in the genre treat the younger female protagonist. Like Mattie (Hailee Steinfeld) in *True Grit*, she is fearless and equally able and willing to act as a perpetrator rather than a victim.

Currently, there is little scholarship on *The Missing*, especially in the contexts of groups of women and the perpetrator–victim binary. One exception is work by Maureen Schwarz (2014) who also claims that the film is a feminist Western, noting that to qualify as such "the plot must constitute a subversion of and a challenge to a mainstream text; the actions of a female protagonist must drive the plot rather than simply provide a reason for the actions of the male character or characters; the dialogue of one or more female protagonists must challenge and subvert masculine discourse as well as convey agency; and meanings must be plural rather than singular" (2014: 45). Schwarz is therefore concerned more with defining the feminist Western rather than the distinctiveness of the film's character grouping whereas this chapter uniquely argues that, while clearly feminist, *The Missing* not only develops the trope of women as a group, but does so in a more realistic way than has been previously projected.

An establishing long shot of an isolated ranch in New Mexico opens the film, the wintry conditions immediately suggesting an element of challenge and physical hardship (to emphasize the endurance of Magdalena and her family).

In addition, the initial sequence signals the film's focus on women by opening with a close-up of Magdalena's face, cast in semi-darkness. As Philip French notes, "We think this is the interior of a stagecoach or a ranch house" (2004). In fact, she is in an outdoor privy (unusual for any character in a Western and perhaps anticipating the more realistic tenor of the film) when she is summoned by Dottie to attend to a sick old woman (she is an unqualified healer). Upon examining the old woman's mouth, which is ulcerated, she indicates her toughness by unhesitatingly pulling out the woman's sole remaining tooth. Dottie assists by preparing the requisite medication and then immobilizing the struggling woman as Magdalena removes the tooth with pliers. Despite being a child, Dottie is therefore closely involved in what is conveyed as a daunting process, while the entire opening comprises only female characters.

In contrast, the subsequent sequence involves male characters and moves to the exterior environment (and therefore, initially, the film appears to conform to generic conventions of tying women to domesticity and men to action and public power). Here, the landscape, although appearing beautiful and unsullied in long shots of blue sky and snow-covered ground, builds on the notion of a harsh frontier existence. This is indicated when we learn from Brake Baldwin (Aaron Eckhart), Magdalena's partner, that lightning has struck one of their cattle. A slow zoom in to the dead animal lying in the snow is closely followed by a long shot of two coyotes framed on the horizon. Brake then comments to their ranch hand, Emiliano (Sergio Calderón), that its calf "won't last the night out here." Just as the two men shoot at the coyotes, a long shot reveals a stranger with long hair and shrouded in a poncho approaching on horseback. "Some kind of an Apache son of a bitch," grunts Emiliano, summoning up the negative reactions common to film Westerns but which do not necessarily reflect real reports about Apaches. As Sandra Myres remarks, even though attacks by Native Americans did occur, these were less frequent than one might think (1982: 59). As the "Apache" draws nearer to Brake, the stranger asks him (speaking with an American accent) if that "is your man over there in the trees" without even glancing in the direction of the trees, giving immediate insight into a superior capacity for perception. It transpires that the "Apache" is Magdalena's father, Samuel Jones, thereby providing the first example of how the boundary between white and Native American is confounded, a trope that persists throughout the film.

Jones is initially shunned by his daughter because it emerges that he had abandoned his wife and family, for which Magdalena is unable to forgive him. Magdalena herself has a strong allegiance to both Christian and family values. She is also committed to the work of the ranch and long shots (that allow emphasis on the physicality of the tasks) frequently frame her carrying out what might be deemed as "men's" tasks, such as chopping wood and tossing hay for the animals. Regardless, she undertakes these tasks dressed in jacket and skirt, so there is no suggestion of her being consciously masculinized as in the case of Doris Day's representation of Calamity Jane. She instils a similar work ethic in her daughters and refuses to let the eldest, Lilly (Evan Rachel Wood), attend a town fair (seeing it as somewhat frivolous), instead insisting that she must help Brake with the calving. Lilly, keen to attend the fair, tries to appeal to Brake by saying "riding all day with this cramping and all," to which Magdalena reacts angrily, telling her, "Don't you ever act helpless and pitiable to win favor with a man." (As Philip French [2004] points out, this is perhaps the first Western to reference such a topic.)

Magdalena's tough feminist qualities therefore soon surface, with Dottie exhibiting similar traits. In fact, Dottie is not at all intimidated by Jones's "Apache" appearance; rather, she is fascinated by him and by the possibility that she may be related to an "Indian" (as she refers to him). This attitude is consistent with real-world attitudes at that time, at least regarding the Sioux whereby, as Myres comments, "[m]ost of the trail women were fascinated by these people" (1982: 56), and "on the southern border as on the northern routes, women's attitudes towards the Indians depended to some extent on whether the Indians were considered hostile or friendly. Women's comments about the Indians, like those of men, were ambivalent, expressing fear, distrust, and contempt on the one hand and curiosity, admiration, and sympathy on the other" (1982: 59). Dottie also paints her face and tries to be friendly toward Jones, albeit in a distinctly Westernized manner, when she comments, "Pleased to make your acquaintance." Her gesture is an attempt to bridge the gap between Apache and white culture but at the same time draws attention to it. Lilly, on the other hand, who seems physically and psychologically less robust and aspires to a more sophisticated lifestyle, reacts negatively to Jones, describing him as a "savage." "They're gut eaters you know," she tells Dottie. The sisters' polarized views therefore epitomize the way in which Native Americans are conceived, both historically and filmically. Ironically, Lilly utters the words "gut-eaters" just as she is skinning and gutting a deer, a task which does not faze her, and in which she appears skilled and methodical, despite being inappropriately attired in dress and hat. Her ranch-hand skills not only reflect those that Myres identifies in real frontier children (1982: 261) but diegetically, later help her to escape from her abductors, albeit temporarily.

This abduction is perpetrated by a band of renegades comprising both Apaches and army deserters and occurs when Brake takes the girls out to help with calving. When they fail to return, Magdalena rides out alone in search of them. The threat to her family is anticipated by the fact that she finds a coyote on the dining table, the animal's easy penetration of their home suggesting the family's vulnerability. Riding through woods, her horse seems to sense danger. This is indicated by a series of rapidly revolving shots of the surrounding trees before the camera cuts to Magdalena's point of view. She first sees their ranch hand, Emiliano, lying face down, viewed initially in a close-up that displays a cluster of arrows embedded in his back, and then from an extreme overhead shot that reveals his naked body. According to Pumphrey:

> Where it is acceptable to make a (naked) woman's body the object of an erotic gaze (a character's or the spectator's), it is taboo to do the same with the male body [. . .] and any significant attention to bodily display in mainstream Westerns [. . .] marks a male character as a villain, city slicker or weakling. (Pumphrey 1990: 182)

The nature of the extreme overhead shot, which renders Emiliano's naked body even more vulnerable, is devoid of erotic possibility signifying it as emasculated. A rapidly edited sequence from Magdalena's point of view, indicating her rising fear, first frames a fire smoldering in extreme long shot, above which swings what vaguely appears to be a suspended animal hide. Further subjective shots then zoom in to take account of clothing scattered on the ground, immediately recognizable as Lilly's before the suspended animal hide slowly revolves to disclose to Magdalena, and the spectator, that Brake's body is bound up in the hide. Like Emiliano, his death, which immobilizes him as horrific spectacle, renders him emasculated. Just as she screams in horror, the camera shifts focus from Brake's body to Dottie, who appears in the distance and is framed in long shot. Traumatized, she tells her mother about the attack and that an "Indian" took Lilly. Both Dottie and Magdalena hastily depart the woods where the murders have occurred, with rapid panning shots of their speeding horses emphasizing their riding expertise. In fact, all the female characters in the film are skilled horse-riders, an important element in the construction of women being independent. As Maria Cecília de Miranda N. Coehlo notes, "the horse acts . . . as an equalizer that gives women as much freedom and power as men" (2017: 113).

However, on reporting Lilly's disappearance, the town sheriff seems preoccupied with the town fair while the US Cavalry do not see the missing girl as a pressing matter despite the fact that other young women are being abducted. Magdalena is forced to turn to her father—who, as has become evident, has Apache skills—to track down the renegades. Jones suggests to Magdalena that the Army is in any case heading in the wrong direction, and his keen Apache tracking instincts reveal that a group (likely of girls) are traveling toward the Mexican border. The implication is that the girls will be sold at the border for prostitution. Dottie, traumatized by Emiliano's death (as he gave her similar instructions to stay in place), refuses to stay at home and accompanies them in their search, her fearlessness being integral to the final plan to release the abducted girls. In one of the scenes that illustrates the corruption and ineffectuality of the US Cavalry which comprises both Native American and white soldiers, we witness them looting the homesteads of those murdered or abducted by Chidin's group. A long shot reveals them carrying domestic artifacts that they have looted, and as one soldier approaches the camera and sweeps past, a zoom in to close-up reveals two dolls that he is stealing. If this close-up highlights the (white) soldier's uncaring corrupt disposition, it also signals him as feminized. Dottie's gaze, which follows the movement of the soldier, emphasizes the loss of her sister in its fixity on the two dolls (implicitly referencing the abduction of the girls).

In a further disregard for the property of others and perhaps instigating even more antipathy in the spectator, the Lieutenant then instructs his men to "butcher a couple of those goats for supper." At the same time, the ethnic composition of the soldiers promotes the blurring of stereotypical representations of Native Americans as savages and is made explicit when the Lieutenant tells Magdalena, "You got Indians running with whites and whites running with Indians."

This disruption of the Native-American-as-perpetrator/white-woman-as-victim binary is again suggested by the fact that the group of kidnappers are comprised of both white men and Native Americans. The white Americans particularly lack any sense of manliness and are instead portrayed as sleazy, debauched drunks, and tend to be filmed in long shot which emphasizes their slightly stooped posture and tendency to fall over. Otherwise, several close-ups of one reveal him constantly scratching his head which is covered with lesions. A photographer whom they capture has similar unpalatable qualities and when taking a photograph of the terrified girls who are concealed in a cave, he merely instructs them to "look your best" even as Lilly pleads with him to help them. However, he is killed by Chidin, and, in another reversal of gender politics, Chidin cuts out his heart, the penetrated male body again made a site of emasculation.

Indeed, the gang's leader, Chidin, is conveyed as particularly dangerous, not only through his behavior but also by his appearance—the camera lingers in extreme close-ups on his irregular and rotting teeth, his pitted skin and various facial disfigurements. The settings too in which he is envisioned include dark, blue-toned forests, the overall effect being one of menace, while the snowy unsullied landscapes associated with the Gilkesons' homestead give way to inhospitable arid desert inhabited by rattlesnakes and vultures. Chidin is frequently framed in low-angle camera shots from the perspective of the girls, and often, from Lilly's point of view, thereby emphasizing his menace and their own vulnerability.

While such abductions did occur in the real world, Lackmann states that "[t]he outrages the Indians committed against Euro-American women were usually exaggerated in the press [. . .] Little, however, was ever said about the atrocities committed against the Indians by white settlers in the developing West" (1997: 133). In a related vein, the threat of rape to the kidnapped girls, who are bound and gagged, arises only from their white abductors.

At one point, Lilly herself is almost attacked. This occurs when the girls are asked by one of the kidnappers if any of them are able to skin a deer. We have already seen Lilly doing this, and she duly volunteers to do this again, quickly exploiting the opportunity to retrieve the arrow that killed the deer. Here, one of the men crouches immediately behind her, holding her hands to guide the knife into the deer's gut, his positioning anticipating the attempted rape of Lilly. The trigger for this attempt occurs when she subsequently uses the arrow to cut the ropes that bind her wrists, demonstrating her resourcefulness in adverse conditions. However, she is recaptured and dragged back by a white hostile, who, intoxicated with laudanum and framed in part shadow, attempts to rape her from behind. Ironically, the attempt is stopped by one of the Apache renegades.

Rape by a white man is also implied by Magdalena's response to Jones regarding Lilly's father, when she tells him that "I never saw his face." In a further subversion of the genre, Schwarz notes:

> Samuel Jones is [. . .] a character who has been tainted by miscegenation because of sexual relations with Native American women [. . .] It is a reversal from [. . .] nearly all previous Westerns where the focus is on White female sexual purity, because here the focus shifts from female sexual purity to *white male* sexual purity. This constitutes a subversion of and a challenge to mainstream texts of the Western genre [original italics]. (Schwarz 2014: 52)

Having tracked the renegades, Dottie, Magdalena and her father plan to ambush the group—but their attempt fails, and as they flee their pursuers, they encounter a Chiricahua Apache named Kayitah (Jay Tavare) and his son, Honesco (Simon Baker). It transpires that Jones has lived with the two Apaches in the past, and Honesco's future bride has been abducted as well. The scenario is therefore one where a group of evil Apache and white kidnappers are pitted against another group that comprises a similar ethnic mix. The moral differences between them are largely signified through physical appearance, and the aforementioned close-ups of Chidin's ravaged features and matted hair which contrasts with the smooth skinned and straight-haired characteristics of Kayitah and Honesco. These differences are extended through figure behavior and vocal intonation and are further suggested by the magic that they each carry out.

Their use of magic is triggered when Magdalena accidentally drops a hairbrush as she flees from the renegades—Chidin retrieves hair from the brush to cast a curse over Magdalena who becomes violently ill. Kayitah and Honesco, together with Jones, chant to resist the curse. The camera focuses first on Chidin, framed in extreme close-up and in blue-toned, high-contrast lighting that emphasizes his cruel and irregular facial features and casts him partly in shade. This imagery intercuts with scenes of the two Chiricahua Apaches who help Magdalena. The scene of the latter is contrastingly warm-toned and features long shots of the two Apaches seated round her, stroking her forehead to comfort her. These are intercut with point-of-view shots from Magdalena's perspective, which are blurred and distorted, indicating her feverish state, as well as medium shots of Dottie who recites Christian prayers intently from the Bible. Such binaries continually permeate the film and echo an earlier scene when Magdalena saved Honesco's life after he was injured by the renegades. These parallel scenarios illustrate some of the ironies in the prejudices of white Americans towards Native Americans. For example, Magdalena tells Dottie to keep away from Honesco as she operates on him, telling her, "You don't know what diseases these people have." Yet, Kayitah and Honesco do not hesitate in touching Magdalena despite her overtly sick appearance. Her attitude reflects that of some real westering women, for, as Myres points out, "some women never became accustomed to Indians, even friendly ones [. . .] To [Mrs Jacob] Stroup and women like her, however an Indian was an Indian and they were all 'dirty, vermin-covered,' and 'untrustworthy, thieving and treacherous'" (1982: 64). Regardless, she saves his life, and he, in turn, saves hers. Subsequently, Kayitah and Honesco work together with Magdalena, Jones, and Dottie to rescue the abducted girls—thereby illustrating a significant point in Myres's study, namely that "[j]ust as immigrants and Indians worked out mutually beneficial relationships along the overland trails, so, too, did settlers and Indians find ways of assisting each other. Frontier women often picture Indians as helpful friends [. . .] For some women, the Indians' knowledge of the surrounding countryside and the uses of various wild plants were an almost indispensable aid" (1982: 62). Alongside this, there is a gradual intermingling of beliefs and values between the two cultures with Magdalena eventually wearing the protective beads offered by Jones while he wears a cross belonging to her mother. They therefore come to accept and respect each other's way of life. Ultimately, however, Kayitah is fatally wounded, and Jones is poisoned and then attacked by Chidin and his followers. The attack presents another example of white masculinity under threat with extreme close-ups of Jones's bleeding face and low-angle shots from his perspective that amplify his helplessness as his attackers look down upon him.

In a final attempt to save the girls, Dottie, despite her fear (indicated by the amplified sounds of her breathing), hides under Kayitah's cloak and physically supports his body on horseback, to make it appear to Chidin's followers that he has come back to life. She therefore not only risks her life by riding directly into the path of the hostiles but is in close proximity to his dead and bleeding corpse. Thereafter, low-angle shots reveal the escaping girls on horseback trampling any surviving captors to death (thereby reversing the visual tropes associated with their own earlier susceptibility), while Magdalena, Dottie, and the released hostages resist attacks by the renegades. Even though Jones kills

Chidin, the retreat of the remaining hostiles depends on Magdalena who shoots at them, and then stands up and boldly orders them to leave. Women and girls act heroically to save each other and though initially cast as victims, retaliate and ultimately seize control.

Conclusion

The Missing is a post-9/11 Western that not only portrays a group of ordinary westering women as key protagonists, as opposed to films that celebrate well-known, real-world individuals, but also blurs divisions between Native and white Americans. If this reflects contemporary attitudes to equality and diversity, it also relates more closely to reported experiences of Native Americans in the Old West as described by Myres (1982). At the same time, the film consistently frames men as weak, emasculated, or vulnerable, this reversal of Western gender politics being somewhat inconsistent with commentaries on the post-9/11 television Western, but nonetheless compatible with the representation of men as physically compromised across a broad range of film genres after 9/11. Such portrayals arguably reflect on America's sense of emasculation following the September 11 attacks.

In contrast, women in *The Missing* are strong, stoic, and resourceful in the face of adversity and work together to overcome Chidin. That groups of women on the Western frontier are generally absent from the Western genre may occur, because, as Lackmann notes, women were outnumbered by men in the nineteenth-century West by approximately ten to one (1997: 120). Second, the nature of classic Hollywood film, which generally centers on a single heroic character who is often male, does not readily accommodate the trajectory of a multi-hero narrative. Moreover, the Western has had few women directors until recently, these late twentieth-century filmmakers contributing to a feminist reclaiming of the Western. Even if accounts of both real-life westering women and academic studies of women in Westerns are increasing, there seems to be a lack of recognition of strong female characters who have had leading roles, although this situation is changing. While women are feminized and made physically attractive in *The Missing*, often differing from real-life accounts of westering women, the film nonetheless gives a more rounded version of female representation than is usually the case. Overall, the film not only disrupts gender politics in its representation of strong women and emasculated men but also interrogates binaries of white American/Native American, and Native American-as-perpetrator/woman-as-victim.

Filmography

3:10 to Yuma, director Delmar Daves, featuring Glenn Ford, Van Heflin, Felicia Farr (Columbia, 1957).

Broken Arrow, director Delmar Daves, featuring James Stewart, Jeff Chandler, Debra Paget (20th Century Fox, 1950).
Dr Quinn, Medicine Woman, creator Beth Sullivan, featuring Jane Seymour, Joe Lando, Beth Tovey (CBS, 1993–8).
Fort Apache, director John Ford, featuring John Wayne, Henry Fonda, Shirley Temple (Argosy Productions, 1948).
Jane Got a Gun, director Gavin O'Connor, featuring Natalie Portman, Joel Edgerton, Ewan McGregor (1821 Pictures, 2015).
Johnny Guitar, director Nicholas Ray, featuring Joan Crawford, Sterling Hayden, Mercedes McCambridge (Republic, 1954).
Meek's Cutoff, director Kelly Reichardt, featuring Michelle Williams, Bruce Greenwood, Paul Dano (Evenstar Films, 2010).
The Ballad of Little Jo, director Maggie Greenwald, featuring Suzy Amis, Bo Hopkins, Ian McKellen (Joco and Polygram Filmed Entertainment, 1993).
The Missing, director Ron Howard, featuring Tommy Lee Jones, Cate Blanchett, Evan Rachel Wood (Revolution Studios, 2003).
True Grit, directors Ethan Coen and Joel Coen, featuring Jeff Bridges, Matt Damon, Hailee Steinfeld (Paramount, 2010).
Westward the Women, director William A. Wellman, featuring Robert Taylor, Denise Darcel, Hope Emerson (MGM, 1951).

BIBLIOGRAPHY

Bandy, Mary Lea and Stoehr, Kevin (2012) *Ride, Boldly Ride: The Evolution of the American Western*. Berkeley, CA: University of California Press.
Benke, Richard (2003) "Apaches Laud Accuracy in 'The Missing' Movie," *Seattle Times*, 18 December <http://community.seattletimes.nwsource.com/archive/?date=20031218&slug=nativespeakers18> (last accessed 4 January 2019).
Calder, Jenni (1977) *There Must Be a Lone Ranger: The American West on Film and Reality*. New York: McGraw-Hill.
Carter, Matthew (2015) *Myth of the Western: New Perspectives on Hollywood's Frontier Narrative*. Edinburgh: Edinburgh University Press.
Cawelti, John (1999) *The Six-Gun Mystique Sequel*. Bowling Green, OH: Bowling Green State University Popular Press.
Coelho, Maria Cecília de M. N. (2017) "Horses for Ladies, High-Ridin' Women and Whores," in Sue Matheson (ed.), *Iconography and Archetypes in Western Film and Television*. Jefferson, NC: McFarland, pp. 113–23.
Cook, Pam (1988) "Women," in Edward Buscombe (ed.), *The BFI Companion to the Western*. London: BFI, pp. 240–3.
Cutshaw, Debra (2013) "Violence, Vixens, and Virgins: Noir-like Women in the Stewart/Mann Westerns," in Sue Matheson (ed.), *Love in Western Film and Television*. London and New York: Palgrave, pp. 35–52.
Evans, Peter William (1996) "Westward the Women: Feminising the Wilderness," in Ian Cameron and Douglas Pye (eds), *The Movie Book of the Western*. London: Studio Vista, pp. 206–13.

French, Philip (2004) "New Lessons from the Old West," *Guardian*, 29 February <https://www.theguardian.com/film/2004/feb/29/philipfrench> (last accessed 28 March 2019).

Gazzaniga, Andrea (2013) "From Whore to Hero: Reassessing Jill in *Once Upon A Time in the West*," in Sue Matheson (ed.), *Love in Western Film and Television*. London and New York: Palgrave, pp. 53–70.

Kitses, Jim (2004) *Horizons West: Directing the Western from John Ford to Clint Eastwood*. London: BFI.

Lackmann, Ron (1997) *Women of the Western Frontier in Fact, Fiction and Film*. Jefferson, NC: McFarland.

Lamont, Victoria (2016) *Westerns: A Women's History*. Lincoln, NE and London: University of Nebraska Press.

Lewis, Helen (2013) "Virgins, Widows, and Whores: The Bride Pool of the John Wayne Westerns," in Sue Matheson (ed.), *Love in Western Film and Television*. London and New York: Palgrave, pp. 7–18.

McGee, Patrick (2007) *From Shane to Kill Bill: Rethinking the Western*. Oxford: Blackwell.

Miller, Cynthia (2013) "'Wild' Women: Interracial Romance on the Western Frontier," in Sue Matheson (ed.), *Love in Western Film and Television*. London and New York: Palgrave, pp. 71–90.

Modleski, Tania (1999) *Old Wives' Tales: Feminist Revisions of Film and Other Fictions*. London: I. B. Tauris.

Myres, Sandra (1982) *Westering Women and the Frontier Experience 1800–1915*. Albuquerque, NM: University of New Mexico Press.

Neale, Steve (2000) *Genre and Hollywood*. London and New York: Routledge.

Nelson, Andrew (2013) "Only a Woman After All? Gender Dynamics in the Westerns of Barbara Stanwyck," in Sue Matheson (ed.), *Love in Western Film and Television*. London and New York: Palgrave, pp. 19–34.

Nelson, Andrew (2016) "Don't Be Too Quick to Dismiss Them: Authorship and the Westerns of Delmer Daves," in Matthew Carter and Andrew Nelson (eds), *ReFocus: The Films of Delmer Daves*. Edinburgh: Edinburgh University Press, pp. 48–62.

Newman, Kim (1990) *Wild West Movies: How the West Was Found, Won, Lost, Lied About, Filmed and Forgotten*. London: Bloomsbury.

Peterson, Jennifer (1996) "The Competing Tunes of 'Johnny Guitar': Liberalism, Sexuality, Masquerade," *Cinema Journal*, 35 (3), pp. 3–18.

Pheasant-Kelly, Fran (2016) "Delmer Daves' 3:10 to Yuma," in Matthew Carter and Andrew Nelson (eds), *ReFocus: The Films of Delmer Daves*. Edinburgh: Edinburgh University Press, pp. 149–65.

Prescott, Cynthia Culver (2007) *Gender and Generation on the Far Western Frontier*. Tucson, AZ: University of Arizona Press.

Pumphrey, Martin (1990) "Masculinity," in Edward Buscombe (ed.), *The BFI Companion to the Western*. London: BFI, pp. 181–3.

Pye, Douglas (1996) "Criticism and the Western," in Ian Cameron and Douglas Pye (eds), *The Movie Book of the Western*. London: Studio Vista, pp. 9–21.

Schwarz, Maureen (2014) "Searching for a Feminist Western: *The Searchers*, *The Hired Hand*, and *The Missing*," *Visual Anthropology*, 27, pp. 45–71.

Spigel, Lynn (2004) "Entertainment Wars: Television Culture after 9/11," *American Quarterly*, 56 (2), pp. 235–70.

White, John (2011) *Westerns*. London and New York: Routledge.

Wildermuth, Mark (2018) *Feminism and the Western in Film and Television*. London and New York: Palgrave.

PART TWO

WOMEN'S ISSUES IN POST-WAR, REVISIONIST, AND FEMINIST WESTERNS

9. TRADING PLACES—TRADING RACES: THE CROSS-CULTURAL ASSIMILATION OF WOMEN IN *THE SEARCHERS* (1956) AND *THE UNFORGIVEN* (1960)

Kelly MacPhail

Although assimilation across cultures and ethnic groups has a long history tied to immigration, economics, and warfare, the colonization of the Americas produced a new degree of cultural imperialism. Soon after Spanish exploration, the *encomienda* system attempted to educate and convert Native American peoples while also using them for slave labor. In the nineteenth century, American and Canadian governments began a program of forced assimilation that aimed to replace Native American religion, language, and culture with the European practices of the colonizers. Apart from such organized efforts at wide-scale assimilation, there were several documented instances of individuals who found themselves transplanted into a new culture, either willingly or unwillingly. Natives famously and forcibly abducted include Squanto, a member of the Patuxet tribe brought to Europe as a slave who later acted as one of the translators for the Mayflower Pilgrims, and Pocahontas, who was kidnapped and held for ransom during hostilities between the English settlers at Jamestown and the tribes led by her father. The white female captivity narrative likewise has a long history in American letters that goes back at least to Mary Rowlandson's 1682 account of her capture during King Philip's War. Another well-known case is that of Cynthia Ann Parker, who was abducted as a ten-year-old by the Comanche in Texas in 1836; she fully assimilated to life with the Comanche, married, had three children, and refused to reintegrate into white society when she was forcibly returned by Texas Rangers in 1860. Such historical abductions have provided ample fodder for several Westerns that treat the cross-cultural assimilation of women.[1]

In his novels *The Searchers* (1954) and *The Unforgiven* (1957), Alan LeMay offers a double thought experiment regarding the possibility of cross-cultural and cross-ethnic assimilation in the cases of two young girls, one white and one Kiowa. The subsequent cinematic adaptations of LeMay's novels by John Ford (1956) and John Huston (1960) continue the experiment; in each case, the majority white community reacts to assimilation with deep-rooted fears of miscegenation about the racial contamination of white women that reflects the cultural homogeneity of Hollywood and of America at the times these films were released. Both films revolve around young girls transplanted from their families and ethnic groups and, to varying degrees, assimilated into another. The questionable success of these assimilations gives rise to a troubling and compelling ambivalence at the heart of these narratives that centers on the fruitful binary of captivity versus adoption. Several battles are fought, partially in order to possess and control women's bodies and thus to define these bodies through concepts of identity focused on purity, contamination, adaptation, and assimilation; the central conflicts particularly arise from white families and communities that struggle with their long-entrenched beliefs surrounding race. By shedding light on the majority culture's fears of the cross-cultural assimilation, miscegenation, and contamination of women, these Westerns challenge such essentialist presuppositions about gender, cultural identity, and notions of power based in racial superiority.

THE SEARCHERS (1956)

The Searchers begins in the Texas of 1868, a period following the Civil War when settlers pressed the federal government for relief from Comanche and Kiowa attacks. The film revolves around Debbie (Natalie Wood), a young white girl who is absent for most of the film after she is taken during a raid that kills her family and then assimilated into Comanche society.[2] Her uncle, Ethan (John Wayne), and adopted brother, Martin (Jeffrey Hunter), set out on a multi-year trek to find her. The film's famous opening and closing shots of Ethan and the rugged landscape framed by the doorway and excluded by the domestic sphere of the interior immediately set up a sharp contrast between categories of wilderness and civilization, which cannot but be further read ethnically. The movie is thus a quest myth—circles, cycles, seasons, and years all pass in a search of the men's goals, whether they be vengeance, the fair maiden, family, home, or belonging.

The two heroes of *The Searchers*, Ethan and Martin, are both marginalized figures searching not only for Debbie, but also themselves. Ethan's fear, anger, and obsession over what has happened to Debbie are clear, and he turns his emotions into perpetual action even as he refused to stop fighting after the Civil War. Ethan is best summed up by his own rejoinders to Reverend Clayton: "I

Figure 9.1 The closing shot of *The Searchers* (1956) excludes Ethan from the domestic sphere and returns him to the rugged landscape where he belongs.

don't believe in surrenders" and, as when he is invited to quit the posse, his oft repeated remark, "That'll be the day."[3] As Jim Kitses further describes the character, "*The Searchers*' dark hero, the obsessed Ethan, is the ultimate example of Ford's alienated and self-destructive characters, his black sheep who act to preserve a community they themselves cannot join" (2004: 34). Indeed, unlike LeMay's novel,[4] Ford's film problematizes race beyond the Comanche plotline by portraying Martin as (at least) one-eighth Cherokee and making Ethan's racial stereotypes against Native Americans much more pronounced. Despite this, Martin is the one who is accepted into the community and family, and at the end his marriage to Laurie Jorgensen (Vera Miles) is assured while Ethan turns away from the home to continue wandering.

Arguably, Ethan (Amos in the novel[5]) and Martin are co-heroes in LeMay's novel, and Martin shares much more of the lead. Indeed, his ethics and loyalty are deeply tested, and, given the death of Ethan/Amos in the novel, Martin is the hero who fulfills the mission of finding Debbie and bringing her home. Macho Ethan is at once a hero and a villain. Many viewers cheer for Ethan given his relentless pursuit of what he sees as justice, his hidden love for Martha, and, of course, because he is played by John Wayne. Other viewers find Ethan's behavior disturbing. He disrupts the funeral for Martha, Aaron, and Ben, which to him is a meaningless trapping of religion, to begin the real business of vengeance. He shows deep racism and ambivalent morality in his racialized dealings with Martin, shooting out the Comanche warrior's eyes, firing at retreating Comanche, and tricking Futterman and his henchmen and then shooting them in the back. Chillingly, Ethan hysterically and irrationally slaughters as many bison as he can so that they will not feed more Comanche over the coming winter.[6] Douglas Pye notes that Ethan's slaughter of the animals is only interrupted by the bugle of the cavalry returning from attacking the Comanche village, which "marks eloquently the way in which Ethan's racial hatred is repeated at the institutional level in the genocidal actions of the US Cavalry" (1996: 229).

Despite the essentialist notions of the time period, Ethan and Martin are struck by how thin the veneer of "whiteness" really is. At one point, when Debbie comes, or is sent, from the Comanche village to warn them off, Martin is distraught by the changes he detects in her. In LeMay's novel, Debbie refuses to leave the Comanche and explains that Scar has agreed to marry her to another warrior for the unprecedented sum of sixty ponies. As they argue, Martin thinks to himself:

> Comanche thoughts, Comanche words—a white woman's voice and form . . . the meeting toward which he had worked for years had turned into a nightmare. Her face was Debbie's face . . . [but she] held it wooden, facing him impassively, as an Indian faces a stranger. Behind the surface of this long-loved face was a Comanche squaw. (LeMay 1954: 269)

He soon finds that she believes whole-heartedly the lies she was told: that her family was killed by another tribe and that she had been rescued and adopted by Scar (LeMay 1954: 271). Later, in conversation with Texas Ranger Charlie MacCorry, who wants to know whether Debbie has "been with the bucks," Martin sidesteps the question but explains, "She takes their part now. She believes them, not us. Like as if they took out her brain, and put in an Indian brain instead. So that she's an Indian now inside" (LeMay 1954: 281–2). Similarly, Laurie is a young white woman who seemingly encourages the searchers in their mission to retrieve and rehabilitate the girl. Yet as the years drag on and she sees that her hoped for marriage with Martin is less and less likely, she insists that he acknowledge that when Ethan finds Debbie he will "put a bullet in her brain," adding, "I tell you Martha would want it now" (LeMay 2012: 234).[7] This rationale, coming from a character seen as moderate to this point, is clear although it is appalling and shocking when she describes Debbie as "the leavings a Comanche buck has sold time and time again to the highest bidder, with savage brats of her own." Although viewers may expect Ethan's to be a minority opinion, Laurie shows that racism is mainstream. Indeed, both films put their most virulently racist comments in the mouths of respectful white women: Laurie here and Mrs Rawlins in *The Unforgiven*.

A crucial female Native character in *The Searchers* is "Look" (Beulah Archuletta), a Comanche woman Martin has accidently purchased while in the guise of a trader. The sale of the woman as chattel is employed for comedy in the film though not as much in the novel. LeMay was invited to add a hundred pages to his serialized story for publication as a novel and as Dan LeMay notes, his father used those pages primarily to develop Martin's character and the Native American culture, partially by adding the character of Look (2012: 164).[8] In LeMay's novel, Ethan/Amos indicates that Look can be killed without reprisal after three days travel from her village (1954: 132–4). He tells Martin to knock her on the head but then offers to show him another way using a knotted rope. Martin, despite using bestial language, defends her, saying, "It's my fault she's here—not hers. She's done all she possibly could to try to be nice, and make herself helpful, and wanted. I never seen no critter try harder to do right" (LeMay 1954: 133).

In the film, Ethan finds the whole predicament of "Mrs Pawley" very funny, but his terrifying racism comes out once again when he demands to know more about Scar from her. She leaves the men, only to be found by them later when they come across Scar's winter camp. This scene points to Ford's attempt at a more balanced presentation of the racism of the Old West, as it is one of the earliest film depictions of the slaughter of Native women and children by the US army and perhaps even reproduces the Washita River Massacre (1868), when George Armstrong Custer's 7th Cavalry attacked a Cheyenne winter camp in western Oklahoma and indiscriminately killed women and children. Indeed, rather than being depicted as a barbaric savage, Scar fights passionately to avenge his two sons, killed by whites. This admission, coupled with the scenes of the village destroyed by the cavalry, show that both groups share blame and the capacity for cruelty. Look's body is discovered in the remains of the massacre, and Martin wonders if she had been at Scar's camp to help find Debbie or if she had come to warn Scar of their approach. This sequence demonstrates Martin's inner compassion; although he does act cruelly towards the woman by assaulting her when she tries to share his bed and by starting every sentence with the command "look," as if he were speaking to a child (hence her name, "Look"), he feels sad when she leaves and then remorse and guilt when her body is discovered.

Sexualized contamination is again apparent with the white women taken captive by the Comanche who are found after the cavalry attack. They are kept apart from the Comanche women, who are herded outside like animals. Surveying the obvious mental and sexual derangement of the women, a soldier remarks, "It's hard to believe they're white," to which Ethan replies, "They ain't white, not anymore. They're Comanch," a sentiment he will later echo: "Living with Comanches ain't being alive." A disgusted Ethan looks at the women as if they would be better off dead. Surviving abduction is an almost ontological change that for Ethan removes not only what makes the women sane or white but also what makes them human. When Ethan makes out his will, he makes Martin, whom he considers a half-breed, his sole inheritor, explaining it is because he "has no blood kin." Martin tries to argue that "Debbie's your kin" against Ethan's insistent "Not anymore, she ain't." These scenes immediately offer the probability that Ethan will kill Debbie; her only hope is that the impossibility of these adult women to adapt or assimilate might be different in the case of those abducted as children.

As the women are suspected to have been "living with a buck," sexual contamination and the miscegenation of offspring are assumed. In these characters' judgment, contamination further arises from the women's apparent consent, as opposed, for example, to the rape and murder of Lucy earlier on.[9] The trauma is inexpressible, although it is symbolized well enough by Ethan's rhythmic and sexualized stabbing of the ground with his knife when he returns from finding and burying Lucy's body. Just as he earlier held Martin away from seeing Martha's raped and mutilated body, Ethan insists to the bereaved Brad, who is about to launch his suicidal run into the Comanche camp, "What do you want me to do? Draw you a picture? Spell it out? Don't ever ask me! Long as you live, don't ever ask me more." When Scar's village is eventually located, the truth is that Debbie was well treated, although deceived, throughout her several years with the Comanche. She appears happy and well integrated into Comanche society, calling them "my people" and urging Martin to depart. Indeed, for Kitses, Debbie, as "another spin on the fallen woman type," becomes a cinematic touchstone through exactly this cultural adaptation into "the hostage wife of the Comanche Scar who initially refuses rescue—'these are my people.' A compelling construct, the character so damaged or driven—or so assimilated and loyal—as to embrace their exile" (Kitses 2004: 34). The great tension of the film is whether Ethan will murder Debbie when he finds her or whether Martin will have to kill him first. In the climactic battle, it is Martin instead of Ethan who kills Scar in defense of Debbie and himself, but it is Ethan, shockingly, who scalps Scar's corpse. Even as he shot the eyes from the earlier Comanche warrior, he here adopts the belief system of the other culture to demonstrate masculine power and conquest that affects the Comanche in the afterlife.

By the film's end, Ethan has shown that he is willing to kill Debbie, especially after finding that she is Scar's wife as opposed, in the novel, to being Scar's virginal adopted daughter. A major difference is the fact that abducted white women were typically shunned by their families and communities after their return. Frank Nugent's original screenplay called for Ethan, upon lifting up Debbie in his arms (even as he had lifted her in the air as a child back in the Edwards home years earlier), to say, "You sure favor your mother," but Ford thought it too obvious a reference to Martha as Ethan's true motivation and cut all dialogue until Ethan's "Let's go home, Debbie" (quoted in Dan LeMay 2012: 173). If this impulse from the screenplay remains in the film, although unsaid, then it is this identification of Debbie with Martha that has changed

Ethan's attitude toward her. Ethan's love for Martha is thus doubly doomed even as she is doubly removed from him, first as his brother's wife and second as the raped and murdered victim of the Comanche. This trauma leads to an identification of Ethan with Scar in their violence and in Scar's actual sexual access to the Edwards women that Ethan also desires covertly but cannot enact or even admit.[10]

THE UNFORGIVEN (1960)

The second half of LeMay's thought experiment is *The Unforgiven*, set in the Texas of 1874. While it is not as successful a film as *The Searchers*, it nonetheless powerfully interrogates racial stereotypes and white American prejudice. This film works as a reverse image of *The Searchers* in that the main concern is Rachel (Audrey Hepburn), who is eventually revealed to be a Kiowa taken as a baby and raised as a white child by the Zachary family. Rachel is never termed a captive, but she is one as much as is Debbie. Rachel has no memory of her Kiowa family, though it is obvious from the deerskin calendar and Lost Bird's attempts to get Rachel back that they mourn for her even as the Edwardses mourn for Lucy and Debbie.

LeMay's authorial intent is to play with epistemological certainty by keeping the truth of Rachel's ancestry obscured—her ethnicity remains undecidable in the novel, but in the film it is slowly made certain. LeMay's novel thus parallels William Faulkner's experiment in *Light in August* (1932), wherein a character struggles with the unanswerable question of whether he might be of partial African ancestry. From the beginning, *The Unforgiven* offers hints of Rachel's "Indian identity," including physical characteristics such as her straight, dark hair and her "tan" that stands in sharp contrast to her paper white mother, Mattilda (Lillian Gish). Other indications rely on Native American stereotypes, such as her innate abilities with animals. Given the overt racism of the white settlers towards anything connected with Native culture, a seemingly odd choice by Huston that further reinforces Rachel's hidden identity is to have her name her horse Guipago, meaning "Lone Wolf" in Kiowa.[11]

As in *The Searchers*, important plot points depend on a delusional old timer, here Abe Kelsey, who spreads rumors, even to the tribe itself, that Rachel is Kiowa. No one pays heed until a local man (Rachel's suitor) is killed by Kiowas, at which point racial hatred is directed toward Rachel as a scapegoat. This sequence allows for the development of another possibly partially Native character, Johnny Portugal. In the novel, he is simply another white (or perhaps Latino) cowhand, but Ben fights him as a warning to the other cowhands not to speak to Rachel (LeMay 1957: 69–71). In the film, as a Native or "half-breed," he is able to tame a wild horse after it throws everyone else by seemingly befriending it, once again reinforcing Native American stereotypes.

Yet he also tells the horse, "It ain't gonna hurt much, not after the first time, anyway," a sexual double entendre that pictures the Native male as a sexual threat. Later, it is Portugal who is sent after Kelsey to bring him to justice for collaborating with the Kiowa. In an obvious reference to Zane Grey's famous horse race in *Riders of the Purple Sage* (1912), Portugal takes four horses, rides bareback, switches mounts at a full gallop, and finally runs down Kelsey on the stolen Guipago despite Cash's warning that an hour ahead is as good as a week on Rachel's powerful white stallion.

The capture of Kelsey allows for his full confession, with a rope around his neck, of his understanding of Rachel's Kiowa birth and the circumstances of how she was taken by Old Zach, a testimony that also reveals his complicity in the murder of the Rawlins's son. Despite or perhaps because of Mattilda's heated reaction, rushing at Kelsey and hitting his horse with a lit stick and thereby hanging him, the white community believes him. Mrs Rawlins slurs Rachel explosively, defining her now as a "red-nigger," a "red-hide nigger," and a "Kiowa squaw" who wanted "a litter of half-breeds" and repeats her accusation that "You killed him," speaking of her son, Rachel's short-lived fiancé; the Zacharys are likewise relegated to "red-nigger lovers" (LeMay 1957: 35, 53, 129, 162, 184). Threateningly, community members determine to strip Rachel naked to see if her skin is dark under her clothes too, as if this will prove whether she is Native or not. The Kiowa take a hand at this point and communicate to the Zacharys that Rachel is indeed Kiowa through their evidence of a deerskin pictorial calendar, at which point Mattilda Zachary finally admits that Rachel is Kiowa. She recounts how her own baby girl died, and Old Zach brought Rachel to her as a substitute. She remembers: "My beautiful little Indian baby. My breasts were hurting with all that milk." This final admission provokes a crisis for all the family members.

Akin to the tension around whether Ethan would murder Debbie in *The Searchers*, tension here develops around Rachel's adopted brothers. While the eldest brother, Ben (Burt Lancaster), bravely defends Rachel from the community members, the middle brother, Cash (Audie Murphy), abandons the family because he cannot accept that his sister is not white. His reaction equates to Ethan's blanket prejudice: he claims, for example, that he can smell Indians from a distance and urges Ben to let him kill three peaceful Kiowa before breakfast. Cash's racist motivation is eventually made clear. Unlike the novel, which has Old Zach drowning during a cattle drive, the film instead indicates that he was killed by the Kiowa.[12] The result is Cash's intense hatred of the Kiowa and even of the "half-breed" Johnny Portugal that stands in contrast to Ben's more rational acceptance of people as people and not as stereotypes.

Meanwhile, Rachel herself undergoes a crisis of racial identity. Perhaps not fully accepting Mattilda's explanation of her Indian ancestry, Rachel examines her bare chest in a mirror and finally determines that the rumors are true. She wipes soot across her forehead in an approximation of Native war paint. Clearly distressed, she now understands why the Kiowa have been trying to trade with Ben for her. Despite the family's insistence to Rachel that "Horses and women are all the same to a Kiowa," the warrior attempting to trade for her is Lost Bird, her natural brother who, like the heroes Ethan and Martin, has come immediately upon learning of his lost sister's whereabouts. Indeed, in the novel, Rachel only finds out that she is even adopted through the interference of Georgia, a red-haired, fair-skinned neighbor intent on marrying Cash (LeMay 1957: 90–3). For Rachel, the news leads to an immediate dissociation from her very identity: "it seemed to her that not a single familiar compass point remained. Her whole identity had been struck away" (LeMay 1957: 94), and she realizes that "All my life I'll wonder who I am" (LeMay 1957: 96). In this story, however, there is no righteous indignation at her kidnapping and no possible return to her birth culture. When Lost Bird returns with the argument that white captives are traded back and he wants the same fair treatment from the whites for his sister, Ben orders the innocent young Andy to kill in cold blood one of the Kiowa who has approached the house under a sign of peace. Rachel had offered to sacrifice herself by going with the Kiowa (almost repeating Debbie, she says she will go with "my people, where I belong") so that the Kiowa would not fight her white family, but Ben's actions mean that the Kiowa will now fight to the end and kill everyone, likely including Rachel.

In the film's lengthy climactic battle, Ben and Rachel, now no longer defined as real brother and sister, reveal their romantic love for one another as they face certain death. Unexpectedly, Cash returns to save the day, but it is Rachel who must shoot Lost Bird herself, thus killing her Kiowa brother in order to marry her adopted white brother. The film ends abruptly after the battle with Rachel

Figure 9.2 During the climactic battle scene, Rachel faces a crisis of identity upon finally meeting Lost Bird, her presumptive brother in *The Unforgiven* (1960).

reinstated into white culture as geese fly by and mesmerize the reorganized family. If the choice before Rachel is to which family and ethnic group her loyalty belongs, shooting Lost Bird is her final act of assimilation and enculturation.

There are further major implications concerning Rachel's identity as a Kiowa. In both novel and film, Rachel has an interest in Ben that is romantic, and he reciprocates these feelings (LeMay 1957: 96–8). While, in the film, Rachel has always known that she is not related by blood to Ben despite their brother–sister relationship, in the novel she thinks that she is. Nonetheless, she is sexually attracted to Ben, which raises the threat not only of miscegenation but also of incest. In the film, Ben in fact only permits Charlie Rawlins to come courting Rachel after she, somewhat jokingly, proposes marriage while she is riding behind Ben on his horse and holding him closely. Armando José Prats posits that the incest theme is compounded because Ben first tells Rachel of the grand wedding they will have only after Mattilda dies and lies just off screen, and their kiss occurs just out of the sight of younger brother Andy (2002: 109, n.36). As Eckstein argues, both LeMay novels and the films demonstrate "the deep connection between overt fear of miscegenation and covert fantasies of incest" (2004b: 198). I would contend that changes in both film versions further compound issues around miscegenation and incest. Indeed, one major decision meant to make Wayne's character the central hero of *The Searchers* was to allow him to live to the end of the film. The novel, though, kills him off and then ends with a form of incest, or at least emotional incest, when Martin finally tracks down his adopted sister Debbie, who is near death from exposure. He warms her with his body, she confesses she has always loved him, and intimate sexual relations are implied. Martin is echoed in *The Unforgiven* by Ben, who acts in a similar sexual fashion to make Rachel his own and to nullify any objections or claims of racial contamination. Conversely, the incestuous implications simultaneously reinforce both racial purity and sexual contamination. In both cases, then, the threat of impurity represented by miscegenation is in fact one of hypodescent, as it is revoked when the male is of the dominant cultural group.

As Rachel finds herself in a very difficult position, she is immediately aware that her possible Kiowa racial identity means that, among all the negatives, there is the positive that she can now pursue a relationship with Ben. A further major difference revolves around the Kiowa parchment. As noted, the film has the Kiowa leave a deerskin calendar on the Zacharys' floor that clearly suggests that Rachel was a Kiowa baby who was abducted by two white men. Over the final pages of the novel, the Kiowa likewise deliver a parchment, but Ben consciously decides to burn it unread, which leaves definitive knowledge of Rachel's true parentage unsettled (LeMay 1957: 273–7). For Prats, "Ben does not so much accept Rachel's Indianness as he *abrogates* it; and Rachel's transformation does not so much legitimate her whiteness as it does Ben's power to erase her Native American racial identity for the sake of possessing her sexually" (2002: 109). Along the same lines, Kitses argues that the film "so clearly defines adoption as one-way, possible only if Indians enter the white world" (2004: 97). Thus Ben takes charge and demonstrates that Rachel's ethnicity does not matter to him by again redefining her. After he has Andy murder the Kiowa warrior so that Rachel cannot leave with them, Ben strokes Rachel's face passionately as if he is about to kiss her, saying, "Little Injun. Little red-hide Injun," turning a racial slur into an almost playful characterization that at once infantilizes and eroticizes Rachel, who nonetheless appears comforted by his words. Soon after, Ben announces that he will marry Rachel during a pause in the battle: "We got to take a trip to Wichita . . . We're gonna fix you out in a fancy dress. A white one, with veils . . . That's what they wear for the occasion, ain't it?" Partially, it is simply through Ben's authority to say that Rachel's Kiowa heritage and their adoptive relationship do not constitute miscegenation or incest that they, in fact, do not. He chooses a romantic relationship and marriage with her based on their compatibility and his sexual desire and not her heritage. Ben, as the head of the household, thus acts as if he believes he has the authority simply to sidestep both charges of miscegenation and incest. Certainly, the rest of the white community might not see it his way on either count, yet Ben's move is one that accepts difference.

Two significant differences here are that the film has Rachel kill her own brother in cold blood and that Ben is present for the battle. In the novel, Ben is away, and, when the Kiowa arrive under a sign of peace, it is Cash who murders Lost Bird to keep Rachel from surrendering herself. In Huston's rendering, Lost Bird is the only significant Native American figure, meaning that he must survive until the end. Viewers alert to the parallels between the two novels cannot help but see Lost Bird as Martin, coming to retrieve his sister from men he believes have knowingly abducted her. Does he similarly fear for her, suspecting rape and miscegenation? Lost Bird is not given time to voice such concerns, but his familial and economic claim that he wants to pay to ransom his sister follows rationally and logically.

Early in the film's battle, Lost Bird cuts close to the house on his horse, sees Rachel and cries out "Sister" to her, first in Kiowa and then in English. Rachel finds herself impossibly drawn between a natural brother and the only life she has known. Ben has already urged her not to scream when they are attacked but to shoot. She asks whether he means her to kill them: "My own kind?" He replies, "By blood yes, but not by anything else." Ultimately, she is forced to decide when Lost Bird later comes to her alone inside the house. It is a tense moment; he advances toward her but not menacingly. What will he say? Will it be the same speech that Martin gives Debbie, saying she is his sister and asking if she remembers him? After a pause, Rachel shoots and kills him without hesitation, using the pistol with one bullet left that Ben had given to her in case she was taken and had to commit suicide instead of suffering the only hinted at fate of what would occur. Lost Bird appears shocked that his sister, for whom he has risked so much, and for whom so many have died, has determined to kill him in cold blood. The look of sorrow and miscomprehension in his eyes as he falls to his knees and dies is heartrending. What then happens to Lost Bird's body? Is it buried on the farm? Does Rachel look at her brother's grave for the rest of her life and wonder what might have been or feel guilt for taking a human life? Or is she now so convinced of her belonging in white culture that she does not give it a second thought, having so Othered the Kiowa that any admission of connection with them is impossible for her?

Importantly, while both films gender abduction by showing only women who had been taken by the Comanche or Kiowa, both male and female babies were in fact abducted. The ability to adapt is based on age and not gender. Indeed, an important secondary character in the novel is Seth, a male white abductee who is raised Kiowa and becomes a famous warrior (LeMay 1957: 105–16). It is Seth who represents the immediate counterpoint to Rachel in race, gender, and experience. The novel's narrator refers to several white or partially white warriors who were

> captured, enslaved, and finally Indianized, when very young ... The white war chiefs had made their names in open competition, by the boldness, ingenuity, and ruthlessness with which they made war on their own race. Most believed the white warriors more savage than the Kiowas of blood, but this was because of the resentment aroused by their anomaly of race. They could equal the cruelty of their adopted people; they could not hope to exceed it. (LeMay 1957: 105)

Although Lost Bird is coming for Rachel, the bigger threat is Seth, who keeps attacking after Lost Bird's death. Again, in the novel, it is Rachel, who must come to terms with Seth and kill him during the final stages of the attack on the homestead.

LeMay's novel has Cash cut off from the ranch and killed by the Kiowa, Mattilda dead, and Andy badly wounded when the final onslaught arrives. It is Rachel alone who must face this attack. Seth and another warrior come up from under the house, figuring rape by invading the domestic space through the "Glory Hole," the space under the floorboards where the Zacharys hide their money. In a reverse penetration, Rachel shoots Seth through the eye socket as he raises his head above the trapdoor. Of course, Hollywood films operate on stars, and Lancaster's character was not about to be sidelined for the big fight anymore than Wayne's Ethan was going to play second to Hunter's Martin. But LeMay's story does just that in both cases. It is as if Huston must reinscribe the male hero by having Ben defend the ranch, force everyone else to keep their heads, and get the girl.

ADAPTATION AND HYBRIDITY

Most viewers would agree that *The Searchers* is the better film. Its direction, performances, cinematography, and setting are widely admired and emulated while *The Unforgiven* is notorious for Huston's claim that he disliked it the most of all his films. While he wanted to make a serious film about race, the studio wanted action and adventure. Hepburn broke her back due to a fall from a horse during rehearsal, which suspended production for several months and may have contributed to her subsequent miscarriage. Although *The Searchers* does add some characterizations of Mose and Charlie MacCorry meant to add some humor, *The Unforgiven* misses its emotional register by flirting with slapstick and the ridiculous in its portrayal of Andy, Charlie's bumbling courtship, and the Kiowa attack on the piano, all of which are additions to the novel. When it comes to the two films, Ford's is more complex due to his brilliant adaptations of the source material and his revolutionary portrayal of the Native and white communities' differing views on race, culture, and identity.

While the two novels are both are serious, well-researched treatments of racism that also tie into LeMay's own Kansas heritage, *The Unforgiven* is actually more complex. LeMay chooses a female protagonist, an uncommon choice in the Western genre. Huston's alterations of LeMay's novel and especially the increased presence of Burt Lancaster's Ben have much to do with the Hollywood of the 1950s and 1960s not knowing how to square the seriousness of a female protagonist with the conventions of the genre.[13] Further, Rachel is a deeply fraught character who, for most of the film, may or may not also be a Native American; as a result, she must endure the constant threat of violence from the Kiowa and from whites who hate her for the threat she represents. Not only do the whites see her as either a Kiowa or the product of miscegenation, they also fear that she is in active alliance with Lost Bird and so is an enemy within their own gates passing for one of them while plotting their downfall. This creates a parallel not only to changes in American race relations in the 1950s, but also to the depths of Cold War Red Scare paranoia. This is a dark psychological Western very much attuned to Rachel's soul-searching as she thinks through her racial identity, her hidden and unknowable past, and the consequences for her future.

The threat of miscegenation is implicit in both narratives, but its fascinating backstory in the films means that the issue of redface is not as black and white as it first appears. Although it was common practice in Westerns of this period to use Native Americans (mainly Navahos for Ford, including in *The Searchers*) as usually uncredited secondary actors while giving white actors the important Native roles, the underlying theme of miscegenation qualifies what is happening in both films. Ford hired Henry Brandon to play Scar specifically because of his physical features (Eckstein 2004a: 13). Although this appears to be another incidence of redface, given that Brandon, who is of German ancestry and was born as

Heinrich von Kleinbach, is playing a Comanche, his blue eyes make his whiteness too apparent for simple miscasting. Indeed, Ford chose Brandon because his blue eyes indicate that his Scar was himself partly white and therefore the product of an interracial pairing (Dan LeMay 2012: 174). Was Scar's white mother also a captive? Did she survive? Was she the one who taught Scar his English that Ethan remarks on sarcastically at their first meeting? Would this parentage mean that Scar would see Debbie as a potential wife similar to his own mother and therefore in a much different light than Ethan could ever guess?

Of course, charges of redface could also be leveled at Hepburn, but here again there is a complication. In the novel, her racial identity must be left undecideable; the best source of knowledge is Ben, who knows that his father did believe Rachel to be Kiowa, although Ben is not sure if his father knew that for certain or not (1957: 155–6). At one point, Kelsey's story is revised to say that Rachel is "a Kiowa quarter-breed baby . . . Lost Bird's half sister, out of a white woman captive" (1957: 139).[14] In the film, there also is room for doubt. While the deer hide calendar shows Rachel's abduction, it does not represent her heritage. This would point to the necessity of having an actress of white or mixed heritage to assume the role of a woman who questions her unknowable identity.

The narratives reflect more than simple fiction. LeMay's interest in these racial questions must stem in part from the Native American and African American experience of racism and the beginnings of the Civil Rights Movement in the 1950s, the same time that he wrote *The Searchers* (1954) and *The Unforgiven* (1957).[15] This was the decade of *Brown v. Board of Education* (1954), the vicious lynching of Emmett Till (1955), the Montgomery Bus Boycott (1955–6), and sit-ins beginning with the Greensboro Woolworths (1960), all of which some whites feared specifically because of what they saw as the threat of miscegenation arising from integration. Kitses is undoubtedly correct, however, when he insists of *The Searchers* that "the notion that the Indian stands in for black can be seen as repeating the disenfranchisement of the Native American, and of blurring the film's focus on the nation's primal events" (2004: 100). Conversely, the Motion Picture Association was troubled by the repeated insult "red nigger" in *The Unforgiven*; yet, their rationale was that "it is bound to be deeply injurious to the feelings of Negroes in our audience" as opposed to offending Native Americans (quoted in Aleiss 2005: 110).

During this period, the Native American community also sought increased human and civil rights. This activism originated in a broken relationship with the American government strained because of treaty rights, the status of tribes as "domestic dependent nations," and the withholding of American citizenship to most Native Americans until 1924. Undoubtedly, the notion of children being removed from one culture and raised in another raises the specter of American and Canadian church-run, off-reservation residential schools and the Sixties Scoop program, the goals of which were to assimilate Native American children into white culture by removing them from their communities and giving them a Western education. Now seen as formalized cultural genocide regulating religion, language, clothing, diet, and even personal names, residential schools are also condemned as being prone to physical and sexual abuse. A national organization in the United States would not be founded until the American Indian Movement and after the passage of the Indian Civil Rights Act (ICRA) in 1968 and the National Indian Education Association (NIEA) a year later. Another notable public protest for Native American rights was Marlon Brando's refusal of his 1973 Academy Award for *The Godfather* (1972) and his choice to ask Native American actress Sacheen Littlefeather to speak instead and highlight America's continued mistreatment of Native peoples. In this light, the novel and film versions of *The Searchers* and *The Unforgiven* both participate in the vitally important conversations of 1950s America that questioned founding mythologies, race relations, and the role of women and Native Americans within wider society.

Notes

1. Examples include *Northwest Passage* (1940), *The Charge at Feather River* (1953), *They Rode West* (1954), *Trooper Hook* (1957), *Two Rode Together* (1961), *The Stalking Moon* (1968), *Little Big Man* (1970), *Soldier Blue* (1970), *The Last of the Mohicans* (1992), and *The Missing* (2004).
2. While such kidnappings of children certainly occurred, neither *The Searchers* nor *The Unforgiven* is based on a specific case. This is despite the claims of some critics who link *The Searchers* particularly to the Cynthia Ann Parker case. Instead, LeMay did extensive research on at least sixty-four abductions in Texas and Kansas (Dan LeMay 2012: 169–71), and these as a group inform his fiction. Likewise, LeMay wrote *The Unforgiven* after extensive research, including a month of first-hand research with the Kiowa in the fall of 1954 (Dan LeMay 2012: 175).
3. Fascinatingly, this phrase directly inspired Buddy Holly and Jerry Allison's song of the same title, which became a number one hit in the fall of 1957 (McBride 2011: 570).
4. For more on the differences between the novel, the screenplay, and the final film, see Eckstein (1998).
5. In LeMay's novel, "Ethan" is actually the name of Martin's father, who died during a Comanche raid when Martin was a little boy who, like Debbie, was sent outside to hide.
6. In what is a perhaps ironic twist, given the mass slaughter and near extinction of plains bison by white hunters during the nineteenth century, this scene was not filmed in the US but rather in Elk Island National Park near Edmonton, Alberta, Canada, with doubles filling in for Wayne and Hunter; Joseph McBride notes that "Some buffalo were actually shot on camera, although the killing was performed by game wardens as part of the regular culling of the herd" (2011: 554).
7. In 1871, General Phil Sheridan reflected a similarly shocking point of view when he refused to authorize the payment of five ponies to ransom a white woman named

Mary Jordan, saying, "I cannot give my approval to any reward for the delivery of this white woman . . . After having her husband and friends murdered, and her own person subjected to the fearful bestiality of perhaps the whole tribe, it is mock humanity to secure what is left of her for the consideration of five ponies" (quoted in Prats 2002: 60, n.28).

8. As Lehman notes, Ethan fears Native American rape of and miscegenation with white women, but he finds the reversal offered by Martin as a white man with Look as a Native woman to be merely funny without any inherent contradiction (1990: 406). The implied threat to white purity does not go both ways; indeed, such pairs have been approved in American literature from the template of John Smith and Pocahontas. For an extended analysis of Look, see Lehman (1990) and Marubbio (2017).

9. Lehman argues that literal or figurative rape is several times indicated or implied in the film, including Scar's rapes of Martha, Lucy, and Debbie; Ethan's entry into his brother's house, his sexual interest in Martha, and knowledge of Martin's mother's hair; Brad's reaction to Lucy's rape; and Ethan riding his horse into Scar's teepee before scalping his corpse (1990: 390, 403).

10. In a notorious interview with film historian Brian Huberman in 1974, Wayne was asked about playing the "villain" in the film, to which he angrily replied "He was a man living in his times. The Indians fucked his wife. What would you have done?" (quoted in McBride 2011: 557). Note Wayne's slippage in wrongly substituting Martha in the role of his character's wife.

11. Lone Wolf is also the name of one of the last Kiowa chiefs, Lone Wolf the Elder (1820–79), a signer of the Little Arkansas Treaty in 1865.

12. Graves in both films are reminders of violence. William Zachary's grave marker reads that he died defending his family from "red Indian devils," and Ethan's mother's gravestone notes that she was killed by a Comanche attack.

13. Some notable exceptions of women in starring roles in serious Westerns are Barbara Stanwyck in Anthony Mann's *The Furies* (1950) and Joan Crawford in Nicholas Ray's *Johnny Guitar* (1954). Women did star in Western musicals or comedies, such as *Annie Get Your Gun* (1950), *Calamity Jane* (1953), and *Cat Ballou* (1965).

14. Likewise, Lost Bird in is played by Carlos Rivas, a Texan born to a German father and Mexican mother.

15. Critics including Brian Henderson (1985), Peter Lehman (1990), and Marty Roth (1991) have argued that the film encodes fears about African American men, partially by displacing them onto another race then not directly feared by white Americans.

Filmography

Annie Get Your Gun, director George Sidney, featuring Betty Hutton, Howard Keel, Louis Kalhern (MGM, 1950).

Calamity Jane, director David Butler, featuring Doris Day, Howard Keel, Allyn Ann McLerie (Warner Bros., 1953).

Cat Ballou, director Elliot Silverstein, featuring Jane Fonda, Lee Marvin, Michael Callan (Columbia, 1965).

Johnny Guitar, director Nicholas Ray, featuring Joan Crawford, Sterling Hayden, Mercedes McCambridge (Republic, 1954).
Little Big Man, director Arthur Penn, featuring Dustin Hoffman, Faye Dunaway, Chief Dan George (Cinema Center Films, 1970).
Northwest Passage, director King Vidor, featuring Spencer Tracy, Robert Young, Walter Brennan (MGM, 1940).
Soldier Blue, director Ralph Nelson, featuring Candice Bergen, Peter Strauss, Donald Pleasence (Embassy Pictures, 1970).
The Charge at Feather River, director Gordon Douglas, featuring Guy Madison, Vera Miles, Frank Lovejoy (Warner Bros., 1953).
The Furies, director Anthony Mann, featuring Barbara Stanwyck, Wendell Corey, Walter Huston (Wallis-Hazen, 1950).
The Last of the Mohicans, director Michael Mann, featuring Daniel Day-Lewis, Madeleine Stowe, Russell Means (Morgan Creek Entertainment, 1992).
The Missing, director Ron Howard, featuring Tommy Lee Jones, Cate Blanchett, Evan Rachel Wood (Revolution Studios, 2003).
The Searchers, director John Ford, featuring John Wayne, Jeffrey Hunter, and Vera Miles (C. V. Whitney Pictures, 1956).
The Stalking Moon, director Robert Mulligan, Gregory Peck, Eva Marie Saint, Robert Forster (National General Production, 1968).
The Unforgiven, director John Huston, featuring Burt Lancaster, Audrey Hepburn, Audie Murphy (Hill-Hecht-Lancaster Productions, 1960).
They Rode West, director Phil Karlson, Robert Francis, Donna Reed, May Wynn (Columbia, 1954).
Trooper Hook, director Charles Warren, featuring Joel McCrea, Barbara Stanwyck, Earl Holliman (Filmaster, 1957).
Two Rode Together, director John Ford, featuring James Stewart, Richard Widmark, Shirley Jones (Columbia, 1961).

Bibliography

Aleiss, Angela (2005) *Making the White Man's Indian: Native Americans and Hollywood Movies*. Westport, CT: Praeger.

Eckstein, Arthur M. (1998) "Darkening Ethan: John Ford's *The Searchers* (1956) from Novel to Screenplay to Screen," *Cinema Journal*, 38 (1), pp. 3–24.

Eckstein, Arthur M. (2004a) "Introduction: Main Critical Issues in *The Searchers*," in Arthur M. Eckstein and Peter Lehman (eds), *The Searchers: Essays and Reflections on John Ford's Classic Western*. Detroit, MI: Wayne State University Press, pp. 1–45.

Eckstein, Arthur M. (2004b) "Incest and Miscegenation in *The Searchers* (1956) and *The Unforgiven* (1959)," in Arthur M. Eckstein and Peter Lehman (eds), *The Searchers: Essays and Reflections on John Ford's Classic Western*. Detroit, MI: Wayne State University Press, pp. 197–221.

Henderson, Brian (1985) "*The Searchers:* An American Dilemma," in Bill Nichols (ed.), *Movies and Methods: An Anthology, Volume II*. Berkeley, CA: University of California Press, pp. 429–49.

Kitses, Jim (2004) *Horizons West: Directing the Western from John Ford to Clint Eastwood*, new edn. London: British Film Institute.

Lehman, Peter (1990) "Texas 1868/America 1956: *The Searchers*," in *Close Viewing: An Anthology of New Film Criticism*. Tallahassee, FL: Florida State University Press, pp. 387–415.

LeMay, Alan (2009 [1954]) *The Searchers*. New York: Leisure Books.

LeMay, Alan (2009 [1957]) *The Unforgiven*. New York: Leisure Books.

LeMay, Dan (2012) *Alan LeMay: A Biography of the Author of The Searchers*. Jefferson, NC: McFarland.

McBride, Joseph (2011) *Searching for John Ford*. Jackson, MS: University Press of Mississippi.

Marubbio, M. Elise (2017) "Look at the Heart of *The Searchers*," in Steve Pavlik, M. Elise Marubbio, and Tom Holm (eds), *Native Apparitions: Critical Perspectives on Hollywood's Indians*. Tucson, AZ: University of Arizona Press, pp. 108–34.

Prats, Armando José (2002) *Invisible Natives: Myth and Identity in the American Western*. Ithaca, NY and London: Cornell University Press.

Pye, Douglas (1996) "Double Vision: Miscegenation and Point of View in *The Searchers*," in Ian Cameron and Douglas Pye (eds), *The Book of Westerns*. New York: Continuum, pp. 229–35.

Roth, Marty (1991) "'Yes, My Darling Daughter': Gender, Miscegenation, and Generation in John Ford's *The Searchers*," *New Orleans Review*, 18 (4), pp. 65–73.

10. WESTERN NOSTALGIA, REVISIONISM, AND NATIVE AMERICAN WOMEN IN *WIND RIVER* (2017)

Robert Spindler

> The death of a beautiful woman is, unquestionably, the most poetical topic in the world.
>
> Edgar Allan Poe

Native American women are probably the most under-represented demographic group in the Western film genre, compared to the proportions of the people involved in the actual historical events that inspired this narrative form. The rudimentary appearances of Native American women characters in Westerns, extant as they are, suffer from a twofold bias towards gender and ethnicity. Even the pro-Native American Westerns in the history of the genre fail to establish and portray self-contained indigenous female characters. In the majority of films eager to present more nuanced portrayals of Native Americans, the visibility of Indian women roles seeks justification solely through their relation to male and, mostly, white protagonists. A recurring topos in this web of interdependencies is the interracial marriage or partnering of native female and white male, which functions as a lever to bestow a hybrid "Anglo-Native" status upon the male. This status legitimizes his function as a patronizing "messenger" for Native Americans, in a mainstream film produced for, and by, a white majority.

Frequently, the Native American woman perishes in the aftermath of the mixed marriage/union, cementing the passivity of the introduced character and restoring the freedom of mobility and action to the male lead, who follows up with heroic deeds of revenge. This motif of the "Celluloid Maiden," as M. Elisa Marubbio calls it in her book *Killing the Indian Maiden*, "the young Native woman who dies as a result of her choice to align herself with a white colonizer" is as old as the Western genre itself (Marubbio 2006: 4–5). Marubbio differentiates between the "Celluloid Princess," who "initiates a cross-racial union and the integration or absorption of one group into another, but by carrying through that union, she transgresses taboos against interracial mixing and must pay the price with her life,"[1] and the "Sexualized Maiden," who "embodies enhanced sexual and racial difference that results in a fetishizing of the figure ... she becomes the female representation of the ignoble savage" (Marubbio 2006: 7). Both of these staples inevitably die in the course of the narrative. From the 1970s onwards, Marubbio argues, Western cinema saw an increasing number of female Native Americans that represented a hybrid between the two. Classics such as Delmer Daves's *Broken Arrow* (1950), Elliot Silverstein's *A Man Called Horse* (1970), or Sydney Pollack's *Jeremiah Johnson* (1972) all feature prototypes of the Celluloid Maiden, although these films had tendencies towards a more pro-Native American stance than their contemporaries (Marubbio 2006: 15, 17). The dominance of this scheme reveals much about Hollywood's agenda on the portrayal of Native Americans, who work as "a colonial rhetorical strategy to promote a national American identity defined against a raced and 'savage' Other" (Marubbio 2006: 5). The recent neo-Western *Wind River* (2017), directed by Taylor Sheridan, continues this design, despite a revisionist stance.

Wind River is a thriller and neo-Western set in the present day. The film tells of an FBI agent (Jane Banner, played by Elizabeth Olsen) who attempts to solve an alleged murder case but finds her work hampered by the fact that the victim, Natalie Hanson, a young Arapahoe woman (Kelsey Asbille), was a resident of

Figure 10.1 Celluloid princess or sexualized maiden? Kelsey Asbille as Natalie Hanson in *Wind River* (2017).

the Wind River Indian Reservation in Wyoming. Jane finds assistance from the conservation officer and professional hunter Cory Lambert (Jeremy Renner), who knows his way around the reservation, and whose unconventional methods clear some of the stumbling blocks of government restrictions out of the FBI agent's way. Cory discovered the body of the young woman in the snow while he was on the hunt for a mountain lion that preyed on livestock. Because it looked like homicide, the FBI was alerted, and during their investigations Cory's ability to read tracks already turns out to be a useful resource. The autopsy reveals that Natalie was raped (not murdered), whereupon she ran away and died of pulmonary haemorrhage because she ran barefoot through the snow for several miles. This makes it a case outside the responsibility of the FBI, and it seems that Jane, although she is emotionally affected by the case, the circumstances, and the lack of clarification, has to pull out and leave the reservation. However, she has the sympathy of Cory, who appears personally affected by the crime as well. Then, another body turns up—that of Natalie's boyfriend Matt Rayburn (Jon Bernthal), who was obviously murdered. Jane is back on the case, and Cory assists her. Together, they track down the delinquents who work on a nearby oil-drilling site, and Jane kills most of them in a shootout. Only the rapist, Pete (James Jordan), escapes. Cory tracks him down and brings him to a mountaintop, where he exacts his cruel revenge. He offers Pete freedom if he manages to escape as Natalie did: barefoot through the snow. Unlike Natalie, Pete collapses after only a few hundred feet, illustrating his degenerative state in contrast to the "warrior" (as Natalie is repeatedly labeled), who ran for several miles before she eventually died.

Despite its modern-day setting, *Wind River* fits well into a series of films that have come out since the 2000s and form a small revival of Westerns with very formulaic structures and iconography, contrasting with the more revisionist Westerns of the later decades of the twentieth century. These films include *3:10 to Yuma* (2007), a remake of the 1950s classic, or Kevin Costner's *Open Range* (2003), which is a far cry from his *Dances with Wolves* (1990) and narrates a highly conventional Western plot, *Appaloosa* (2008), also a very personal work, directed by and starring Ed Harris, *Seraphim Falls* (2006) and other neo-Westerns like *The Three Burials of Melquiades Estrada* (2005), and other genre variants like the "meat pie Western" *The Proposition* (2005).[2] While all of these films feature minor revisionist elements, their rather obvious serious and nostalgic character outweighs these. A number of successful and truly revisionist Westerns, like *Brokeback Mountain* (2005), *The Assassination of Jesse James by the Coward Robert Ford* (2007), *Meek's Cutoff* (2010), or the very recent (and Native American-themed) *Hostiles* (2017), *The Rider* (2017), and *Woman Walks Ahead* (2018) complement the more "nostalgic" recent Westerns and, through their gravity, contrast strongly with the more light-hearted revisionist attempts of the 1990s, like *Posse* (1993) or *The Quick and the Dead* (1995). Thus Western cinema after 9/11 seems to follow along two parallel and contradictory lines that either attempt to resurrect the traditional Western and the supposedly proto-American values the genre represents, or deconstruct its rigid norms further, as has happened continuously since the 1950s (Spindler 2008). Occasionally, these two lines cross in films that feature Western nostalgia but deconstruct at least some of its conventions, like *The Missing* (2003), which recalls John Ford's *The Searchers* (1956) but presents an alternative perspective on women in the West. At first sight, *Wind River* seems to fall exactly into that category. Although it presents a rather clear-cut revenge story plot with a traditional Western complex of characters, it promises a novel deconstruction of portrayals of Native Americans in the Western in general, and female Native Americans in particular, by depicting the social realities of a present-day Indian reservation, and by closing with a title that points to the number of unresolved violent crimes on Native women in reservations. However, a close look reveals that its revisionist stance is overshadowed by an incapability to do away with conservative genre conventions.

In the first place, *Wind River* combines its murder mystery elements with prototypical Western iconography, characters, and plot structures, creating a neo-Western that fulfills the post-9/11 desire for the proto-American genre without obtrusive anachronisms, pathos, or meta-references. It manages this mainly by positioning the setting, the Wind River Indian Reservation, at its centre. John G. Cawelti points out the importance of the setting for the Western, arguing that a popular genre has to be defined in terms of narrative structure, but that ultimately "the Western is initially defined by its setting," as the plot patterns necessitate a backdrop of "ten-gallon hats and horses" (Cawelti 1999: 19). He points out that a Western typically takes place "on or near a frontier," and thus, by Frederick Turner's Frontier Thesis, is "set at a particular moment in the past" (Cawelti 1999: 20). This is obviously not true of *Wind River*, which is explicitly not set in the (far) past. However, its setting (the Wind River Indian Reservation) is comparable to Cawelti's definition of the frontier (based on Turner's thesis), and its quintessential role in the Western genre (Cawelti 1999: 19–20). Much of this definition rests on the opposition of Whites versus Native Americans. According to Cawelti, the frontier is a setting of contact and confrontation between civilization and a more "savage" alternative, which might be represented by outlaws or Native Americans, the latter personifying a purer, more natural way of life. Nevertheless, the gradual disappearance of Native Americans along the Western genre's frontier is never questioned (Cawelti 1999: 20). They represent no relevant alternative to, or critique of, the "American way of life," but merely provide a setting for suspenseful action. Cawelti concludes that "the Indian remains a stereotypical figure in all but the most complex and interesting Westerns . . . he was usually in the process of vanishing," and argues further: "Even in Westerns quite sympathetic to the Indian . . . the focus of the action usually shifts from the

Indians themselves to the dilemmas their situation poses for the white hero and heroine" (Cawelti 1999: 21–2).³ Cawelti goes on to quote Armando Prat's "firsting" of the White American," in films that "justify the destruction of the Indian by having him hand on the torch to a sympathetic and understanding white character" (Cawelti 1999: 22). From this, Cawelti concludes that the Native American functions more as a setting in the Western than as part of a complex of characters: "If the Indian represented a significant way of life rather than a declining savagery, it would be far more difficult to resolve the story with reaffirmation of the values of American society" (Cawelti 1999: 22). This is an astonishingly accurate summary of *Wind River*'s portrayal of white–Native American relations, despite its pro-Native American marketing.

In addition, the reservation is characterized as a heart of darkness,⁴ and thus a present-day pendant to the nineteenth-century frontier, for Jane, who represents a technologically advanced, urbanized, and feminized America. The actual Wind River Indian Reservation is located in Wyoming, the least populated state of the US, and the "Cowboy State," as license plates proudly declare. It is as close as present-day America gets to the Old West, with near intact Western towns, unpredictable weather extremes, and guns carried visibly in the open street. The conquest of the West and its repercussions have an uncanny immediacy in Wyoming and the Wind River Indian Reservation. In Fort Washakie, huge stone letters against a hillside celebrate the famous name giver of the community, the Shoshone chief who realized the futility of resisting the advancing whites and ensured the survival of his people by paving the way for friendly relationships, and thus the establishment of the reservation.⁵ In this world, typical Western elements are not out of place. They are not the "ten-gallon hats and horses," but certainly cowboy hats, guns, and horse-equivalents like pickup trucks and snowmobiles, which blend well into the remote and desolate landscape of the reservation.

Also Cawelti's complex of characters is reflected in the film, albeit on a more complex level. The three character types that Cawelti identifies are "the townspeople or agents of civilization, the savages or outlaws ... and the heroes, who are above all 'men in the middle'" (Cawelti 1999: 29). Despite some heroic features in Jane's character, the hero is clearly Cory. He is the "big, strong, and silent" (Peterson 1996: 14) type that represents the traditional interface between civilization and the wild, not only through his connection to Native Americans (he lives on the reservation, is well integrated into its society, and was married to a Native American woman), but also through his atavistic job, which opens the movie and sets the scene: he hunts down predators that endanger sheep and cattle herds inside the reservation.⁶ In contrast to other Native American-themed revisionist films, Cory is neither the ridiculed hero of *Little Big Man* (1970), nor the un-American British aristocrat of *A Man Called Horse*, nor the psychologically unstable protagonist of *Jeremiah Johnson* (Marubbio 2006: 194). However, what is less clear is who "the townspeople or agents of civilization," and who the "savages or outlaws" are. Jane clearly represents a supposedly more "civilized" group, that of First World America, which contrasts with the less affluent reservation society. Although she is in fact the stranger that comes to town, she is much more of the prototypical schoolmarm type—blonde, fragile, inexperienced, overly civilized, and in need of Cory's help (at least in the beginning—later on, she does get to demonstrate her toughness and gun fighting skills in the shootout). However, within the reservation there are Native American "townspeople" as well, like the family of the murder victim, or the sheriff, played convincingly by Graham Greene, whose prime function, however, is to illustrate that the hands of the under-staffed law enforcement are tied in the pristine world of the reservation—legitimizing the near-vigilante intervention of Cory. The "savages or outlaws," on the one hand, are ruined Native American reservation residents, living in a hell of drugs, and, on the other hand, immoral workers on an oil drilling site of a remote area within the reservation, who are not of any visible Native American ancestry. There appears to be a complex triangle of First World America (Jane), reservation community (the sheriff, for example), and reservation hinterland (the oil workers and thugs). Cory stands between all three.

Wind River contains all the gaming pieces of a classic Western, and combines them into a very straightforward plot that ties up with the formulaic Western as well. As Cawelti points out, the variety of Western plots is vast if the basic aspects of setting and complex of characters are given. According to Cawelti, a basic Western plot develops when "society stands balanced against savage wilderness" (1999: 45):

> The situation involves a hero who possesses some of the urges toward violence as well as the skills, heroism and personal honour ascribed to the wilderness way of life. It places this hero in a position where he[7] becomes involved with or committed to the agents and values of civilization. The nature of this situation, and of the conflict between town and wilderness which lies behind it imply that the formulaic pattern of action is that of chase and pursuit because it is in this pattern that the clash of savages and townspeople manifests itself. (Cawelti 1999: 45)

One story variation involving this complex of characters could be, for example, that the hero initially identifies more with the savages and gradually adapts to the townspeople (Cawelti 1999: 29). In the case of *Wind River*, this is the case to a certain degree. It is obvious that Cory sees himself as belonging to the reservation community. However, his gradual approximation to and final union with Jane reads like an adaptation to the dominant American society: an urban, sterile, First World lifestyle. Marubbio says, about Westerns that feature Native American women: "The films often position the Native American maiden as culturally and socially inferior to a refined and pure white woman whose ultimate union with the hero signifies the moral and social acceptability of this choice" (Marubbio 2006: 20). This is exactly the case in *Wind River*, where the Native American still fulfills the vanishing role. Cory, as the hero, is the white man to "take up the torch." Even the final scene does not manage to take away this feeling of a downward spiral, although Cory sits down side by side with the war-paint wearing father of the victim, Martin Hanson (Gil Birmingham), to mourn in unison the deaths of their daughters: in contrast to Martin, Cory was the active part who hunted down the rapist, and he looks forward to a silver lining on the horizon, the union with Jane. Martin, however, is left with his wife's shattered psyche.

Wind River's plot also conforms to Will Wright's definition of the "classical [Western] plot" to a certain degree, the "story of the lone stranger who rides into a troubled town and cleans it up, winning the respect of the townsfolk and the love of the schoolmarm" (Wright 1975: 32). However, even though the film qualifies as a proper Western with almost nostalgic genre conventions, it has some revisionist elements. These are its treatment of, on the one hand, women, and, on the other hand, Native Americans. Thus *Wind River* contains a kind of reversal of the principal gender roles, in that Jane is the one "riding" into the "troubled town." But although the film thus attributes some relevance to Jane, she clearly plays second fiddle to the lead Cory, as the film centers around his backstory. Jane does get some screen time where she can demonstrate her skills as an FBI agent, in particular in contrast to the supposedly streetwise police officers, but apart from this, she is little more than a foil to Cory, a plot motivation as the love interest, and the personification of a more affluent and materialist America. Comparing her to one of the earliest revisionist women roles of Western cinema, Vienna in *Johnny Guitar* (1954), it appears that there are some parallels. The female lead of the classic 1950s Western, played by Joan Crawford, "is financially independent, runs her own saloon, and is the boss of several male employees" (Peterson 1996: 11). Likewise, *Wind River*'s Jane is in a powerful operating position as principal investigator of an FBI unit. However, as Peterson argues, *Johnny Guitar*'s Vienna is "also in control of her sexual relationships, able to choose for herself which man she wants . . . rather than being chosen by them" (Peterson 1996: 11). In *Wind River*, it is Cory who makes the conscious choice to enter into a romantic relationship with Jane, as he is also the one who has to overcome the trauma of his broken marriage. Hence, although Jane is granted professional prestige and independence, as well as martial skill, she lacks the sexual self-determination of Vienna. Also, Jane lacks the autonomy as a character that *Johnny Guitar*'s Vienna boasted more than sixty years earlier:

> Despite her gender . . . Vienna is allowed to stand as a self-sufficient individualistic western hero. Vienna is certainly not a depiction of the female

as lack, nor is she entirely a castrating woman. She has phallic presence and is unable to be possessed unless she allows it. At the same time, however, this presence is a spectacle. Her male saloon employees make a point of commenting on this unusual gender behaviour. Sam says, in a nearly direct address to the camera and the viewer: "Never seen a woman who was more a man. She thinks like one, acts like one, and sometimes makes me feel like I'm not." (Peterson 1996: 15)

While *Wind River* certainly attempts to portray a comparably strong woman, the film fails by not going beyond a superficial level of staged masculinity, starting out with Jane's arrogant first appearance (soon curbed by her obvious unpreparedness for the rough Wyoming climate) and culminating in her authority and leadership skills demonstrated in the initial de-escalation with the oil site workers and, following that, her martial skill in the actual gun fight (in which she does "castrate" some of the male offenders). Nevertheless, her character retains a dependence on the male lead Cory, who drives the plot forward as the skilled (man-) hunter and troubled ex-husband and father, who is granted the privilege of settling the final score with the rapist.

Apart from this attempt at a more differentiated gender perspective, the film has a major agenda of portraying present-day Native American societies. That the perspective remains one of white America is obvious. The film is not Native American-produced, and both male and female leads are white and dominate the screen time. Although some of the thugs and more adverse characters are of European descent, Native American characters (and actors) make up most of the remaining cast, naturally, as one of the largest Indian reservations in the US serves as a setting. The film takes most of its dramatic tension from the fact that the action is set in a society probably unknown to the majority of the film's audience. In a way, this justifies the perspective of white America, and the film succeeds in portraying the world of Native American reservations only effectively because of its outside perspective, mostly devoid of pathos and moralizing.

This reservation world is one of the first images viewers receive before they get to know individual Native American characters. As Jane drives through the desolate roads of the reservation, sweat lodges built of scrap and an upside-down stars-and-stripes suggest an otherworldly and hostile environment. The disparaging looks of Natives remind of the occasional sightings, or suspicions, of "savages" along the river in heart-of-darkness-films like *Apocalypse Now* (1979) or Werner Herzog's *Aguirre* (1972). It is a dark and threatening atmosphere of rejection and hostility that cries cry out against a capitalist America.[8]

The few Native American characters introduced represent a relatively even mixture. Nevertheless, the characters are stereotyped and reaffirm the feeling that something is wrong with this place. The father of the missing young woman,

Martin, is a tall, long-haired warrior-type, who remains, or believes he has to remain, stoic in the face of his daughter's death. His wife, the victim's mother, is a hysterical "wild" woman (Miller 2013), who tries to cut open her wrists out of grief for her daughter's death, in a scene reminiscent of Stands With a Fist's suicide attempt in *Dances With Wolves*. The murdered woman's brother Chip (Martin Sensmeier) is a good-for-nothing, who spends his dreary days with characters from the bottom of the reservation society: intoxicated junkies, who, so it seems at first sight, might be connected to Natalie's death, and who remind one of the staple of the "drunken Indian whose weakness and inability to assimilate surface in his or her alcoholism" (Marubbio 2006: 4). Two Native American characters personify a pleasant relief of humaneness: Cory's ex-mother-in-law, Alice Crowheart (Tantoo Cardinal), a "spiritual earth mother" type (Marubbio 2006: 172), and the sheriff Ben Shoyo (Graham Greene).

This cast of Native American characters, incapable of acting, whether inadvertently or not, centers around the omnipotent white cowboy Cory. However, his otherness is relativized by a crucial plot detail: he once had a Native American wife, and a daughter, who fell victim to a crime very similar to the one that has just happened. It is this little backstory that breaks through his reserve and provides character motivation for him to assist Jane in solving the crime with unconventional methods at the edges of legality.

In sum, there are three to four Native American women relevant to the plot: the murder victim herself, who is dead from the beginning of the film, as is Cory's daughter. Cory's ex-mother-in-law receives little screen time, and even less the mother of the murdered Natalie, who is portrayed as little more than a madwoman in the attic. However, the viewer does get to know Natalie better in a conclusive flashback scene, which confirms the premise that she was raped, but not murdered, as the coroner decided, and which technically excluded Jane from the case. When Jane comes to the oil-drilling site, the scene cuts from the outside of a trailer to the inside and jumps to several days earlier. Matt, Natalie's boyfriend, is alone in the trailer, obviously after the work shift has ended, and, answering a knock on the trailer door, opens up to a smiling Natalie. It becomes clear for the first time that Matt is the person Natalie's brother Chip designated a "white asshole" earlier, thematizing the implied immorality of mixed-race unions in the classic Western. Natalie has made it all the way to the drilling station were Matt works, to be with him for a night—a not untypical accentuation of female sexual openness in the Celluloid/Sexualized Maiden, which is "underscored as a component of her Native heritage" (Marubbio 2006: 168). However, Natalie's visit is not an unproblematic act in an environment with exclusively male workers confined in a cramped trailer with little privacy for long time periods, and in a desolate no-man's-land. Matt's colleagues promptly return from a night of heavy drinking, and start to molest the couple, reminiscent of the outlaw gang as a staple of the classic Western. The whole scene is a prototypical premise of a Western-plot, familiar, for example, from Kenny Rogers's country song *Coward of the County*:

> One day while he was working, the Gatlin boys came calling
> They took turns at Becky (and there was three of them).
> Tommy opened up the door, and saw Becky crying.
> The torn dress, the shattered look was more than he could stand.
>
> (*Coward of the County*)

The boyfriend (up to this point, the viewer has not developed much sympathy for him) turns out to be a heroic warrior. He fights fiercely to protect his Native American girlfriend from the drunken lot, but (unlike Kenny Roger's Tommy) he succumbs to the superior number of thugs. He is beaten unconscious, as is Natalie. Pete, the most despicable member of the "gang," rapes her in this state, until Matt regains consciousness and starts another vicious attack, for which he pays with his life. However, he gives Natalie the chance to run away. With no time to put on her shoes, she runs several miles through the snow barefoot, until she collapses and dies of pulmonary haemorrhage, as Cory predicted at the start of the film. It is this fate that pulled Cory into the case, as it almost paralleled the death of his own daughter.

This is a highly interesting plot detail. It is interesting because it is banal and repeats the classic motif of the deceased Indian maiden, failing to essentially revise the treatment of Native American women in the (neo-)Western. As in *Broken Arrow*, *A Man Called Horse*, or *Jeremiah Johnson*, Cory becomes the white avenger of these deceased Native American maidens. The deaths of his part Native American daughter and Natalie legitimize his violent act of revenge.

But there is a crucial twist that spins this tale further: the fact that the FBI agent Jane, white, blonde, and civilized, eventually becomes Cory's love interest. It suggests that even though a mess is left behind on the reservation, order is restored at least on a racial level. The white leads form a union that turns its back to the problems of interracial marriage, and implies that harmony can only be found if the world of Native Americans is left aside.

In sum, *Wind River* is a typical post-9/11 Western that combines nostalgic with revisionist elements. On the revisionist side, the film achieves—or attempts— a few notable things. It is probably the first major studio production dedicated to Native American women in present-day Native American reservations. However, a closer look at the portrayal of these women in *Wind River* shows that this element is treated in a quite conventional way. In her 2006 work, Marubbio asks why Native American female roles have experienced a decline, and are

> seen mostly behind the main male figure or as an extra who creates a more realistic image of Native communities. While the early 1990s

Hollywood films pay particular attention to creating more substantial Native male characters, why does the Native woman decline in her screen presence? The revisionist attempts of the 1990s pay no real attention to the Native woman. (Marubbio 2006: 224)

In the more than ten years since the publication of Marubbio's book, this trend has hardly changed. Instead, the films that have come out since 9/11, and since the publication of Marubbio's book, "continue to rely on standard generic figures and themes: the noble/ignoble savage, the sexualized young Princess figure, and the vanishing Indian" (Marubbio 2006: 228), as this analysis of *Wind River* (2017), where "the Native American woman symbolically vanishes allowing for the culturally sanctioned union of the white heterosexual couple," has shown (Marubbio 2006: 20).[9]

John G. Cawelti's explanation of the popularity of Westerns in the 1950s, and at the same time its demarcation from the "Post-Western," which is the central theme of the "role of the gunfighter or marshal called upon to save a somewhat unwilling town from the domination of outlaws, a mythic parable which seemed increasingly to define America's perception of her role on the international scene during World War II and in the early years of the Cold War" (Cawelti 1999: 98), may account for the resurgence of very classical Western plots after 9/11 and during Bush's War on Terror (Teissl 2011: 23). However, it remains to be seen how far this trend will continue under the Trump administration. There is, in fact, an ironic twist in the distribution history of *Wind River* that is indirectly connected to the onset of Donald Trump's presidency and its socio-political atmosphere. The film, which promotes equal rights for women of an ethnic minority within the US, is a production of the Weinstein Company. With the cementation of the accusations against Harvey Weinstein, and the evolving #MeToo movement, the director, producers, and members of the cast of *Wind River* sought distance from Weinstein's production firm. The rights for DVD and online distribution were passed on to other companies, and revenues from theatrical distribution were channeled into the National Indigenous Women's Resource Center (Schröder 2018).

Notes

1. The textbook example of the Celluloid Princess is Pocahontas and her popularized union with John Smith. To German readers, the Wild West adventure stories of Karl May come to mind, who lets the omnipotent white male I-narrator of *Winnetou*, Old Shatterhand, rebut the advances of the Mescalero Apache chief's daughter Nscho-Tschi, with the argument that he currently has no plans for marriage. Only when malignant Kiowa warriors kill her in an attack does he discover that he had

something like feelings for her, and joins in a retaliation campaign against the hostile tribe with vigorous energy.
2. *The Three Burials* is set in present-day America, *The Proposition* in Australia.
3. Kevin Costner's *Dances with Wolves* would be a typical example.
4. John G. Cawelti draws a connection between Joseph Conrad's *Heart of Darkness* and the Western, a shared "ambiguous antithesis between man and jungle," and juxtaposes Conrad's work with John Ford's *The Searchers* (Cawelti 1999: 25).
5. A graveyard on the reservation also contains the alleged grave of one of the most famous Native American women in US history, Sacajawea, who accompanied Lewis and Clark on their expedition.
6. In the documentary *Reel Injun* (2009) by native filmmaker Neil Diamond, Jim Jarmusch sums up the essential Western hero image: "A John Wayne type who embodies America and its values. A tall, broad-shouldered white man. Not very clever, but doing the right thing. Chasing out the Indians, marrying the schoolmarm, and riding towards the sunset" (my translation of the German subtitles). Apart from the chasing of Indians, this stereotypical depiction fits perfectly with Cory.
7. Note the exclusively male pronoun.
8. Apart from the upside-down stars-and-stripes, I can confirm the authenticity of the portrayal of the reservation, having been so lucky as to be able to visit the Wind River reservation in the fall of 2017 and get to know some its friendly residents. I am indebted to Nico Holt and Prof. Harald Stadler for this opportunity.
9. In her reading of the science fiction Western *Cowboys & Aliens* (2011), Cynthia Miller has also observed "that even the Westerns of a new century continue to embrace the tropes of decades long since past" (2013: 86).

Filmography

3:10 to Yuma, director James Mangold, featuring Russell Crowe, Christian Bale, Ben Foster (Lionsgate, 2007).

A Man Called Horse, director Elliot Silverstein, featuring Richard Harris, Judith Anderson, Jean Gascon (National General Pictures, 1970).

Aguirre, the Wrath of God, director Werner Herzog, featuring Klaus Kinsi, Ruy Guerra, Helena Rojo (Filmverlag der Autoren, 1972).

Apocalypse Now, director Francis Ford Coppola, featuring Martin Sheen, Marlon Brando, Robert Duvall (United Artists, 1979).

Appaloosa, director Ed Harris, featuring Ed Harris, Viggo Mortensen, Renée Zellweger (New Line Cinema, 2008).

Brokeback Mountain, director Ang Lee, featuring Jake Gyllenhaal, Heath Ledger, Michelle Williams (Focus Features, 2005).

Broken Arrow, director Delmer Daves, featuring James Stewart, Jeff Chandler, Debra Paget (20th Century Fox, 1950).

Dances with Wolves, director Kevin Costner, featuring Kevin Costner, Mary McDonnell, Grahame Greene (Orion Pictures, 1990).

Hostiles, director Scott Cooper, featuring Scott Shepherd, Rosamund Pike, Ava Cooper (Entertainment Studios, 2017).

Jeremiah Johnson, director Sydney Pollack, featuring Robert Redford, Will Geer, Delle Bolton (Warner Brothers, 1972).
Johnny Guitar, director Nicholas Ray, featuring Joan Crawford, Sterling Hayden, Mercedes McCambridge (Republic Pictures, 1954).
Little Big Man, director Arthur Penn, featuring Dustin Hoffman, Faye Dunawaye, Chief Dan George (National General Pictures, 1970).
Meek's Cutoff, Kelly Reichardt, featuring Michelle Williams, Bruce Greenwood, Paul Dano (Oscilloscope Laboratories, 2010).
Open Range, director by Kevin Costner, featuring Kevin Costner, Robert Duvall, Diego Luna (Buena Vista Pictures, 2003).
Posse, director Mario Van Peebles, featuring Mario Van Peebles, Stephen Baldwin, Charles Lane (Gramercy Pictures, 1993).
Reel Injun, director Neil Diamond, featuring Adam Beach, Chris Eyre, Russell Means (Domino Film, 2009).
Seraphim Falls, director David Von Ancken, featuring Pierce Brosnan, Liam Neeson, Anjelica Huston (Samuel Goldwyn Films, 2006).
The Assassination of Jesse James by the Coward Robert Ford, director Andrew Dominik, featuring Brad Pitt, Casey Affleck, Sam Shepard (Warner Brothers, 2007).
The Missing, Ron Howard, featuring Tommy Lee Jones, Cate Blanchett, Evan Rachel Wood (Columbia Pictures, 2003).
The Proposition, director John Hillcoat, featuring Ray Winstone, Guy Pearce, Emily Watson (First Look Pictures, 2005).
The Quick and the Dead, director Sam Raimi, featuring Sharon Stone, Gene Hackman, Russell Crowe (TriStar Pictures, 1995).
The Rider, director Chloé Zhao, featuring Brady Jandreau, Moody, Tim Jandreau (Sony Pictures Classics, 2017).
The Searchers, director John Ford, featuring John Wayne, Jeffrey Hunter, Vera Miles (C. V. Whitney Pictures, 1956).
The Three Burials of Melquiades Estrada, director Tommy Lee Jones, featuring Tommy Lee Jones, Barry Pepper, Dwight Yokum (Sony Pictures Classics, 2005).
Wind River, director Taylor Sheridan, featuring Kelsey Asbille, Jeremy Renner, Julia Jones (Weinstein Company, 2017).
Woman Walks Ahead, director Susanna White, featuring Jessica Chastain, Louisa Krause, Boots Southerland (A24, 2017).

Bibliography

Bowling, Roger and Wheeler, Billy Ed (1979) *Coward of the County*, performed by Kenny Rogers (United Artists Group, record).
Cawelti, John G. (1999) *The Six-Gun Mystique Sequel*. Bowling Green, OH: Bowling Green State University Popular Press.
Marubbio, M. Elise (2006) *Killing the Indian Maiden: Images of Native American Women in Film*. Lexington, KY: University Press of Kentucky.
May, Karl (1992 [1893]) *Winnetou I*. Bamberg: Karl-May-Verlag.

Miller, Cynthia J. (2013) "'Wild' Women: Interracial Romance on the Western Frontier," in Sue Matheson (ed.), *Love in Western Film and Television*. New York: Palgrave Macmillan, pp. 71–89.

Peterson, Jennifer (1996) "The Competing Tunes of 'Johnny Guitar': Liberalism, Sexuality, Masquerade," *Cinema Journal*, 35 (3), pp. 3–18.

Schröder, Christoph (2018) "'Wind River': Kälte als Daseinsform," *Zeit Online*, 6 February <www.zeit.de/kultur/film/2018-02/wind-river-taylor-sheridan-film>.

Spindler, Robert (2008) *Recent Westerns: Deconstruction and Nostalgia in Contemporary Western Film*. Marburg: Tectum.

Teissl, Christian (2011) "Ins Dunkle Herz Amerikas: Notizen zum Western nach 9/11," *Celluloid*, February, pp. 20–3.

Wright, Will (1975) *Sixguns and Society: A Structural Study of the Western*. Berkeley, CA: University of California Press.

11. MOSTLY WHORES WITH A (VERY) FEW ANGELS: ASIAN WOMEN IN THE WESTERN

Vincent Piturro

Hollywood's West has been notorious for either under-representing people of color or leaving them out completely. One group left out, nearly completely, has been that of the Asian woman. In "Portrayals of Chinese Women's Images in Hollywood Mainstream Films—An Analysis of Four Representative Films of Different Periods," Hanying Wang notes "Hollywood's portrayal of Eastern women has not changed significantly over time" (2013: 79). Considering the prominence of Asians in the historical West—in particular the Chinese who helped to build the railroads and the huge immigration of Chinese before the Chinese Exclusion Acts began in 1882—the most striking aspects of their depiction in the Hollywood Western has either been their absence or the singular representation of Asian women as whores. Compounding this problem, film theory has also contributed to the stereotyping of Asian women. As Shoba Sharad Rajgopal points out, feminist film theory, "concerned with film as a signifying practice, as a locus of pleasure and entertainment, and as an instrument of dominant ideology, or conversely as a tool for political resistance and subversion" (2010: 143), has responded to the presence of white women in film, excluding women of color and, specifically, Asian women.

To appreciate the difficult, and sometimes conflicting historical, cultural, and filmic contexts of these representations, it is first necessary to understand the Chinese immigration to America, and then consider how this history underpins, informs, and underlies the Western's cinematic representations of Asian women. This chapter explores the representation of Asian women in

Hollywood Westerns—their presence as well as their absence—in films such as *McCabe and Mrs Miller* (1971), *Gunless* (2010), and their representations in TV iterations such as *Broken Trail* (2006). Comparing the depictions in these films with representations of women in Asian Westerns (in particular *Yojimbo* (1961) and *Sukiyaki Western Django* (2007)), this chapter also interrogates how depictions of Asian women as prostitutes in the Hollywood cinema, American television, and then Asian Westerns have changed (or not).

First, the historical basis of these cinematic representations of Asian women—the time period in question, the social realities on which those representations are based, and the cultural milieu of contemporaneous societies—calls for consideration. The historical record reveals that America has always been somewhat hostile to immigrants, and the history of Chinese immigrants, in particular, demonstrates this point. The largest immigration in American history was from 1890 to 1920, but the majority of those immigrants were from Europe. Chinese immigration to the United States started in the early to mid-1800s; this period included most of the Chinese laborers and many who worked on building the railroads that began to crisscross the country during the fertile period of the American West. Since the Chinese immigrants worked cheaply, the American workers viewed them as competition for their jobs. These economic concerns eventually reached a public breaking point in the 1880s. A combination of economics and racism spurred the United States government to pass the Chinese Exclusion Act of 1882, which prohibited Chinese immigration into the US for ten years. It was then extended for ten more years (which is why we now refer to it in the plural form—the Chinese Exclusion Acts). The Exclusion Act was the first law in the history of the United States to prevent immigration based on race. The Chinese were one of many groups to find themselves excluded from America for both economic reasons and ethnic reasons.

The Japanese have another story in the making of their way to the United States. The first Japanese came to the US around 1868. Their departures coincided with massive social changes in Japan, including the Meiji Restoration. They initially landed in Hawaii and did not make their way to the American West until later—mainly in the 1880s, after the Chinese Exclusion Act was enacted. Later, the Japanese were essentially banned from entering the US by the Immigration Act of 1924 (popularly known as the Johnson-Reed Act), the express purpose of which was "to preserve the ideal of American homogeneity." After the bombing of Pearl Harbor and the advent of the World War II, Executive Order 9066 from President Roosevelt initiated the internments that would place 120,000 Japanese-Americans in detention camps, many of whom had been born in the US, since no Japanese entered the US after 1924.

The history of Chinese and Japanese immigration to the United States, then, is not just a casual racism toward Asian peoples, but rather a systematic, institutionalized policy of racism that dates back to the mid-1800s. The Chinese were first banned from the US during the time of westward expansion in the post-Civil War era—the same time that shaped the events of the Wild West—and then the Japanese were subsequently and summarily excluded. The representations of Asians who did manage to break into Hollywood followed the lines of the institutionalized attitudes of the country. The first Asian woman to star on screen was Anna May Wong, born in Los Angeles in 1905 to second-generation Chinese-American parents. Her screen career started in the early 1920s, and she initially found favor in *The Toll of the Sea* (1922). During her long career, she was generally typecast into one of two roles: either the "butterfly," the demure, submissive Asian, or the "dragon lady," a masculinized, ruthless character who, in most instances, was a sidekick to the real (male) antagonist. These were the binary stereotypes of cinematic Asians during the era. Hanying Wang notes of Wong's dragon lady roles, "Of course she didn't originate the stereotype, but her on-screen representations of it helped make the image an unforgettable part of Western consciousness" (2013: 76). Wong herself was not satisfied playing Western stereotypes and representations, and she moved back and forth between the US and Europe in search of different and more diverse roles. In one of her many opinion pieces written during her career to trade magazines, she remarks, "Why should we [screen Chinese] always scheme, rob, kill? I got so weary of it all—the scenarist's concepts of Chinese characters" (in Wang 2013: 77). Wong's representations also perpetuated notions of exotic and hyper-sexualized Asian women, and many of her roles were cautionary tales of men falling under such spells. This recurring stereotype found lasting favor in Hollywood. Such characters were passive antagonists for (mostly white) audiences. Even though Wong was extremely popular and played many of these types of roles, she, like many other Asian actors and actresses, was routinely passed over for signature parts that would break these stereotypes. As Shoba Sharad Rajgopal notes in "*The Daughter of Fu Manchu*: The Pedagogy of Deconstructing Representation of Asian Women in Film and Fiction":

> [T]he racism of mainstream American cinema is revealed in its treatment of Asian actors as well. In the 1932 film *Shanghai Express* the great Asian American actress Anna May Wong enacts a wicked Asian vamp, but when it came to playing a good Chinese woman such as O-Lan in *The Good Earth* (1937) from Nobel Prize-winning author Pearl S. Buck's book, Wong was not permitted to play the role even though she was the most famous Asian American actress of her time. Instead it was Luise Rainier, a white woman in yellow face, with her eyelids taped back, who played the Chinese woman and won the coveted Oscar. (Rajgopal 2010: 149)

Rajgopal goes on to note that Katherine Hepburn also performed as a Chinese woman in yellow face in *Dragon Seed* (1944). Rajgopal argues that "[t]he rationale behind these bizarre decisions taken by the Hollywood moguls was not hard to understand. Miscegenation laws were still in effect all over the country, and no Asian actress could play a lead role opposite a white man. Thus Asian actresses played only negative roles, such as the evil henchmaiden to the Asian villain" (Rajgopal 2010: 149). It was not until the miscegenation laws relaxed in the 1950s and 1960s (due in part to the Korean War and the practice of American servicemen marrying Korean women), that Asian-American women could take parts where they played opposite white male partners on screen.

The next big Asian star was Nancy Kwan in *The World of Suzie Wong* (1960). This filmic adaptation of the stage play and novel concerns an American painter (William Holden) who moves to Hong Kong, hires a local prostitute (Nancy Kwan) as a model, and they eventually fall in love. The white savior narrative plays out here amid the backdrop of Hong Kong and Hollywood with a white male and an Asian woman in the leading roles. Notably *The World of Suzie Wong* not only perpetuated the same Asian stereotypes established with Ana May Wong, it also began to institutionalize them in a new era, while sexualizing them, objectifying them, and exoticizing them for mainly white audiences. Hanying Wang notes about the film:

> This big-budget Hollywood film organizes its elaborate production around the Asian Woman lead, considering her life worthy of narration, with her as both desiring subject and object of desire. The otherness, symbolized by Suzie's dress, obviously was the desire of the western characters in the film as well as the western audience outside of the film. (Wang 2013: 76)

The exotic, sexual, and submissive Asian temptress became a staple of this new era in Hollywood, and the newest of the stereotypes of Asian women. In fact, the film title became part of the lexicon for white males romantically involved with subservient Asian females. As Balaji and Worawongs note, "Hence, the 'Suzy Wong' dynamic can be seen in television advertisements, maintaining the idea of Asian exoticism and perceived assimilation through the White Male" (2010: 225). These representations have hardly abated in recent history. As the Japanese American Citizens League noted about Katy Perry's 2013 performance at the American Music Awards:

> Katy Perry's recent geisha-styled performance on the American Music Awards (AMA), broadcast nationally on ABC television, served as the latest rendition of the bad movie we've all seen before. There is a persistent strain in our culture that refuses to move beyond the stereotype of Asian women as exotic and subservient. These stereotypes have been reinforced in our popular culture through plays and movies from our distant past such as *Madame Butterfly* and *The World of Suzie Wong*. Moreover, stereotypes aren't confined to those that denigrate Asian women as depicted in more

recent characterizations that tarnished all Asians as dog-eaters by Tonight Show host, Jay Leno. (JACL 2013)

Stereotypical representations of Asian women throughout Hollywood film history continue to be found in popular culture today, but the representation of Asian women in the West is virtually non-existent in the era of the classic Western (1930s–50s). Among the later Westerns in which Asian women appear, *McCabe and Mrs Miller* (1971) tells the story of a rakish gambler (Warren Beatty as McCabe) who arrives in a Washington town circa 1902, and proceeds to use his gambling winnings to set up a brothel and bathhouse. His partner in the brothel business, Mrs Miller (Julie Christie), is a confident white Cockney whose independent characterization contrasts with that of the other women in the film. McCabe and Mrs Miller bring a new crop of prostitutes to the town, one of whom is an Asian woman. The men, in anticipation of her arrival, discuss her "exotic" nature and probe each other to determine if anyone has been with an Asian woman before, drawing on the familiar stereotype of exotic and hypersexualized Asian women. Upon arrival, the Asian prostitute seems happy and congenial in her station, and she is even shown playing and bathing together with the other women. All of these women (the Asian woman among them) appear to be content in their lives and profession. The other notable scene is of the Asian woman standing with the other prostitutes at a funeral in the town. The final representation of an Asian woman that takes place at the end of the film continues to reinforce the stereotype. Mrs Miller leaves town to escape the posse and ends up in a San Francisco opium den. As she passes out with a pipe in her hands, an Asian woman attends to her and removes the pipe. That is all we see of her. The Asian prostitute is replaced by a drug-pusher.

The TV mini-series *Broken Trail*, first aired on the AMC network in 2006, challenges the narrative of the Asian prostitute found in *McCabe and Mrs Miller*. As he began the *Broken Trail* screenplay, Alan Geoffrion was interested in telling the story of British immigrant Harry Haythornwaite, who drove a herd of 700 horses from Oregon to the Rosebud Indian Reservation in South Dakota sometime in the 1880s. But as Geoffrion researched the time period further, he then joined that story to another, true story: "the neglected chronicle of Chinese girls—thousands of them—who were brought to America throughout the 19th Century and forced into prostitution across the West" (in Holley 2006). As Laura Woodworth-Ney remarks in "Women and the Myth of the American West," while white women in the post-Civil War West gained more independence and rights, the same was not true for Asian and Native American women.

> During the post-Civil War period in the American West (1865–1910), middle-class and upper-class white women often did enjoy more flexibility and more freedom—to travel, to own land in their name, to exercise

control over their children. Minority women—particularly Chinese and Native American—did not experience greater freedoms. For these groups, the idea of an American "West" was meaningless. For Chinese women who immigrated during the late-19th century to work in the laundries, saloons, and grimy inns of mining camps scattered throughout California and the Rocky Mountain interior, the West was not west at all but rather east, and it was often not a voyage of choice. Impoverished families in China were encouraged to sell their daughters, who were shipped to San Francisco, held in "pens," and taken to mining camps. Even though slavery had been outlawed after the Civil War, the isolation of these camps—in places like Warrens, Idaho—meant that slavery existed in fact if not in law. (Woodworth-Ney 2018)

The story of an aging rancher (Robert Duvall as Prentice Ritter) and his nephew (Thomas Hayden Church as Tom Hart) transporting 500 horses from Oregon to Wyoming, *Broken Trail* takes place in 1898. In the striking opening sequence, another Westerner (a henchman employed by a whorehouse madam) is shown buying young Chinese girls in San Francisco whom he will transport to a Montana mining town where they will serve as prostitutes. The two different groups cross paths on their way East, and the cowboys kill the henchman and take the girls. A posse hired by the madam then hunts the girls and the cowboys. As Joe Holley notes in "Hitch Your Wagon," Geoffrion was moved by several stories he read about Chinese girls being abused in this era: "From his reading, Geoffrion discovered that the young women had been ripped from their families in China and lived an average of five years in

Figure 11.1 Thomas Hayden Church and Gwendoline Yeo in *Broken Trails*.

America before succumbing to suicide, violence, or disease." Geoffrion found a true account of a Chinese woman who married a Wyoming rancher and then merged the two stories into one, bringing the saga of the Chinese girls to the forefront. The scene of an American male buying young Chinese girls to serve as sex slaves is the opening sequence of the show, taken directly from an unfortunate history. As Jacquie Rogers notes in "Tragic Tales: Chinese Slave Girls of the Barbary Coast," "[i]n China girls weren't valued, and many girls, even babies, were sold to 'entrepreneurs' who took them to America to be used as sex slaves. In San Francisco, girls were bought and sold—a baby sold for a little over $100. These girls were raised to prostitute themselves."

After the opening sequence of the girls being sold into slavery, *Broken Trail* takes its viewer into classic Western territory: there are shots of cowboys wrangling horses, cattle herding and branding, sweeping Western vistas teeming with livestock, and other images of a busy working ranch. When the old cowboy rides in with news of Tom's mother's death, Prentice convinces Tom go back to Wyoming with him after buying the horses for transport. They will start a family business. The juxtaposition of these opening sequences in *Broken Trails* is strikingly reminiscent of Charlie Chaplin's opening sequence in *Modern Times*. In Chaplin, the viewer is offered a simple dialectical montage: a shot of cramped factory workers barreling up the stairs to work is juxtaposed with a shot of crowded sheep being corralled. The conclusion here is clear: the people are being treated like sheep. The same montage opens *Broken Trail*: the juxtaposition of the girls being bought by the whorehouse henchman colliding with the shots of the cattle being branded also creates a clear statement: the women are being treated like cattle. They are a simple commodity.

The setting in *Broken Trail* is also important and telling: the story starts in San Francisco, and moves to a ranch in Oregon. Then the respective parties make their way to Wyoming, a path that takes them across the Northwest, reversing the journey from East to West that is taken by most Westerns, and aligning the cowboys traveling East with more civilized Eastern values and not the brutal, lawlessness of the West. Richard Slotkin's famous theory of how the Western participates in the idea of a "regeneration through violence" is important here. Slotkin's theory plays out in many classic Westerns as the Frontier is cleared for expansion (1973: 3). The classic of classic Westerns, *Stagecoach*, clearly illuminates the process: the small group on the stagecoach must fight off Geronimo and his men so that the genteel Eastern woman and her baby are saved, along with the other travelers. The violence of the fight leads to a more open and safer West—one where the Eastern values can thrive and live "peacefully." In *Broken Trails*, before the men take the girls, they must first murder the madam's henchman. Later, the men must also fight the posse to keep the girls away from the madam. Both instances force the men into violence before the women are "saved"—a regeneration through violence. But the men also show compassion, restraint, and remorse, speaking to their journey eastward and away from the cycle of violence that so plagued the westward expansion. Even while reversing the physical course of the classical Westerns, they must still revert to the regenerative violence to restore order; the difference here is that the "order" is not clearing the way for a western expansion of whites, but rather the de-commodification of human beings (in the case the Chinese girls who had been sold as cattle).

The girls also change during the journey—moving from despair and resignation to steely resolve and strength. Midway through the journey, one of the girls, so distraught at the whole endeavor, kills herself by jumping in front of stampeding horses. And when several of the girls wish to stay with Prentice and Tom because they felt safe, another girl retorts that "There is nowhere in this land where we are safe." Yet the remaining girls do find their voices and engage the men on different levels, giving them a humanity and individuality that is missing from any other representation. The eldest of the girls, their unofficial leader, begins to learn English and communicate with Tom. Prentice teaches them to ride the horses in one of the lighter moments of the show. In the end, one of the girls stays with Tom, and the remainder are taken back to San Francisco (where who knows what fate waits for them). Before the credits roll, the audience is finally told, that the couple stayed in the West, started a family, and the descendants of that family still remain in Wyoming. There was a happy ending for some, at least.

A Canadian Western spoof that tells the story of an American gunslinger (the Montana Kid) in a small town in Western Canada, *Gunless* (2010), offers another representation of Asian females not seen in Hollywood Westerns. As he makes his way through the town for the first time, "Mr Montana Kid" (as the locals call him) encounters an Asian family curiously watching him. When he meets the young Asian girl in the group, he asks her, "*Do you speakee English?*" She responds in perfect English. Later, as a group of Chinese railworkers land in the town, the young girl tells the Montana Kid what the men are doing there. She even mocks him, using the stereotypical slur from earlier in the film, a common refrain from Americans of a certain period: "*They no speakee Engwish*," she tells the gunslinger. The Asian family owns a laundry and a kitchen, like many Chinese immigrants of the era. The family doesn't speak English, save for the little girl, so she speaks on the behalf of the family. The father even takes English lessons in the local school, although his parroting of singular words comes out as stereotypical and is used for comic effect. The respresentations go beyond spoof, however: they highlight the racism inherent in the Western and the limited range of those representations. Further, the fact that the Westernized member of the family is a female is significant, in that it marks a generational change: the next generation of Asians will integrate into this society and become more prominent. Notably, there are no Asian prostitutes in the film.

Yet another episode from *Gunless* finds an Asian family camping in the wilderness far from any town. A posse approaches and asks if anyone has seen the Montana Kid, and it is only the women who can speak perfect English as they answer. Again, the Asian women seem to be the most intelligent and best communicators of the group. Yet we also see the clan as marginalized; they are living far from town, they are isolated, and there is no sense that they can be integrated into the community. The women, and their ability to communicate, keep them connected to the world. Unlike *McCabe and Mrs Miller*, the Asian women are given a voice in this film, and they also portend a bright future.

To a certain extent, the same is true of representations of women in Japanese Westerns. In Akira Kurasowa's Samurai Western *Yojimbo* (1961) set in 1860 Japan, the shogun warriors have been released from service and no longer serve a master. Mirroring the classic Western story of the Civil War soldier who makes his way to the West after the war, the *ronin* Saguro wanders into a small town with two warring factions.[1] Saguro plays both sides against one another to improve his station. An allegory about blind capitalism and the state of Japan in the post-World War II era, *Yojimbo* also comments on the roles of women. There are three different types of women: the group who is "bought" by one of the local factions and serve at the pleasure of the men; women like Nui, who was taken away from a farmer and who now "belongs" to the son of one of the faction leaders; and the families' matriarchs or matrons like Orin, who pull the strings behind the scenes but is not the public face of the group. In all of these representations, women are viewed in terms of their economic use-value. There are shades of the Hollywood Western in the first two of these representations: the group of women bought for the pleasure of the men parallels representations of brothel-kept women in the Western and the group of Chinese girls bought and sold into sex slavery in *Broken Trail*. Consider the brothels in *Mc Cabe and Mrs Miller* (the women bought and sold as mere commodity, including Asian women) or the brothel in *Unforgiven* (1992). In *Broken Trail*, we get to see the entire commodifying process, rather than just the end result in the brothel. In *Yojimbo*, the woman who is essentially stolen from the farmer and held captive accords with the Western's representations of whores in that the woman is bought and sold at the whim of the male. She is also eventually saved by Sanjuro and returned to her husband and son, a male savior narrative that is also typical in the Western and Hollywood in general (including *Broken Trail*).

The wife/mother character of Orin is a slightly different representation. As a matriarch, Orin is in a position of power. She obviously holds sway over the men in certain respects. She schemes to betray Sanjuro, and she even meets with him with hopes of turning him into an ally. As one of the leaders of the group, she has clear agency: as the other men in the group flounder in how to deal with Sanjuro, Orin directs the boys and sets the terms of the negotiatons, even warning her son that he must be stronger and more ruthless (qualities she obviously has!) should he wish to be the family heir. We can certainly categorize her as the

Dragon-lady type in contemporaneous Hollywood films, but she is not entirely subservient to the males. Operating at the top of the food chain, Orin is refreshingly disdainful and powerful for a female character.

Finally, Takashi Miike's *Sukiyaki Western Django* (2007) is an English-language Japanese Western that pays homage to both classic Westerns and Spaghetti Westerns. This postmodern pastiche of styles and genres also shades into parody at times, so some of the representations and characterizations need to be viewed through that lens. The story is familiar: a lone gunslinger rides into a town with two warring factions, the *Heike* (or the Reds) and the *Genji* (or the Whites). The gunslinger then attempts to rescue a woman thrust into prostitution in hopes of saving her son (after her husband is killed by the *Heike*). Gunfights and gruesome killing ensue. Obviously, the story takes from various genres and Miike gives it his own bloody, horror-film touch (Miike also helmed such horror classics as *Ichi the Killer* and *Audition*). The only two women of note in the film are the mother/prostitute Shizuka and her mother-in-law, Ruriko. Ruriko is a figure drawn directly from *Yojimbo* and *A Fistful of Dollars*. She operates in a liminal space much like Orin in *Yojimbo* or Consuelo Baxter in *A Fistful of Dollars*—she offers strong advice, intercedes in squabbles, and directs the men from the sidelines at the start. We first meet her as she saves the gunslinger by interceding and taking him out of harm. Her character then turns into something else entirely.

Shizuka is also a combination of the angel/whore trope from the Hollywood Western. She starts out as an angel: she arrives in town, pregnant, with her husband—a *Heike* man named Akira. She is a *Genji*, so their son, as one character calls him, is a "half-breed." Akira and Shizuka wish to get past the simplistic *Genji/Heike* feud and (naively, certainly) see their marriage and son to be healing symbols or even talismans. But they are wrong, and Akira is shot dead by the *Heike* in front of both Shizuka and their son. The *Heike* man then drags Shizuka through the mud (literally), attempting to rape her, but she gets away. She escapes to the *Genji* where she is raped by the leader, but she is able to make a deal with them. At once an angel and a whore, she is the *Genji*'s prostitute as long as her son is kept safe. Ultimately, Shizuka is killed when she tries to escape the town with her mother and son.

Her mother Ruriko is another interesting study. When she enters the film, she is a neutral character in the town—taking care of the boy, swigging whiskey, and saving the gunslinger from an initial fight. She gives the gunslinger the film's entire backstory and seems to act as a conscience for the town. But later, as she, Shizuka, and the boy are escaping from the town, she leaps into action, revealing herself as the legendary gunslinger "Bloody Benten" (about whom rumors abounded). She dispatches men with ease, saving both the boy and the gunslinger (although she is unable to save Shizuka). Her character develops agency, action, and formidable skill that is usually the domain of the male characters. While she differs from Orin in *Yojimbo* in terms of her action, she stands apart as a character who is allowed a voice, independence, and the ability to act out as fiercely as the men.

What is clear from these representations of Asian women throughout the history of film is that their absence is just as telling as their presence. Their absence in early Hollywood Westerns, through the classic Westerns and, even into the revisionist Westerns of the late 1950s, 1960s, and 1970s, speak not only to their actual absence during the historical time period in which the stories were made (post-Civil War) but also to the innate racist tendencies among the population, the specific legislation throughout American history, the denial of venal and abusive practices in the Wild West, and the social practices that surrounded American society throughout the late nineteenth century and well into the twentieth. Even when the women become present on screen (whether it be in American Westerns or Japanese Westerns), their representations leave much to be desired—falling into tired stereotypes with long filmic histories, bereft of independence of agency, or when they are allowed such qualities, it usually does not end well for them. There is validity in the argument that the same can be said for *all women* in the history of cinema, but the Asian women occupy an interesting space because they were completely absent for so long, and then showed up in such regressive representations that even film theorists ignored them. They are mostly portrayed, as shown, as prostitutes. The most positive representations of the woman who lived out a (seemingly) happy life on a Wyoming farm (after being sold into sex slavery before being saved by a white male) and the young girl in a small Western Canadian town augur hope for a more vibrant on-screen future for Asian women. Perhaps the fate of Asian women in the Western may follow along the more positive and progressive path of more recent Westerns in general—as seen in such films as *The Ballad of Little Jo* or *Brokeback Mountain*. Yet one question this study raises is what was the actual role of Asian women in westward expansion? Is it as limited as we see in the representatons above? Or are there other, as yet unrecovered, stories that might depict a more diverse reality?

Note

1. This was the film/narrative that Sergio Leone famously copied, without obtaining the rights, in *A Fistful of Dollars*.

Filmography

A Fistful of Dollars, director Sergio Leone, featuring Clint Eastwood, Gian Maria Volontè, Marianne Koch (Jolly Film, 1964).

Audition, director Takashi Miike, featuring Ryo Ishibashi, Eihi Shiinia, Tetsu Sewaki (Basara Pictures, 1999).

Brokeback Mountain, director Ang Lee, featuring Jake Gyllenhaal, Heath Ledger, Michelle Williams (Focus Features, 2005).
Broken Trail, director Walter Hill, featuring Robert Duvall, Thomas Haden Church, Greta Scacchi (American Movie Classics, 2006).
Dragon Seed, directors Harold S. Bucquet and Jack Conway, featuring Katherine Hepburn, Walter Huston, Aline MacMahon (MGM, 1944).
Gunless, director William Phillips, featuring Paul Gross, Sienna Guillory, Dustin Milligan (Alliance, 2006).
Ichi the Killer, director Takashi Miike, featuring Tadanobu Asano, Nao Omori, Shin'ya Tsukamoto (Omega Project, 2001).
McCabe and Mrs Miller, director Robert Altman, featuring Warren Beatty, Julie Christie, Rene Auberjonois (Warner Brothers, 1971).
Stagecoach, director John Ford, featuring John Wayne, Claire Trevor, Andy Devine (Walter Wanger Productions, 1939).
Sukiyaki Western Django, director Takashi Miike, featuring Hideaki Itô, Kôichi Satô, Quentin Tarantino (A-Team and Dentsu, 2007).
The Ballad of Little Jo, director Maggie Greenwald, featuring Suzy Amis, Bo Hopkins, Ian McKellen, (Joco and PolyGram Filmed Entertainment, 1993).
The Toll of the Sea, director Chester M. Franklin, featuring Anna May Wong, Kenneth Harlan, Beatrice Bentley (Technicolor Motion Picture Corp., 1922).
The World of Suzie Wong, director Richard Quine, featuring William Holden, Nancy Kwan, Sylvia Syms (World Enterprises, 1922).
Unforgiven, director Clint Eastwood, featuring Clint Eastwood, Gene Hackman, Morgan Freeman (Warner Bros., 1992).
Yojimbo, director Akira Kurasowa, featuring Tshirô Mifune, Eijirô Tôno, Tatsuya Nakadi (Kurasowa Production Co., and Toho Pictures, 1955).

Bibliography

Balaji, Murali and Worawongs, Tina (2010 [2018]) "The New Suzie Wong: Normative Assumptions of White Male and Asian Female Relationships," *Communication, Culture & Critique*, 3 (2) <https://onlinelibrary.wiley.com/doi/full/10.1111/j.1753-9137.2010.01068.x> (last accessed 11 August 2018).

Holley, Joe (2006), "Hitch Your Wagon," *Washington Post*, 22 June <https://www.washingtonpost.com/archive/lifestyle/2006/06/22/hitch-your-wagon-span-class-bankheada-would-be-writers-dream-came-true-with-the-help-of-star-robert-duvallspan/30edeed2-5721-4848-aded-bd5c0be83a42/?utm_term=.4934e963a229> (last accessed 11 August 2018).

Rajgopal, Shoba Sharad (2010) "*The Daughter of Fu Manchu*: The Pedagogy of Deconstructing Representation of Asian Women in Film and Fiction," *Meridians*, 10 (2), pp. 141–62.

Rogers, Jacquie (2018) "Tragic Tales: Chinese Slave Girls of the Barbary Coast," *Unusual Historicals* <http://unusualhistoricals.blogspot.com/2010/08/tragic-tales-chinese-slave-girls-of.html> (last accessed 21 August 2018).

Slotkin, Richard (1973) *Regeneration through Violence*. Middletown, CT: Wesleyan University Press.
"Statement on Katy Perry AMA Performance" (2013) Japanese American Citizens League, 27 November <https://jacl.org/jacl-statement-on-katy-perry-performance/> (last accessed 15 August 2018). Cited parenthetically as JACL (2013).
Wang, Hanying (2013) "Portrayals of Chinese Women's Images in Hollywood Mainstream Films—An Analysis of Four Representative Films of Different Periods," *China Media Research*, 9 (1), pp. 75–9.

12. "WE BEEN HAUNTED A LONG TIME"—RAPED WOMEN IN WESTERNS

Maria Cecília de Miranda N. Coelho

In her introduction to *Reading Rape: The Rhetoric of Sexual Violence in American Literature and Culture*, Sabine Sielke defines the representation of rape as a rhetorical device while tracing the evolution of what is a specifically an American rhetoric regarding sexual violence (2002: 1–2). Transposed into discourse (and into images in the case of Diane Wolfthal's focus in *Reading Rape: The Rhetoric of Sexual Violence in American Literature and Culture* on the *heroization* of rape in mythological narratives), rape is often metaphorical, "an insistent figure for the social, political and economic concerns and conflicts" (Sielke 2002: 2). Speaking of representations of rape in *Rape-Revenge Films: A Critical Study*, Alexandra Heller-Nicholas concurs with Wolfthal's observation that "rape imagery shows a broad range in tone and meaning" (2011: 5). Pointing to historically entrenched, artistic representations of rape, she also remarks that the "heroic" tradition of rape imagery stems from Renaissance artworks in which rapes performed by Roman and Greek heroes and gods indicate power (2011: 5–6). The pervasiveness of this tradition, Heller-Nicolas notes, should be attributed to images of rape being used as a narrative device to address issues other than those of sexual violence, for example those of political, sexual, ethnic, class, or gender differences.

As Henry N. Smith's title of his study, *The Virgin Land: The American West as Symbol and Myth* indicates,[1] the metaphor of land (and property) as a caste woman to be possessed acts as a powerful literary convention, expressing the nature of westering in nineteenth-century writings as different as Walt

Whitman's *Leaves of Grass*, Frederick Jackson Turner's *The Frontier in American History*, and the popular tales of the Dime Novel. A familiar leitmotif of the "heroic" tradition in the American West, rape (or the attempt to rape) in the Western, shown (explicitly), indicated, or reported by women and men, is part of a cinematic tradition modeled on epic and tragic patterns. This chapter explores how the "heroic" tradition of rape underpins the rape-triggering plots and representations of rape in *Sergeant Rutledge* (Ford, 1960), *Duel in the Sun* (Vidor, 1946), *The Searchers* (Ford, 1956), *Man of West* (Mann, 1958), *The Bravados* (King, 1958), *For a Few Dollars More* (Leone, 1965), *Hang 'em High* (Post, 1968), *Cemetery Without Crosses* (Hossein, 1969), and *The Ballad of Little Jo* (Greenwald, 1993).

On screen, Shakespearean tragedy acts as a touchstone for these patterns illustrating: (a) the choices a director makes and the concerns he/she has while displaying rape by images, gestures, signs, and discourse; (b) the values (implicit) in actions of the avenger; and (c) the intertextuality of the tradition (literally and imagetic) in a chain of reception. A complicated and conflicted trope, rape, transmitted as a matter of (dis)honor, is readily recognizable in Julie Taymor's *Titus* (1999), her adaptation of Shakespeare's *Titus Andronicus* to cinema. Her choice of the film's dissonant soundtrack in a rape scene, made with Elliot Goldenthal, aligns with the horror of the defloration perpetrated by the two sons of Tamora (Jessica Lange), the queen of the Goths which follows the pattern of the myth of Philomela.[2] In *Titus*, the rape is not shown the moment it occurs. It is indicated when Tamora's sons cut the black dress of Titus's daughter, Lavinia (Laura Frazer), after her future husband is killed and while she is pleading with the queen to pity her. Lavinia's uncle finds his niece with tree branches instead of hands and a red strip, representing blood, coming from her mouth. She is shown on a tree stump, wearing only a white slip, and the first sight of her shocks the viewer as it does her uncle. Later, the rape carries with it a double reference: reading Ovid's *Metamorphoses*, Lavinia recognizes the pattern her rapists followed, and after she shows the illustration to her relatives with a stick in her mouth (a very phallic image). With her arms holding the stick, she writes in the sand the names of Tamora's sons. While she is writing, images of her rape come to her mind, so the spectator sees (in fast motion) what happened via her "experience." After her male relatives know who attacked her, they plan their revenge. Tamora will be murdered after being informed that she has eaten the flesh of her sons in a dinner prepared by Titus. Lavinia will also die at the hands of Titus, with the approval of the Emperor, who affirms that a girl who was raped should be killed by her father to regain her/his honor (*Titus Andronicus*, V, iii, quoted in the film).[3] Following this (literary) pattern, Titus kills Lavinia (dressed in white with a veil covering her face) by breaking her neck.

As Phillip Loy points out, "with the development of the rating system and society's willingness to confront the severity of sex crimes, [W]esterns were willingly to treat the issue [of sexual assault] openly," and "[m]ore frequently after 1955, women were portrayed as victims of unwanted sexual advances and rape" (2014: 277, 276). Combining racism and rape, *Sergeant Rutledge* gives special visibility to the representation of rape and calls for a (re)consideration of the work of John Ford, a director so representative of the Western.[4] Filmed in the iconic landscape of Monument Valley (Utah), the film presents the court martial in 1881 of a black US Cavalry seargent, Braxton Rutledge (Woody Strode), accused of the rape and murder of a white girl, Lucy Dabney (Toby Michaels), whose father, Major Dabney, was also killed. Rutledge is defended from these charges by his troop officer, Lt Tom Cantrell (Jeffrey Hunter). Structured in flashbacks, the film conducts us through the testimonies of men and women. The prosecution's accusation is aggravated by Rutledge's desertion after the death of his commanding officer. However, the fact that he voluntarily returns to his troop to warn of an attack by Native Americans and his protection of a white woman, Mary (Constance Towers), speak in his favor. While Cantrell and Braxton (handcuffed) ride back to the fort, the former remarks: "What if you did get away? Why, this thing would haunt you until you couldn't stand it." Targeting the theme of Civil Rights explicitly addressed in the film, Braxton answers incisively: "You forget, sir. We been haunted a long time. Too much to worry. Yeah, it was all right for Mr Lincoln to say we were free. But that ain't so! Not yet! Maybe some day, but not yet!"

In the end, the white military court, with their racist innuendos—and also the spectators of the judgment and of the film—have to face the fact that the rape was perpetrated by the sutler Chandler Hubble (Fred Libby), an old man who confesses his (pathological) attraction to the young Lucy. The element that triggers his self-accusation is the gold cross that Lucy received years earlier from her father, sold to him by Chandler, and left in the pocket of his hunting jacket (stolen by a native whose body Cantrell had found). Lucy first appears dressed in pants, on a horse, at Chandler's store. Criticized by Mrs Fosgate for riding astride, Lucy answers in a sweet but disruptive manner: "Papa says as long as I say my prayers and behave myself with the young lieutenants, he doesn't care if I ride like Lady Godiva." However, Lucy's reply (and behavior) is less disturbing to her neighbors than her friendship with the black Sergeant. Mrs Fosgate's (and her friend Mrs Hackett's), Chandler's and his son's expressions when she leaves the store in the company of her old friend Braxton not only indicate their disapproval, but also the difficulties that Cantrell will have defending the accused in that community. The next image of Lucy is of her body, seen by Cantrell, after he discovered the Major's corpse. The camera first shows his startled eyes, and then Lucy's bare legs, which are covered by the doctor with a colored, native-patterned blanket. The doctor says she was strangled and raped. Her scarred neck is explained by Cantrell after he sees in a picture Lucy wearing the gold cross. Ripped off, the necklace is missing. The doctor argues that her body was probably covered and the cross taken, so the murderer could hide (even from himself) the shameful act. In spite of the film's happy ending –Cantrell kisses his fiancée and Rutledge is reintegrated into his troupe—Chandler's outburst in court and his subsequent confession which closes the case remain disturbing, because the wrongdoer is a respected citizen. A similar situation occurs in *The Bravados* (1958), the focus of which is a misleading perception that condemns and kills the innocents. In *The Bravados*, Jim Douglass's (Gregory Peck) wife is not raped and killed by a group of outlaws, as the spectator is led to think, but by a neighbor, John Butler (Gene Evans), who also steals Douglass's money. The victim's picture (in a cameo pocket watch) also plays an important role, but *The Bravados* does not address issues of racism and pathological sexual desire as *Sergeant Rutledge* does.

In *Duel in the Sun*, Pearl Chavez (Jennifer Jones) cannot escape her family history and is portrayed as a seductress. She goes to live with her distant relatives after her father is sentenced to death for killing his wife and her lover. There she is not respected. The father (Lionel Barrymore) calls her a half-breed. Caught between two brothers, the gentle and gentlemanly Jesse (Joseph Cotten) and the rude and lecherous Lewt (Gregory Peck), she is unable to control her temper (and sexuality). Even though she tries to follow the advice of her stepmother (Lillian Gish), she succumbs to Lewt's advances. Ashamed of her desire, Pearl later shows regret, when she realizes that Lewt did not intend to marry her. In part, her fall is also attributed to Eve's curse by the preacher, who is brought to support her to avoid temptation. In this (almost comic) scene, she is covered by a blanket sporting native patterns, parts of her naked body are shown as claims like this are made: "Under that heathen blanket, there's a full-blossomed woman built by the devil to drive men crazy."

Pearl's diabolic, innately lewd trait, which Lewt also shares, conflates sexuality and desire in the couple's tragedy. Lewt enters Pearl's room as she is crouched, moving her body while cleaning the floor. Looking at him with fear and desire, Pearl blurs the line between her rape and her seduction. Indeed, the tragic history of hybristic passion in this film also suggests that Pearl's rape is only a corollary of her own burning sexuality, which is also attributed to her half-breed nature and to her mother's adultery, something that the film's final message seems to condemn and repress in order to create the reconstruction of an "honorable" family. Having shot his own brother, Lewt becomes a wanted man, a menace to his own blood. Pitying Jesse, Pearl decides to kill Lewt in a moment of reparation. Their famous duel looks like a dance of death between damned lovers. In part, Pearl is redeemed by her desire to help Jesse and his kind wife reconstruct their honor. Because of this poignant heroic scenario, enhanced by a touching soundtrack and lovers dying embracing one another, the rape scene pales in significance.

Complicated and conflicted, representations of rape are also used to drive film narratives. The implied rape of Debbie (Natalie Wood in *The Searchers*) is a well-known case in point. In a review of Glenn Frankel's *The Searchers: The Making of an American Legend*,[5] James Hoberman remarks that this "psychological epic,"[6] announced by Ford, is "steeped in pathology—not just the director's, but ours. No American movie has ever so directly addressed the psychosexual underpinnings of racism or advanced a protagonist so consumed by race hatred" (Hoberman 2013: 17). But what, as Sielke says, is rape as a rhetorical device to talk about? In Taymor's *Titus*, Philomena and Lavinia have silence imposed on them. In *The Searchers*, silence is also the means by which characters cope with the horror felt in the place of another, who is silenced by death. One of the more touching and meaningful scenes illustrating the trauma that follows rape is contained in the brief dialogue that takes place between Ethan (John Wayne) and Brad (Harry Carey Jr), when they are searching for the sisters, Debbie and Lucy (Pippa Scot), who have been abducted by Comanche. The dialogue between the mature and downcast Ethan and the broken young man who is searching for his sweetheart is meta-referential. Following the scene in which Brad tells he had seen Lucy, and wants to go to get her, Brad is stopped by Ethan, who says: "What you saw was a buck wearin' Lucy's dress. I found Lucy back in the canyon. Wrapped her in my coat [a confederate coat caressed tenderly by Martha], buried her with my own hands. I thought it best to keep it from ya." Shocked, Brad shows the impossibility of naming such a terrible thing. "Did they . . . ? Was she . . . ?" The lack of words is followed by the impossibility of describing the rape, as Ethan snarls, "What do you want me to do? Draw you a picture? Spell it out? Don't ever ask me! Long as you live, don't ever ask me more."

Here it is important to note that Ethan sees (off-screen) the body of his beloved sister-in-law Martha (Dorothy Jordan) and finds Debbie's blanket and doll, nearby the grave of his mother, who was also killed by the Comanche. These absences of the grandmother and granddaughter empower one another. Similarly, after discovering Lucy's body, Ethan encounters a group of women refugees,[7] who are mentally unbalanced. Ethan's comment—"They ain't white, not anymore"—and his face half hidden in darkness reveal his hatred of Native Americans is generated by the way they corrupt and destroy women. Later, this hatred is emphasized when he declares his intent to kill his niece, explaining to an enraged Martin that Debbie should be considered dead: "Livin' with Comanches ain't being alive." However, as we know, he changes his mind. Scalping Scar, the Comanche chief, off screen seems to give Ethan the catharsis he has been seeking, and Debbie is tenderly nestled in his arms at the end of the film.

As in *The Searchers*, tragic patterns underlie the representation of rape in *Man of the West*. This Western features Link Jones (Gary Cooper) facing his former life as a criminal, when he encounters a gang of outlaws led by his "uncle" Dock Tobin (Lee J. Cobb). Jones leaves his wife and child to travel to hire a schoolteacher for his new town, Good Hope. Carrying the savings of his fellow citizens, he is shown to be reliable, but like so many Western heroes he has a past. On the trail, he meets Billie Ellis (Julie London), a saloon singer, on a train. Elegant and discreet, she expresses her solitude and dissatisfaction, complaining to him that men "all think they have a right to put their hands on me." When Jones and Ellis are captured by the outlaws, Jones presents her as his woman, but this is not enough for the group to respect him (and her), even when they are trying to get his cooperation to rob a bank in Lasso.

Interviewed, Mann said that he wanted to change the script and make Ellis Link's wife: "Just *imagine* if the *wife* had to do what she has to do [. . .] Sure, if it had been his wife he was getting even for, it would have been terrifying! It would have been a great film. It was almost, but it could have had that difference. There was this evil, and a man trying to destroy his own evil" (Wicking and Pattinson, 1969: 51). Here, Mann is referring to the scene in which Billie is forced by one of the outlaws, Coaley (Jack London), to strip, while the others watch. Holding a knife to Jones's throat, he screams: "Now undress. Start with the shoes. Do you want to see me cut him? Heh? Ha-ha! The stockings . . . Get up. That shirt thing, now, peel it off . . . I don't have to tell you what's next, do I? Come on. Come on!" Tobin waits until Billie is almost undressed before stopping the performance (and Jones's humiliation) and sending the couple to sleep in the barn.[8] Later, Jones's repressed fury is evident when he takes revenge on Coaley in a fight during which he strips him. In spite of his rage, Jones does not intend to kill Coaley, even while beating and stripping him, as he shouts, "How does it feel?!" Jones, however, does intend to kill Dock after the old man rapes Billie. The rape is reported briefly, as Link sees Billie's half-naked back. The camera then shows Jones's and Ellis's faces, as she lies devastated in a wagon. It is the actual rape that makes Link, outraged, chase and kill his (incestuous) uncle. Significantly, critics have emphasized the complexity of both characters and posed a difficult question to answer—"Who is the Man of the West?"[9]—but they have not questioned the woman's role in this film. She is the element that triggers the desire for revenge and creates the psychological landscape in which the men fight for honor, property (Jones's money), and even redemption.

This psychological landscape is also apparent in *The Bravados*, in which the four men who are believed to have raped and killed Jim Douglass's wife (whom we know only by her image, with a baby, in his cameo pocket watch) are innocent. Three of them die as Douglass avenges his wife's death. This film also houses a second rape, of a girl, Emma (Kathleen Gallant), who was taken as a hostage when the gang escaped from the city where they were imprisoned and condemned to be hung for other murders. While Emma is being raped, inside Jim's neighbor cabin, we listen to her screaming, but we do not see her. The members of the posse, Jim and Josefa (Joan Collins), a former sweetheart of Jim, arrive after the rape. The camera, from outside the cabin, shows the men—Emma's father and groom—looking for her, all of them injured and ashamed. The focus, however, occurs in the reaction of Josefa, the first person to see Emma. Before this rape, Josefa asked Jim to stop his manhunt, because the men may have been innocent. After seeing Emma, she runs to Jim and asks him to kill them. Her request endorses Jim's previous and later actions. Emma's rape minimizes Douglass's guilt about killing innocent men and fuels and justifies his acts of revenge. There are no further scenes with Emma, who is discharged from the plot.[10]

Also about a manhunt, *For a Few Dollars More* (1965) offers a *heroicized* representation of rape. In spite of their differences, two bounty hunters, Colonel Douglas Mortimer (Lee van Cleef) and Monco (Clint Eastwood) work together to capture a psychopathic villain, Indio (Gian Marie Volonté) who has escaped from jail. Like Mortimer, Indio carries a musical pocket watch, a trophy which belonged to a woman (Rosemary Dexter), who killed herself after he entered her bedroom, shot her husband, and raped her. In a very poignant scene, she uses Indio's gun to kill herself. Shown from above in a beautiful close-up shot, her eyes are wide open in death, and her face is *heroiciced*. During the film's final showdown, Mortimer recovers the woman's pocket watch and responds to Monco's comment that he bears a family resemblance to the picture of the woman that it contains—"Naturally, between brother and sister." Unlike Monco who calculates how much he will earn with the corpses they kill, Mortimer's reward is his family's honor. His sister, whose name is not given, follows the familial precedent set by Lavinia/Titus. Shown heroic in death, hers is an honorable suicide, and her brother's revenge empowers her memory.

To understand this pattern of heroism and empowerment, it is necessary to consider two other Westerns, Charles M. Warren's *Trooper Hook* (1957) and Robert Mulligan's *The Stalking Moon* (1968). Both consider white women captives who bear half-breed children and return to the civilization. In *Trooper Hook*, Cora (Barbara Stanwyck), traveling to meet her husband, is raped and has a boy with an Apache chief. Returning home, she is well received, but her son is not. After her ruthless husband's death, she accepts Sgt Clovis Hook's (John McCrea) proposal of marriage. The happy ending of a complex problem—the assimilation of the half-breed child (whose condition is similar to Martin Pawley's in *The Searchers*)—does not, however, hide the difficult condition of women who have been "defiled."[11] Earlier, the commanding officer's wife showed sympathy for Cora and asked her husband to see himself in Cora's place, but he said he could not imagine this, because he thinks his wife would "kill herself before she let that happen to her." That "a woman should kill herself before she permits an Indian male to have sexual intercourse with her" (Loy, 2014: 278) is clearly demonstrated by Sarah (Eva Marie Saint) in *The Stalking Moon*. When Sam (Gregory Peck) shows a romantic feeling for Sara, a rescued woman who had a child with Salvaje (Nathaniel Narciso), an Apache chief, she is ashamed. Tellingly, she says: "I didn't have the courage to die." As Prat points out, Sarah's redemption and reintegration into white society while resisting a second attack by Salvage, leaves her "beaten but not ruined," and demonstrates how "the hero remythifies the fallen woman" (2012: 40–6).

In Budd Boethicher's *Comanche Station* (1960), Cody (Randolph Scott), who has been searching a long time for his wife, kidnapped by natives, helps another woman, Nancy (Nancy Gates) return home. Afraid of her husband's reaction, Nancy asks Cody, "If . . . if you had a woman taken by the Comanche and . . . and you got her back . . . how would you feel knowing . . ." (her silence announces the act). In Cody's assurance that if her husband loved her, "It wouldn't matter at all" (and also in Sam's to Sarah in *The Stalking Moon*), there is a significant deviation from *Titus*'s mythic pattern in which dishonor is publicly resolved by death; Nancy's salvation and her honor remain in the hands/heart of her husband, not the public's. Another film which also deviates from *Titus*'s pattern is *Hang 'em High* (Ted Post, 1968). An innocent who is almost killed after being hung by a posse, Jed Cooper (Clint Eastwood) becomes friends with Rachel Warren (Inger Stevens), who searches the prisoners arriving at Fort Grant for the men who killed her husband and raped her. One day, after avoiding Jed's kiss at a picnic, she explains her trauma. The close-ups of her face and Jed's compassionate eyes[12] emphasize the horror of her rape as she says, "[A]nd then they came, again and again." Before she answers Jed's question about what she will do when and if she finds those men, a tempest arrives. She helps Jed, who is ill, to the shelter of a shack, and she protects his trembling body with her body. Talking to Jeb is a cathartic experience for Nancy.[13] With him she is able to love again. Like Cora and Sara, she is able to reintegrate into society and the world because of her erotic encounter with a man.

Robert Hossein's *Cemetery Without Crosses* (1969) and Susan Greenwald's *The Ballad of Little Jo* (1993) are singular films because of their unusual treatment of the tragic woman as avenger and protagonist.[14] In *Cemetery Without Crosses*, Maria (Michèle Mercier) is a widow who asks her ex-lover, Manuel (Robert Houssein), to help her to take revenge on an oppressive cattle rancher, Will Rogers (Daniel Vargas), whose sons hung her husband in front of her and later burned the house of her brothers-in-law. Manuel manages to be received as a friend by Rogers and even gets a job working for the rancher. He then kidnaps Roger's daughter, Diana (Anne Marie-Balin), taking her to the ghost town he earlier had made his home. There, Maria's brothers-in-law rape Diana, while Maria and Manuel, listening to her scream, wait outside the house. Maria's knowledge that Diana will be raped brings to mind Tamora's part in Lavinia's rape in *Titus*. However, her act of revenge to honor her husband's memory and her confession while dying mitigate her resemblance to the queen of the Goths. After the rape, Maria has the decent funeral for her husband that she demanded in exchange for Diana, but she and Manuel are betrayed by her brothers-in-law, and their plans to escape are frustrated. Wounded by Roger's sons, Maria dies in Manuel's arms, confessing her love for him, in spite of having married his friend. After killing Diana's brother in a duel, Manuel is killed by Diana, who shoots him with a rifle. His death, however, reads as a suicide, because he removes his "killing glove"– which he always donned before fighting.

Directed by a woman, *The Ballad of Little Jo* portrays an attempted rape. Inspired by a true story, the tale of Josephine Monaghan, Josephine (Suzy Amis) is an Eastern woman, who after being seduced by a photographer and delivering her baby, is expelled from her home and has her child given to her sister. Josephine goes West, and after almost being sold as a whore by her employer and running from a group of men (who, it is implied, intend to rape her), she makes a radical decision to survive. Because living as a woman will invite more men to abuse her, Jo dresses like a man, cuts her hair and even her face, to look unattractive.[15] Disgusted by the misogyny of a man whom she considered her friend and who tried to rape her when he discovered her secret, she lives alone, working as a shepherd on a ranch and fighting against powerful landowners. Her solitary and celibate life changes when she meets an outsider like herself. She saves Tinman Wong (David Chung) from being lynched, and they become involved in an intimacy that ends only with his death. Later, when Jo dies, the people of Ruby City, who have always respected that man they considered a bit strange, but so kind, feel betrayed. The last image of Jo is that of her body tied to her horse for a photograph. If we think of rape as the possession of a woman's body, this final image is devasting. In the end, Jo loses control of the representation of herself, reminding spectators and audiences of the violence of the relationships she experienced in both the East and the West.

At the beginning of this chapter, I introduced influential patterns regarding tragedy and the representation of rape in works by Ovid and Shakespeare. I would like to end by remembering Homer in the chain of reception to which these patterns belong. If Borges is correct, Westerns should be seen as the heir of the epic.[16] When considering rape in Westerns, it is important to remember the passage in the *Iliad*, in which old Nestor, a wise and venerable man, gives a disturbing counsel to the Greek warriors: "Wherefore let no man make haste to depart homewards until each have lain with the wife of some Trojan, and have got him requital for his strivings and groanings for Helen's sake" (*Il.* 2, 354–6).[17] Abducted and raped in some narratives, Helen was the device that began a war in which men could show their courage and make their fame (*kleos*).[18] Herodotus also initiated his *History* explaining the rape of women (Europa, Ino, Medea, and Helen, I: 1–5) as the cause of wars.[19] After World War II, the Western's film narrative has often been a martial tale of conquest, frequently housing the rape-revenge story. Paraphrasing Godard when thinking about *eros* and *eris* in Hollywood (or Troy), it seems that a weapon and a (disputed) girl is all that is needed for a film (or a war). Despite feminist advances throughout the the twentieth century, representations of sexual violence in *Duel in the Sun* (1946), *The Searchers* (1956), *Man of the West* (1958), *The Bravados* (1958), *For a Few Dollars More* (1965), *Sergeant Rutledge* (1960), *Hang 'em High* (1968), *Cemetery Without Crosses* (1969), and *The Ballad of Little Jo* (1993) reveal the pervasiveness of rape-revenge narratives embedded in the tragedy and the epic. Portrayed as victims and avengers in a chain of reception stretching back to the *Illiad*, women have long been haunted by ancient patterns in what is America's quintessential story. The Western is indeed an heir to the epic, but further improvements in the status of women in the twenty-first century suggest filmic representations of rape and rape-revenge are ready to change. One can only hope that this will happen when writers and directors recognize the Western's *heroicization* of rape (and come to terms with what Susan Estrich terms "real rape"). As Sergeant Rutledge says, "Maybe some day, but not yet, it will not be anymore."

Notes

1. The feminine body as a territory is an old image. A paradigmatic example is that of King Creon, who tells Ismene in the famous tragedy *Antigone*, when she asks if he is going to kill his son's bride: "Why not? There are other fields for him to plough" (l. 589). Incidently, it is worth remembering Creon's discussion with his Haemon. Creon accuses his son of being ruled by a woman, instead of thinking that the (other) land, Thebas is the property of the man in power (ll. 728–89). Regarding the allegory of land as a woman from a postcolonial perspective, see *Virgin Territory—Women, Gender and History in Contemporary Brazilian Art*, a catalog related to an international celebration of the 500th anniversary of Brazil's discovery by the Portuguese.
2. Philomela was the Greek princess raped by her brother-in-law, King Tereus, who cut off her tongue to avoid her denouncing him to her sister Procne. In Ovid's *Metamorphoses* (6, 438–74), Philomela manages to weave her story in a tapestry, informing her sister of Tereus' crime. The revenge of Procne, "rendered in silence" when she knew (ibid., 584–5), was to kill her son, Itys, by chopping him up and cooking him to serve to her husband—in a symbolic gesture cutting away the possibility of fatherhood.
3.
    Titus: My lord the Emperor, resolve me this: / Was it well done of rash Virginius / To slay his daughter with his own right hand, / Because she was enforc'd, stain'd, and deflower'd?
    Saturninus: It was, Andronicus. [. . .]
    Titus: A pattern, precedent, and lively warrant / For me, most wretched, to perform the like. Die, die, Lavinia, and thy shame with thee; [He kills her] And with thy shame thy father's sorrow die!

4. Ford defined himself in terms of the genre, saying, "My name's John Ford. I make Westerns." See Anderson (1981: 150). On the film, see Matheson (2016: 231–51) and Kitses (2007: 107–9).

5. London: Bloomsbury, 2013. On race, rape, and captivity, see especially Gaylyn Studlar (2004). On female captivity and denying male responsability, see Heller-Nicholas (2011: 71–2).
6. On how the genre epic made Ethan's "semi-psychotic" character more complex, see Matheson (2016: 204). The connection with classical literature came from articles in magazines like *Look*, naming *The Searchers* a "Homeric odyssey" to the French filmmaker Godard, who "compared the movie's ending to "Ulysses being reunited with Telemachus" (*Cahiers du Cinema*, 1959, *apud* Hoberman). On comparison to the *Iliad*, see Winkler (2004).
7. A subject Ford addresses again in *Two Rode Together* (1961).
8. The scene was seen as an allegory of a gang rape, but inside a family group. This subject can be found in *Ride the High Country* (Sam Peckinpah, 1962), when Elsa is almost raped by her four brothers-in-law with whom her husband wants to share his bride. Rape was also a fundamental device Peckinpah used in the polemical *Straw Dogs* (1971)—Susan George agreed to play the scene on the condition that the rape was controlled "through her eyes and body" (see Polanski's conversation with Heller-Nichols (2011: 48)). Also in *Hannie Coulder* (Burt Kennedy, 1971), a family—three brothers—rape the protagonist in a grotesque sequence.
9. Wicking and Pattinson (1969) and Basinger (2007), for instance.
10. It is interesting to compare her situation to Helen Caldwell's (Zohra Lampert) in *Posse from Hell* (Herbert Coleman, 1961). Caldwell deals openly with the personal shock of being gang raped and with the social constraints and shame a woman has to face, even if is known that she was forced.
11. Seeing the rescued women was shot from Ethan's perspective. For further discussion, see Studlar (2004). About Indians and women in Westerns, see Loy (2014), chapters 10 and 11, respectively.
12. A very different character, compared to Clint Eastwood's personae in films like *High Plains Drifter* (Clint Eastwood, 1973) or even *Sudden Impact* (Clint Eastwood, 1983), in which part of the revenge of the "hero" involves a rape. About the similarities between Dirty Harry and Western themes and characters and violation, see McClelland and Clayton (2014: 160–72).
13. In *The Forty Guns* (Samuel Fuller, 1957), an old shack during a wind storm is also where Jessica (Barbara Stanwyck) and Griff (Barry Sulivan) make love, after she tells him how she was, as a teen, attacked in that place by a "saddle tramp"—a "rattler" who tried to bite her and killed her father—and how she managed to "step on the rattler."
14. While talking about Westerns in which women take revenge, I cannot avoid mentioning *The Belle Starr Story* (Lina Wertmuller, 1968) and *Hannie Calder* (Burt Kennedy, 1971)—see, for instance, Heller-Nicholas (2011: 75–9). In both of these films, the exploration of women's body and sexuality are contradictory when one considers the violence which seems to be denounced and punished.
15. Making themselves unattractive was a common practice used by women to avoid rape, according to Wolfthal (2000: 62–7). For one of Jo's strategies to look more masculine, see Coelho (2017).
16. Here it is worthwhile to remember the famous comment by J. L. Borges: "I think nowadays, while literary men seem to have neglected their epic duties, the epic has

been saved for us, strangely enough, by the Western." In *The Paris Review Interview* 40 (1967), pp. 16–64, 123).
17. Regarding rape as a strategy of war, see Wolfthal (2000).
18. *Helen of Troy* (J. Harrison, 2003) is the only film that explicitly shows Helen's contact with Theseus, and, in a disturbing scene, at the end of the war and the film, Helen, held by Greek soldiers, is raped by a fierce Agamemnon, in front of his brother Menelaus. For further discussion, see Coelho (2016).
19. Helen is a paradigmatic case in which being abducted (and raped) is seen as her fault due to the power of her beauty: "Beauty, then, is part and parcel of the *fiction* of rape. And within these fictions, it serves a particular purpose: it attributes more power to the victim than she indeed has" (Duggan 2010: 137).

Filmography

Cemetery Without Crosses, director Robert Hossein, featuring Michèle Mercier, Robert Hossein, Guido Lollobrigida (Loisirs du Monde, 1969).
Comanche Station, director Budd Boethicher, featuring Randolph Scott, Nancy Gates, Claude Akins (Columbia, 1960).
Duel in the Sun, director KingVidor, featuring Jennifer Jones, Joseph Cotten, Gregory Peck (Selzick International, 1946).
For a Few Dollars More, director Sergio Leone, featuring Clint Eastwood, Lee Van Cleef, Gian Maria Volontè (Produzioni Europee Associate, 1965).
Forty Guns, director Samuel Fuller, featuring Barbara Stanwyck, Barry Sullivan, Dean Jagger (21st Century Fox, 1957).
Hang 'em High, director Ted Post, featuring Clint Eastwood, Inger Stevens, Pat Hingle (Leonard Freeman Production, 1968).
Hannie Calder, director Burt Kennedy, featuring Raquel Welch, Robert Culp, Ernest Borgnine (Tigon British Film Productions, 1971).
Helen of Troy, director John Harrison, featuring Emilia Fox, James Callis, Daniel Lapaine (Fuel Entertainment, 2003).
High Plains Drifter, director Clint Eastwood, featuring Clint Eastwood, Verna Bloom, Marianna Hill (The Malpaso Company, 1973).
Lights! Action! Music!, director Dan Lieberstein, featuring John Barry, Terence Blanchard, Carte Burwell (The Wild Project, 2007).
Man of the West, director Anthony Mann, featuring Gary Cooper, Julie London, Lee J. Cobb (Aston Productions and Walter Mirisch Productions, 1958).
Posse from Hell, director Herbert Coleman, featuring Audie Murphy, John Saxon, Zohra Lampert (Universal, 1961).
Ride the High Country, director Sam Peckinpah, featuring Joel McCrea, Randolph Scott, Mariett Hartley (MGM, 1962).
Sergeant Rutledge, director John Ford, featuring Jeffrey Hunter, Woody Strode, Constance Towers (Warner Bros., 1960).
Straw Dogs, director Sam Peckinpah, featuring Dustin Hoffman, Susan George, Peter Vaughan (ABC Pictures, 1971).
Sudden Impact, director Clint Eastwood, featuring Clint Eastwood, Sondra Locke, Pat Hingle (Warner Bros., 1983).

The Ballad of Little Jo, director Susan Greenwald, featuring Suzy Amis, Bo Hopkins, Ian McKellen (Joco and Polygram Filmed Entertainment, 1993).
The Belle Starr Story, director Lina Wertmuller, featuring Elsa Martinelli, Robert Woods, George Eastman (Eureka Films, 1968).
The Bravados, director Henry King, featuring Gregory Peck, Joan Collins, Stephen Boyd (20th Century Fox, 1958).
The Searchers, director John Ford, featuring John Wayne, Jeffrey Hunter, Vera Miles (C. V. Whitney Pictures, 1956).
The Stalking Moon, director Robert Mulligan, featuring Gregory Peck, Eva Marie Saint, Robert Forster (National General Production, 1968).
Titus, director Julie Taymor, featuring Anthony Hopkins, Jessica Lange, Osheen Jones (Clear Blu Sky Productions, 1999).
Trooper Hook, director Charles M. Warren, featuring Joel McCrea, Barbara Stanwyck, Earl Holliman (Filmaster, 1957).
Two Rode Together, director John Ford, featuring James Stewart, Richard Widmark, Shirley Jones (Columbia, 1961).

Bibliography

Anderson, Lindsay (1981) *About John Ford*. New York: McGraw-Hill.
Aquila, Richard (2015), *The Sagebrush Trail: Western Movies and Twentieth-Century America*. Tucson, AZ: University of Arizona Press.
Basinger, Jeanine (2007) *Anthony Mann*. Middletown, CT: Wesleyan University Press.
Coelho, Maria Cecília de M. N. (2016) "Elena troiana: A fama de um nome e o desejo de vingança no cinema," *Artefilosafia*, 20, pp. 17–34.
Coelho, Maria Cecília de M. N. (2017) "Horses for Ladies, High-Ridin' Women and Whores," in Sue Matheson (ed.), *Iconography and Archetypes in Western Film and Television*. Jefferson, NC: McFarland, pp. 113–23.
Duggan, Anne (2010) "Rape and Sociopolitical Positioning in the *Histoire tragique*," *Early Modern Women: An Interdisciplinary Journal*, 5, pp. 137–65.
Estrich, Susan (1988) *Real Rape*. Cambridge, MA: Harvard University Press.
Frayling, Christopher (2012) *Sergio Leone, Something to Do with Death*, Minneapolis, MN: University of Minnesota Press.
Heller-Nicholas, Alexandra (2011) *Rape-Revenge Films: A Critical Study*. Jefferson, NC: McFarland.
Hoberman, James (2013) "The Searchers: An American Obsession," *New York Times Review*, 25 February <https://www.nytimes.com/2013/02/24/books/review/the-searchers-by-glenn-frankel.html> (last accessed 13 December 2018).
Kitses, Jim (2007) *Horizons West: Directing the Western from John Ford to Clint Eastwood*, 2nd edition. London: British Film Institute.
Loy, Phillip R. (2014) *Westerns in a Changing America, 1955–2000*. Jefferson, NC: McFarland.
McClelland, Richard T. and Clayton, Brian B. (eds) (2014) *The Philosophy of Clint Eastwood*. Lexington, KY: University Press of Kentucky.
Matheson, Sue (2016) *The Westerns and War Films of John Ford*. Lanham, MD: Rowman & Littlefield.

Prats, Armando J. (2002) *Invisible Natives: Myth and Identity in the American Western.* Ithaca, NY: Cornell University Press.

Read, Jacinta (2010) *The New Avengers: Feminism, Feminity and the Rape-Revenge Cycle.* Manchester: Manchester University Press.

Sielke, Sabine (2002) *Reading Rape: The Rhetoric of Sexual Violence in American Literature and Culture.* Princeton, NJ: Princeton University Press.

Smith, Henry N. (1970) *The Virgin Land: The American West as Symbol and Myth.* Cambridge, MA: Harvard University Press.

Studlar, Gaylyn (2004) "What Would Martha Want? Captivity, Purity, and Feminine Values in *The Searchers*," in Arthur M. Eckstein and Peter Lehman (eds), *The Searchers: Essays and Reflections on John Ford's Classic Western.* Detroit, MI: Wayne State University Press, pp. 171–96.

Virgin Territory—Women, Gender and History in Contemporary Brazilian Art (2001) National Museum of Women in Art. Washington, DC (catalog).

Wicking, Christopher and Pattinson, Barrie (1969) Interview with Anthony Mann, *Screen*, 10 (4), pp. 32–54.

Winkler, Martin M. (2004) "Homer's *Iliad* and John Ford's *The Searchers*," in Arthur M. Eckstein and Peter Lehman (eds), *The Searchers: Essays and Reflections on John Ford's Classic Western.* Detroit, MI: Wayne State University Press, pp. 145–70.

Wolfthal, Diane (2000) *Images of Rape: The "Heroic" Tradition and its Alternatives.* Cambridge: Cambridge University Press.

13. "MY BODY FOR A HAND OF POKER": THE BELLE STARR STORY IN ITS CONTEXTS

Erin Lee Mock

It is nothing new to say that the Western is a male-dominated genre, measured by its practitioners, presumed audiences, and the characters it represents. However, the genre has sometimes offered rich, developed female characters, including several historical figures who are portrayed time and again as times require. Though not as recognized as Calamity Jane or Annie Oakley, the figure of Belle Starr has appeared at least nineteen times in film and television since 1928's *Court-Martial* (directed by George Seitz and produced by Harry Cohn). Well before she appeared on screen, Starr was a staple of dime novels and an obsession of the Western popular press. A verified outlaw of the American West associated with the James Gang and other criminal outfits, Starr stands apart from Oakley and Calamity Jane, embodying a Western heroine who might seem in keeping with the "psychological Western" protagonist, in part because unlike these other female Western icons, she did not participate in self-mythology.

As the "classic Western" gave way to the "psychological Western" gave way to the Spaghetti Western and other revisionist interpretations of the genre, portrayals of women did not necessarily advance. While some directors of the American Western made an effort to investigate the motivations and experiences of women of the West—Elliott Silverstein's comic Western *Cat Ballou* (1965) and Robert Altman's *McCabe and Mrs Miller* (1971) come to mind — the Spaghetti Western was nearly void of female protagonists and its portrayals of women were especially problematic.[1] William McClain recounts *Time* magazine's 1967 summary of Sergio Leone's style: "Be mean, mean, mean. Don't punch cattle, punch a few women instead. Never waste a punch when a knee in the groin will do" (2010: 57). The Spaghetti Westerns were in keeping with their circumstances: both the European art film and the exploitation films of the 1960s–70s were preoccupied with lurid representations of violence against women as feminist critics have documented (Brizio-Skov 2011a: 89; Broughton 2016: 57–72; Haskell 1974: 323; Waddell 2018: 48).

The Belle Starr Story (*Il mio corpo per un poker*, Lina Wertmüller, 1968) is worthy of closer examination in these contexts. The only Spaghetti Western directed by a woman and one of very few featuring a female protagonist, *The Belle Starr Story* similarly incorporates the tropes of exploitation cinema, in this case revising the historical record into a more explicitly "feminized" tale, which emphasizes her psychological motivations in response to sexual trauma. In one of the only discussions of the film, Bert Fridlund argues that it creates a relationship between Belle and Blackie (George Eastman), her love interest, which mimics the partnerships in the earlier Spaghetti Westerns, specifically Leone's, in some sense masculinizing her (2007: 160). While this may be so, the film also uses flashback effects more in keeping with the rape revenge films popular in horror and exploitation cinema of the time and narratively locates the source of Belle's criminality in past abuse, isolating her in a way which also deviates from historical facts as we know them, and privileges a (non-sexual) relationship with a female partner. Given that the historical record shows that Starr was a victim of murder, but, not to anyone's knowledge, sexual abuse, Wertmüller's decision as writer and director to make Belle a victim of assault is remarkably contextual: she makes the abused woman of the Spaghetti Westerns a protagonist, the "punched woman" bringing to bear her own violence. Furthermore, Wertmüller, operating under an Anglophone male pseudonym (Nathan Wich), was able to smuggle this "female rape-revenge" plot into the male-dominated genre in which men were typically responsible for avenging a woman's "honor," while revising the traumatized gunfighter in a way which validates women's experiences of trauma.

This article considers the situation which produced *The Belle Starr Story*, including the figure of Belle Starr, narrative deviations from the historical record, changes in the Western as a genre and Spaghetti Westerns specifically, rape-revenge and exploitation films, and Wertmüller's body of work, in order to assess the film's radical revisions of female subjectivity in perhaps the most aggressively masculine subgenre of the typically male genre.

Belle Star, the Bandit Queen, the Petticoat Terror of the Plains, or the Female Jesse James

It is not within the scope of this paper to trace every contour of "Belle Starr" the woman, the legend, and the character: books have been written on the subject. Like all name-brand heroes of the old West from Buffalo Bill to Jesse

James, she appears in different guises in different eras for different reasons. As I note above, Belle Starr was not herself active in constructing her legend, so the room for "interpretation" is especially broad. According to Glenn Shirley in *Belle Starr and Her Times* (1982), the most thorough account to date, Starr's biography was radically inaccurate from the moment it was made public in the *Fort Smith Elevator* announcing her death on 6 February 1889. The death announcement was sent to other newspapers, so readers of the *New York Times* and *Dallas Morning News* got the same misinformation. Immediately, she became fodder for dime novels read by a majority of the male population in the United States (of course, women read them too). By the end of the year of her death, she was famous. As Shirley puts it:

> Almost overnight, the name of Belle Starr became a household word throughout the nation. She had been elevated to a seat of immortal glory as a sex-crazed hellion with the morals of an alley cat, a harborer and consort of horse and cattle thieves, a petty blackmailer who dabbled in every crime from murder to the dark sin of incest, as a female Robin Hood who robbed the rich to feed the poor, an exhibitionistic and clever she-devil on horseback and leader of the most bloodthirsty band of cutthroats in the American West. All this despite the lack of a contemporary account or court record to show that she ever held up a train, bank, or stagecoach; or killed anybody; the renegades she supposedly led or kept out of the tangles of the law were only figments of a vivid imagination. (Shirley1982: 3)

Though she was indeed arrested and jailed for horse theft, this is as far as she got from the law. As radically as reports and portrayals differed from the facts of her life, several things about Belle Starr's story made her "useful" to the mythology of the Old West and open to artistic exploration. For example, unlike Calamity Jane whose mother was a sex worker and father a gambler, Starr came from a well-to-do Virginia family. She loved showing off her fine horses and velvet clothes and rode side-saddle like a "lady," not astride (Shirley 1982: 39). She was formally educated in a private girl's school and studied classical music. She was also married at least three times and invariably attracted to the dangerous type: every man she married or was involved with either was already or became a criminal. Though this has often been underplayed, Starr was not only part Cherokee, but, more importantly, married into the tribe more than once, and was believed to be in another relationship with a member of the Creek Indian tribe. Among the outlaws she rode with were not the famous James brothers—they were her just friends—but, in fact, some of the most fearsome Indian bandits. She bore children—one of whom, Pearl, would develop notoriety of her own. And, though some historians and commentators have taken pains to correct the widespread assumption that she was beautiful—Buck Rainey (2015) is only one of many who use the terms "hatchet-faced" and "flat-chested"—this correction never quite took hold (131, in Holland 2007: 161).

By 1941, she was a glamour girl, played by Gene Tierney in Twentieth Century Fox's *Belle Starr* alongside Randolph Scott (looking strikingly like Vivien Leigh's Scarlett O'Hara in Victor Fleming's *Gone with the Wind* two years earlier).[2] After two other films about Starr, Jane Russell famously played the role in *Montana Belle* (Allan Dwan, 1952).[3] The publicity kit offers a poster split across the middle. On top, Russell adopts her familiar pin-up pose, reclining, looking over her shoulder with her blue dress falling off, and a quote, "Let's get friendly . . . stranger!" On the bottom, she stands to the right of a gunfight, pistol at her side, in men's clothing (though her top buttons have come loose). After *Montana Belle* and before *The Belle Starr Story* in 1968, Starr appeared in a handful of television episodes (she was never given more than one guest spot per program) and was played by Sally Starr in the *The Outlaws Is Coming* (Norman Maurer), a Three Stooges comedy, in 1965.[4] Clearly, the potential of "Belle Starr" to expand the stable and scope of female Western protagonists had yet to be realized.

ENTER THE SPAGHETTI WESTERN

As Belle Starr evolved from Jane Russell's tough Hollywood pinup to a character in a Three Stoogies film, changes were taking place in the Western film genre. As Hollywood was investing less in Western film, Leone's *A Fistful of Dollars* (*Per un pugno di dollari*) came out in 1964 (released in the US in 1967), "filled a void and became a classic," occasioning even heavier Italian investment in popular genre films, especially Westerns (Walle, 2000: 166; Wagstaff, 1992: 246). The shifts in the genre were not, of course, simply issues of money and volume. Stephen McVeigh is in agreement with a long line of critics when he claims that "Spaghetti Westerns . . . reinvented the genre so it could again be politically, socially, and culturally relevant," and that the European film industry—in Italy in particular—"saved" the Western (2007: 168; Buscombe 1998: 1).[5] The Spaghetti Western was not, however, just a savior of or a cure for an American film genre. As Austin Fisher writes in the introduction to *Spaghetti Westerns at the Crossroads*, the Spaghetti Western is "a transatlantic meeting place," which requires scholars to consider these films "in international contexts" (2016: 1). Fisher's volume builds on the twenty-first-century scholarship on Spaghetti Westerns, which has largely pursued a broader outlook, considering genre, style, and national and international filmmaking, distribution, and reception. Dmitri Eleftheriotis urges scholars to consider that there are

> several layers superimposed in the Spaghetti western that describe a process of transculturation: the growing confidence of the Italian film

industry, the strategic decision of the industry to export films masquerading as American, the fact that this strategy goes hand-in-hand with an elaborate system of re-inventing and re-launching the careers of numerous Italian actors and directors, that this necessitates a playful process of reimagining and re-negotiating identity and, finally, that there is no evidence that audiences around the world watched Spaghetti westerns as if they were genuine American movies. (Eleftheriotis 2002: 108)

The "playful process of reimagining and re-negotiating identity" that Eleftheriotis mentions helps make sense of the very odd cultural artifact which is *The Belle Starr Story*.

To many feminist critics, the Western has always been inhospitable to women. Books and articles on the topic abound. In Maria Cecília de Miranda N. Coehlo's words: "women are important insofar as they motivate and direct men's actions, often as wife or sister, kidnapped, murdered or raped and so cause for revenge, their presence in the narrative tends to be ephemeral since protagonists are nearly always male" (2017: 114). More harshly, "[w]oman in the Western was a sawdust doll" (Hutchison 1979: 34). And, in the Spaghetti Western, "[t]he heroine may suffer at the hands of the villain even when she plays only a peripheral role. Director Sergio Leone's violent Western world was a male one, for example, with a general absence of women's leading roles, though secondary women are included, often as rape victims" (Agnew 2015: 167). In her monograph, *Italian Cinema*, Mary Wood argues that, in fact, gender roles in Italian films changed dramatically in both art and popular Italian cinema in the 1960s, such that Spaghetti Westerns were of a piece (2005: 169).

Though we tend to associate Spaghetti Westerns with "new characters" which became themselves iconic—Man with No Name, Django, Ringo, Trinity, and others—*The Belle Starr Story* is not the first to capitalize on the known legends of Western American history (Betts 1992: xii). Several of the first handful of Spaghetti Westerns did just that. In 1964, Mario Costa (under the delightful pseudonym John Fordson) made *Buffalo Bill, Hero of the Far West* (*Buffalo Bill, L'eroe del Far West*) starring Gordon Scott in the title role and Mirko Ellis as Yellow Hand (143). Also in 1964, Mario Caiano's *Bullets Don't Argue/Pistols Don't Argue/Guns Don't Argue* (*Le pistole non discutono*) featured versions of Pat Garrett and the Clanton Brothers. And in 1965, Joaquín Luis Romero Marchent (as José Hernandez) directed *Seven Hours of Gunfire* (*Sette ore di fuoco*), and used the characters of Buffalo Bill, Wild Bill Hickok, Calamity Jane, and Red Cloud. Clearly, even in its earliest days, the Spaghetti Western was engaged with the Western's mythology which permeated American cinema, television, and literature. However, as Aliza Wong puts it, "Spaghetti Westerns played with the 'myth of the myth', rather than worrying about questions of 'authenticity,'" and Brizio-Skav takes the same notion further: "[t]he Spaghetti

[W]estern deals with 'the myth of the myth' that by now has nothing to do with the historical events that occurred in the Far West and, as a consequence, does not show any preoccupation with historical verisimilitude, nor does it share the same initial ideals . . . only the present exists" (Wong 2016: 75; Brizio-Skov 2011a: 85). This looseness with the historical record is but one example of Eleftheriotis's "playfulness" at work. I argue that the "present" is not just a response to cultural norms of the 1960s, but to the genre itself. What, the films ask, is the Western genre in the present time?

Rape Revenge and the Western

No one would dispute the prevalence of rape in both mainstream and exploitation film, both before and after *The Belle Starr Story* and before and after the Spaghetti Western, and, indeed, as Agnew reminds us, the genre gave audiences what they'd become accustomed to. Just after *The Belle Starr Story*'s release, a wave of rape revenge films hit theaters, especially in the United States and in the horror genre. As Carol Clover writes:

> Rape, real or imagined, has been a staple of cinema more or less from the beginning. Until the early 70s, however, it was typically a side theme—a psychopathic flourish in a suspense plot, or one of several atrocities Indians might visit on whites in the Western. One 1972 film changed that: *Last House on the Left* (Wes Craven). It moved rape from the periphery to the centre—turned what had been a sideshow in any kind of movie to the main act, the central motivation, [*sic*] of that American favorite, the revenge plot. (Clover 1993: 76)

While analyzing the same period, Jacinda Read departs from Clover's argument that these rape revenge films constitute a "genre," positing instead that the early 1970s inaugurated a "cycle," which was grounded in a particular moment in American history (2000: 25). Whether genre, cycle, or structure, Clover and Reed agree that these rape revenge films from the 1970s belong to the era of second-wave feminism and are, indeed, a response to it.[6] While films like *Last House on the Left*, *I Spit on Your Grave* (Meir Zarchi, 1978), and *Ms .45* (Abel Ferrara, 1981) likely spring to mind as examples of rape revenge film, both Heller-Nicholas and Read point out that, in fact, rape has not been simply "one of several atrocities Indian might visit on whites in the Western," but is a cinematic narrative as old as the 1910s (and likely before) and a trope visited by nearly every national cinema.[7] "Despite its common association with the horror film in the United States during the 1970s in particular, it spans genres, time and national borders" (Heller-Nicholas 2011: 5). Reading the narrative structure of rape revenge across genres, Read makes plain what, to a scholar of the cinematic and literary Western is incontrovertible: rape and revenge "are intimately connected," rather than "one of several atrocities" in the genre. If early American captivity narratives are proto-Westerns, as many scholars attest, it could not be otherwise.[8] Departing, however, from the captivity narrative, the Indian man-white women perpetrator-victim formula does not cover all or most of these atrocities in the later Westerns, especially and including in the Spaghetti Western. Generally, most rape revenge films and films involving rape contained white victims and white perpetrators after the first third of the twentieth century (Heller-Nicholas 2011: 71). According to Clover, the "other" was defined in the 1970s by region; Lehman describes the otherness of the perpetrators as "extremely repulsive, a characterization which frequently employs stereotypes about class and ethnicity" (1993: 112). After all, white male protagonists do not *need* a motive to attack Indians and/or Latinx (or, in cases mostly outside the Western, African-Americans) who are presumed guilty. By the second half of the twentieth century, the reverse is just as likely: films like *Chato's Land* (Michael Winner, 1972) and *The Man Who Loved Cat Dancing* (Richard Sarafian, 1973) feature the rapes of and vengeance on behalf of Native American women; here, white settlers are both the rapists and, at times, the avengers. (While there are other films we could semantically or syntactically consider "rape revenge Westerns," Leone's 1965 *For a Few Dollars More* is likely the one that comes to mind first.) In the case of *The Belle Starr Story*, the victims are both female, one white and one Indian, and they are also the avengers against white perpetrators.

In *Watching Rape*, Sarah Projansky argues that one distinction among these films is most fundamental and contains serious political/ideological implications:

> Sometimes revenge is taken by a man who loses his wife or daughter to a rape/murder, and sometimes the revenge is taken by women who have faced rape themselves. The films in the first category depend on rape to motivate and justify a particularly violent version of masculinity, relegating women to minor "props" in the narrative. The films of the second category, however can be understood as feminist narratives in which women face rape, recognize that the law will neither protect nor avenge them, and then take the law into their own hands. (Projansky 2001: 60)

How does *The Belle Starr Story* fit into this schema? Beautifully, it doesn't . . . quite.

The Belle Starr Story: A Woman's "Traumatic Western"

Counterintuitively, by invoking the rape revenge structure, the film becomes an example of what Janet Walker calls the "traumatic Western": positioning Belle as a Western hero in the mode of a male protagonist, while accounting for her trauma. Walker describes this subgenre:

> I have come to the realization that westerns are not only grandly historical (peopled by historical personages and referencing actual occurrences), but that very many of them are *internally* historical as well. In countless westerns, events of disturbing proportions, events that are markedly anterior to the fictive present, propel the actions and retaliatory violence of the narrative. (Walker 2001: 220)

While Belle herself is the victim of an assault, it is the harm that comes to her Indian friend and former servant, Rafika (Francesca Righini), which is most foundational to her development as a Western hero.[9] As such, Belle functions as the familiar female victim-character with the ubiquitous (typically male) protagonist driven by vengeance on behalf of a woman. To use a more canonical Spaghetti Western as a touchstone, she is both rape victim Marisol (Rosemary Dexter) and her brother Mortimer (Lee Van Cleef) whose mission is to avenge her rape and related suicide (*For a Few Dollars More*/*Per qualche dollaro in più*, Sergio Leone, 1965).

In order to think through the structure and meaning of rape, sex, and romance in the film, we must immediately concede that the film's apparent definition of sexual "consent" is one that Euro-American culture has fortunately (if perhaps superficially) eschewed by 2019.[10] Between Belle and her lover, Blackie, "yes means yes" and "no means yes," and sadomasochism is a given, barely remarked upon except in jest. Because the film is a love story which seems designed to draw distinctions between the man Belle loves (and later, the man who loves Rafika) and the men who have wronged them, it conforms to the sexual norms of almost all other Spaghetti Westerns, including and especially in Leone's *Once Upon a Time in the West* (*C'era una volta il West*, 1968), *Face to Face* (*Faccia a faccia*, Sergio Sollima, 1967), and *I Want Him Dead* (*Lo voglio morto*, Paolo Bianchini, 1967). Wood explains that the sexual norms of the Spaghetti Western square with the rest of Italian culture of the period and, therefore, cinema broadly: [there was a] "transference of desires for greater sexual and social freedom onto the bodies of female protagonists. The preponderance of excessive representations of the female body and material prosperity indicates the level of male unease at a new and more modern way of making relationships with women, and dealing with female autonomy" (2005: 169). According to Marcia Landy, it was not just Italian genre cinema that evinced confusion over changing gender roles and sexual mores: "the so-called Spaghetti western shares some [of these] concerns with the 'art cinema' identified with Fellini, Rossellini, Antonioni, Visconti, Pasolini, and Wertmüller" (2000: 181). In *The Belle Starr Story*, these common tropes and images are weighted with genre-specific meaning.

Figure 13.1   Elsa Martinelli is Belle Starr in *The Belle Starr Story/Il mio corpo per un poker* (Lina Wertmüller, 1968).

The film's opening scene features Belle (Elsa Martinelli) at the poker table, handily beating the men and the one other woman in competition. Her unmitigated dominance is interrupted by Larry Blackie (played by George Eastman and as yet unnamed) who claims to be the best poker player around. He quickly turns the tables until she finally admits: "That's it. I'm afraid I have nothing more to lose." Blackie suggests a different wager: he'll bet on the chance to sleep with her, with the caveat: "Of course, you'd never agree to bet that. A woman has to hold her honor very seriously."

It is at this moment, after establishing both her dominance and vulnerability, that the viewers are given access to her subjective experience as she considers the offer. Her flashback is rendered in a series of shots so quick-cut as to be nearly inscrutable.[11] After a whip pan over a wooded landscape: a man lying face-down on a slight hill with a knife in his back; Belle tumbles down the hill with that man rolling over her; close-up of Belle's frightened and struggling face; repeat shot of the man with the knife in his back; an older white-haired white man tries to pry up Rafika's skirts as she fights him; another repeat shot of the man with the knife in his back; shot of Rafika pulling the man off of Belle in the woods; repeat shot of the man with the knife in his back; whip pan through the wooded area around him; cut back to a close-up of Belle considering Blackie's proposal. Throughout rapid-fire editing, Wertmüller "display[s] the formal and stylistic characteristics of the traumatic mindscape in which disturbances of memory are prominent" before surprising the audience (and Blackie): Belle agrees to make the bet (Walker 2001: 225). He cuts, she deals, and, with a close-up on her cards, we see that she has four queens. She calls a draw, laying down only three. She has not only decided to bet "her body for a hand of poker," but clearly wants to lose it. The Italian title—*Il mio corpo per un poker*—is implicitly reinterpreted in Belle's favor.

What follows is (at least initially) unpleasant, even repellant. He circles her, undressing, eyeing her like predator does prey. As she undresses, he watches her in the mirror and says, "It's not every day a woman gets undressed and takes off a pair of trousers." Beneath her masculine attire, she is wearing highly feminine undergarments of satin and lace (but with riding socks). Laughing, he reveals that he looked at her cards ("I'm sorry. I'm afraid I suffer from curiosity.") and knows that she misrepresented her hand in order to sleep with him. Embarrassed, she pulls a gun on him. He yanks the carpet to knock her off her feet and the gun out of her hand. She punches him, he holds her back, they fight for some time. Finally, he slaps her across the face, throws her on the bed, holds her down, and puts his hand around her throat: "You threw a hand so you could go to bed with me, didn't you? Now you're going to enjoy it. Be a good girl." When he mentions that she must have been with other men, the flashback series returns to her in a different order with new shots: whip pan over the woods; rolling downhill; man with the knife in his back; Rafika being held from behind by the same old man; man with the knife in his back; Rafika and Belle struggle with the man on the hill; whip pan over the woods; and Belle's face in the present of the film, remembering as Blackie "has his way with her." She bites his hand, but he kisses her mouth slowly and music swells (an instrumental version of the film's romantic theme), as she begins to run her hands through his hair, awkwardly, but with honest romantic passion. He acknowledges aloud and she by assent that she "needed an excuse" to make love: these flashbacks and experiences they represent have made it impossible for her to fall in love up to this point.

Belle's flashbacks depict several acts of violence: all three of these events are in some way conflated by being cut together. She seems just as—if not more—disturbed by Rafika's murder of her (Belle's) assailant (a man who had been Belle's best friend) as she is by the two attempted rapes, since the image of the man with the knife in his back recurs more than others. Her trauma is complex: it is violence upon violence upon violence, seen and perpetrated, in the time-honored tradition of the Western gunfighter. This violent past and the gunfighter's attachment (willing or unwilling) to it threatens any possibility for love and stability. She must keep running, she says, even though Rafika appears to be the perfect homesteader "wife." Her violent past, however, makes her especially able to "clean up" the town and community: at a saloon the night after meeting Blackie, Belle shoots several men who are harassing a young woman whom she does not even know. In her words, "I really became what everybody already said I was." Because of her traumatic history, she becomes the quintessential Western protagonist, trapped in her legend and in what she has done.

Though the film does not begin with the scene of her assault, it enacts a mini-narrative of a rape revenge Western in its first ten minutes. Critics argue that central to the rape revenge film is the transformation of the heroine; in Schubart's words, "rape is the initiation rite that pushes women from being 'soft' victims to becoming 'hard' avengers" (Projansky 2001: 258; Schubart 2007: 95). That Belle is "hard" is apparent from the first moment of the credits sequence, which could belong to nearly any Spaghetti Western. We focus on a pair of hard, pencil-sketched eyes, framed in the standard Spaghetti Western disembodied extreme close-up, accompanied by Morricone-influenced whistling (the film's music was composed by Charles Dumont). The sound of gunshots accompanies each name as it appears until the title, after which a trumpet blows and the credits are superimposed over Belle riding her horse in medium long shot, superimposed too over the eyes, pulling back to reveal that we are looking at a wanted poster/mug shot. The first 56 seconds of the film are in keeping with the Spaghetti Western inaugurated by Leone. Suddenly, this sequence is interrupted by Wertmüller's very unusual choice: the Morricone-style music breaks into "No Time for Love," the film's romantic theme played on a classical guitar with a woman's voice over a sequence of "glamour shots" of Belle (Martinelli, a former model). She looks soft and dreamy. She is longing for love. The trumpet/bugle blasts back in and the mug shot image returns, this time exposed fully, over her on horseback. Of the Spaghetti Western style, Mitchell writes that the "prolonged close-ups serve a formal, structural purpose far more than a customary emotional one. That is, the camera follows faces not to probe psychology but simply to register the impossibility of any greater knowledge of character than one has at first glance" (Mitchell 1996: 230). Wertmüller's prolonged close-ups, however, introduce Belle as a soft, beautiful woman yearning for romance who is also as rough and tough as any man of the West.

This soft, beautiful romantic protagonist reappears later in the film, following their first sexual encounter and again when Blackie visits her at her homestead. She sings and plays a melancholy "No Time For Love" on a classical guitar: "I only want a love that's true / And what my heart is looking for / is love to last forevermore . . . Love comes along / I run away / But I will stay until the day / I see my love at last has come to me." Blackie approaches her from behind and, validating the song's lyrics, she growls, "Just what are you after?" What comes next is not a cute *tête-à-tête*, but an authentic fight in which she proves herself the mean gunfighter, not the romantic balladeer. Blackie provokes her by questioning her mettle: "You're the terrible Belle Starr. It's easy to start a legend. Talk is cheap in bar and saloons. Before I believe you show me." She shows him by shooting the fence on which he's leaning, the heels off his boots, and his hat off.

Unsurprisingly, however, they embrace and kiss (and a close-up reveals her loosening her grip on the pistol between them) and make love (offscreen) in a haystack. Here, Belle takes a different approach to her legend. When Blackie says, "You're so different now. So sweet and tender. Sort of helpless. You're not Belle Starr," she responds: "Belle Starr doesn't exist, she's just a cover for what's left of a life gone wrong." Her line here is standard for the Western, but can also be generically bisected: she is the avenger of the rape revenge film and has the vulnerable heart that beats in the legendary gunfighter. He affirms the latter: "All of us hide our lives behind guns and tough talk." Perhaps because he relates to her, she shares her story, via narration and flashbacks, of "a life gone wrong." Viewers too get context for the earlier flashbacks. Her story is incontrovertibly a story of lifelong gendered and sexual violence: naked, she is threatened and taunted by a voyeur; her abusive uncle attempts to marry her to an older colleague for political gain; this uncle attempts to rape Rafika (during which he admits to raping Rafika's mother) and Belle saves her from being hanged for resisting, which requires her to shoot the town sheriff, among others; Rafika herself rescues Belle when she is sexually assaulted by the only man she trusted, her best friend. The story is punctuated by verbal abuse, e.g. the advice her uncle offers to her intended: "I say she needs a good horsewhipping . . . These white little savages make the best wives for a man to dominate them." Belle's story is of gendered abuse and her reaction to it, but Blackie again relates to her: "Our stories are a lot alike." He draws a beard and mustache on her wanted poster. By interpreting her rape revenge story as the gunfighter narrative, he certainly improves his lot as a romantic partner, but, through both language and image, he asserts the film as a Western for the viewer. Blackie presumably equates sexual trauma with other violence, which some viewers might find problematic.[12] In my view, it reconciles her status as a victim with her menacing behavior and legend. This conversation also prepares viewers for what comes next: though the two compete for a heist, Belle rescues Blackie—shirtless and whipped—from the Pinkertons. It is Blackie, however, who rides off into the sunset, suggesting that neither have the capacity for partnership and family.

THE BELLE STARR STORY BY LINA WERTMÜLLER

It is the Western genre itself which reconciles the victim and the perpetrator, making women seem obvious protagonists of the genre: Belle is the gunfighter who yearns for a life she is too traumatized and violent to truly embrace. Belle belongs therefore in the tradition of Wyatt Earp (Henry Fonda) in John Ford's classic *My Darling Clementine* (1946) and the title character of *Shane* (Alan Ladd), directed by George Stevens in 1953, though Wertmüller is not a director known for her dialogue with classic Hollywood or even Spaghetti Westerns.

Considering *The Belle Starr Story* as a prelude to Wertmüller's most acclaimed body of work opens up re-readings of the director's *oeuvre*. Importantly, after her debut film *I basilischi* (*The Lizards*, 1963) made her beloved among the intelligentsia, she turned toward film and television in popular genres. Her second film, *Questa volta parliamo di uomini* (*This Time Let's Talk About Men*, 1965) was an episodic comedy, and she spent the years between it and *The Belle Starr Story* working on television *musicarellos*. She did these projects not because she was forced to, but because she actively disliked feeling that "the people" were not enjoying her work. After *The Belle Starr Story*, she began making films which, though considered "art films" by American audiences, were crude comedies in the Italian tradition (Bullaro 2006: xviii). As Fabio Vighi writes, "the director who best epitomises this . . . unrestrained masculine vulgarity" is Wertmüller (2006: 100). Radically revising female subjectivity, Belle embodies the confusion of changing gender roles and sexual mores found in the 1960s in Italy. Although the violence she experiences masculinizes her, she also retains her femininity; in fact, her very specifically female story suggests that women might make ideal Western protagonists. According to the genre-specific meaning of Wertmüller's Western tropes, Belle is a gunfighter who longs for what she may be too damaged to attain. It is both a possible and worthy effort to contextualize *The Belle Starr Story* within Wertmüller's career without looking to check a box for feminist credentials.[13] It is enough to consider that gender is both an important feature in her work and a feature to which most all viewers and critics have been drawn and that it is possible that Wertmüller's gender played a role in her writing and directing of *The Belle Starr Story*. Julia Erhart offers a conclusion from her research: "[In] historical film subtypes, female filmmakers create new understandings of women and history, reframe generic concepts such as fame, heroism, and historical worthiness . . . Their films add complexity to the understanding of the past" (2018: 34). Wertmüller does add complexity, but this complexity is not always welcome. Wertmüller's approach has frustrated critics of all stripes: "Wertmuller poses the problems, not solutions, and attempts to entertain us while stripping away the romantic myths with which we have all been fed" (McCormick 1977: 60). As she admits to Grace Russo Ballaro, she does not and did not feel that she owes her audiences answers to the questions her films raise (2006: 129). What conclusions we may draw from *The Belle Starr Story* might derive from our understandings of genre past and present, rather than our understanding of the enigmatic Wertmüller herself. As Fisher writes about the Spaghetti Western, "If this *filone* is indeed to be read as a document of 'time and place,' which times and which places? The immediate concerns of 1960s and 1970s Italy are certainly pivotal to understanding these films' cultural-political significance, but so too are their varied antecedents and legacies" (2016: 4). Every Western tells us something about both.

Notes

1. Certainly, characters like Jill (Claudia Cardinale) in Sergio Leone's *Once Upon a Time in the West* (*C'era una volta il West*, 1968) may be interpreted with more complexity, as Andrea Gazzaniga does (2013: 53–70). But Jill was a rarity indeed.
2. This appearance is preceded by George Seitz's *Court Martial* (1928), in which Belle is played by Betty Compson.
3. Tim Whelan's *Badman's Territory* and Lesley Salander's *Belle Starr's Daughter* came out in 1946. Isabel Jewell played Belle in both.
4. Belle appeared in: "Belle Starr," *Stories of the Century* (synd., 1954), played by Marie Windsor; "Belle Starr," *Tales of Wells Fargo* (NBC, 1957) and "Shadow of Jesse James," *Bronco* (ABC, 1958–62), played by Jeanne Cooper; "Full House," *Maverick* (ABC, 1957–62), played by Jean Wiles; "Perilous Passage," *Overland Trail* (NBC, 1960), played by Lynn Bari; "A Bullet for the D.A.," *Death Valley Days* (synd. 1952–70), played by Carol Matthews.
5. Italy had partners in this effort. See Miller and Van Riper (2014: xv).
6. It's important to keep in mind that the women's liberation movement ran parallel with other struggles, including the war in Vietnam, in which rape was a battle tactic and spoil of war, and the Red Power Movement which—however intermittently—addressed the rape of Native women in the conquest of the United States and, further, that second-wave feminism looked different in Italy than in the United States.
7. Lest we forget: *Last House on the Left* is a remake of Ingmar Bergman's 1960 *The Virgin Spring*.
8. Frankel (2014: 34–5), Lusted (2003: 81–2), Miller (2013: 72, 80–1), Slotkin (1998: 14–15), to name a few.
9. It is worth considering whether Rafika, the native woman, ex-servant, is an Indian "prop" meant to support a "white savior" narrative. In fact, on one level, she must be. It is she who gives Belle the chance to be a "savior" and there is no question that her race plays a role in the plot: the man who attempts to rape Rafika is her employer just returned from the Civil War and he indicates that her mother was a victim as well, reminding viewers that rape was considered a prerogative of slaveholders, whether those slaves were black or Native American. Ultimately, having gotten out of the rape, it is her scheduled lynching that brings Belle back home to save her. Another reading is available, which does not contradict the "white savior narrative" but can stand alongside it, complicating it in a way which develops both characters and contributes something original to the Spaghetti Western subgenre. Rafika too becomes a "savior," interrupting an attempted rape on Belle, and killing the perpetrator. Neither kills her own attacker but saves the other from harm. Belle Starr, the woman behind the legend, was a spoiled Southern belle early in her life, but, later, she was also the partner, wife, and mother of Indians who lived much of her life on Indian territory and was, as noted above, part Cherokee herself. What if, instead of merely a "prop," Rafika is another form of Belle? What if we read the film as offering a "Belle Starr" split in two for a profoundly different narrative that broadens possible definitions for femininity and partnership in the Western (with a dash of solidarity)? What if this "split personality" is necessary in the context of mid-nineteenth-century America? In a Western territory for men, two women are better than one.

10. The fact that this view of sexuality was commonplace does not mean it was unintentional. According to Dominique Russell, Wertmüller "used the dynamics of power in the sexual realm, and rape itself, to comment on political power" in much of her work (2010: 5).
11. Though it is also a key aesthetic element of the "traumatic Western," Wertmüller was known for using it in her later film comedies (Marcus 2002: 283).
12. It is, of course, possible that Blackie was also the victim of attempted rape, but this seems unlikely.
13. Bondanella assures readers that, contrary to most feminist critics, "Wertmüller is 'feminist'" and her first film is a "feminist interpretation of Italian provincial life" (2009: 193).

Filmography

"A Bullet for the DA," *Death Valley Days*, Season 10, Episode 9 (Flying "A" Productions, 1961).

A Fistful of Dollars (Per un pugno di dollari), director Sergio Leone, featuring Clint Eastwood, Gian Maria Volontè, Marianne Koch (Jolly Film, 1964).

"Archive: *The Belle Starr Story (Il mio corpo per un poker),*" *Internationales Frauen Film Festival*, The Belle Starr Story *(Il mio corpo per un poker)* <https://www.frauenfilmfestival.eu/index.php?id=2743>.

"Baby Outlaws," *Dr Quinn, Medicine Woman*, Season 3, Episode 21 (CBS Entertainment Production, 1995).

Badman's Territory, director Tim Whelan, featuring Randolph Scott, Ann Richards, George "Gabby" Hayes (RKO Radio Productions, 1946).

Bass Reeves, director Brett W. Mauser, featuring Wesley Blake, Leroy Branch, Ed Burlett (Ponderous Productions, 2010).

Belle Starr, director Irving Cummings, featuring Randolph Scott, Gene Tierney, Dana Andrews (20th Century Fox, 1941).

"Belle Starr," *Stories of the Century*, Season 1, Episode 1 (Studio City Television Productions, 1954).

Belle Starr Bandits, director Akihiro Ito (Kadokawa, 1993).

Buffalo Bill, Hero of the Far West (Buffalo Bill, L'eroe del Far West), director Mario Costa, featuring Gordon Scott, Ingeborg Schöner, Catherine Ribiero (1964).

Bullets Don't Argue/Pistols Don't Argue/Guns Don't Argue (Le pistole non discutono), director Mario Caiano, featuring Rod Cameron, Angel Aranda, Horst Frank (Jolly Film, 1964).

Cat Ballou, director Elliot Silverstein, featuring Jane Fonda, Lee Marvin, Michael Callan (Columbia, 1965).

Chato's Land, director Michael Winner, featuring Charles Bronson, Jack Palance, James Whitmore (Scimitar Films, 1972).

Court-Martial, director George B. Seitz, featuring Jack Holt, Betty Compson, Pat Harmon (Columbia, 1928).

Face to Face (Faccia a faccia, Sergio Sollima, 1967), director Ingmar Bergman, featuring Liv Ullman, Erland Josephson, Aino Taube (Cinematograph AB, 1976).

For a Few Dollars More (*Per qualche dollaro in più*), director Sergio Leone, featuring Clint Eastwood, Lee Van Cleef, Gian Maria Volontè (Produzioni Europee Associate, 1965).

Gone with the Wind, director Victor Fleming, featuring Clark Gable, Vivien Leigh, Thomas Mitchell (Selznick International, 1939).

Guns Blaze West, director Nobuhiro Watsuki (Shueisha, 2001).

I Spit on Your Grave, director Meir Zarchi, featuring Camille Keaton, Eron Tabor, Richard Pace (Barquel Creations, 1978).

I Want Him Dead (*Lo voglio morto*), director Paolo Bianchini, featuring Craig Hill, Lea Massari, José Manuel Martin (Centauro Films, 1967).

Last House on the Left, director Wes Craven, featuring Sandra Peabody, Lucy Grantham, David Hess (Sean S. Cunningham Films, 1972).

"Lions, Loves (... And Lies)," *Internationales Frauen Film Festival*, 2016 <www.frauenfilmfestival.eu/index.php?id=2650&id=2650&L=1>.

McCabe and Mrs Miller, director Robert Altman, featuring Warren Beatty, Julie Christie, Rene Auberjonois (David Foster Productions and Warner Bros., 1971).

Montana Belle, director Dwan, Allan, featuring Jane Russell, George Brent, Scott Brady (RKO Radio Productions, 1952).

Ms .45, director Abel Ferrara, featuring Zoë Lund, Bogey, Albert Sinkys (Navaron Films, 1981).

My Darling Clementine, director John Ford, featuring Henry Fonda, Linda Darnell, Victor Mature (20th Century Fox, 1946).

Once Upon a Time in the West (*C'era una volta il West*), director Sergio Leone, featuring Henry Fonda, Charles Bronson, Claudia Cardinale (Rafran Cinematografica, 1968).

"Perilous Passage," *Overland Trail*, Season 1, Episode 1 (Overland Stage-Bilben Productions, 1960).

Seven Hours of Gunfire (*Sette ore di fuoco*), director Joaquín Luis Romero Marchent, featuring Rik Van Nutter, Adrian Hoven, Gloria Milland (Centauro Films, 1965).

Shane, director George Stevens, featuring Alan Ladd, Jean Arthur, Van Heflin (Paramount, 1953).

The Belle Starr Story (*Il mio corpo per un poker*), director Lina Wertmuller, featuring Elsa Martinelli, Robert Woods, George Eastman (Eureka Films, 1968).

"The Legend of Belle Starr," *Quick Draw*, created by Nancy Hower and John Lehr, Season 2, Episode 2 (Hulu, 2013).

The Lizards (*I basilischi*), director Lina Wertmüller, featuring Antonio Petruzzi, Stefano Satta Flores, Sergio Ferranino (Galatea Film, 1963).

The Long Rider, director Walter Hill, featuring David Carradine, Stacey Keach, Dennis Quaid (Huka Productions, 1980).

The Man Who Loved Cat Dancing, director Richard Sarafian, featuring Burt Reynolds, Sara Miles, Lee J. Cobb (MGM, 1973).

The Three Stooges: The Outlaws Is Coming, director Norman Maurer, featuring Larry Fine, Joe DeRita, Moe Howard (Columbia, 1959).

The Virgin Spring, director Ingmar Bergman, featuring Max von Sydow, Birgitta Valberg, Gunnel Lindblum (Svensk Filmindustri, 1960).

This Time Let's Talk About Men (*Questa volta parliamo di uomini*), director Lina Wertmüller, featuring Nino Manfredi, Luciana Paluzzi, Milena Vukotic (Archimese Films, 1965).

BIBLIOGRAPHY

Agnew, Jeremy (2015) *The Old West in Fact and Film: History Versus Hollywood*. Jefferson, NC: McFarland.
Bayman, Louis and Rigloetto, Sergio (2013) "The Fair and the Museum: Framing the Popular," in Louis Bayman and Sergio Rigoletto (eds), *Popular Italian Cinema*. New York: Palgrave Macmillan, pp. 1–28.
Betts, Tom (1992) "Westerns . . . All'Italiana!" *The Spaghetti Western Database* <www.spaghetti-western.net/index.php/Westerns..._All%27Italiana!> (last accessed 5 November 2019).
Blumenfeld, Gina (1974) "The (Next to) Last Word on Lina Wertmuller," *Cineaste*, 7 (2), pp. 2–5.
Bondanella, Peter (2009) *A History of Italian Cinema*. New York: Continuum Books.
Brizio-Skov, Flavia (2011a) "Dollars, Bullets and Success: The Spaghetti Western Phenomenon," in Flavia Brizio-Skov (ed.), *Popular Italian Cinema: Culture and Politics in a Postwar Society*. London: I. B. Tauris, pp. 83–106.
Brizio-Skov, Flavia (2011b) "Popular Cinema and Violence: The Western Genre," in Flavia Brizio-Skov (ed.) *Popular Italian Cinema: Culture and Politics in a Postwar Society*. London: I. B. Tauris, pp. 189–228.
Broughton, Lee (2016a) *Euro-Western: Reframing Gender, Race, and the "Other" in Film*. London: I. B. Tauris.
Broughton, Lee (2016b) "Rethinking the Representation of Race and Gender in American Exploitation Westerns from the 1960s," in Lee Broughton (ed.), *Critical Perspectives on the Western: From A Fistful of Dollars to Django Unchained*. Lanham, MD: Rowan & Littlefield, pp. 57–72.
Bruno, Giuliana and Nadotti, Maria (2016) *Off Screen: Women and Film in Italy: Seminar on Italian and American Directions*, 1st edn. London: Routledge.
Bullaro, Grace Russo (2006a) *Man in Disorder: The Cinema of Lina Wertmüller in the 1970s*. Leicester: Troubador.
Bullaro, Grace Russo (2006b) "The Fictitious Genius of Lina Wertmuller's 1970s Films? A Look at the American and Italian Views," *Forum Italicum*, 40 (2), pp. 487–99.
Buscombe, Edward (1993) *The B.F.I. Companion to the Western*, 1st edn. Atheneum.
Buscombe, Edward and Pearson, Roberta E. (1998) "Introduction," in Edward Buscombe and Roberta E. Pearson (eds), *Back in the Saddle Again: New Essays on the Western*. London: BFI Publishing.
Cantini, M. (2013) "Italian Women Filmmakers and the Gendered Screen," *Italian and Italian American Studies*. New York: Palgrave Macmillan, pp. 1–11.
Carter, David (2008) *The Western*. Harpenden: Kamera Books.
Chapman Peek, Wendy (2003) "The Romance of Competence: Rethinking Masculinity in the Western," *Journal of Popular Film and Television*, 30 (4), pp. 206–19.

Clover, Carol (1993) "High and Low: The Transformation of the Rape-Revenge Movie," in Pam Cook and Phillip Dodd (eds), *Women in Film: A Sight and Sound Reader*. Philadelphia, PA: Temple University Press, pp. 76–85.

Coehlo, Maria Cecília de Miranda N. (2017) "Horses for Ladies, High-Ridin' Women and Whores," in Sue Matheson (ed.), *A Fistful of Icons: Essays on Frontier Fixtures of the American Western*. Jefferson, NC: McFarland, pp. 113–23.

Cook, Pam (1993) "Border Crossings: Women and Film in Context," in Pam Cook and Phillip Dodd (eds), *Women in Film: A Sight and Sound Reader*. Philadelphia, PA: Temple University Press, pp. 9–23.

Cuklanz, Lisa M. (2000) *Rape on Prime Time Television, Masculinity, and Sexual Violence*. Philadelphia, PA: University of Pennsylvania Press.

Davis, Robert Murray (1992) *Playing Cowboys: Low Culture and High Art in the Western*. Norman, OK: University of Oklahoma Press.

Deleas, Josetta (2002) "Lina Wertmuller: The Grotesque in *Seven Beauties*," in Jacqueline Levitin, Judith Plessis, Valerie Raoul (eds), *Women Filmmakers: Refocusing*. (Vancouver: University of British Columbia Press, 2002), pp. 151–63.

Dworkin, Mark J. (2015) *American Mythmaker: Walter Noble Burns and the Legends of Billy the Kid, Wyatt Earp, and Joaquín Murrieta*, 1st edn. Norman, OK: University of Oklahoma Press.

Edson, J. T. (1968) *The Floating Outfit* (series). Charter Books.

Erhart, Julia (2018) *Gendering History on Screen: Women Filmmakers and Historical Films*. New York: I. B. Tauris.

Estlemen, Loren D. (2009) *The Branch and the Scaffold: The True Story of the West's Hanging Judge*, 1st edn. New York: Forge/Tom Doherty.

Ferlita, Ernest and May, John R. (1977) *The Parables of Lina Wertmuller*, 1st edn. Mahwah, NJ: Paulist Press.

Fischer, Lucy (1989) *Shot/Countershot: Film Tradition and Women's Cinema*. Princeton, NJ: Princeton University Press.

Fisher, Austin (2014) *Radical Frontiers in the Spaghetti Western: Politics, Violence and Popular Italian Cinema*, 1st edn. London: I. B. Taurus.

Fisher, Austin (ed.) (2016) *Spaghetti Westerns at the Crossroads: Studies in Relocation, Transition and Appropriation*. Edinburgh: Edinburgh University Press.

Forshaw, Barry (2017) *Italian Cinema: Arthouse to Exploitation*. Harpenden: Kamera Books.

Foster, Gwendolyn Audrey (1995) *Women Film Directors: An International Bio-Critical Dictionary*. Westport, CT: Greenwood Press.

Frankel, Glenn (2014) *The Searchers: The Making of an American Legend*. New York: Bloomsbury.

Franklin, Mark (2107) "The Belle Starr Story (1968)," *Once Upon a Time in a Western*, 21 January <onceuponatimeinawestern.com/the-belle-starr-story-1968/> (last accessed 5 November 2019).

Fridlund, Bert (2007) *The Spaghetti Western: A Thematic Analysis*. Jefferson, NC: McFarland.

Gazzaniga, Andrea (2013) "From Whore to Hero: Reassessing Jill in *Once Upon a Time in the West*," in Sue Matheson (ed.), *Love in Western Film and Television: Lonely Hearts and Happy Trails*. New York: Palgrave, pp. 53–69.

Gaines, Anne Marie and Herzog, Charlotte Cornelia (1998) "The Fantasy of Authenticity in Western Costume," in Edward Buscombe and Roberta E. Pearson (eds), *Back in the Saddle Again: New Essays on the Western*. London: BFI, pp. 178–9.

Giusti, Marco (2007) *Dizionario del western all'italiana*. Milan: Mondadori, pp. 45–7.

Gragasin, Angeline (1979) "The Belle Star Story," *Screen Slate*, 2018, <www.screenslate.com/features/930>.

Hamilton, Emma (2016) *Masculinities in American Western Films: A Hyper-Linear History*. Oxford: Peter Lang.

Hardcastle, Stoney (1979) *The Legend of Belle Starr*, 1st edn. New York: Carlyle Books.

Haskell, Molly (1974) *From Reverence to Rape: The Treatment of Women in the Movies*. New York: Holt, Reinhardt & Winston.

Haskell, Molly and Dargis, Manohla (2016) *From Reverence to Rape: The Treatment of Women in the Movies*, 2nd edn. Chicago: University of Chicago Press.

Heller-Nicholas, A. (2011) *Rape-Revenge Films: A Critical Study*. Jefferson, NC: McFarland.

Henry, Claire (2014) *Revisionist Rape-Revenge: Redefining a Film Genre*. New York: Palgrave Macmillan.

Holland, Barbara (2007) *They Went Whistling: Women Wayfarers, Warriors, Runaways, and Renegades*. New York: Random House.

Hopkins, Lidia Hwa Soon Anchisi and Cuculis, Luke (2013) "Don't Bring a Gun to a Fistfight: Deconstructing Hegemonic Masculinity through the Gun in Lina Wertmuller's *Pasqualino Settebellezze*," in Maristella Cantini (ed.), *Italian Women Filmmakers and the Gendered Screen*. New York: Palgrave, pp. 53–72.

Hughes, Howard (2011) *Cinema Italiano: The Complete Guide From Classics to Cult*. London: I. B. Tauris.

Hughes, Howard (2004) *Once Upon a Time in the Italian West: A Filmgoers' Guide to Spaghetti Westerns*. London: I. B. Tauris.

Hutchison, W. H. (1979) "Virgins, Villains, and Varmints," in James K. Folsom (ed.), *The Western: A Collection of Critical Essays*. Englewood Cliffs, NJ: Prentice Hall, pp. 31–49.

"Image Et Son" (n.d.) *Objectif Cinema* <www.objectif-cinema.com/spip.php?article5533&artsuite=1>.

Johnson, Claire (1974) "Women's Cinema as Counter-Cinema," *Notes on Women's Cinema: Screen Pamphlet*, No. 2, pp. 24–31.

Jones, Douglas C. (1991) *The Search for Temperance Moon*, 1st edn. New York: Henry Holt.

Kay, Karen and Peary, Gerald (eds) (1977) *Women and the Cinema: A Critical Anthology*. New York: E. P. Dutton.

Kuhn, Annette and Radstone, Susannah (1990) *The Women's Companion to International Film*. London: Virago.

Lamont, Victoria (2016) *Westerns: A Women's History*. Lincoln, NE: University of Nebraska Press.
Landy, Marcia (2000) *Italian Film*. Cambridge: Cambridge University Press.
Lusted, David (2003) *The Western*. London: Routledge.
McClain, William (2010) "Western, Go Home! Sergio Leone and the 'Death of the Western' in American Film Criticism," *Journal of Film and Video*, 62 (1–2), pp. 52–66.
McCormick, Ruth (1977) "Swept Away by Romano Cardarelli, Lina Wertmüller," *Cineaste*, 7 (2), pp. 41–2.
McIsaac P. and Blumenfeld, G. (1974) "You cannot make the revolution on film": An Interview with Lina Wertmuller," *Cineaste*, 7 (2), pp. 7–9.
McLennan, Jim (2017) "The Belle Starr Story: 'A Blandly Over-Cooked Platter of Spaghetti,'" *Girls with Guns: Home of the Action Heroine* <girlswithguns.org/belle-starr-story/> (last accessed 5 November 2019).
McVeigh, Stephen (2007) *The American Western*. Edinburgh: Edinburgh University Press.
Marcus, Millicent (2002) *After Fellini: National Cinema in the Postmodern Age*. Baltimore, MD: Johns Hopkins University Press.
Mathijs, Ernest and Mendik, Xavier (2004) *Alternative Europe: Eurotrash and Exploitation Cinema since 1945*. London: Wallflower.
Mayne, J. (1990) *The Woman at the Keyhole: Feminism and Women's Cinema (Theories of Representation and Difference)*. Bloomington, IN: Indiana University Press.
Meier, Allison (2013) "Belle Starr the Bandit Queen: How a Southern Girl Became a Legendary Western Outlaw," *Altas Obscura* <https://www.atlasobscura.com/articles/belle-starr-the-bandit-queen> (last accessed 5 November 2019).
Mellen, J. (1980) "Lina Wertmuller," in A. A. Berger (ed.), *Film in Society*. New Brunswick, NJ: Transaction, pp. 99–108.
Miller, Cynthia J. (2103) "'Wild' Women: Interracial Romance of the Western Frontier," in Sue Matheson (ed.), *Love in Western Film and Television: Lonely Hearts and Happy Trails*. New York: Palgrave, pp. 71–89.
Miller, Cynthia J. and Van Riper, A. Bowdoin (2014) "Introduction," in Cynthia J. Miller and A. Bowdoin Van Riper (eds), *International Westerns: Relocating the Frontier*. Lanham, MA: Scarecrow Press, pp. ix–xxvii.
Mitchell, Lee Clark (1996) *Westerns: Making the Man in Fiction and Film*. Chicago: University of Chicago Press.
Modleski, Tania (2004) "Wertmuller's Women: *Swept Away* by the Usual Destiny," *Jump Cut: A Review of Contemporary Media*, 10–11, pp. 1–16.
Morgan, Speer (1979) *Belle Starr*, 1st edn. Boston: Little, Brown.
Nelson, John S. (2017) *Cowboy Politics: Myths and Discourses in Popular Westerns from The Virginian to Unforgiven and Deadwood*. Lanham, MD: Lexington Books.
Nowell-Smith, Geoffrey (2013) *Making Waves: New Cinemas of the 1960s*. London: Bloomsbury Press.
O'Healy, Annie (1990) "Reframing Desire in Lina Wertmüller's *Sotto . . . Sotto*," *Spectatator*, 10 (2), pp. 45–7.

Parke, Henry C. (2018) "DVD Review: Black Jack & the Belle Starr Story," *True West: History of the American Frontier* <truewestmagazine.com/dvd-review-black-jack-the-belle-starr-story/> (last accessed 5 November 2019).

Pheasant-Kelly, Fran (2017) "The Sexual Signification of the Gun in Western Film," in Sue Matheson (ed.), *A Fistful of Icons: Essays on Frontier Fixtures of the American Western*. Jefferson, NC: McFarland, pp. 124–41.

Projansky, Sarah (2001) *Watching Rape Film and Television in Postfeminist Culture*, 1st edn. New York: New York University Press.

Quacinella, L. (1974) "How Left is Lina?" *Cineaste*, 7 (3), pp. 7–9.

Quart, Barbara (1988) *Women Directors: The Emergence of a New Cinema*. New York: Praeger.

Rainey, Buck (2015) Western Gunslingers in Fact and on Film: Hollywoods Famous Lawmen and Outlaws. Jefferson, NC: McFarland, pp. 131–44.

Ramirez, Juan (2017) "Bonnets, Guns and Trails: Westerns Made by Women," *Brattle Theatre Film Notes* <www.brattleblog.brattlefilm.org/2017/06/25/bonnets-guns-and-trails-westerns-made-by-women-5284/> (last accessed 5 November 2019).

Read, Jacinda (2000) *The New Avengers: Feminism, Femininity and the Rape-Revenge Cycle*. Manchester: Manchester University Press.

Rickman, Gregg and Kitses, Jim (1998) *The Western Reader*. New York: Limelight Editions.

Rigoletto, Sergio (2013) "Laughter and the Popular in Lina Wertmuller's *The Seduction of Mimi*," in Sergio Rigoletto and Louis Bayman (eds), *Popular Italian Cinema*. New York: Palgrave Macmillan, pp. 117–32.

Roberts, Gary L. (2006) *Doc Holiday: The Life and Legend*, 1st edn. Hoboken, NJ: Wiley.

Robinson, Lillian S. (1985) "Treason Our Text: Feminist Challenges to the Literary Canon," in Elaine Showalter (ed.), *The New Feminist Criticism: Essays on Women, Literature, and Theory*. New York: Pantheon, p. 109.

Rosa, Joseph G. (1996) *Wild Bill Hickok: The Man and His Myth*. Lawrence, KS: University Press of Kansas.

Russell, D. (2010) *Rape in Art Cinema*. New York: Continuum.

Scott, Kenneth (1963) *Belle Starr in Velvet*. New York: Pan Press.

Schubart, Rikkie (2007) *Super Bitches and Action Babes: The Female Hero in Popular Cinema, 1970–2006*. Jefferson, NC: McFarland.

Shirley, Glenn (1982) *Belle Starr and Her Times: The Literature, the Facts, and the Legends*, reprint. Norman, OK: University of Oklahoma Press.

Slotkin, Richard (1998) *Gunfighter Nation: Myth of the Frontier in Twentieth-Century America*. Norman, OK: University of Oklahoma Press.

Smith, Paul (1993) *Clint Eastwood: A Cultural Production*, 1st edn. Minneapolis, MN: University of Minnesota Press.

Steele, Phillip W. (2002) "Belle Starr: Petticoat Wildcat," *True West: History of the American Frontier* <truewestmagazine.com/belle-starr/> (last accessed 5 November 2019).

Sutherland, John (1981) *Bestsellers: Popular Fiction from the 1970s*. London: Routledge, pp. 33–7, 154–66.

"The Belle Starr Story," *Revolvy*, <www.revolvy.com/page/The-Belle-Starr-Story/>.
"The Belle Starr Story" (2019) *Sensecritique* <www.senscritique.com/film/The_Belle_Starr_Story/13587880>.
Tompkins, Jane (1992) *West of Everything: The Inner Life of Westerns*. Oxford: Oxford University Press.
Vighi, Fabio (2006) *Traumatic Encounters in Italian Film: Locating the Cinematic Unconscious*. Bristol: Intellect.
Vitti, Antonio C. (1989–90) "The Critics 'Swept Away' by Wertmüller's Sexual Politics," *NEMLA Italian Studies*, 13–14, pp. 121–31.
Vogel, Art (1974) *Film as a Subversive Art*. New York: Random House.
Waddell, Calum (2018) *The Style of Sleaze: The American Exploitation Film, 1959–1977*, 1st edn. Edinburgh: Edinburgh University Press.
Wagstaff, Christopher (1992) "A Forkful of Westerns: Industry, Audiences and the Italian Western," in Richard Dyer and Ginette Vincendeau (eds), *Popular European Cinema*. London: Routledge, pp. 245–62.
Wagstaff, Christopher (2013) "Italian Cinema: Popular?" in Louis Bayman and Sergio Rigoletto (eds), *Popular Italian Cinema*. New York: Palgrave Macmillan, pp. 29–51.
Walker, (2001) *Westerns: Films Through History*. London: Routledge.
Walle, Alf H. (2000) *The Cowboy Hero and Its Audience*. Bowling Green, OH: Bowling Green State University Popular Press.
Winter, Nina (1978) *Interview with the Muse: Remarkable Women Speak on Creativity and Power*. Berkeley, CA: Moon Books.
Wong, Aliza S (2016) "Malaysian Pirates, American Cowboys, and the Marginalized Outlaw: Constructing Other-ed Adventurers in Italian Film," in Austin Fisher (ed.), *Spaghetti Westerns at the Crossroads: Studies in Relocation, Transition, and Appropriation*. Edinburgh: Edinburgh University Press, pp. 67–85.
Wood, Mary (2005) *Italian Cinema*. Oxford: Berg.
Yates, Norris (1995) *Gender and Genre: An Introduction to Women Writers of Formula Westerns, 1900–1950*. Albuquerque, NM: University of New Mexico Press.

14. THE FEMALE AVENGER IN POST-9/11 WESTERNS

Martin Holtz

INTRODUCTION

After a decade of relatively sporadic output, 9/11 certainly reinvigorated the Western. Not only did the terror attacks and the ensuing climate of righteous retaliation conjure up the established metaphors of the genre's inventory, its relevance was also confirmed by the subtle modifications in its repertoire. President Bush availed himself in frontier rhetoric to galvanize a traumatized nation into support for his global War on Terror. The frontier was drawn between American democracy and Middle East terrorism with the threatening claim, "either you are with us or you are with the terrorists" (Bush 2001), Bin Laden was "wanted dead or alive," and the army would "smoke out" the Taliban fighters from their mountain caves (qtd. in Knowlton 2001). As Dixon points out, many films followed suit:

> While some contemporary films offer escapism, the bulk of mainstream American cinema since 9/11, whether the films were in production before the events of that day or not, seems centered on a desire to replicate the idea of the "just war," in which military reprisals, and the concomitant escalation of warfare, seem simultaneously inevitable and justified. (Dixon 2004: 1)

The Western appeared to satisfy this desire in its classical incarnation of providing fantasies of justified revenge unencumbered by institutionalized law in a frontier environment. A film like *Open Range* (2003) illustrates both the appeal of a return to genre classicism and the subtle modifications that the immediate post-9/11 context seemed to spawn. The film follows the pattern of what Will Wright calls the "vengeance variation" of the classical plot and consciously evokes such classics as *My Darling Clementine* (1946) and *Shane* (1953) (cf. Wright 1975: 59–74). A peaceful free-grazing cattle-herding outfit is attacked by an evil landbaron who simultaneously keeps a town's population in his thrall. The free-grazers take revenge and rid the town of evil. The personal interests of the heroes are united by communal benefit. Their violence is "regenerative" (cf. Slotkin 1988: 234). So far, so classical, and so apt for the times. But the crucial difference to the classical model can be found in the depiction of the woman. In Wright's conception and in the ur-text of the genre, Owen Wister's *The Virginian* (1902), the woman, as a representative of the peaceful and victimized community, is a spokesperson for pacifism. She opposes the violent ways of the hero, and, even if her pleas are subdued by the necessity of violence, her pacifist ideology guarantees the future blossoming of the town once it has rid itself of evil (cf. Wright 1975: 68). When, in a crucial scene in *Open Range*, Kevin Costner's hero tells the nurse Sue, played by Annette Bening, "Men are gonna get killed today, Sue, and I'm gonna kill them. Do you understand?" she calmly and matter-of-factly replies, "Yes" and gives him a talisman for good luck. Instead of opposing violence, she endorses it.

Bell-Metereau points out that there is a general trend in post-9/11 films to portray women as "participants in 'justified' revenge" (2004: 143), which contributes to an atmosphere of universal, cross-gender, national determination. She concentrates on the film *Panic Room* (2002) as an example for the determined mother action heroine that builds on the post-*Alien* cultivation of female heroines in the action/adventure genre. "With the repositioning of women in traditionally masculine genres, images of domesticity and consumption are also retooled and refigured, and instead of featuring Rosie the Riveter on the home front, filmmakers give viewers something more like Rosie the Robocop" (2004: 146).[1] Why has the violence-prone woman become a trend in post-9/11 cinema? Landy suggests that the "dramatization of the violation of innocence" (2004: 87), including the depiction of the terrorist attacks in terms of alternately rape or castration (2004: 82), pervades cultural expressions of that time. They revel in victimhood in order to secure a moral authority that legitimizes the ensuing retaliation. Women, stereotypically associated with victimhood *and* moral authority, fulfill the pathos of the violated and therefore automatically assume a moral high ground when pursuing their revenge. In other words, if even the traditional pacifist cries for revenge following her violation, who would disagree with her? Furthermore, on the surface, the female avenger is presented as an icon of progressive feminism, which seeks to promote a revision of established stereotypes. Yet, this progressive appeal is put to the service of a pro-violence message of justified retaliation in the wake of 9/11, as a sort of liberal catalyst for an essentially conservative agenda.[2]

This contribution will explore three post-9/11 Westerns in which the female avenger figure is featured and show how her initial ideological function receives an ongoing modification in subsequent films and changing political and cultural climates. *The Missing* (2003) is the prototype, *Bandidas* (2006) the comedic variation, and *True Grit* (2011) the deconstruction. Collectively, these three films display the importance of the female avenger as a by now established innovation in recent Western history and also its flexibility in accommodating different moods, political leanings, and contexts as a sort of ideological barometer for the genre as a whole.

THE MISSING

The Missing is the prototype of female avenger Westerns after 9/11 not only because it was the first one, but also because it set the standard for the ideological effectiveness of the model as described above. As a film made shortly after the terrorist attacks it reflects an attitude of righteous retaliation, albeit one softened in its hawkishness, and thereby all the more persuasive, by an astute management of gender and ethnicity politics. Essentially an Indian captivity tale, the film explicitly references John Ford's *The Searchers* (1956) and can be seen as reversing its ideological trajectory (cf. Bischoff and Nocon 2004: 117). *The Searchers* starts from a clearly delineated conservative scenario: a seemingly unmotivated Indian raid on a white settlement prompts a rescue mission to return two girl captives back to white society. But in the course of the film this scenario is complicated by the explicit racism displayed by the white society, the victimization of the Indians, and the kidnapped girl's refusal to return to her home, by which the conservative implications of its traditionally happy ending are exposed as delusional fantasy. In contrast, *The Missing* has a progressive premise: a female heroine and a multidimensional ethnic spectrum on both sides of the dramatic conflict. But it manages to reduce this complexity to conservative simplicity by advocating the supremacy of the ethnically pure family, the preservation of which justifies any means available. In this way, it presents a narrative that proposes a return to a simplistic good vs. evil scenario by smothering intimations of moral complexity and relativity and thereby aligning itself with a post-9/11 spirit of righteous retaliation in favor of a more nuanced and balanced conflict resolution.

The protagonist Maggie (Cate Blanchett) is introduced as a character uniting traditional and progressive features. As a doctor living in an isolated homestead, she is economically self-reliant and highly respected among the local, mostly Spanish-speaking population. She takes care of two daughters and has a lover without being married to him. Hence she is responsible without being dependent, interculturally adept with a strong sense of familial bonding. But her protective motherhood also harbors potential conflict. Her teenage daughter Lilly (Evan Rachel Wood) seeks independence from the drab life on a farm and fantasizes about fancy clothes and urban sophistication so much so that she feels "born into the wrong family," which is met by her mother's tenacious insistence on curbing her "daintiness" and staying where she belongs. Complicating this conflict of overprotection vs. teenage rebellion is the arrival of Samuel Jones (Tommy Lee Jones), a white man who "went Indian" and is the source of much fascination on the part of Maggie's younger daughter Dot (Jenna Boyd) and much anti-Indian resentment on the part of her mother. Jones turns out to be Maggie's father who left the family to fend for itself when she was still a young girl, which "broke" her mother and left Maggie first praying for his return, then embittered over his departure. It becomes clear that her overprotection of her daughters (as well as her unwillingness to enter into dependencies with other men) is an overcompensation for her abandonment as a child. Jones, on the other hand, is presented as a free spirit, an artist, a man imbued with Native American spirituality, but also one who is "good at killing things," as his daughter says. He has come to seek forgiveness, full of remorse for his selfish neglect of the family and willing to support her and her daughters. Where Maggie appears aggressive and resentful in her insistence on kinship loyalty, Jones appears level-headed and respectful of cultural difference *because* of the neglect of his kin. Both have their points and our sympathies as both can be seen as representing contrastive political positions regarding the protection of domestic integrity, the pursuit of intercultural dialogue, and the cultivation of force, befitting a pre-9/11 ideological indecisiveness.

Then tragedy strikes. When her lover Brake (Aaron Eckhardt) and her two daughters ride to the town's fair, they are attacked by an Indian band. Brake is killed, Lilly is abducted, but Dot is able to hide. Lilly's abduction is explicitly related to her quest for independence as she is the one who instigates the trip in the first place. When Maggie comes looking for them, she only finds the mutilated corpse of Brake and Dot, who, as the traumatized survivor, can only stammer about having been abandoned. This is the film's 9/11. Maggie, as the representative of a cautionary but ultimately unassertive America, feels riddled by guilt (just as the country) berating her lack of vigilance and immediately planning for revenge in the form of a rescue mission. The allegorical dimensions of the film at this point have ambivalent ideological implications. Maggie cannot count on the law enforcement authorities to help her. The sheriff denies responsibility and is busy (or so he claims) policing the town's fairgrounds.[3] The army is portrayed as being composed of selfish looters and inexperienced officers following ineffective orders. Both are emblems of a decadent society, a wayward America that has forgotten about self-sacrificial civic engagement and hides its refusal of responsibility behind conformist bureaucracy. While this portrayal can be seen as a critical comment on the representatives of the state that have turned a blind eye to the threats that face the nation, it can also (in a similarly hawkish vein) be seen as a critical comment on the international skepticism of the US path of revenge, which ultimately, in true Western fashion, led to the country's break away from a "decadent" UN diplomacy in order to take the law into its own hands.

Yet Maggie does not go wholly alone. Jones is eager to make up for his past mistakes by assisting Maggie in finding her daughter, and, as the man who knows Indians, he has the skill to track down the Indian band that took her. This intercultural collaboration is at the center of the film's ethnic complexities, which are exemplified by the army officer's assessment that "the whole territory turned topsy-turvy, whites running with Indians, Indians with whites," suggesting a lack of order due to racial intermingling. Rather than sharing the officer's explicit racism, the film can be seen in line with a post-Vietnam War "politically correct" redefinition of frontier binarism (cf. Bischoff and Nocon 2004: 120). The frontier does not run along the lines of a racial divide anymore but along the lines of an ideological divide, in this case pro-family vs. anti-family attitudes, which once again suggest a Manichean worldview of American vs. anti-American factions comparable to post-9/11 warmongering rhetoric. Accordingly, the villains are not exclusively Indian, they also include a token white guy and so combine the worst features of white civilization and Indian savagery. White complicity is also suggested in the emergence of villainy. The Indians are former army scouts who went rogue when their chief was hanged, suggesting a commentary on America's erstwhile support of the Taliban and subsequent abandonment. Just like Al-Quaida, the Indians are essentially religious fundamentalists bent on terrorizing their former allies. The main villain is a caricature of the savage Indian, a monstrous shaman, ugly, sadistic, evil, his band hiding in caves. "It is difficult not to identify him with Osama Bin Laden," French writes (2005: 201), or rather with the image of Bin Laden in the American media as an enemy of Western civilization. This "unholy alliance" (Bischoff and Nocon 2004: 120) of Indians and disgruntled whites tries to sell the kidnapped girls across the border in Mexico, combining terror with greed and playing into a post-9/11 fear of open borders. Their dressing up the girls in garish clothes and make-up to spruce up their merchandise becomes a sardonic comment on the decadent culture they despise. It is this unqualified hatred of Western culture that marks them as wholly irredeemable.

The one-sided fundamentalism of the villains not only supports the legitimacy of retaliation, it is also contrasted with the collaborative trajectory of the heroes. Maggie's quest for revenge involves her successive acceptance of Indian culture. This gradual approach is depicted on a distinctly religious level, with Maggie's crucifix and Jones's Indian paraphernalia such as beads and even moccasins as well as ritualistic chants working as talismans that protect the group from the spells of the shaman. There are clearly supernatural aspects to the story. A spring tide, summoned by the shaman, almost kills Dot were it not for a bracelet Jones has given her, Maggie suddenly falls ill and is only saved by a ritual that combines Dot's prayers with Jones's chants, and, most baldly, Jones turns into a bird to escape the Indian band after he gets caught. Late in the film, the searchers are joined by a Chiricahua warrior and his son, who have also been victimized by the renegades. So does the film advocate intercultural harmony? Yes and no. The multicultural alliance can be seen as a "coalition of the willing" under American leadership. The presence of Indians among them further legitimizes the pursuit of the villains along the lines of the Iraq War justification: the bad Indians harm their own people, who, as good Indians, join in the fight against the oppressor. Additionally, in line with the genre's classical depiction of ethnic frontiers, intercultural collaboration is portrayed as a wholly pragmatic "know your foe" scenario. It is necessary to be able to vanquish the enemy and rescue the girls (cf. Bischoff and Nocon 2004: 120–1).[4] Its function is not the propagation of peaceful diplomacy but the assembly of the greatest amount of militant effectiveness. The point is to kill the enemy, exemplified in a telling scene when Maggie instructs Dot to say a little prayer before firing a weapon to ease her conscience, and Jones wholeheartedly agrees. The two otherwise disparate cultures and religions are united in supporting revenge, and the woman becomes the fulcrum of unifying civilization and violence.

The resolution of the conflict comes in the form of a surprise attack, mirroring the ambush scenario of the "9/11" attack at the beginning. After the first attempt to get Lilly back peacefully by offering a trade (corresponding to a diplomatic conflict resolution) ends in the Chiricahua's loss of life amid the mocking brutality of the shaman's band, the stage is set for a violent raid that crucially eschews any decorum of the "fair" Western duel. The scenario requires and justifies extreme measures to guarantee success. This abandonment of fairness corresponds to the contemporary justification of pre-emptive war, the feeling of moral righteousness in subordinating notions of rules of engagement to victory by all means, because "they did it first," which justifies even the most uncompromising "shock and awe" tactics. Jones and Maggie sneak up on the band and are able to kill enough of them before they get a chance to defend themselves. The girls are rescued, but they are not safe until the shaman is defeated after a counterattack at night, in which Jones selflessly throws himself and the villain across a cliff, which results in their mutual death. After the leader is killed, Maggie is able to discourage his followers from taking revenge, confirming the myth of the surgical strike and the spinelessness of the villains. Jones's trajectory is thereby completed. He has overcome the selfish impulses that led to the abandonment of his family and given his life in order to protect it. This sacrifice absolves him from his daughter's resentment who in turn forgives him. Crucially, it is the Chiricahua companion who spells out the conservative rebuttal of Jones's ethnic transcendence in stating that the biological family is the most precious. By having the minority member as the spokesperson for conservative values, the film mirrors the strategy of having the female as the spokesperson for violent revenge. Also Lilly falls in line with the conservative conclusion, in a way reversing the trajectory of the kidnapped Debbie (Natalie Wood) in *The Searchers*. Where Debbie embraces Indian culture, Lilly regrets her rebellion against her mother, realizes her guilt, and is forgiven her transgressions. In the reunification of the ethnically pure white family, Maggie's initially dubious overprotectiveness is wholly vindicated as all the forces harmful to the family (the shaman, Jones, Lilly) are either killed off or reeled in, and so her "Let's go home" which ends the film carries none of the ironic implications of John Wayne's delivery in *The Searchers*. Defending "home" by all means is the message and the essence of the film, and with Maggie the film finds the perfect purveyor, as she emerges as the textbook balance of feminist appeal and family-mindedness in her incarnation as the vigilant avenger and persuasive incarnation of a post-9/11 American retaliatory spirit, whose wrath and force is justified by the experience of loss, the concern for loved ones, and the tolerance for cultural Otherness.

Bandidas

Even though there are only three years between the releases of *The Missing* and *Bandidas*, the political climate changes dramatically in between. Where *The Missing* reflects the dominant national mood of righteous revenge immediately after 9/11, *Bandidas* addresses the international and domestic resentments that America's War on Terror generated, particularly with the unpopular Iraq War that was widely criticized as imperialist and unethical, given the obvious rejection of the occupation by the local population, the mounting rate of casualties, and finally the Abu Ghraib torture scandal in 2004. The ideological thrust of the two films, however, is remarkably similar, even if their structural organization of the revenge plot appears to be at odds. *The Missing* legitimizes US revenge, *Bandidas* defuses vengeful resentments towards US international politics. The female gender of the heroines, as portrayed by Mexican Salma Hayek and Spanish Penelope Cruz, contributes to their presentation as essentially loveable and harmless in their nonchalant sexiness, safely embedded in a star discourse of Hollywood establishment. Utilizing elements of the classical vengeance variation, the film is less concerned with the legitimization of revenge and more with channeling its subversive implications into safe and ultimately US affirmative ideological territory.

The initial situation sets up a scenario that clearly addresses legitimate concerns with the way the US conducted itself internationally after 9/11 and earlier. The villain is Jackson (Dwight Yoakam), a representative of an American railroad company who is sent by his boss to Mexico[5] in order to expand the railway system there under the aegis of corporate interest. In practice this is manifested in the established stereotype of the land-grabbing railroad magnate of the populist Western, who uses economic power to push through his greed-driven interests, controls the corrupt law, and victimizes the population (cf. Slotkin 1992: 278–312). The victimization occurs on two levels. Economically, Jackson gains control over the local banks and land tracts by collaborating with local elites, in particular Don Diego (Ismael "East" Carlo), a rich hacienda owner, whom he coaxes into signing a contract only to kill him by poison afterwards by which he secures monopolistic power. Militarily, Jackson secures the control of the land by having his minions raid the homesteads that the contract allows him to buy up and, in the case of resistance by the owner, to violently take over. Too poor and too powerless to mount a defence, farmers are easy victims. The film therefore reflects the perfidious convergence of globalized capitalism under US control and American military expansionism, thereby addressing the sinister avaricious history and underpinnings that led to and inform America's War on Terror, particularly considering US interests in Middle East resources. Jackson is a clearly marked and one-dimensionally presented projection screen for all these highly combustive resentments. He is dressed in a dandified black outfit, he is heartless, condescending, racist, and sexist. The audience is emotionally manipulated to focus all its anger onto him.

As Jackson's foray into Mexico produces two different victims, it also produces two different avengers: Don Diego's daughter Sara (Salma Hayek) and farmer's daughter Maria (Penelope Cruz). At this stage, the film delves into class politics, given the potential criticism of Don Diego's and hence the local elite's collaboration with the enemy to the chagrin of the poorer population. Sara is, like her father, highly privileged and not a little snobbish, flaunting her European education and lack of concern for the lower classes, but also impressive with her intelligence and sophistication given the predominant stereotype of the Mexican "greaser" who is poor and lazy. Maria, on the other hand, is a simple farmer's daughter with a strong connection to the rural community, albeit outspoken, crafty, glib, and just as pretty as Maria. The two clash early on in the film and again after they start their respective paths of revenge by robbing the banks of the enemy. Where Maria, befitting her class, is a true social bandit who takes from the rich to give to the poor (cf. Hobsbawm 2000: 30), Sara's concern is purely selfish. She wants to keep the loot for herself to satisfy her grief over her father's death and restore the lost money to her wealth in order to go back to Europe and leave Mexico behind. In this way, the two women embody the conflicting motivations of the classical Western avenger, whose self-centered revenge requires a socially regenerative dimension in order to be justified. Sara must learn to curb her selfishness and discover compassion and social responsibility, something she accomplishes due to Maria's persuasion and the local priest's guidance and confrontation with all those suffering from Jackson's "cleansings" and organized resistance. If Sara learns social responsibility, Maria learns pragmatism and organization from Sara, by which the film creates a utopian idea of cross-class collaboration in which the elite is shown to be capable of compassionate concern for the lower classes and even helpful in addressing their concerns and organizing their reformative action. Rather than social overthrow, the film suggests a shared lot to conservatively advocate class harmony (cf. Ruiz-Alfaro 2014: 202). But this conservative utopia carries a considerable subversive note, as the two Mexican women embody a class-crossing righteousness in their revenge against the *American* villain, and by extension America's post-9/11 imperialism, let alone a potential for lesbian romance. One thing is sure, the two have all the sympathies from the audience.

This is the point where other American characters enter the plot. Sam Shepard plays a Butch Cassidy type former bandit who lives alone on a small homestead in Mexico and does not let himself be scared away by Jackson's men. By establishing him as clearly anti-Jackson, the film introduces a different image of the American that is in line with the attractiveness of the Western hero, one that is marked by rebelliousness, a sense of liberty and justice, and above all pragmatic competence. As an experienced gunman, Shepard becomes the mentor of the two women who seek out his expertise and defer to him. An amusing training montage ensues, which derives its humor from the bungling exploits of the women and the calmly bemused patience of their teacher. Not only does this sequence display a superior competence of American professionalism over Mexican amateurism, but also his moral sanction and guidance of their revenge. In fact, he tells them not to kill anyone, laying down the rules of what their revenge is supposed to look like. By establishing the American Western hero as the purveyor of skill and ethics that are sought out by the national Other, the film constructs a fantasy of the US as a sympathetic governing force over world affairs while retaining a safe distance to trouble spots, the ideal of the military advisor who outsources and controls solutions to problems he himself has created, as a kind of idealized version of the American efforts to reduce its presence in Iraq by training a local military force to keep the country stable.

Another sympathetic American enters the film once the two *bandidas* have started their successful run of bank robberies. Quentin Cooke (Steve Zahn), a detective well-versed in the art of science and future son-in-law of Jackson's corporate boss, is sent to Mexico to investigate the robberies and find the culprits. His east coast naivety is another source of humor but also sympathy, which is shared by the two women, who kidnap him, fall for him, and ultimately fight over him while he discovers that Jackson poisoned Don Diego and decides to side with them. As the unlikely love interest of the *bandidas*, Quentin fulfills several important functions in the narrative. First, he provides the decisive proof that morally sanctions their revenge. Second, the attractiveness he exudes suggests that even in all his awkwardness he represents an ideal that Mexico (and, metaphorically, the Middle East) looks up to. As Ruiz-Alfaro puts it:

> he is an educated man who believes in the new scientific technology he uses and his own intelligence as his best weapons for fighting injustice, underscoring with his personality the radical difference between the "modern" United States—a technologically advanced, scientific oriented new society—and the old, "uncivilized" Mexico, with its rural peasants and its wild and fierce *bandidas*. (Ruiz-Alfaro 2014: 204)

Third, his sanctioning function goes further than proving Jackson's murder of Don Diego. His sympathy for the Mexican cause also makes him appear more idealistic than the two heroines who are more interested in winning his favor. He sees "nobility" in the struggle, and it is his approval of the Revolution that immediately precedes Sara's participation in shouts of "Viva la Mexico" and her statement that she "will not let her country down" and stay in Mexico. As another ethical authority, Quentin therefore not just judges and approves the avengers' actions, he positively guides their behavior and even renders safe the subversive potential of the Mexican Revolution by making it appear as if it were conducted in unison with American interests. Fourth, as Quentin commands the interest of the *bandidas* he also dispels any notions of a homosexual romance between them and thereby takes over the role of many women in classical Westerns, whose presence guarantees a safely rendered homosociality. More than that, the efforts they go through to accentuate their attractiveness for Quentin creates a gendered "spectacle in which these bodies are rendered consumable for both the man in the scene as well as for the audience outside of it" (Ruiz-Alfaro 2014: 205). This sexualized consumability of their female bodies further defuses the subversive implications of their actions. They exist to be looked at, and their concern is geared towards confirming their objectification.

The resolution completes the film's innocuous trajectory. Late in the story, the Mexican governor is introduced. His collaboration with Jackson and function as a state representative should mark him as a villain, given the film's sympathy for the Revolutionary forces. But he consistently expresses his care for the Mexican people and likes to see their money safe in Jackson's bank. He is presented as the idealized kind of strong man leader that the US has routinely backed throughout history and across the world regardless of their anti-democratic stance in efforts to keep revolutionary and subversive political forces in check. Jackson, assuaging the governor's concerns, suggests they deposit their gold in Texas where it would be safe from the *bandidas*. To this end he wants to transport the money on a fortified train across the border and, to prove his goodwill, his boss and the governor will be invited to join the ride. Once on the train, however, Jackson shows his true face by throwing the governor from the train and intending to kill his boss, both of whom, it becomes apparent, had the people's interest in mind at all times. Jackson's villainy thereby vindicates both state power and corporate interest who are equally appalled at and victimized by the individualized villain. In fact, the plot construction even suggests that the whole Revolution is essentially unnecessary as long as the aberrant corruptor of peaceful and mutually enriching economic relations between the US and Mexico is removed. The removal is accomplished by Sara, who, in line with the classical vengeance variation plot, kills Jackson in defence of Maria's life, not to satisfy her bloodlust but to protect the life of her partner. With as little bloodshed as possible, Maria and Sara are something like the antithesis to the suicide bomber, their violence being considerate and restrained, even reluctant, and, most importantly, in line with US interest. Quentin goes back to the States to marry his fiancée, leaving the two wistful *bandidas* behind in what seems like a fantasy conclusion to the Iraq War, as the threat is neutralized, economic relations established, and responsibility for damage and turmoil evaporates.

Bandidas is a comedy, and as such one has to consider the degree of seriousness with which it treats the ideological implications of its plot. Clearly, the ironic tone is pervasive, but above all the irony is geared towards what is constructed as a threat to, i.e. legitimate criticism of US conduct, not so much the innocuous and affirmative solution to the threat that the film offers. By presenting the female avengers, representative of Mexican and by extension global discontent with American xenophobia and imperialism, as on the one hand acting in line with US interests and on the other hand as charmingly sexy, consumable bodies to be looked at, the film takes the wind out of their subversive potential and projects all offences onto a clearly marked individualized rogue villain in order to vindicate America at large. It is a film that makes audiences feel good about the general dynamics that underlie America's involvement in the world.

True Grit

True Grit belongs to yet another Western cycle that gained prominence in the wake of the Iraq War and critically interrogates and deconstructs the intimations of regenerative violence that the earlier revenge Westerns propagated. Films like *The Proposition* (2006), *Seraphim Falls* (2006), *3:10 to Yuma* (2007), and the Coens' *No Country for Old Men* (2007) present a much more morally dubious environment of universal corruption, perennial and inevitable violence, and a disbelief in the advancement of civilization. Obama-era Westerns like *Django Unchained* (2012), *The Homesman* (2014), and *The Hateful Eight* (2015) continue in the same vein. *True Grit* is part of the latter group. In fact, it can be read quite effectively as a scathing allegory of America's recent military endeavors, its understanding of justice and morality, and its post-war disillusionment. The film is about the attempt to impose a capitalist regime, represented by an infantile avenger and clad in the rhetoric of justice, on a "wilderness" which refuses to yield to the avenger's demands and instead charges a price from her that not only transcends her rigorously financial mathematics but also figuratively and literally destroys her innocence, her physical wholeness, and her emotional faculty.

The female avenger, Mattie Ross (Hailee Steinfeld), is introduced via voice-over: "People do not give it credence that a young girl could leave home and go off in the wintertime to avenge her father's blood. But it did happen." At forty years of age, she looks back at this episode of her youth trying to establish two things, to the audience as much as to herself: credence and justification. While the sepia-toned, iris-framed flicker image zooms in on the corpse of the slain father, the voice continues: "I was just 14 years of age when a coward by the name of Tom Chaney shot my father down and robbed him of his life and his horse and two California gold pieces that he carried in his trouser band." The reverence for the father, then, is Mattie's prime justification for her version of justice and consequently for her version of the truth. The rhetorical establishment of credence and righteousness is part of the elusive quality of grit that Mattie seeks, finds, and embodies in the course of the film.

Mattie's gender and youth is expressed in her rigorous pragmatism, severity, and sense of entitlement. She invokes her age and sex several times in the movie in various situations, most often in order to have her way with adults without relinquishing a certain air of innocence. Sex and age make her unassailable and obnoxiously persevering. She uses adults for her purposes, just as she ultimately devotes her cause to the memory of the father. Twice she expertly rolls a cigarette and sticks it in Rooster's mouth as if to manipulate him into action by "remasculinizing" him. And before she joins the posse, she puts on her father's clothes, trying to make them fit by stuffing them with newspaper, thereby masculinizing herself.[6] She is, then, a child who has grasped the rules of the adult world to such a degree that she exposes their childishness in turn, a childishness that can be funny and frightening at the same time.

Mattie's pursuit of justice, contrary to what she may believe, illustrates its arbitrariness and relativity. The law does not exert itself naturally, the law must be paid to start working. It is thus not a sovereign and impartial entity, but dependent on whoever wields the most (financial) influence and thus it is at the very least subjective and morally incoherent (cf. LaRocca 2012: 313). *True Grit* shows that vengeance is no longer regenerative for a society, but that it works on purely individual economic interests based on financial compensation. The pursuit of justice is a matter of individual business enterprise, of having the means to hire the right men who are professional enough to get the job done. Pretensions of moral rectitude are hypocritical at best.

Appropriately, Mattie chooses Rooster Cogburn (Jeff Bridges) over the more impartial L. T. Quinn who "always brings in his prisoners alive" but "might slip one by every now and then," because Rooster is "the meanest," "a pitiless man, double tough, fear don't enter into his thinking." His potential ruthlessness in the execution of Mattie's will is not his only quality of "grit" though. His ability to withstand legal inquiry into his more than questionable understanding of self-defense is crucial for the justification of the retaliatory punishment Mattie intends to hire him for. Just as Mattie, he can give "credence" to his side of the story (cf. Millard 2011: 473), even if it amounts to nothing more than legal toleration, but this is enough to satisfy Mattie's understanding of moral sanction.

With the introduction of LaBoeuf (Matt Damon), the film further complicates the notion of the professionalization of justice. LaBoeuf is hired to bring Chaney (Josh Brolin) back to Texas, there to receive his just punishment for the killing of a senator and LaBoeuf to receive his reward. As someone who has the same job as Rooster, he is either an accomplice or a rival professional. Mattie insists that Chaney be punished for killing her father and not for killing the senator, thus enforcing a rivalry between Cogburn and LaBoeuf. Why is this insistence so important for her? Her insistence implies that what she bought is not only the death of Chaney by an agent of the law, but his death as a result of his guilt at killing her father. In other words, she claims to have bought the moral supremacy of *her* revenge over the revenge of anyone else. It is this presumption of a financial control over the exercise of the law and over the assumption of an absolute moral righteousness that makes Mattie a frightening and vicious comment on America's wars after 9/11.[7] It is not only that revenge can be bought, but also the moral legitimacy of one's retribution is a matter of wielding the right economic power.

With her financially sanctioned moral righteousness Mattie starts her crusade by crossing the river that deceptively neatly separates civilization from wilderness in order to join Rooster and LaBoeuf. Their immediate rejection of Mattie's presence can be easily explained by the potential burden she poses to the effective pursuit of Chaney. But more than that, her presence disturbs the frontier equilibrium which the agents of the law are there to uphold. Mattie, as a representative of civilization, must be protected from the potential corruption of the wilderness. The task to protect Mattie's innocence in the wilderness becomes a symbolic theme in the movie, which starts with a stylized shot of Mattie picking up shiny red apples (using the arm she will later lose) as supplies for her beloved horse Little Blackie (cf. Cumbow 2011). She will throw one apple at the ferryman in order to break away and cross the river. If the apple stands at the gateway to corruption, the snake is its agent. The practice of putting a rope around Mattie's sleeping place in order to ward off snakes is emphasized twice in the film. Rooster feels responsible for maintaining a bubble of innocence around the little representative of civilization. She enters the wilderness in the belief of imposing her will on it while staying free of any influence coming the other way. The film shows that such arrogance is certain to crumble.

If we take Rooster (and LaBoeuf) to be a representation of contemporary war activities and attitudes, we find in him a sarcastic comment on America's conduct. Both Rooster and LaBoeuf spend a considerable amount of time waxing eloquent about their professional skills while doing little to turn their bragging into action. Theirs is not a functioning "coalition of the willing." Instead of finding the thing they are looking for, they spend more time wasting their energies (and corn dogs) in futile competitions for superior marksmanship, trying to appear efficient rather than being it and failing in both. At one point they split up in a fight, only to be reunited in a failed ambush with LaBoeuf hurt by friendly fire. For all their ineffectiveness, they do show a willingness to employ all means necessary to acquire their target. Rooster's treatment of Quincy (Paul Rae) and Moon (Domhnall Gleeson) evinces a particularly ruthless shade of his "grit" when he threatens the delinquent acquaintances of the Ned Pepper gang with medical non-assistance and shoots Quincy point-blank after the man chops his friend's fingers off. If getting information out of a dying kid does not qualify as torture, it at least comes close to showing what a man of grit is capable of. In the long run, however, they are unable to track Chaney down.

Ultimately, it is not torture or tracking skill that leads to Chaney but sheer accident. Chaney, in fact, comes closest to the classical Coen hero (and he is quite appropriately played by Brolin, who was the lead actor of *No Country for Old Men*): a loser who feels mistreated by the unfathomable powers of the universe, believing that everything is against him and using these feelings of victimization as an excuse for his errant criminal activities, encountering mischance and absurdity along the way (cf. Palmer 2004: 16, 39, 54; Seeßlen 2000: 253–4, 268–76). As obnoxiously obstinate as they may be, Chaney's laments relativize Mattie's claims to moral absolutes by introducing his side of the story. He may have a point when he says that Frank Ross had no business meddling in his affairs (Frank tried to stop Chaney from getting into trouble with the law after he lost in a card game). His resolute egocentricity is a mirror to Mattie she refuses to recognize herself in. They are two sides of the same coin, both proclaiming an absolute validity to their own point of view by which they justify their questionable actions. By positing the two against each other, the film dismantles their very claims.

While Rooster and LaBoeuf take care of the gang, it is Mattie who has to shoot Chaney, and, as opposed to the novel and the 1969 version, she actually kills him. The recoil from the gun immediately catapults her into the snake pit behind her where she is bitten. Her innocence lost, she will also lose her arm as a mark of the grit that comes with the exposure to the wilderness and constitutes the price she has to pay for her revenge regardless of her financial deal. What Mattie's killing makes clear is the undeniable guilt and "fall from grace" as a result of her participation. Rooster does not manage to keep her from killing Chaney just as he does not manage to save her arm. In fact, Rooster's attempts to salvage a situation that is past salvaging leads to further harm. In their ride to the nearest homestead, past the strewn corpses of the criminals, Little Blackie is sacrificed as an innocent victim of Mattie's quest for revenge.

The point is, Mattie got exactly the kind of justice she wanted, but the price she has to pay for it is the realization of the extent of the damage her rigor has claimed. What the film shows, critically analogous to the Iraq War, is that even though "civilization," i.e. the US, may have triumphed in its pursuit of retaliation, it did so receiving unforeseeable harm and causing more harm than good in the wake of triumph, isolating itself in the process while stubbornly insisting on its everlasting righteousness, as Mattie ends up as an embittered, one-armed spinster at Rooster's grave.

Conclusion

The female avenger emerged in the Western after 9/11 as a versatile metaphor to reflect the nation's conduct in the retaliatory wars spawned by the terrorist attacks. As such the figure has reflected divergent attitudes towards war by both incorporating the stereotypical connotations of women in Westerns and introducing feminist modifications. *The Missing* presents the heroine as (stereotypically) a victim of traumatic loss and an embodiment of moral righteousness, whose (progressive) decision to embark on a vengeance/rescue mission holds considerable feminist appeal for its pragmatist activism. Yet, despite her acceptance of cultural diversity as a means of defeating the enemy, the film carries a decisively conservative message of protecting and recovering the ethnically pure white family by any means necessary and by annihilating all the forces, whether internal or external, that threaten its integrity, whereby it functions as an effective pro-war treatise and summation of the nation's self-image as justified avenger emerging from unwarranted suffering with moral authority. Three years later, *Bandidas* tackles the growing international resentment against the US War on Terror and its imperialist swagger with the two Mexican avengers embodying a militant potential of justified outrage. However, their stylized femininity as well as the villain's aberrational status and the inclusion of sympathetic, sanctioning American characters contributes to defusing the subversive implications of anti-American notions and reaffirming the structural conditions of America's conduct in the world. With the increase in a critical self-inspection of the ravages of America's War on Terror in the late 2000s, *True Grit* presents the female avenger as a misguided, stubborn, and arrogant agent of violence, whose infantile girlhood serves to emphasize her presumption in imposing her selfish morality onto a world that resists her intrusion and charges a price from her that leaves her crippled and embittered. Through all its different incarnations, the female avenger has proven to be a particularly apt character through which to explore America's changing attitudes to its post-9/11 wars, reaffirming the genre's adaptability and relevance in the process.

But the female avenger has by now also emancipated herself from concrete war contexts and references. In *Sweetwater* (2013) she emerges as the only moral figure in a universally corrupt world in which religious fundamentalism on the one hand and a harsh (and insane) law and order vehemence on the other hand square off against each other and victimize her. Devoid of male assistance or social obligation, she performs the role of the whore that a hypocritical and sexually abusive masculinity has imposed on her only to take revenge on those who have wronged her. With its baroque scenario of female emancipation from a grotesquely despotic patriarchy, the film brings out the subversive feminist potential of the female avenger at the same time as it affirms the significance of this innovative character for the genre's and its gender politics' continued relevance.

Notes

1. Further examples of women participating in justified revenge can be found in *The Sum of All Fears* (2002) and *Pearl Harbor* (2001) (Bell-Metereau 2004: 146), perhaps culminating in the figure of Maya in Kathryn Bigelow's *Zero Dark Thirty* (2012), which makes the metaphorical implications of the former films concrete by providing an explicit War on Terror scenario.
2. Exploring a more recent incarnation of the type in *Jane Got a Gun* (2016), John White comes to similar conclusions about that film's political implications: "a reactionary film presenting itself as feminist but only possessing the most rudimentary surface credentials with which to do so" (2018: 76). In fact, White argues, the film illustrates (unwittingly) an anxious ideological ambivalence of combining the progressivism of a "'girlpower' female action hero full of her own inner strength and independence" with the conservatism of a "rather weaker woman who needs to be brought by a man to an understanding of the true nature of the world" (66), i.e. accepting and participating in the necessity of violence. Ultimately, however, "rather than an empowerment of the feminine, what we have is a taming within violence of the assertive woman, a re-domestication of the overly confident woman" (82).
3. The town enjoys the technological advancements of the gramophone and telegraph but, the film seems to suggest, these advances do not contribute to any effective action, they rather stifle the kind of pragmatic agency that is required under the circumstances.
4. That this sort of collaboration does not automatically run smoothly is exemplified by Lilly's resistance to being saved by an Indian, which sabotages the first rescue attempt by the searchers. The captive does not accept her rescue by the racial Other. Too ingrained are the prejudices. It is this sort of racist thinking that almost undoes the rescue mission and adds to the complexity of the film in matters of race and ethnicity.
5. Mexico Westerns have traditionally been read as allegorical comments on America's foreign policy towards Third World countries in military conflicts, particularly in the Vietnam age (cf. Slotkin 1992: 405–86), and *Bandidas* is no exception in offering such an allegorical perspective with Mexico as a stand-in for the Middle East. Ruiz-Alfaro, however, points out how the film should also be seen as dealing very

concretely with Mexico–US relations as affected by the War on Terror: "The period between 2004 and 2006, the years in which *Bandidas* was filmed, produced, and finally released, coincided with a period of nativist backlash against immigration and the emergence of alarmist voices that pointed to the potential 'terrorism' coming across the southern border. The xenophobic climate after 9/11 and the anxiety about illegal aliens traversing the US–Mexico border became the breeding ground for what is known as the 'Latino Threat Narrative'" (200).
6. This scene can also be read as establishing an analogy between Mattie and George W. Bush. Bush Jr's foray into Iraq has occasionally been interpreted in an Oedipal fashion as trying to step out of the shadow of Bush Sr by finishing a job his father started (cf. Yetiv 2008: 120–35).
7. Not only did the "coalition of the willing" consist of countries that promised themselves better economic relations with the US, it also featured considerable support from mercenary organizations such as Blackwater and the like.

Filmography

3:10 to Yuma, director James Mangold, featuring Russell Crowe, Christian Bale, Ben Foster (Lionsgate, 2007).

Bandidas, directors Joachim Rønning and Espen Sandberg, featuring Penélope Cruz, Salma Hayek, Steve Zahn (EuropaCorp, 2006).

Django Unchained, director Quentin Tarantino, featuring Jamie Foxx, Christoph Waltz, Leonardo DiCaprio (Weinstein Company, 2012).

My Darling Clementine, director John Ford, featuring Henry Fonda, Linda Darnell, Walter Brennan (20th Century Fox, 1946).

No Country for Old Men, directors Ethan Coen and Joel Coen, featuring Tommy Lee Jones, Javier Bardem, Josh Brolin (Paramount Vantage, 2007).

Open Range, director Kevin Costner, featuring Kevin Coster, Robert Duvall, Diego Luna (Touchstone Pictures, 2003).

Panic Room, director David Fincher, featuring Jodie Foster, Kristen Stewart, Forest Whitaker (Columbia, 2002).

Pearl Harbor, director Michael Bay, featuring Ben Affleck, Kate Beckinsale, Josh Hartnett (Touchstone 2001).

Seraphim Falls, director David Von Ancken, featuring Pierce Brosnan, Liam Neeson, Anjelica Huston (Icon Productions, 2006).

Shane, director George Stevens, featuring Alan Ladd, Jean Arthur, Van Heflin (Paramount, 1953).

Sweetwater, director Logan Miller, featuring Ed Harris, January Jones, Jason Isaacs (Kickstart Productions, 2013).

The Hateful Eight, director Quentin Tarantino, featuring Samuel L. Jackson, Kurt Russell, Jennifer Jason Leigh (Visiona Romantica, 2015).

The Homesman, director Tommy Lee Jones, featuring Tommy Lee Jones, Hilary Swank, Grace Gummer (EuropaCorp, 2014).

The Missing, director Ron Howard, featuring Tommy Lee Jones, Cate Blanchett, Evan Rachel Wood (Revolution Studios, 2003).

The Proposition, director John Hillcoat, featuring Ray Winstone, Guy Pearce, Emily Watson (UK Film Council, 2005).

The Searchers, director John Ford, featuring John Wayne, Jeffrey Hunter, Vera Miles (C. V. Whitney Pictures, 1956).

The Sum of All Fears, director Phil Alden Robinson, featuring Ben Affleck, Morgan Freeman, Ian Mongrain (Paramount, 2002).

True Grit, directors Ethan Coen and Joel Coen, featuring Jeff Bridges, Matt Damon, Hailee Steinfeld (Paramount, 2011).

Zero Dark Thirty, director Kathryn Bigelow, featuring Jessica Chastain, Joel Edgerton, Chris Pratt (Columbia, 2012).

Bibliography

Bell-Metereau, Rebecca (2004) "The How-To Manual, the Prequel, and the Sequel in Post-9/11 Cinema," Wheeler Winston Dixon (ed.), *Film and Television After 9/11*. Carbondale, IL: Southern Illinois University Press, pp. 142–62.

Bischoff, Peter and Nocon, Peter (2004) "*The Missing*: Gender- and Ethnicity-Correct Constructs," *Studies in the Western*, 12, pp. 117–22.

Bush, George W. (2001 [2014]) "President Bush Addresses the Nation," *Washington Post*, 20 September 2001, web 22 June 2014 <https://www.washingtonpost.com/wp-srv/nation/specials/attacked/transcripts/bushaddress_092001.html?noredirect=on> (last accessed 21 August 2018).

Cumbow, Robert C. (2011 [2014]) "A Great Adventure: 59 Seconds of 'True Grit,'" in *Parallax View*, 6 June 2011, web 25 October 2014 <http://parallax-view.org/2011/06/06/a-great-adventure-59-seconds-of-true-grit/> (last accessed 21 August 2018).

Dixon, Wheeler Winston (2004) "Introduction: Something Lost—Film after 9/11," in Wheeler Winston Dixon (ed.), *Film and Television after 9/11*. Carbondale, IL: Southern Illinois University Press, pp. 1–27.

French, Philip (2005) *Westerns: Aspects of a Movie Genre and Westerns Revisited*. Manchester: Carcanet.

Hobsbawm, Eric (2000) *Bandits*. London: Weidenfeld & Nicolson.

Knowlton, Brian (2001 [2014]) "Terror in America / 'We're Going to Smoke Them Out': President Airs His Anger," *New York Times*, 19 September 2001, web 22 June 2014 <www.nytimes.com/2001/09/19/news/19iht-t4_30.html> (last accessed 21 August 2018).

Landy, Marcia (2004) "America under Attack: Pearl Harbor, 9/11, and History in the Media," in Wheeler Winston Dixon (ed.), *Film and Television after 9/11*. Carbondale, IL: Southern Illinois University Press, pp. 79–100.

LaRocca, David (2012) "'A Lead Ball of Justice': The Logic of Retribution and the Ethics of Instruction in *True Grit*," in Mark T. Conrad (ed.), *The Philosophy of the Coen Brothers*. Lexington, KY: University Press of Kentucky, pp. 307–31.

Millard, Kenneth (2011) "History, Fiction and Ethics: The Search for the True West in *True Grit*," *Philological Quarterly*, 90 (4), pp. 463–79.

Palmer, R. Barton (2004) *Joel and Ethan Coen*. Urbana, IL: University of Illinois Press.

Ruiz-Alfaro, Sofia (2014) "Between Women: *Bandidas* and the Construction of Latinidad in the U.S.-Mexico Borderlands," *Quarterly Review of Film and Video*, 31, pp. 199–210.
Seeßlen, Georg (2000) "Spiel. Regel. Verletzung. Auf Spurensuche in Coen Country," in Peter Körte and George Seeßlen (eds), *Joel & Ethan Coen*, 2nd edn. Berlin: Bertz, pp. 229–98.
Slotkin, Richard (1988) "Violence," in Edward Buscombe (ed.), *The BFI Companion to the Western*. London: BFI, pp. 232–6.
Slotkin, Richard (1992) *Gunfighter Nation: The Myth of the Frontier in Twentieth-Century America*. New York: HarperPerennial.
White, John (2018) *The Contemporary Western: An American Genre Post 9/11*. Edinburgh: Edinburgh University Press.
Wright, Will (1975) *Six Guns and Society: A Structural Study of the Western*. Berkeley, CA: California University Press.
Yetiv, Steven A. (2008) *The Absence of Grand Strategy: The United States in the Persian Gulf, 1972–2005*. Baltimore, MD: Johns Hopkins University Press.

15. YOU'VE GOT SOMETHING: FEMALE AGENCY IN *JUSTIFIED*

Paul Zinder

The female characters in *Justified* (2010–15), the televised Western based on Elmore Leonard's short story *Fire in the Hole* (2001), relate to the narrative drive and the male leads of the series in ways that both defy and surrender to generic expectations established in the classic Western. Although US Marshal Raylan Givens (Timothy Olyphant), the series protagonist, and additional male characters inhabit most of the series' screen time, the women in the series leave a profound mark on its direction. Four of the principal characters in *Justified* are women, and each holds a central position in the serialized construct of its narrative. Criminal masterminds Mags Bennett (Margo Martindale) and Katherine Hale (Mary Steenburgen), Raylan's ex-wife, Winona Givens (Natalie Zea), as well as the series' female lead, Ava Crowder (Joelle Carter), all command significant story arcs in *Justified*. Mags, as matriarch of the Bennett family and her own marijuana empire in Harlan County, defends both her business and the livelihoods of her fellow countryfolk when threatened by Black Pike, an outside urban force. Katherine, a formidable woman who seeks both land and revenge in the final two seasons of the series, rejects the man who loves her in pursuit of a very personal agenda. Winona, Raylan's ex-wife and the mother of his only child, does not abide Raylan's anti-hero status, making clear that his responsibilities lie with the family that he continuously rejects. Ava, the female protagonist in *Justified*, in killing her abusive husband at the opening of the series, catalyzes the involvement of both Raylan and Boyd Crowder (Walton Goggins) in her affairs, marshalling both of them into a series-long male rivalry impacted by her own considered actions.

While a deconstructive narrative structure that challenges both genders' traditional portrayals in the Western does feel at least part of the fabric of *Justified*, an equally formidable defense of the aged values of the genre marginalizes the power that these and other women maintain during the series' six-season run. This paradox is never resolved in *Justified*, a show that utilizes Western female archetypes that float between deconstruction and concession in their engagement with the history of the genre.[1] From its early roots, the Western denied female agency in a male-dominated genre. Winona Howe and Michael Coyne acknowledge the secondary roles that women have often occupied since the birth of the Western, these characters' lack of importance sidelining potentially compelling female voices. The films' representations of non-consequential women undermine the potential of their three-dimensional development. Howe cites classic Westerns, including *The Searchers* (1956), *The Magnificent Seven* (1960), and *Once Upon a Time in the West* (1968), all of which include female leads that serve a primarily sexual objective or as an inconsequential plot device (2005: 198–9).

In *Justified*, the "Myth of the West" defines Raylan Givens's conduct and its import, designating him a traditional cowboy who gains and maintains audience support throughout the series, no matter the consequences of his actions.[2] While Raylan's heroics serve as the lynchpin of the series' Western designation, the women of *Justified* encourage an expanded reading of the show's position as a genre text. As a contemporary rebuttal to a singular (and classical) approach to genre, the organizational design of *Justified* frequently evokes the mingling of genres in televised Westerns of the postmodern era. According to Neil Campbell, Joss Whedon's *Firefly*, a Western disguised in part by semantic elements of science fiction, particularly in its iconography and narrative concerns, offers progressive female portraits that favor diversity over tradition (in Johnson 2012: 129). Post-Westerns like *Firefly* eschew stereotype to favor a different kind of woman (in Johnson 2012: 129). But the intermingling of genres in television does not always lend Western archetypes a progressive hand. Michael K. Johnson argues that the contemporary AMC Western *Hell on Wheels* offers both a revisionist portrait of Native Americans and a more traditional portrayal of its female lead, Lily Bell, whose strength and ineptitude become interchangeable (2012: 12). Johnson infers that the multi-generic elements of *Hell on Wheels* separate the show from revisionist Westerns like the nineteenth-century-set HBO series *Deadwood*, which offers three-dimensional characterizations of the series' businesswomen, prostitutes, and other female camp-dwellers (2012: 127). While both series invite revisionist readings, only *Deadwood* seriously respects the authority of women in the television Western.

Justified is a multi-generic series that favors the syntax of a Western, primarily due to Raylan Givens's function as a loner cowboy, but many of its semantic components (including its visual strategy, use of archetypes, and its narrative make-up) marry the Western with both Gangster and *film noir* texts.[3] Neil Campbell contends that the Western's survival has depended on its ability to transcend its own generic guidelines by incorporating various attributes from other forms in an effort to attract an audience familiar with a contemporary televised landscape, one that both crosses and destroys the "rules" established by classic genre texts (in Johnson 2012: 125). *Justified* functions as one of these hybrid forms, and its major female characters are molded by fundamental generic attributes of the Western, the Gangster text, and the *film noir*, which encourages multiple readings of each woman's placement in its story-design, thereby commenting on female agency in the series.[4] This essay offers a reading of the representation of primary female characters in *Justified*, including Mags Bennett, Katherine Hale, Winona Givens, and Ava Crowder, each woman's characteristics encouraging the viewer to question how the series operates as a Western.[5]

Legacy vs. Lace

You've got something. Power you haven't even begun to understand.

Mags Bennett to Loretta McCready[6]

Justified's positioning as a multi-generic series with a Western syntax sometimes supersedes its more traditional Western tropes. The shootout at the opening of the pilot of *Justified* establishes the place of the Western hero, Raylan Givens, a man shrouded in moral ambiguity. This foundational introduction also produces an archetype of a contemporary gangster, Tommy Bucks (Peter Greene), who occupies the same diegesis and comes into conflict with Raylan, thereby establishing a connection between the two genres in the series' very first sequence. While that world shifts from Miami (where the shooting occurs) to Raylan's boyhood home, Harlan County, Kentucky, the two genres continue to butt heads throughout the series.[7]

Martha P. Nochimson contends that gangsters and law-abiding American citizens are quite similar, particularly when one considers each person's relationship to the capitalist society in which he or she lives (2007: 7). In *Justified*, some of the women in Harlan County are quite formidable, but the continued challenges associated with their blue-collar upbringings prompt a turn to criminal enterprises that are more commonly housed in an urban setting. Portrayed as a county lacking concern for the customary mores of justice, Harlan's frontier-like mentality feels reminiscent of the lawlessness of *Deadwood*, a setting (and series) preoccupied with the perils of a "civilized" existence. The country, in the case of *Justified*, is the scene of the gangsters' crimes (in Howe 2005; 198).[8]

Mags Bennett, a widower, single mother, and the shrewd antagonist in the second season of *Justified*, operates her expansive marijuana enterprise from her pseudo-headquarters in a small country store in Harlan County, out of reach of the law and with the ardent support of her three sons, who both fear and respect her.⁹ Mags's sons, Doyle (Joseph Lyle Taylor), the dissolute town sheriff, Dickie (Jeremy Davies), a bumbling, inept interferer, and Coover (Brad William Henke), a weed-addicted giant, trail behind her, attempting to keep in line with Mags's wishes while failing to avoid the pitfalls that result from their own inability to capably exist in a world of crime. Considering that male business leaders dominate traditional Western narratives (Neale 2000: 141), Mags's savvy and brutal approach to her own capitalist syndicate galvanizes her to torment the men who threaten her, while masculinizing her as a Western outlaw.

Mags does not, however, allow her familial challenges to negatively impact her empire. Yvonne Tasker contends that the "white woman in the Western has, at least some of the time, a strength and an independence to match the struggles that she faces" (1998: 53). While managing the plethora of trials perpetrated by her often incompetent sons, Mags welcomes the young rebel Loretta McCready (Kaitlyn Dever) into the fold after having Loretta's father, Walt (Chris Mulkey), killed for secretly growing marijuana on Bennett land. Mags operates as a surrogate mother of sorts (Hagelin and Silverman: 2017: 854), strongly implying that she trusts Loretta more than her own blood to successfully inherit her business.[10] Though Westerfelhaus and Lacroix argue that in a traditional Western "villains and their actions are depicted as unambiguously evil, with little to render them sympathetic" (2009: 31), Mags proves herself a very different kind of antagonist. As Hagelin and Silverman remark, Mags's "pro-community," convincing, and charismatic speech at the Black Pike meeting helps to monopolize viewer support (2017: 856). The television audience cannot help but root for her, placing them in direct conflict with the mission assigned Raylan by the US Marshal Service. Mags's partial function as a master criminal also buttresses the argument that *Justified* can be read as both a Western and a Gangster text since the latter is chiefly identifiable by its point of view (Nochimson 2007: 8), one that belongs to a lead gangster with iniquitous characteristics similar to those of the Bennett matriarch.

The arrival of the Black Pike Mining Company most keenly tests her resolve. For Mags, Black Pike's activity in Harlan Country will endanger both the land and the independence of its citizenry.[11] Western narratives turn on the fight for land (Metz 2008: 65), and Mags's initial response to Black Pike's predatory strategy is to prepare for a violent engagement. Interestingly, in this instance, Mags, the Western antagonist, faces a new foe with the same land-coveting goals, Black Pike, with audience sympathies falling firmly in line with the woman who governs local resources from outside of the law.[12] However, Mags's actual strategy surprises all who watch her every move, including Raylan. As one of the savviest characters in the series' run, Mags recognizes that her best option is to partner-up with that other local criminal, Boyd Crowder, and strike the out-of-towners at their own corporate game. In doing so, she replaces cowboy Raylan as the heroic savior of her local community.[13]

Metz maintains that "the end result of the American Western narrative will remain stable, culminating in the noble and happy production of the normative family unit" (Metz 2008: 69). But such a convention does not permit Mags to triumph. After Loretta abandons her in anger for killing Walt, and the authorities mercilessly kill her sons, Mags chooses suicide over a continuing fight, her loss of both the surrogate and genetic roles of mother the final straw.[14] While immense power lay in her own choice to die, the removal of her deconstructive position as a power-wielding female character in *Justified* drives criminality and its associated power back into the hands of men.[15]

Katherine Hale, the female antagonist in the final two seasons of *Justified*, would probably liken herself a *femme fatale*. Her affair with the mobster Avery Markham (Sam Elliott) directly links to her focused aim in the show's final season, to avenge Grady, her fallen husband, by finding and killing the person responsible for his murder. But Katherine neither pines for Grady nor feels for her current lover. On the contrary, she notes that Grady "was the face and I got it done," and promises that if Avery was involved in Grady's murder, he will also die, as "A man as much as kills your husband, you got to do something about it."[16] Here, the character of Katherine Hale ignores prescriptive Western convention in favor of that of a classic *noir*. As Avery Markham's partner and lover, Katherine fronts the plan by Avery to purchase land around Harlan County, his intentions echoing those of Black Pike in the second season of *Justified*. Avery longs for something more personal than real estate, however. When Katherine ignores Avery's proposal of marriage, she rejects his most serious advance, also acknowledging the behavior of widow-characters in classic Westerns.[17] Tasker writes that women in the Western are sometimes positioned to accept "'male' responsibilities following the loss or failure of a significant man" (1998: 57). Katherine both acknowledges Grady as her deceased partner and establishes a relationship with Markham as a means to avenge her fallen husband.[18]

Avery Markham is not her only focus. Like Mags before her, she recognizes the usefulness of Boyd Crowder. Katherine needles Boyd on her suspicion that his partner, Ava Crowder, has been released from prison for questionable purposes[19] and flirts with him as well, calling him "the man of my dreams."[20] Unlike Mags, however, Katherine dismisses the importance of motherhood when she tells Avery (while they share a post-coital joint, another moment with shadings of *noir*) that she's not happy that she's a grandmother, as "I don't even know what they're saying half the time."[21] For Katherine, suicide isn't a befitting response to the loss of family. Ultimately, Katherine, as powerful and threatening as any character in the series, ultimately fails in all of her personal business, even after discovering and confronting Grady's killer, Wynn Duffy (Jere Burns). Her brutal death at the hands of Wynn's assistant as she prepares to fulfill her season-long objective silences yet another dominant female character, one who shrank from nobody.[22]

DECONSTRUCTIVE IMPULSES AND CONCILIATORY ADJUSTMENTS

> You going to take care of me? Like you did when you came to my door after Bowman? The answer to my prayers?
>
> Ava Crowder to Raylan Givens[23]

In the Western, the male hero's independence prevents the development of a happy marriage, as marital contentment would indicate an assimilation of the husband into the local populace, thus taking him off the frontier (McDonough 2005: 106.). Raylan Givens is no different, avoiding the opportunity to achieve a successful relationship with Winona Givens or his young daughter.[24] From her first appearance on *Justified*, Winona Givens establishes herself as an assured woman inherently committed to Raylan, but her disappointment over his inability to reciprocate breaches their intimacy. As she and Raylan reunite during the first season of the series, Raylan does not conceal that Winona is the love of his life. Kylo-Patrick R. Hart writes that "Winona is the kind of good woman who may one day enable Raylan to prove he has overcome his past emotional deficiencies and achieve fulfilling masculine domesticity" (2013: 300). But Raylan won't oblige. When Winona informs him that she is pregnant with their first child, Raylan still refuses to sacrifice the independence of his cowboy roots to become a reliable partner and father. Although Winona openly suspects that their relationship will not survive, she continues to pine for Raylan through most of the series, even after he proves himself incapable of equal devotion. Raylan would rather continue the fight in Harlan County, leaving the opportunity of familial love behind, a decision similar to the one made by characters like Wyatt Earp in the classic Western *My Darling Clementine* (1946). Andrew Patrick Nelson labels such protagonists as reveling in the "myth of the prototypical frontier lawman," a characteristic easily applied to Raylan (2015: 51). Winona, as a woman incredibly patient with a man unfit for her care, fulfills the classical Western criterion that pigeonholes the female character as one unable to domesticate her cowboy.

In the episode "Bloody Harlan," Raylan claims that he will leave the Marshal's service to be with Winona if his transfer out of Lexington is not approved, but his fear of personal transformation keeps him in Harlan County, denying the couple a "traditional" American family.[25] During the third season of the series, Winona leaves him, recognizing that this Marshal will not change.[26] By the series finale, she has happily settled in Florida with a new partner while continuing to encourage Raylan as he visits their daughter, seemingly at peace with her decision to move on from her past.[27] While Winona's proactivity frees her to pursue her own interests, her decision to partner with yet another man proves a conservative (and predictable) choice. Although Winona offers Raylan every opportunity over the series' six seasons to re-establish their erstwhile relationship, her final decision to shift her focus to motherhood and a new marriage allows a move away from Raylan, the traditional loner-lawman, to finally discover her independence once freed from his damaging pull.[28] The Western's emphasis on customary familial harmony simply does not apply to *Justified* (Metz 2008: 69).

Both Western and Gangster *noir* tropes impact Ava Crowder, the female lead in *Justified*, as her character develops over the course of the series. Steven Cohan argues that 1950s American media texts trained men "to fear blondness as a threatening form of female sexuality . . . as part of a package suggesting the double-standard of a lady/whore" (quoted in Hart 2013: 299), and although Ava utilizes her sexuality to achieve personal goals, she never does so to destroy a man who does not catalyze his own downfall. Ava's first foray into violence, the killing of Bowman Crowder, her abusive husband, puts down a vicious man as a means of both self-defence and revenge, not murder.[29] Westerfelhaus and Lacroix argue that retribution in the classic Western is a completely natural, morally acceptable version of justice (Westerfelhaus and Lacroix 2009: 30), marking Ava as a traditional Western killer at the onset of the series. Except that she isn't really "traditional" at all. She is a woman who exerts her power over a malevolent partner, an affront to those male characters that victimize so many women in the genre. Frontier mythmaking has pigeonholed female characters as reliant on heroic men for rescue (Slatta 2010: 88). The fact that the viewing audience may struggle to condemn Ava for her courageous act plays into a revisionist Western's hands.

Figure 15.1   Ava Crowder (Joelle Carter) alternates between an archetypical Western power figure and a stereotypical female submissive throughout the course of the series.

Boyd Crowder, Bowman's brother, does not blame Ava for his sibling's death; in fact, her show of strength initiates *Justified*'s most enduring love story, the relationship between Ava and Boyd. This pairing, however, could not have developed without the aid of a certain, reckless cowboy. When Raylan shoots two separate people in two separate incidents inside the same house where Bowman was killed, one of the victim's deaths leads directly to Boyd's release from prison. The second shooting occurs after Raylan and Ava begin an affair, against the advice of his superior, Art Mullen (Nick Searcy). Raylan's reckless gunplay inadvertently credits him with Ava's opportunity to experience a loving relationship with Boyd.[30] Throughout the run of *Justified*, Ava faces crossfire as Boyd colludes with characters that fit the gangster mold, including Nicky Augustine (Mike O'Malley), Wynn Duffy, and Theo Tonin (Adam Arkin). Although Ava challenges Boyd on his decision to partner with such shifty men,[31] he convinces her that she should participate in any scheme that will provide them with the financial means to escape the impoverishment that has formed their lives. After securing an association with the Detroit mobster, Augustine, in the fourth season of the series,[32] Boyd again convinces Ava to partner with him, arguing, "This is our time. Let's break through that glass ceiling." And in *Justified*'s final season premiere, Boyd argues that the city awaits, convincing his love that "Harlan's dying ... If there's a chance for us ... it's not here."[33] Each time, Ava proffers her independence, convinced by her lover that his collusion with gangsters will improve both of their lives. By the time Raylan enlists Ava as a secret informant in an effort to bust Boyd, she finds herself in the onerous yet empowered position of deceiving both men in an effort to save herself. Raylan warns her that she is "of no use to us" if she does not satisfy the Marshal's Service by providing the evidence necessary to put Boyd away.[34] When a suspicious Boyd insists, "I feel like I don't know who you are anymore," Ava offers him her body to "remind" him, prostituting herself to maintain her cover. Ava is a pawn manipulated by both men throughout the final season of the series, her independence shrouded by male rivalry. She finally decides to reclaim her power and betray both men to save herself.

Ava does eventually recognize that Boyd's personal machinations represent a different kind of abuse than the sort she suffered at the hands of his brother, and she again chooses to conclude her relationship with a Crowder. While she does not kill Boyd as an act of retribution, she does evade him (as well as Raylan's arrest), quitting herself of Boyd's influence in the series finale of *Justified*. When Raylan tracks her down years later after her solitary flight from Harlan County (and after his final archetypical Western shootout with another would-be cowboy), he finds that Ava has become a single mother to Boyd's young, clandestine son. Raylan decides to both (illegally) release Ava from a Marshal arrest warrant and visit Boyd in prison to convince him that Ava is dead.[35] In the end, Raylan, a Western male protagonist who defines "ethical" behavior according to fluctuating personal agendas, protects Ava, the initially autonomous Western female lead, the same woman whose own violent initiative liberated herself from male dominance in the series premiere of *Justified*.

Tasker argues that freedom remains the Western's principal concern (1998: 3). Ava's escape in the series finale offers her an independence that is arguably revisionist, in that she chooses to renounce her relationship with the gangster-affiliated Boyd in order to avoid a life as a single mother behind bars. Raylan, however, in sanctioning her freedom, becomes the man who "allowed" her independence, shadowing her achievement with old-school genre sexism. Ava Crowder both denies and relies on the rules of the Western and survives.

The major female characters in *Justified*, whether instilled with the hallmarks of the Western, the Gangster film, *film noir*, or a combination of the three textual formulas, are all linked by single motherhood. These women do not belong to orthodox families that function as peaceful nuclei (Zinder 2013: 127). This single motherhood, coupled with the multi-generic construct of *Justified*, conditions each of these women's agency in the series. Mags Bennett, after losing her position as a biological and surrogate mother who operates in both Western and Gangster spheres, ends her own life, because her mistakes are too difficult to bear. Katherine Hale, a *femme fatale* who endeavors to exact revenge in a classical Western sphere usually controlled by men, is gunned down for overstepping her semantic station(s). Winona Givens, a woman whose classical dependence on the cowboy Raylan fades by the end of the series, finds a "replacement" man to help her to raise her daughter out of the confines of the Harlan County frontier, choosing to settle into a more traditional family than the one she longed for with Raylan. And Ava Crowder, in outsmarting both Boyd and Raylan, temporarily evades the conventions of a Western/Gangster mash-up by settling into a happy life of single motherhood, but one which hinges on Raylan-the-Marshal's aid. In the final analysis, a Western narrative's representation of gender remains crucial to the reading of an individual text (Tasker 1998: 51). Ultimately, the agency of these four steadfast women steer much of the action in *Justified*, yet the series does not resolve to free female characters from marginalization similar to that found in old-fashioned Westerns. Considering that the series also includes both semantic and syntactic elements of both Gangster and *film noir* texts, perhaps such displacement makes narrative sense. The women who inhabit the diegesis of *Justified* face multi-generic obstacles that refuse to give way.

Notes

1. As Yvonne Tasker notes, "The perception that genres might in some senses be gendered has . . . persisted with narratives of . . . the Western acquiring and retaining a reputation as male spaces" (1998: 51).

2. See Carter for a discussion of the cowboy's function in the "myth of the West" (2015: 115).
3. Sarah Hagelin and Gillian Silverman argue that *Justified* combines elements of the Western and the "antihero police procedural." While the series considers the relationship between the "rogue cop" and the "criminal antihero," I contend that both the Gangster text and *film noir* are crucial generic partners as well, due to *Justified*'s extensive use of underworld archetypes and the *femme fatale* (2017: 851).
4. Carter notes that Richard Slotkin recognized the inclusion of features of *film noir* in certain Cold War Westerns.
5. While secondary female characters like Rachel Brooks, Aunt Helen, and Ellen May and others have agency in *Justified*, their lack of extensive development does not make them ideal subjects for this essay.
6. From "Brother's Keeper," 2.9.
7. See Crossley for how *Justified* is designated a contemporary Western partially due to its pilot's multi-generic opening (2014: 58).
8. Sandra Schackel comments on stereotypical women in the Western as usually pigeonholed into the role of "nurturer/civilizer" or "*femme fatale*/vamp" (in Howe 2005: 198).
9. See "The I of the Storm," 2.3.
10. See "The Moonshine War," 2.1. Considering that Tasker argues that a traditional Western generally avoids a focus on female relationships (1998: 61), the pairing of Mags and Loretta lends *Justified* another opportunity to revel in change.
11. Joanna Crosby contends that Mags recalls the "strong Appalachian women" who defended their own against outside interests beginning at the end of the eighteenth century (in Carveth and Arp 2015: 140).
12. Mags's position as a cruel and yet empathetic antagonist preoccupied with both her own interests and those of her countryfolk echoes characters in range war films (including *Shane* [1953]), as well as that of the saloon keeper Al Swearengen in *Deadwood*, a series that focuses on external threats from gold baron George Hearst, who fiercely amasses local resources. Swearengen combines both magnanimity and brutal power to (unsuccessfully) safeguard the Deadwood camp. Like Mags, he seeks to protect the freedom afforded those settlers who developed their land while maintaining his *de facto* position as local ruler.
13. See "Brother's Keeper," 2.9. Also see my discussion in "'Osama bin Laden Ain't Here.' *Justified* as a 9/11 Western" (Zinder 2013: 129/130).
14. In "Bloody Harlan," 2.13.
15. In "Burned," 6.9, Loretta earns her place as Mags's surrogate daughter. When Avery makes his own sales pitch to Harlan's gathered masses, Loretta becomes the local spokesperson, verbalizing her alliance with Boyd for Avery, Katherine, and Raylan to hear. Her confidence is one rooted in local resources, including her own ability to carry on a powerful woman's legacy.
16. See "The Trash and the Snake," 6.4.
17. See "Alive Day," 6.6.
18. In "Alive Day," 6.6, Katherine tells mob-tied Wynn Duffy that if Avery is "playing me, we're going to have to kill him slow."

19. See "Cash Game," 6.2.
20. In "Noblesse Oblige," 6.3. Hagelin and Silverman recognize that Carol Johnson of Black Pike is also "characterized by *femme fatale* eroticism," placing her in concert with Katherine Hale's handling of male characters in the series (2017: 859).
21. See "Cash Game," 6.2.
22. Katherine's death in "Fugitive Number One," 6.11, acknowledges traditional mores of both the Western and *film noir*, as female characters in both types of narrative are often punished for attempting to outgun a man.
23. See "Sounding," 6.5.
24. Michael Graves notes that the televised adaptation of *Justified* includes interesting alterations to the Elmore Leonard short story that inspired the series (2016: 8). In Leonard's original text, Raylan and Winona have two sons while in *Justified*, they have one daughter, a noticeable change, particularly when considering Raylan's lack of action regarding his only (female) child.
25. "Bloody Harlan," 2.13.
26. "Thick as Mud," 3.5.
27. "The Promise," 6.13.
28. McDonough notes that the "domesticating woman in the classic Western is frequently an obstacle to the hero's quest . . . Typically, the hero first agrees to avoid the conflict but ultimately fights the outlaws" (2005: 107). In the case of *Justified*, Raylan proves himself a conservative classic cowboy, choosing to pursue Boyd over the potential of familial happiness.
29. While Howe notes that the poor treatment of women in the Western is a stereotypical element of the genre (2005: 199), Ava's response to Bowman's abuse separates herself from generic expectation.
30. Even considering Raylan's machinations, Ava and Boyd prove compatible in their criminal alliance throughout the series. But when Ava successfully abandons Boyd in "The Promise," 6.13, to avoid incarceration, she (temporarily) proves herself a more competent lawbreaker than her erstwhile partner, leaving Boyd both stunned and emasculated.
31. See "For Blood of Money," 2.4.
32. See "Outlaw," 4.8.
33. See "Fate's Right Hand," 6.1
34. Ibid.
35. See "The Promise," 6.13.

Filmography

"Alive Day," *Justified*, Season 6, Episode 6 (FX, 24 February 2015).
"Bloody Harlan," *Justified*, Season 2, Episode 13 (FX, 4 May 2011).
"Brother's Keeper," *Justified*, Season 2, Episode 9 (FX, 6 April 2011).
"Burned," *Justified*, Season 6, Episode 9 (FX, 17 March 2015).
"Cash Game," *Justified*, Season 6, Episode 2 (FX, 27 January 2015).
"Fate's Right Hand," *Justified*, Season 6, Episode 1 (FX, 20 January 2015).
"For Blood of Money," *Justified*, Season 2, Episode 4 (FX, 2 March 2011).

"Fugitive Number One," *Justified*, Season 6, Episode 11 (FX, 31 March 2015).
"Noblesse Oblige," *Justified*, Season 6, Episode 3 (FX, 3 February 2015).
"Outlaw," *Justified*, Season 4, Episode 8 (FX, 26 February 2013).
"Sounding," *Justified*, Season 6, Episode 5 (FX, 17 February 2015).
"The I of the Storm," *Justified*, Season 2, Episode 3 (FX, 23 February 2011).
"The Moonshine War," *Justified*, Season 2, Episode 1 (FX, 9 February 2011).
"The Promise," *Justified*, Season 6, Episode 13 (FX, 14 April 2015).
"The Trash and the Snake," *Justified*, Season 6, Episode 4 (FX, 10 February 2015).
"Thick as Mud," *Justified*, Season 3, Episode 5 (FX, 14 February 2012).

Bibliography

Carter, Matthew (2015) *Myth of the Western: New Perspectives on Hollywood's Frontier Narrative*. Edinburgh: Edinburgh University Press.

Carveth, Rod and Arp, Robert (2105) *Justified and Philosophy: Shoot First, Think Later*. Chicago and LaSalle, IL: Open Court.

Crosby, Joanna (2015) "We Are Not Your Savages," in Rod Carveth and Robert Arp (eds), *Justified and Philosophy: Shoot First, Think Later*. Chicago and LaSalle, IL: Open Court Press, pp. 133–43.

Crossley, Laura (2014) "Gangstagrass: Hybridity and Popular Culture in *Justified*," *Journal of Popular Television*, 2 (1), pp. 57–75.

Graves, Michael (2016) "Transmedia Storytelling, Adaptation, and the Reversing of *Jusitifed*," *Adaptation*, 10 (1), pp. 1–17.

Hagelin, Sarah and Silverman, Gillian (2017) "The Female Antihero and Police Power in FX's *Justified*," *Feminist Media Studies*, 17 (5), pp. 851–65.

Hart, Kylo-Patrick (2013) "The (Law)Man in the Cattleman Hat: Hegemonic Masculinity Redux," *Journal of Men's Studies*, 21 (3), pp. 291–304.

Howe, Winona (2005) "Almost Angels, Almost Feminists: Women in *The Professionals*," in Peter C. Rollins and John E. O'Connor (eds), *Hollywood's West: The American Frontier in Film, Television, and History*. Lexington, KY: University Press of Kentucky, pp. 198–217.

Johnson, Michael K. (2012) "Introduction: Television and the Depiction of the American West," *Western American Literature*, 47 (2), pp. 123–31.

Leonard, Elmore (2001) *Fire in the Hole*. Los Angeles: Contentville Press.

McDonough, Kathleen A. (2005) "Wee Willie Winkie Goes West: The Influence of the British Empire on Ford's Cavalry Trilogy," in Peter C. Rollins and John E. O'Connor (eds), *Hollywood's West: The American Frontier in Film, Television, and History*. Lexington, KY: University Press of Kentucky, pp. 99–114.

Metz, Walter (2008) "'Mother Needs You': Kevin Costner's *Open Range* and the Melodramatics of the American Western," in Murray Pomerance (ed.), *A Family Affair: Cinema Calls Home*. London and New York: Wallflower Press, pp. 63–76.

Neale, Steven (2000) *Genre and Hollywood*. London: Routledge.

Nelson, Andrew Patrick (2015) *Still in the Saddle: The Hollywood Western, 1969–1980*. Norman, OK: University of Oklahoma Press.

Nochimson, Martha P. (2007) *Dying to Belong: Gangster Movies in Hollywood and Hong Kong*. Malden, MA: Blackwell.
Slatta, Richard W. (2010) "Making and Unmaking Myths of the American Frontier," *European Journal of American Culture*, 29 (2), pp. 81–92.
Tasker, Yvonne (1998) *Working Girls: Gender and Sexuality in Popular Cinema*. London: Routledge.
Westerfelhaus, Robert and Lacroix, Celeste (2009) "Waiting for the Barbarians: HBO's *Deadwood* as a Post-9/11 Ritual of Disquiet," *Southern Communication Journal*, 74 (1), pp. 18–39.
Zinder, Paul (2013) "'Osama bin Laden Ain't Here.' *Justified* as a 9/11 Western," in Andrew Patrick Nelson (ed.), *Contemporary Westerns: Film and Television since 1990*. Plymouth: Scarecrow Press, pp. 119–34.

16. EASTWARD THE WOMEN: REMAPPING WOMEN'S JOURNEYS IN TOMMY LEE JONES'S *THE HOMESMAN* (2014)

J Paul Johnson

Promoting the release of his 2014 feature *The Homesman*, director and star Tommy Lee Jones expressed a far greater resolve about what his film was not than what it was. It was not, Jones articulated with his characteristic mixture of down-home charm and weathered *gravitas*, "a Western." For Jones, *Western* "is a term that people use so often that I don't think it has much meaning anymore [. . .] I don't know *what* a Western is" (2015: 6, emphasis added). For that matter, according to Jones, not only was the film not necessarily a Western but it was not necessarily a *feminist* Western, either, although it did address women's issues in a way he hoped would reveal "the origins of the female condition today" (2015: 6). The film's reviewers and critics were far less reticent about employing the term "Western" to describe the film and "feminist" to modify that description more precisely. In fact, in the weeks following its US release, nearly every major US review (the aggregator site Rotten Tomatoes' 39 "Top Critics") characterized the film as a Western, if often modifying it as an unconventional, revisionist, or—most frequently—"feminist" Western. In the *New York Times*, A. O. Scott called it "both a captivating western and a meticulous, devastating feminist critique of the genre" (2015). In fact, other than the names of the principals, place names, and characters, the terms, "Western" and "feminist" were the two terms more frequently used to describe the film than any other.

As this general critical consensus would seem to demonstrate, *The Homesman*, despite its director's claims to the contrary, takes place in a rich and long context of American Western films, and like most revisionist—and feminist—Westerns, aims to revise traditional expectations to focus on a story or perspective not previously told. In the case of *The Homesman*, that story is clearly oppositional, particularly in highlighting matters of the debilitating conditions faced by some pioneer women, emphasizing the resolute character and strength of its female lead, and charting a journey back East as a story of failure and regression. In an era where Western films generally struggle to connect with audiences, *The Homesman* aims to tell an untold story—one of silenced women and their struggles—yet its narrative ultimately renders mute the very women to whom it aspires to give voice.

Adapted faithfully from the 1988 novel of the same name by Glendon Swarthout (*Bless the Beasts and Children*, *The Shootist*), *The Homesman* debuted in competition for the Jury Prize at Cannes in 2014 and was later released in the US to generally strong reviews that November. Its box-office performance was tepid: in limited release on a weekend dominated by *Dumb and Dumber To*, the film opened with just $139,322 in receipts after its first weekend and eventually earned only $2,428,883 against its reported $16 million budget.[1] After the surprise commercial success of the Coen brothers' remake of *True Grit* in 2010 and the epic failure of Disney's *Lone Ranger* update in 2013, the box office landscape in which *The Homesman* appeared did not look friendly for Westerns of any ilk—whether traditional, revisionist, satirical, comic, animated, or hybridized. With Kieran Fitzgerald and Wesley Oliver, Jones co-wrote the script, directed (his third feature, following *The Three Burials of Melquiades Estrada* and *The Sunset Limited*), and stars in one of its two top-billed roles as George Briggs, the crusty squatter whose help Hilary Swank as Mary Bee Cuddy must enlist to complete a treacherous journey across difficult terrain and with significant hindrances.

Figure 16.1 Hilary Swank as Mary Bee Cuddy and Tommy Lee Jones as George Briggs form an unlikely bond in *The Homesman* (2014).

For Jones and Swank both, the roles seem deliberately cast to take full advantage of each's iconography. Jones's down-home cantankerous charm suits him well as the curmudgeonly Briggs, the nearly-lynched claim jumper whose life is saved by Cuddy. Now in his late sixties, Jones, once a college footballer and still today a cattle-rancher and polo player, retains a creaky athleticism, and his prior portrayals as lawmen in *Lonesome Dove*, *The Fugitive*, and *No Country for Old Men* (and even in the Marvel Cinematic Universe) bring to the actor's presentation a comfort in the saddle of authority—even if the character he portrays is a deserter, claim jumper, and general ne'er-do-well, a man who has failed at farming, at service, and at life in general.

In stark contrast to Briggs is Mary Bee Cuddy, the unmarried homesteader whose journey west to Nebraska territory has been successful in every aspect except one. Two-time Academy Award for Best Actress winner Hilary Swank's career has been one of crossing gender borders even from her very first lead role in a *Karate Kid* sequel, to Brandon Teena in Kimberly Peirce's *Boys Don't Cry*, the boxer Maggie in Clint Eastwood's *Million Dollar Baby*, and Amelia Earhart in Mira Nair's biopic *Amelia*. Swank is most often, and most successfully, cast in roles that allow her to project a steely resolve more traditionally associated with masculinity; many of these roles call for either a strength of physicality, an ability to sublimate traditionally feminine features and qualities, or both. Conversely, her few roles that do not tap into this masculinity, such as the romantic comedy *P.S. I Love You*, have met with critical scorn. As Mary Bee Cuddy, she is, as *The Homesman*'s Buster Shaver (Barry Corbin) says, speaking for the townsfolk, "more a man than any man 'round here."

"It's Not a Lone Woman's Place"

Mary Bee Cuddy's journey in *The Homesman* is an unusual one in the context of the Western film genre. Well before the narrative proper, she has already accomplished a significant goal, and done so largely without the help of a man. The film's initial scenes depict her silhouetted against the solitude of a desolate plains, plowing her fields, stabling her horses, and tending to her small homestead with confidence and aplomb. These initial scenes, captured by cinematographer Rodrigo Prieto with meticulously arranged compositions, elide what surely must have been years and years of challenge and toil. Indeed, for any pioneer woman to move West on her own—to establish a homestead, supervise construction, till the land, and manage a household—must have been a remarkable feat. Historical pioneer women like Pamelia Fergus and Kitturah Penton Belknap, whose migrations to the frontiers of the Midwest are featured in Peavey and Smith's *Pioneer Women: The Lives of Women on the Frontier* (1996), faced challenging journeys, complex preparations, and arduous domestic responsibilities—and once arrived, their husbands shared the tasks that Cuddy tackles largely alone. As Americans migrated westward, women were very much in demand to become wives: males outnumbered females by a significant margin, and in the establishment of a homestead there was much work to be done, both in the home and in the bearing of children (Riley 1994: 13). Further, it should be noted, the move westward was itself a radical disruption, perhaps especially so in a time when women were valued for their passivity as much as their domesticity (Riley 1994: 1). Cuddy emigrated west from New York, where her sister is married to a doctor, a life, we are meant to assume, far more leisurely by contrast, and their mother died young. Despite all of this, Cuddy's home is far more elaborately finished and furnished than any of the simple sod huts built by the male homesteaders. The narrative, though, is far less concerned with Cuddy's earlier journey westward to settle in Nebraska Territory than it is with the journey eastward to Iowa that will follow—one motivated in no small part by the one failure of Cuddy's adult life the film depicts: to marry.

Of course, if there is any journey that the Western has charted thoroughly, it is that of the perilous journey west. The struggle of pioneers and their families to navigate and settle the unfamiliar frontier of the West, from *Drums along the Mohawk* (dir. John Ford, 1939) to *Shane* (dir. George Stevens, 1953) and *How the West Was Won* (dir. Ford and Henry Hathaway, 1962) is one familiar to even the most casual students of the form. In most of these, as Pam Cook points out, females fill a dual, contradictory role, simultaneously secondary to the action of the plot and central to its conflicts and thematics (1998: 293). They are often secondary characters whose own desires are subordinated to the quest of the male, even if their own traits—like Amy Kane's (Grace Kelly) pacifism in *High Noon* (dir. Fred Zinneman, 1952) or Marian Starrett's (Jean Arthur) sexual desires in *Shane*—impact directly upon each film's themes. Even when a Western foregrounds the story of women as portrayed by stars like Barbara Stanwyck and Joan Crawford, it does so in ways that frequently overtly sexualize (as in Samuel Fuller's 1955 *Forty Guns*) or ironically subvert (as in Nicholas Ray's 1955 *Johnny Guitar*) gender expectations. A better point of comparison, albeit lacking the star power of a Stanwyck or Crawford (and the camp appeal of those films and their directors) may be *Westward the Women* (dir. William Wellman, 1951), in which a caravan of resourceful proto-pioneer women are led westward along the California Trail by wagon master Buck Wyatt, played by Robert Taylor. *Westward the Women* is one of the few earnest attempts at telling the story of women's journeys to settle the West, even if it does so with a male as guide, lead, and savior. As the classic phase of the traditional Western drew to a close, characters like Hallie (Vera Miles) in *The Man Who Shot Liberty Valance* (dir. John Ford, 1962) and Jill (Claudia Cardinale) in *Once Upon a Time in the West* (dir. Sergio Leone, 1968) brought a transfigured strength and resolve to the role of women (Lucas 1998: 318–20). Later revisionist and feminist Westerns like *The Battle of Little Jo* (dir. Maggie Greenwald, 1993) would do more to examine the plight of women faced with the societal scorn and dangerous terrain of the Western frontier.

From the start of *The Homesman*, Cuddy's narrative appears front and center. Following the initial sequence that demonstrates the success of her homesteading, Cuddy proposes marriage to Bob Giffen with the cold logic of rational argument and the accompaniment of canned peach pie and a post-prandial hymn but is soundly rejected. The film does not specify Cuddy's age, but a marriageable woman past the age of sixteen was generally considered a cause for wonder in her day and age (Peavy and Smith 1996: 42). When three mentally ill women need a "homesman" to shepherd them to a church in Iowa, Cuddy's story proper begins. *The Homesman*, then, is highly unusual for a Western in that its primary journey is eastward. Assuming what is traditionally a man's role, Cuddy takes on a journey that inverts that of the traditional Western. The film's geography is a little ambiguous, indicating only "Nebraska Territory" as the general location of Cuddy's stead and Loup (City) as the nearest town. Created by the Kansas–Nebraska Act of 1854 and existing until the admittance of the state of Nebraska to the union in 1867, the territory encompassed most of the northern Great Plains, much of the upper Missouri River basin and the eastern portions of the northern Rocky Mountains, including areas of what is today Nebraska, Wyoming, South Dakota, North Dakota, Colorado, and Montana. Cuddy worships and purchases goods in Loup, the county seat on the Loup River's south fork; the trip to Hebron, the filmmakers say, covers 400 miles, with a treacherous pass over the Missouri River near Omaha.

A group's travel across dangerous territory is of course a trope common to the Western, especially given such iconic journeys as those depicted in *The Big Trail* (dir. Raoul Walsh, 1930), *Stagecoach* (dir. John Ford, 1939) or the cattle drive of *Red River* (dir. Howard Hawks, 1948). But the fact that this group in *The Homesman*—Cuddy, Briggs, and their three passengers—must travel East after the early settlement of Loup and other small Nebraska Territory towns marks this journey not as one of progress but of regress. Cuddy and Briggs have failed, and the women they transport are each victims of a debilitating madness brought on by the challenges of frontier life. Collectively, their communal narrative is not one that looks forward to the prospects of settlement, the challenges of frontier life, and the Manifest Destiny of westward expansion. To go West, in this era and as the myth that followed, is to brave uncharted horizons, to settle uncharted territory, to make a new civilization, to triumph over wilderness, and to fulfill a preordained destiny. But to go back East is, simply, to fail.

"There's been some trouble with some women hereabouts"

Although none of them speaks more than a few lines in the narrative, *The Homesman*'s three mentally ill women represent the unfortunate alternative to Cuddy's nearly superhuman taming of the frontier. None of them possesses Cuddy's indomitable will or physical strength, and for that matter, nor do any of their husbands. Each of the three—Gro Svendsen (Sonja Richter), Arabella Sours (Grace Gummer), and Theoline Belknapp (Miranda Otto)—succumbs to a madness related to the very conditions of pioneer life. Gro is a Norwegian wife whose husband Thor's attempts at impregnation are delivered with oaths of potency: "You will give me a son! You will take my seed!" When Gro abandons her marital bed to sleep with her mother, her husband redoubles his efforts, sometimes with her mother as silent witness; when her mother dies, leaving Gro to endure the Nebraskan winter with her husband, she is driven to insanity, threatening to kill him. On the journey, she hisses, howls, and bites like a feral wolf. Arabella, just nineteen, refuses to move or speak, clutching the rag doll that is her substitute for the three children she lost to diphtheria in three days. Her husband Garn, twenty-one, is the only one of the three husbands shown to care for his wife, recognizing the value of a family keepsake, but even he, unable to accept her illness, damns his wife to hell as she goes. Incapacitated by her losses, she can only say "goodbye" repeatedly, no matter the situation. The third woman, Theoline ("Line") Belknap (Miranda Otto) succumbs to the challenge of child-rearing in an inhospitable territory. Theoline and her husband lose their cattle, then their crops; the pressure of motherhood leads her to kill her own infant, leaving it to die in an outhouse, while two young girls remain. (In the novel, Theoline, forty-three, has given birth to six children and kills the last of them.) On the trip, glassy-eyed and disheveled, she never speaks or acts but simply stares, a silent witness to and victim of the harsh conditions of the Plains.

The challenges of frontier life were indeed many: thin-walled tents provided little protection against freezing cold, and night fears of Indian and predator attacks prevented sound sleep. Attacks were uncommon, but their fears not unfounded; accidents and illness plagued travelers; and non-contaminated water sources were precious. Wet beds and freezing rains sometimes resulted in pneumonia; typhoid, diphtheria, and other diseases could prove sudden and deadly. For women the challenges of childbirth and childrearing were doubled by such conditions (Peavy and Smith 1996: 34–42). Forced often to engage in the commerce more traditionally assigned to men—or, in some cases, left to fend for themselves during a husband's long absence—these women often faced new and daunting challenges (Peavy and Smith 1994: 3–4). Yet, as Nancy Wilson Ross wrote in her early study of pioneer women, *Westward the Women*—an uncredited source for Wellman's 1951 film—"in spite of all their fears the women came by the hundreds. And having come, they stayed" (1944: 12). Except, as Jones's film indicates, when they could not.

These fears and hardships are the very conditions on which *The Homesman*'s central conceit is established, and the mentally ill women being escorted back to Iowa have each suffered debilitating loss. The cinematic presentation of their stories is for the most part rendered elliptically and non-chronologically, their three situations compressed into brief montages. For instance, Gro is first introduced as grieving her dead mother, who reappears alive (if mortified!) a time later; just after she is given over to Cuddy's care she is shown in bed with her very-much-alive mother, being penetrated by her husband. Later still is her self-mutilation and garment-rending. Co-writer Kieran Fitzgerald claims that "the hardest thing in writing the screenplay was to fill in the blanks that Glendon Swarthout left in the novel" (Oliver and Fitzgerald 2015: 18), but in many ways the film's screenplay and direction exhibit not an *expansion* of their stories but a significant *contraction* of them. In fact, Swarthout's novel foregrounds their narratives far more fully and immediately: for instance, Theoline Belknap's killing of her infant child begins the novel and takes place over a richly described twelve pages, far more fully developing the series of natural disasters that over a period of time claim their cattle (blackleg), their corn (wind), their oxen (warbles) and their hogs (cold)—not to mention Theoline's mental struggle to persuade herself she is capable of raising a sixth child at the age of forty-three when her God "must be angry" with her (Swarthout 1988: 3). Theoline's situation, like Arabella's and Gro's, is radically contracted in Jones's film, the three backstories all compressed into ninety-second flashes of nonsequential, if visually evocative and historically valid, segments.

Theirs are not the only women's stories so silenced. In Swarthout's novel, Cuddy and Briggs must deliver a fourth woman, Hedda Petzke, a thirty-six-year-old wife and mother of two boys, driven mad with fear after fending off a series of wolf attacks. Although in the novel these scenes appear in flashback, even after readers know that Hedda survived them, they are among the novel's most visceral and suspenseful. Unlike the madnesses experienced by the others, brought on by the cruelties of childbirth, disease, and rape, Hedda's is one of the fear of predators in the natural world: with only her wits and her firearm to protect herself, the near-death experience drives her insane. According to co-writer Fitzgerald, "the logistics of carrying four women in the wagon and creating four distinct arcs in the story would have been awkward [. . .]. Having a fourth woman on board didn't bring much to the narrative" (Oliver and Fitzgerald 2015: 18). But in a film that aims to make clear the challenges faced by frontier women and the not-uncommon fate of those driven mad by circumstance, the elision of Hedda Petzke's story from the film serves as yet one more reminder of how many pioneer women's stories remain untold onscreen.

"I LIVE UNCOMMON ALONE"

The three women's backstories in the film are presented so quickly—thirty seconds here, twenty there—as to render them nearly if not quite unintelligible.

These changes and alterations I have described, however much they might alter the focus and emphasis of the women's stories told and not told, hardly characterize the overall approach to adaptation of *The Homesman*. In most other regards, Jones's film is a scrupulously faithful adaptation of Swarthout's novel, dutifully keeping every character name, place and setting, nearly all major plot events (and some minor ones), inventing only one or two scenes not in the novel. Swarthout's novel employs a loose and limited omniscience, moving freely between key third-person points of view—primarily, Cuddy's and Briggs's but occasionally others—in a way that lends itself well to the camera, and without the complications of first-person voice. Aside from the contraction of each woman's backstory, the omission of Hedda Petzke and her fearful encounter with a terrorizing wolfpack is the only significant alteration from Swarthout's novel. One smaller change is that in the novel, Briggs's final journey across the Missouri—he must bring each of the three across by foot, without Cuddy's or anyone's help—is fraught with tension, and Briggs nearly loses consciousness and drowns due to fatigue. In the film, Briggs crosses without danger, suffering only some mild agitation completing a task as mundane as his having helped the women urinate. But having deleted both a predator attack and a near-drowning, Jones and his writers have elected to downplay the first-hand physical threats of the natural world and focus instead on the psychological consequences that follow from them. In his adaptation of *The Homesman*, even brief scenes of suspense and action are omitted in favor of a more mannered, measured character study.

Although the omission—indeed the silencing—of Hedda Petzke's story and the contraction of each of the other women's plights might suggest otherwise, Jones's film seems clearly aimed at offering a feminist perspective. That women have historically been silenced during this era is a given, and that none of the three speaks anything other than a brief threat, epithet, or exclamation in the film is telling. But these are not the only women who are silenced. For a full two-thirds of the narrative, its protagonist Mary Bee Cuddy, having tamed the frontier and built a homestead, having bravely volunteered in other men's places for the role of the "homesman," and having saved Briggs from death-by-lynching, has proved herself "as much a man as any man hereabouts." (She is also told more than once that she is "plain as an old tin pail," a quality no reviewer has ascribed to Hilary Swank.) Among her qualities are a devotion to her church and community, her love of hymns and music, and her domestic prowess, all shown elaborately in the film's first act. Her proposals of marriage to neighbor Bob Giffen first, and Briggs later, each of them vouched in terms of a profitable domestic merger, show her heteronormative desire for a traditional marriage.

While Swarthout's novel makes use of a narrative strategy that allows for a degree of filtered omniscience and frequently employs both indirect and free indirect discourse to articulate both protagonists' thinking, Jones's film must rely instead on more traditionally cinematic means of conveying character motivation—facial expression, *mise-en-scène*, lighting, editing, and music—all of which are as skillful as one might imagine, given the pedigree and accomplishments of the principal actors and especially of cinematographer Rodrigo Prieto and composer Marco Beltrami. Prieto's stark, carefully structured compositions often posit Cuddy alone, in extreme long shot, dwarfed by the immensity and the austerity of the Nebraska Territory (actually New Mexico) plain. Beltrami's otherwise traditionalist score employs a 175-foot wired piano outdoor wind harp that makes use of the Santa Ana winds to help convey the incessant, maddening force of the wind (D'Alessandro 2015).

Swarthout's novel is simply more direct in articulating Cuddy's mounting despair. Having rejected Cuddy's proposal, Briggs, relieved to be alone, is shown to think, "She may make it, she may not. She's hollow in the head, all right. No telling what she'll do, one minute to the next. I better bow low to her and do-si-do. I better handle her like a cracked egg, because she's about to bust. Or has already" (Swarthout 1988: 172). Furthermore, when Cuddy later approaches Briggs for sex, Swarthout's free indirect discourse makes both characters' unspoken motivations and sentiments clear: Briggs is perturbed but aroused, concerned about "bedding down with a woman out of her mind" (1988: 173), and Cuddy is inexperienced but resolute. Perhaps most telling is this line with which Swarthout concludes the scene: "When, later, it was done, and she went back to her bed on the far side of the wagon, Mary Bee Cuddy knew in her soul that the women were awake, and had seen it, and so had He" (1988: 174). This simple line evokes both Cuddy's closer alignment to the women who have already gone insane and her fear of a wrathful God whom she has worshipped all her life.

In Swarthout's novel, this is the last moment at which there exists any interior characterization of Cuddy. From this moment on, the novel hews strictly to Briggs's perspective, showing him waking, finding Cuddy gone, and searching for her. Swarthout shows nothing further of Cuddy's remorse or of her approaching suicide. Jones's film follows suit, keeping the narrative perspective much as it had been in the novel, showing Briggs alone and searching for Cuddy (and limiting the viewers' perspective to what Briggs does and does not know). The consequence here is that even *before* her suicide, Mary Bee Cuddy is silenced—and viewers have little insight as to the state of mind that would drive her to an act as desperate as any by the women known to be insane. Cuddy's increasing desperation is, in contrast, more apparent in Swarthout's novel, which in comparison more fully establishes two key facts: one, that Briggs (hardly the most astute observer of female behavior) had recognized Cuddy's mounting despair; and two, that Cuddy's most immediate thought following her sex with Briggs was to fear her God.

If there is any single fault found most often with Jones's film by critics, it seems to be this particular sequence of events. Even those few who panned the film complimented Jones's direction, Beltrami's score, Prieto's cinematography, the principals' acting, and in general the bleak, austere, and unforgiving *mise-en-scène* and production design. But Cuddy's proposals (marriage first and sex second) and subsequent suicide seem to have been the plot points to which many reviewers (professional and lay viewers alike) took exception. Todd McCarthy in *The Hollywood Reporter* described the narrative turn as "a huge dramatic left hook [that] comes out of the blue at the 80-minute mark" (2014). *Grantland* reviewer Wesley Morris complains that that act "is a complete betrayal of Swank's performance and the radiance she emits" (2014). Calvin Wilson in the *St Louis Post-Dispatch* says that this "late and wholly unexpected narrative turn severely undermines the story, which never quite recovers" (2014). And Associated Press reviewer Jake Coyle writes that Cuddy's fate is "a conclusion at odds with Swank's excellent, sturdy performance of her" (2014).

Although these and other reviewers avoid "spoiling" the specifics of Cuddy's proposals of marriage and sex and subsequent suicide, for them the actions seem at odds with the development of her character as indicated earlier in the film and as a consequence leave audiences without sufficient motivation for what seems like a sudden betrayal of character. Perhaps these and other viewers overlooked the subtleties of the preceding scenes which detail Cuddy's experience of finding the shallow grave of an eleven-year-old Cissy Hahn, dug up for clothes and the carcass devoured by wolves, sending Cuddy on a long and circuitous solo journey alone across the plains looking for a suitable gravesite. Pioneer families knew well that predators might dig up any such shallow grave, and little four-year-old Eva Ingram is just one pioneer girl whose gravesite was marked along the trail by a scrawled headstone (Peavy and Smith 1998: 40). As Cuddy wanders lost through the territory, Beltrami's ethereal score and Prieto's night-time cinematography suggest her approaching the insanity that had already descended upon the others. The scene is followed shortly by Cuddy's playing the quilted keyboard by the riverbank and then her proposal to Briggs. The presentation of young Cissy Hahn's shallow grave and Cuddy's difficult journey to relocate her headstone is conveyed nearly wordlessly, and it seems intended clearly to suggest Cuddy's worsening condition—one in which she might offer herself, first in marriage and then in sex, to George Briggs.

There may be another reason why some critics reject Cuddy's actions here. Though only one reviewer mentions it, Cuddy's offering of herself to Briggs, even if presented in the least romantic of methods and warranted by the faithful approach to adaptation of the source novel, also smacks of the long-held, imbalanced, and generally sexist tendency of Hollywood films to pair older leading men with much younger women: at the time of the film's Cannes debut, Swank was thirty-nine, Jones sixty-seven. One recent study found that in 91 percent of 311 Hollywood films starring male actors over the age of thirty-five, the female lead was younger; for male actors in their sixties, female co-stars were on average more than a decade younger ("Hollywood Gender Age Gap" 2015). *The Homesman*'s pairing of Jones and Swank greatly exceeds by decades what is already a dramatic bias in pairing older men with much younger women.

For a film that so carefully and intentionally aligns itself with the plight and perspective of pioneer women, examining what would be nearly a century later "the problem that has no name" and would still resonate with viewers of a twenty-first-century film set in the long-distant past, the consequences are these: an astonishingly strong, brave, pious, and resolute pioneer woman must lower herself for sex with a much older, much lesser man and is silenced by the narrative nearly immediately after having done so. The strong woman is removed; the insane women, silenced by their madness, remain, now safely delivered and under hospice care, no longer a threat to their husbands, their children, or society; and Briggs, though he has already lost what little he gained in the venture, is headed "back West," restoring the narrative to a state where women are absent and the eternal drive westward is one towards progress.

"You can go on now"

At the film's conclusion Briggs finds himself, despite his honorable actions in delivering the women to safety and donating the wagon and goods, rather abruptly dismissed by the pastor's wife Altha Carter (Meryl Streep), and then again by Tabitha Hutchinson (Hailee Stenifeld), who works at the nearby inn. In quick order, Briggs spends a good bit of the money he earned on a suit of clothes, a few good meals, and a headboard for Cuddy, before he learns that his notes from the Bank of Loup are worthless. Undercapitalized banks often printed their own money, as Swarthout discovered during his research for the novel (1988: 246). Once again without a home and without resources other than the clothes on his back, Briggs is shown—again, just as per Swarthout's novel—back to his old ways, dancing and singing his drunken jig about Charley's "Weevily Ways" and firing his handgun for emphasis. The narrative that had begun with Cuddy's triumphing over the Nebraska plain concludes with Briggs alone. Indeed, in his drunken stupor Briggs forgets the headstone he has had carved for Cuddy, and it is unceremoniously dumped off the ferry he boards to float away ignominiously in the muddy Missouri river. The ending features no triumph of the spirit but only a return to a pathetic, drunken jig fading like a glowing ember. For the *Globe and Mail*'s Geoff Pevere, "*The Homesman* itself ultimately gives in to what Mary Bee and her damaged cargo are seeking to escape: an Old West where men and their guns are not only the ultimate authority, but the last word and final hope for the future" (2014). But this is not an ending with hope, as Prieto's camera tracks out and Briggs's jig fades slowly from view as a distant memory of a past long gone.

Although Cuddy's suicide renders a strong woman a martyr to social norms, her beliefs and intentions at least for a time promote a change in Briggs. In this way, Cuddy's journey is completed, as each of the three troubled women in Cuddy's charge is ultimately delivered safely "home." And *The Homesman* helpfully reminds viewers that the settlement of the West was not without victims, not without challenges lost as well as won. For some 1850s pioneer women the conditions of frontier life were simply too much to bear. Few films have prioritized their stories. Even in 2014, to encounter a film that addresses such concerns in any significant way is still too rare a thing. As a recent study published by the Annenberg School for Communication at the University of Southern California demonstrates, only 30 percent of over 30,000 speaking characters in the 700 top-grossing films from 2007 to 2014 were female: a gender ratio of 2.3 males to every one female (Smith et al. 2015: 7). Only 11 percent of these same 700 films had gender-balanced casts or featured females in roughly half of the speaking roles. And in *The Homesman*'s year of release, 2014, only twenty-one of the top 100 box-office-grossing films featured a female lead or roughly equal co-lead (Smith et al. 2015: 7). Having not cracked the list of top 100 films in 2014, *The Homesman* was not included in the Annenberg study—further evidence that a film featuring a female co-lead in a non-sexualized role with significant attention to feminist concerns has little commercial appeal. Yet *The Homesman* has much to offer anyone interested in the Western genre, the study of adaptation, the representation of women onscreen, and the ongoing disparity so problematic to Hollywood. *The Homesman* may not give full voice to silenced women, and its commercially non-viable genre and attention to feminist concerns may preclude widespread commercial success, but its content and reception both illustrate the ongoing problem of gender disparity in Hollywood—and Jones's direction, whether he is willing to allow for the film being "a Western" or not, makes for a challenging and rewarding cinematic experience.

Note

1. See "Box Office" at IMDb <https://www.imdb.com/title/tt2398231/?ref_=fn_al_tt_1>.

Filmography

Bless the Beasts and Children, director Stanley Kramer, featuring Billy Mumy, Barry Robins, Miles Chapin (Stanley Kramer Productions, 1971).
Dumb and Dumber To, director Bobby Farrelly and Peter Farrelly, featuring Jim Carrey, Jeff Daniels, Rob Riggle (Universal. 2014).
Lone Ranger, director Gore Verbinski, featuring Johnny Depp, Armie Hammer, William Fichtner (Walt Disney Pictures, 2013).

The Homesman, director Tommy Lee Jones, featuring Tommy Lee Jones, Grace Gummer (EuropaCorp, 2014).
The Shootist, director Don Siegel, featuring John Wayne, Lauren Bacall, Ron Howard (Paramount, 1976).
The Sunset Limited, director Tommy Lee Jones, featuring Samuel L. Jackson, Tommy Lee Jones (HBO Films, 2011).
The Three Burials of Melquiades Estrada, director Tommy Lee Jones, featuring Tommy Lee Jones, Barry Pepper, Dwight Yokum (EuropaCorp, 2005).
True Grit, directors Ethan Coen and Joel Coen, featuring Jeff Bridges, Matt Damon, Hailee Steinfeld (Paramount, 2010).

Bibliography

Cook, Pam (1998) "Women and the Western," in Jim Kitses and Gregg Rickman (eds), *The Western Reader*. New York: Limelight, pp. 293–300.

Coyle, Jake (2014 [2015]) "*Homesman* Reverses the Western's Course," *San Jose Mercury News*, 18 November 2014, web, 1 August 2015 <https://www.courier-postonline.com/story/entertainment/2014/11/14/homesman-reverses-westerns-course/19017395/> (last accessed 15 November 2018).

D'Alessandro, Anthony (2014 [2105]) "The Biggest Outdoor Wind Harp in Malibu," *LA Weekly*, 20 November 2014, web, 1 August 2015 <https://www.laweekly.com/the-biggest-outdoor-wind-harp-in-malibu/> (last accessed 15 November 2018).

Jones, Tommy Lee (2015) "Q&A with Tommy Lee Jones," *The Homesman*: A Film by Tommy Lee Jones. EuropaCorps and Premier Communications, web, 1 August, pp. 6–9, pdf file.

Kitses, Jim and Rickman, Gregg (eds) (1998) *The Western Reader*. New York: Limelight.

Lucas, Blake (1998) "Saloon Girls and Ranchers' Daughters: The Woman in the Western," in Jim Kitses and Gregg Rickman (eds), *The Western Reader*. New York: Limelight, pp. 301–20.

McCarthy, Todd (2014 [2015]) "*The Homesman*: Cannes Review," *Hollywood Reporter*, 18 May 2014, web, 1 August 2015 <https://www.hollywoodreporter.com/review/homesman-cannes-review-705259> (last accessed 15 November 2018).

Morris, Wesley (2014 [2015]) "Review," *Grantland*, 18 November 2014, web, 1 August 2015 <http://grantland.com/hollywood-prospectus/dumb-and-dumber-to-rosewater-beyond-the-lights-homesman-review/> (last accessed 15 November 2018).

Oliver, Wes and Fitzgerald, Keiran (2015) "Q&A with Wes Oliver and Keiran Fitzgerald," web, 1 August 2015, pp. 18–21, pdf file <https://medias.unifrance.org/medias/254/230/124670/presse/the-homesman-dossier-de-presse-anglais.pdf> (last accessed 15 November 2018).

Peavy, Linda and Smith, Ursula (1996) *Pioneer Women: The Lives of Women on the Frontier*. Norman, OK: University of Oklahoma Press.

Peavy, Linda and Smith, Ursula (eds) (1994) *Women in Waiting in the Westward Movement: Life on the Home Frontier*. Norman, OK: University of Oklahoma Press.

Pevere, Geoff (2014 [2105]) "*The Homesman*: On the Frontier of Madness," *Globe and Mail*, 21 November 2014, web, 1 August 2015 <https://www.theglobeandmail.

com/arts/film/film-reviews/the-homesman-on-the-frontier-of-madness/article 21676164/> (last accessed 15 November 2018).

Riley, Glenda (1994) *Women and Indians on the Frontier, 1825–1915*. Albuquerque, NM: University of New Mexico Press.

Ross, Nancy Wilson (1944) *Westward the Women*. New York: Random.

Scott, A. O. (2014) "Plain on the Plains," *New York Times*, 14 November 2014, web, 1 August 2015 <https://www.nytimes.com/2014/11/14/movies/the-homesman-stars-hilary-swank-and-tommy-lee-jones.html> (last accessed 15 November 2018).

Smith, Stacy L. et al. (2015) *Inequality in 700 Popular Films: Examining Portrayals of Gender, Race, & LGBT Status from 2007 to 2014*, in Media, Diversity, & Social Change Initiative, Los Angeles, University of Southern California, 2014, web, 6 August 2015 <https://annenberg.usc.edu/sites/default/files/MDSCI_Inequality_in-700_Popular.pdf> (last accessed 15 November 2018).

Swarthout, Glendon (1988) *The Homesman*. New York: Simon & Schuster.

Swarthout, Miles (1988) "Afterword," in *The Homesman*. New York: Simon & Schuster, pp. 243–8.

"The Hollywood Gender Age Gap" (2015) *Graphjoy.com*, 16 August, web, 23 August 2015 <http://graphjoy.com/2015/08/the-hollywood-gender-age-gap-part-1/> (last accessed 15 November 2018).

"*The Homesman* Reviews: Top Critics" (2015) *Rotten Tomatoes*, 1 August <https://www.rottentomatoes.com/m/the_homesman> (last accessed 15 November 2018).

Wilson, Calvin (2014 [2015]) "Hilary Swank is Outstanding in *The Homesman*," *St Louis Press Dispatch*, 28 November 2014, web, 1 August 2015 <https://www.stltoday.com/entertainment/movies/reviews/hilary-swank-is-outstanding-in-homesman/article_3961ca17-fe00-528a-9578-212299c4c198.html> (last accessed 15 November 2018).

17. WOMEN GOTTA GUN? ICONOGRAPHY AND FEMALE REPRESENTATION IN *GODLESS*

Stella Hockenhull

Godless is a US TV drama that commenced production in September 2016 and aired in 2017 on Netflix. It is comprised of seven episodes, has a number of narrative strands, and includes many unusual and outrageous characters. In the serial, outlaw Frank Griffin (Jeff Daniels) has been betrayed by his protégé, Roy Goode (Jack O'Connell), and is out for revenge causing carnage in his search. Frank and his gang eventually arrive at the local mining town of La Belle where the inhabitants are comprised largely of women; this gender imbalance is a consequence of a mining disaster that virtually wiped out the male population. One of the town's people, Alice Fletcher (Michelle Dockery), operates a horse stud, but she is unpopular with the locals who believe she is a witch who has brought bad luck to the town. One of the reasons for this is that, having been rescued from a brutal rape by the town's sheriff, Bill McNue (Scoot McNairy), she moved in to live with a family of Native Americans, one of whom she married and who was later murdered by the townspeople. Subsequent to this the mining disaster occurred. She takes in the fugitive, Roy, and protects him from capture. Ultimately, the two form a relationship, and he becomes her lover and a father figure and role model for her son, Truckee (Samuel Marty). Roy's parents died when he was young, and, later he was abandoned by his elder brother whom he makes it his mission in life to find. Another key character, Mary Agnes McNue (Merritt Wever), the sheriff's sister, is one of the many widows of the town. She has adapted to the change by dressing in men's clothing and engaging in a lesbian relationship with local whore, Callie Dunne (Tess Frazer). At the end of the serial, Roy leaves Alice to find his long-lost brother in California, but not before he joins the local townswomen in a shootout and kills Frank and the gang of outlaws. Finally, one must presume that Alice develops a relationship with Sheriff Bill NcNue when they are seen from a distance, accompanied by her son, walking towards the farmhouse deep in conversation. Eventually Roy arrives in California and is pictured on his horse overlooking the sea. Soon, one supposes, having reached his destination, he will be reunited with his brother.

Alice is one of the central protagonists in the serial, and in this, and other examples of the genre where women are the focal point of the narrative,[1] she is desirable and beautiful, but becomes masculinized in order to succeed (Jeffers McDonald 2010). Forced to adopt traits and expertise normally associated with traditional male iconography in the Western (Matheson 2017), Alice has no option but to cast aside her elegant clothing in favor of a functional felt hat and workmanlike trousers. She has to become a proficient horsewoman and manage livestock and, furthermore, she is an able markswoman capable of protecting herself. Indeed, horses and guns are phallic tropes in the Western and, as Stella Bruzzi suggests, "the possession of a detached phallic symbol is a survival imperative" (1997: 181). Responding in part to Alice's masculinization, critical reviews of the serial at the time of its release suggest that, owing to its largely female cast, *Godless* is a feminist Western. As one commentator contends, it is "a proto-feminist pasture, shot in a sweeping 2.39:1 aspect ratio where horses roam and women rule. And the show sets itself up for those women to stand their ground against Griffin's outlaws" (Nevins 2017). However, despite the tough central female characters and the predominance of women in the serial, *Godless* fails to deliver a Western that replaces traditional patriarchal society associated with the genre. Indeed, the Western iconography that identifies the woman's place within the serial's nexus presents a complicated scenario in which the tradition of a male hierarchical figure is retained, violence rules, and women either conform or are eventually subjugated. Alice and the townswomen seem to be independent and to have adopted those masculine traits associated with the cowboy, yet they are never entirely bestowed equal status and ultimately conform to being feminine stereotypes.[2]

Masculine Traits and the Western Hero

In classic Westerns, concepts of manliness are embodied in the cowboy figure. Traditionally he is a national hero, and is identified romantically through his bravery and rugged individualism. As Lee Clark Mitchell points out, albeit referring to the nineteenth-century Colonel, Richard Irving Dodge, "For fidelity to duty, for promptness and vigor of action, for resources in difficulty, and unshaken courage in danger, the cow-boy has no superior among men" (Mitchell 1996: 25). In addition, the cowboy is feted for his liberty to roam and escape from civilized life. As Mitchell later remarks, "In a period of increasing pressure on the nuclear family, the cowboy represented a nostalgic dream of escape from middle-class obligations, and in particular from family ties (a basic theme elaborated in the frequency of the phrase 'just passin' through' or the popularity of the western songs like 'Don't Fence Me In' and 'Wayfarin' Stranger')" (Mitchell 1996: 27).

The Western hero roams freely, he is enigmatic, and his masculinity is a performance displayed through gestures and mannerisms. Indeed, the cowboy is characterized as "[t]he strong individual (almost always a straight white male) standing 'tall in the saddle' and using righteous violence (his gun) to protect the expanding American community from those who would harm it" (Benshoff and Griffin 2009: 105). Because the Western is a genre of contrasts, men and women are seen as opposites and the latter are also constructed in terms of contradictions. As Jane Tompkins comments, this

> set of oppositions [are] fundamental to the way the Western thinks about the world. There are two choices: either you can remain in a world of illusions, by which is understood religion, culture, and class distinctions, a world of fancy words and pretty actions, of "manners for the parlour and the ball room, and . . . womanly tricks for courting"; or you can face life as it really is—blood, death, a cold wind blowing, and a gun in the hand. (Tompkins 1992: 48)

Not only is masculinity in the Western displayed through body language, but also through the ownership and use of the gun. As Fran Pheasant-Kelly points out, weaponry is a symbol of manliness and "[c]onventionally, the gun in film is a marker of masculinity and its recognition as a phallic symbol abounds across all genres" (Pheasant-Kelly 2017: 124). Additionally, an arms weapon offers a means of protection for the protagonists where there is no other solution. Indeed, "[t]he gun symbolizes the individual's right to self-protection in a society where the law is unreliable or absent altogether" (Buscombe 1993: 137).

Generally, expertise with a gun is a symbol of heterosexual power for the Western male, but in *Godless* both Alice and Mary Agnes are also proficient and adept. This is demonstrated in the first episode, when the central male protagonist and love interest, Roy, first meets Alice. The sequence commences as he appears out of the gloom on his horse. When the door of Alice's small timber homestead opens, and before anyone is visible to the spectator, a woman's voice demands of the stranger, "Who's there? Declare yourself or I'll shoot." The camera frames a raised shotgun in close-up, before revealing its owner, Alice. Cast in shadow, she seems menacing and moves slowly towards the rider. When he fails to respond to her question, she raises the rifle and shoots the already injured stranger who falls from his horse. There is no doubt that Alice is an expert with the firearm and prepared to defend herself and her property, but her victim is already rendered vulnerable. Thus, although Alice exercises her right to protect herself and demonstrates her ability with a gun, she also attacks a defenceless individual. Hers is not a laudable gesture.

A little later, following Roy's arrest (he is a wanted man), Alice further reveals her prowess with weaponry. She realizes that she needs his help around the property and, therefore, must break him out of jail. Subsequently, and again signifying grim determination, she is seen returning to the house to ride into town to effect his release. As she walks to the door, Alice purposefully grabs the gun and explains to her mother-in-law, Iyovi (Tantoo Cardinal), and her son, Truckee, that she will be back later. An upright figure, she walks with an erect and purposeful stride as she marches away from the homestead demonstrating her strong disposition. As Deborah Kitchen-Døderlein points out, posture, a significant feature of character in both men and women, is "an important marker among female characters ... White women tend to have good posture ... In general, erect posture marks pride and a sense of authority for both men and women and for Indians and Whites" (Kitchen-Døderlein 2017: 81).

A little later Alice enters into the sheriff's office and, this time, her gun is raised at shoulder height, a symbol of phallic masculinity. Seen in medium shot and half light, her mannish felt hat is pulled over her eyes making her appear mysterious yet threatening. She cocks the gun and forces the fairly inept local sheriff's assistant, Whitey Winn (Thomas Brodie-Sangster), to remove his gun belt and open up the cell where Roy is held. "Do it or you're gonna be awful damn sick from a bullet in your chest," she states in ominous tones, and a cut from her face to an apprehensive Roy, who is behind bars, confirms that she means business. The camera reframes her as she follows Whitey to the jail where she locks him up, her rifle remaining erect and aimed at the young man. Despite the gun operating as phallic symbol, and Alice's threatening demeanor, a victory over Whitey is not that impressive. He is not a robust character and is represented as immature and inept throughout the serial. Furthermore, although he is eventually freed from imprisonment in the next episode, to instigate this he is forced to beseech a woman, Mary Agnes, for help from behind a barred window, an act which presents a comedic aspect to the narrative. Ultimately, due to his immaturity, Whitey meets an untimely death as a result of his bravado. This occurs at the end of the serial when Frank and his gang raid the town; the boy attempts to tackle them alone, spinning his pistols in a showy manner, but he is too slow firing, and is stabbed in the chest. Whitey's lack of expertise with a firearm has cost him his life; previously, it seems Alice's earlier act emasculated him.

Towards the end of the serial, all the women are forced to use guns because they have to defend themselves from the vengeful Frank and his men, who believe that they have been harboring Roy. The defence of the town is initially led by Mary Agnes who strategically directs each woman to a particular point of the main hotel in La Belle. Mary Agnes has already proved herself useful with a gun on a previous occasion. Accompanied by her niece and nephew, she is shopping for supplies in the local grocer's store, and part of her order includes bullets. On this matter she is very knowledgeable and precise in her requirements. The grocer tries to sell her a lesser size than she wants but she is firm in her request for a larger cartridge. Mocking her he exclaims, "Why, you huntin' buffalo?," to which she sarcastically answers, "Why you seen any?" Meanwhile, her niece, Trudy McNue (Marie Wagenman), is tampering with some of the contents in the shop and the shopkeeper threatens her. Mary Agnes is immediately antagonistic and pulls a gun on him. Seen in medium shot, the camera positioned from over her shoulder, she continues to keep the grocer in her aim until he calms down and becomes less intimidating. However, her act is against a defenceless old man, again rendering her threats with the gun impotent and, in this instance, she fails to act like a cowboy.

The women ultimately make a valiant attempt to defend the town in the final siege in the hotel. Here, an initially reluctant Alice ultimately agrees to help after observing the poor attempt that one of the townswomen, Charlotte Temple (Samantha Soule), makes while firing a gun. She is hopeless and Alice sees she must be of assistance. The final shootout commences and the camera cuts to a distance shot of Frank and his men approaching the town on horseback in a cloud of dust. An edit shows the town buildings, which now seem deserted, and a silence reigns. Rising above the hotel in a crane shot, the camera reveals Alice and Mary Agnes poised with their guns ready for action. The sound of galloping horses is heard as the women gaze out into the distance, wherefrom the men commence their assault. In keeping with the traditions of the Western the action speeds up, and intercuts between the women with their guns raised ready to fire and the marauding men, thus creating the appearance of a shooting frenzy. Alice and Mary Agnes are the focus of this exchange, and frequently the camera frames the two together as a strong and capable duo, guns raised at their attackers picking them off one by one. Inside the hotel the other women flounder a little, but they hold their own, and even Charlotte manages to aim accurately and fire. The section is balletic: filmed in slow motion, an unusual technique for television but certainly owing a debt to the Bloody Porch sequence in the *The Wild Bunch* (Peckinpah, 1969), the women's prowess is championed as a result.[3] However, despite this display, when it seems that they may be overpowered, it is Bill and Roy who step in and kill the remainder of the gang, apart from Frank who is despatched at the end of the film by Roy.

Costume

While guns are key to masculinity in the Western, clothing also makes a significant contribution. Generally and historically, men wear buckskin fringe which reveals the character's identification with the wilderness. This use of leather is natural and, as Sue Matheson points out, "the more elaborately trimmed the buckskin garment, the more primitive and therefore more noble the character of its wearer is" (Matheson 2017: 25). Buckskin is linked to notorious heroes such as Buffalo Bill and Shane and is "a reliable indicator of a good man" (Matheson 2017: 30). In the Western, buckskin is a man's apparel. Fringe-wearing women such as Annie (Barbara Stanwyck) in *Annie Oakley* (1935) and Calamity (Doris Day) in *Calamity Jane* (1953) leave their buckskins behind when they fall in love and marry. In *Godless*, there is little use of buckskin, but the female focal figures in the narrative wear masculine clothes, or, in the case of Mary Agnes, men's attire. When the spectator is first introduced to her she is dressed in a man's shirt and waistcoat, and she sports a gun and holster at all times. She also has the erect posture and demeanor associated with the cowboy: she adopts an upright, purposeful stance and takes long strides. Furthermore, her hat is a Ridge Top which is a traditional cowboy hat but slightly taller than the most common varieties worn (the Cattleman and the Cutter). Because of her appearance, Mary Agnes is frequently the object of speculation from the townspeople and visitors. Indeed, her brother, Bill McNue, suggests that she has changed in personality since the death of her husband in the mining disaster, and, as a result, she has "lost her maternal ability." Later, Charlotte Temple admonishes her over her masculine appearance when the company that are trying to take over the mine visits the town. The "least you could have done was put on a dress," she states. When the men arrive, they look at her with curiosity because she appears unfeminine and at odds with the other local women who wear dresses. Callie, in particular, is clad in pretty, pale-colored dresses with ruffles and a bonnet. Despite having been the local prostitute, she now teaches at the town's school that is set up in the old whorehouse, Magdalena's. Here, her surroundings further emphasize her femininity. They are opulent and luxurious in contrast to Alice's stark living accommodation. When at one point Alice asks to speak privately with Callie, she enters the schoolroom for the first time, and her expression is one of amazement. From her point of view, the camera surveys the lavish room, panning around to encompass the red velvet-covered walls, glass chandeliers, and extravagant fixtures. It is only when the townswomen are forced to defend themselves that some (not all) exchange their gowns for functional, and more masculine, practical attire, sporting trousers held up by braces, and men's shirts.

In a similar vein to Mary Agnes, Alice wears trousers and "Boss of the Plains" brown felt hats, the original cowboy hats which were later molded and creased to suit preferences. Her attire is sombre in tone and workmanlike, an aesthetic which enables her to blend with the environment. As Tania Modleski observes, when referring to the film *The Ballad of Little Jo*, "woman transforms the Western itself when she enters its landscape wearing the clothes that allow her to range freely across it" (Modleski 1999: 178). However, despite her adoption of trousers and workmanlike hat and unlike Mary Agnes, Alice retains some aspects of femininity in *Godless*, often wearing dresses or fitted tops in line with the townswomen.

Horses and Equine Expertise

The horse is always a key feature of the Western and a symbol of masculinity. As noted by Modleski, it offers liberty, and, as John Cawelti argues:

> The hero is a man with a horse and the horse is his direct tie to the freedom of the wilderness, for it embodies his ability to move freely across it and to dominate and control its spirit. Through the intensity of his relationship to his horse, the cowboy excites that human fantasy of unity with natural creatures. (Cawelti 1970: 57)

Often the cowboy hero demonstrates his masculinity through taming and breaking his horse, thus displaying his prowess, manliness, and proficiency. Indeed, the Western succeeded in glamorizing the cowboy because of his relationship with his steed. Not only did it represent him as an able horseman, but also as an authority, and someone whose job it is to fight evil and Native Americans. As Roderick McGillis indicates, the cowboy's mount, "draws attention to the body. Horses are beautiful to look at and so are horse and rider together" (2009: 111). The Western hero wears spurs and chaps and has an elaborate saddle and clothing to correspond with this riding expertise. Further, the horse is both free spirited and courageous, traits that are transferable to the rider. Through his equine skills, the cowboy is linked to strength, freedom, and the wild.

If women want to belong to this masculine world then they also must demonstrate their power and strength, and a major element of this lies in their equestrian skills and ability to deal in business with men as their equals. Yet, as Maria Cecília De Miranda N. Coelho maintains, while they reaffirm the values of the male world of the West, "these 'high-ridin' women' later hand their power over to the men they choose to follow" (2017: 116). *Godless* is no exception.[4] Indeed, while Alice is the person who owns and breeds horses, it is Roy who is represented as an equine expert. He is unafraid to handle the animals, and they appear to understand and obey him. At one point he maneuvers around the herd to make the horses lie down. Seen in close-up, he carefully strokes and manipulates the horses' necks encouraging them each in turn to recline. Eventually every animal complies with his wishes. Shown in extreme close-up and slow motion, his hands caress their bodies, the activity appearing poetic and tactile. Throughout this sequence of events he is watched by Truckee and Alice. A point-of-view shot shows the wonder in Truckee's eyes and, from this moment on, Roy becomes a hero and the object of both the boy's and Alice's gaze. Strangely, given that Alice has owned the farm for some years, she is not as proficient in handling horses as Roy and is represented as his inferior. At one juncture, she attempts to rope a horse, which she partially succeeds in doing, until the animal becomes unmanageable and pulls her through a fence. Seen from an overhead shot, she falls to the ground and the remainder of the horses break out of their corral making her appear inept, and thus she is forced to hand over all the training of the herd to Roy.

A little later in the serial, Roy agrees to break the horses at Alice's ranch in return for reading lessons. He wants to become literate in order to decipher a letter from his brother revealing the latter's whereabouts. The horse training sequence commences when Roy takes a rope and walks towards the paddock where a wild, black horse, one that had previously struck him down, stands. Seen in slow motion, and again watched by Truckee, Roy opens the gate and releases the animal, which gallops out towards him. The camera cuts to a close-up of the animal's ferocious eye, and then tracks Roy as he sidesteps backwards and forwards in an attempt to lasso the feral animal, which careers up and down the fence before stopping to paw the ground. Observed by Iyovi, who is rolling a cigarette, and Truckee, Roy ropes the animal's leg before eventually taming the wild and previously unyielding horse. Alice who has joined the party, also gazes in awe. This is the animal that had seemed rebellious and had previously dragged her along the ground; Roy's expert equine skills and talent is depicted in extreme close-up and slow motion, emphasizing his masculinity, as opposed to Alice's previous clumsy attempt. His facial expression infers concentration and he strokes the horse, soothing it as he removes the rope, the animal remaining motionless. When it eventually reclines, Roy climbs on the back of the beast and rides around the corral, the horse bucking and throwing him to the ground. He remounts and asks Truckee to open the gate and, without a bridle and bareback, he gallops out into the landscape. Viewed from a distance, he is represented as the lone figure/Westerner against the backdrop of the mountains, adopting what is traditionally seen as his rightful place. He pauses and the camera frames his face as he says "Good to see you again boy," a statement which could only mean the landscape, thus heralding freedom and his impending departure.

Roy is not only a competent rider himself, he also teaches Truckee to ride. The boy is resistant and overprotected by his mother and grandmother, but Roy encourages him to experiment with a bigger horse. Even though Truckee falls, Roy persuades the boy to remount and become the horse's boss. Alice and Iyovi are filled with trepidation, and the camera cuts to reveal the pair running to the boy's rescue. However, Roy halts them, suggesting that they are trying to shield the boy too much, and Truckee remounts and falls off a number of times before eventually succeeding. This new skill that the boy has learned enables him to participate in the cowboy's world, and he and his new father figure ride out into the landscape together leaving the women at the homestead.

Alice is a competent rider, but it is Roy who teaches her to ride a recently broken horse. After watching him train numerous animals, she mounts in the corral and rides out through the gate into the landscape, yet she is not permitted the same amount of screen time as was Roy. Briefly, the camera frames her but she does not venture as far afield as her male counterpart, clearly not experiencing the same draw of the wild. In the Western, as Anthony Easthope avers, men on horseback evince "phallic" power: "Once on the horse the lone male will have harnessed its previously unbridled natural power. Instead of running wild it will carry him in planned directions across the terrain . . . Such mastery depends on his phallic power" (Easthope 1990: 47). Alice does not possess this same "phallic" power, preferring to remain on her homestead or with the townswomen and rarely venturing far afield. Indeed, in general the women of the village are not riders, preferring to travel by carriage and only entering the landscape when accompanied by men.

Psyche of the Western Hero

Another way in which women are less influential in *Godless* rests in how their inner psyches are revealed. According to Modleski, men in the Western traditionally are unknowable and mysterious whereas women are readily psychologized. As she maintains, the Western hero is often hard to read and not overly complicated:

> Western heroes are supposed to be enigmatic . . . Indeed, to supply a hero with motives that lie outside him would diminish his phallic self-sufficiency, which is revealed in his typically tautological appeal to a gendered identity whenever he is asked to give a reason for his actions . . . By contrast, the woman must be psychologised and understood for she represents an intolerable double enigma: the enigma of the Westerner superimposed, as it were, on the enigma of woman. (Modleski 1999: 155–6)

In *Godless*, the women's behavior can be interpreted and explained in detail. Mary Agnes has become a lesbian since the death of her husband and has probably always had such leanings we are told. She has subsequently formed a relationship with Callie, whose decisions are also easily decipherable. Having been a prostitute, Callie is dissatisfied with men and prefers relationships with women. At one point, she describes her liaison with her new lover, Mary Agnes. The couple are seated close together in Callie's home, illuminated by the fire that bathes them in a soft light. Melodic non-diegetic music further enhances the romance of the scene as she speaks, enabling the spectator an understanding of her personality. Indeed, Callie is reduced to tears as she states the various aspects of Mary Agnes's character that she esteems, thus permitting insight into her feelings:

> Well, I remember the first time I saw you. It was one afternoon. I'm on Magdalena's porch, reading the paper, when you come galloping into town on that bay mare you used to have. As usual, you were all mad at something or other. Well, I watched you glide off that horse in a big flurry of skirts and hair and that was it for me. I still watch you. All the time. I know everything about you. How you feel. How you taste. How you smell. Hell, lady, I could find you in the dark!

Subsequently the two kiss and embrace.

Alice's motives in the serial are also easily understood. She was the victim of a brutal rape, the viewer is informed, and she has difficulty forming a relationship. Events of the attack are revealed through flashbacks as the story unfolds from her point of view, enabling insights into Alice's psyche and resultant fear of men. Revealing her past, the camera cuts from a close-up of her traumatized expression in the present, and then to a flashback which is a memory of her sprawling body, clad in a yellow dress, in a forest clearing. A point-of-view shot from her perspective reveals a group of figures disguised with buffalo heads replete with horns. Forming a circle, these attackers tower menacingly above her, and then begin to rape her one by one, watched by a group of women and children who are also being held captive by her assailants. Ultimately, Alice is rescued by Bill NcNue, but not before she violently stabs one of the aggressors, repeatedly thrusting a knife into his torso.

Landscape and Setting

Nature in the Western is not merely background, it is a central character and, historically, has been characterized as masculine. As noted, generally, men are provided liberty and autonomy in this genre, and they ride off into the mountains, eventually absorbed by the backdrop and setting. As Roger Horrocks maintains, "Men are dwarfed by this gargantuan landscape; their activities seem to shrink to those of tiny ants, ephemeral beneath the eternal rocks. The land is also austere, hard, sculptural: one might say a homoerotic landscape!" (Horrocks 1995: 71). This landscape is always predominantly a desert. As Tompkins remarks, "The land revealed on the opening pages or in the opening shot of a Western is a land defined by absence: of trees, of greenery, of houses, of the signs of civilization, above all, absence of water and shade" (1992: 71). In this setting, the Westerner is an exposed figure with no place to hide and only the strong and brave can survive. He adopts and imitates the qualities of the landscape and bears adversity courageously. The land is to be respected and acquires a spiritual quality which cannot be dominated: "Nature is the one transcendent thing, the one thing larger than man (and it is constantly portrayed as immense), the ideal toward which human nature strives" (Tompkins 1992: 72). For Tompkins, the wasteland complements the human figure whereas a forest engulfs that person. As she argues, the former occurs "by making it [the figure] seem dominant and unique, dark against light, vertical against horizontal, solid against plane, detail against blankness" (Tompkins 1992: 74). Men in particular emulate the harsh and rocky land and aim to appear as "natural" as possible merging with their surroundings. This occurs through costume, as well as via their dirty and rugged appearance, a point made by Tompkins who contends:

> For the setting by its harshness and austerity seems to have selected its heroes from among strong men in the prime of life, people who have a certain build, complexion, facial type, carriage, gesture, and demeanour; who dress a certain way, carry certain accoutrements, have few or no social ties, are experts at certain skills (riding, tracking, roping, fistfighting, shooting) and terrible at others (dancing, talking to ladies). (Tompkins 1992: 73)

This notion of a harsh landscape supports the idea that men are superior to women in the Western. As Tompkins states, "The female, the dusky, and the dressed up are not harsh and hard and pure like the desert. Not strong and silent and unforgiving" (Tompkins 1992: 74). Coded as masculine, the desert provides freedom of movement and does not hamper the hero who traverses it, lighting a campfire, cooking himself food, finding running water, and pasture for his horse. Celibate and alone, the Western male protagonist exists in a situation described by Tompkins as "desert monasticism" (Tompkins 1992: 84).

Although women are the key protagonists in *Godless*, it is the men that are given liberty to traverse the landscape whereas the women remain static and are hampered by their surroundings. In episode 1, for example, Frank Griffin and his gang roam wild, building campfires, murdering and raping. They appear to have no base and move from settlement to settlement creating havoc. In a similar vein, the sheriff wanders the countryside between visiting Alice's house and in pursuit of Roy, and it is he who eventually becomes the hero and goes off in search of Frank alone. This is visible through a distance shot of horse and rider set against a magnificent, mountainous backdrop. Riding at speed, he throws up a band of dust clouds as he gallops the plains, blending harmoniously with these natural surroundings. As Anthony Easthope maintains, beauty and the magnificence of the landscape are associated with masculinity: "Man is most himself when he is spontaneously at one with nature. Several aspects of the image equate this man with nature, the cowboy (or Cow-*boy*). His hair fades almost imperceptibly into the flowing tail and mane of the horses, just as the colour of his face runs into the red of the prairie" (Easthope 1990: 47).

Roy's links to and love of the landscape are always apparent. At one point, when Truckee has fallen from his horse while being taught to ride, Roy averts his gaze to the mountains beyond. In a point-of-view 180-degree panoramic shot, the spectator is enabled a view of the distant peaks, the camera then returning to rest on the empty paddock: all the horses have now been broken and this spectacle beckons the cowboy away from domesticity, to a place that Alice cannot go. Nowhere are these concepts more accurate than when, at the end, Roy decides that the pull of finding his brother is too much, and he chooses this course of action over his affection for Alice. Watched by Alice, he bids her goodbye and leaves the ranch astride his horse. The lone figure becomes a silhouette on the horizon as a series of shots aid this location transition, demonstrating his move west to track down his brother.

Whereas Roy, Bill, and even Frank are represented as being comfortable in the wilderness, women in this serial are curtailed in that relationship. Mary Agnes remains within the confines of the town, her task to protect the other women, including her lover, from attack rather than to venture out in pursuit of the Griffin gang. Furthermore, she appears to have taken on the role of caring for her brother's children whose mother died in childbirth. The other townswomen accept her guidance and only travel when it is entirely necessary, and then are accompanied as they do so. While Alice does ride out onto the prairie, she does not travel far. Initially, she stays principally in the house preparing food alongside the only other woman on the ranch, Iyovi. At one point, however, as noted previously, she ventures out alone in search of Truckee who has gone missing following the disappearance of Roy. Seen from a distance, she first appears to integrate with her surroundings and visually blends in, suggesting a similar status to her male counterparts. However, when she sees Frank and his men, she is rapidly forced to return to the town, ostensibly to warn the women of the impending attack. This open space that suits Roy and the other men so well is unwelcoming and unappealing for Alice who is ill equipped to confront the dangers it holds.

Conclusion

Although *Godless* uses female characters as center points to the narrative, there is no suggestion of either a feminist production or a change in structure to the Western. Indeed, the serial contains characters and iconography consistent with the traditions of the classic films of the genre. While Alice is a robust female character who can competently ride and shoot, she ultimately conforms to stereotypical representations of femininity. She is the focus of a love triangle between Roy and Bill, and, while she works the land and owns horses, she rarely ventures out alone. She has to be instructed on how to manage her livestock, not having the personal touch with horses that Roy possesses. Roy and, to a certain extent, Bill are manly cowboys who save the day and rescue the women, thus restoring order to La Belle. This takes place with a final shootout typical of the genre, demonstrating that, although the women are capable, the traditions of the Western are upheld. Women in *Godless* further conform to Western stereotypes in that they are not very comfortable in the environment if too far from civilization. Alice, because of her past, is afraid to shift far from home. Her forays into the wilderness are instigated through necessity rather than a desire for adventure, and it is Roy who eventually leaves to push west. In addition, Alice and Mary Agnes appear to be rebellious, but they ultimately desire stable romantic relationships, as exemplified when Alice remains with Bill. Roy tells Bill to "look after" Alice and Truckee and, from his point of view, the camera frames Alice and Bill together. She takes him by the arm and leads him towards the house. Truckee takes Bill's horse's reins and leads the animal away, suggesting a return to a patriarchal household and order for the family. As Victoria Lamont avers, Westerns emphasize the fact that the female protagonist is alone and vulnerable. Even if she is mutinous, then she is really a true woman underneath. In fact, "[t]he self-reliant woman of the West was a mainstay of *Romantic Range* stories [which] often introduced these heroines as lone figures in the wilderness, sometimes engaged in feats of heroic action. The reader is soon reassured, however, that a 'true woman' lies beneath these masculine appearances" (Lamont 2016: 45). Alice is solitary and susceptible, but the true woman emerges as the serial progresses, and she settles into a heterosexual relationship and family unit.

Notes

1. Examples include *Cat Ballou* (Silverstein, 1965), *The Ballad of Little Jo* (Greenwald, 1993) and *True Grit* (Coen and Coen, 2010).
2. In *The Contemporary Western: An American Genre Post 9/11*, John White also explores the role of strong central women characters in films such as *Jane Got a Gun* (O'Connor, 2016), *Open Range* (Costner, 2003), and *True Grit* (Coen and Coen, 2010). He suggests that these works reflect the anxieties of a post 9/11 America. Furthermore, for him, they fulfill the need for US patriotism as well as a societal desire for self-defense in the face of adversity.
3. This is reminiscent of the "Bloody Porch" sequence in Sam Peckinpah's *The Wild Bunch* (1969) where the director uses slow motion combined with fast editing to create a dramatic and memorable effect.
4. In a small number of films, women defy gender conventions. As De Miranda N. Coelho points out, "In addition to being good riders and wearing male attire, they are smart and witty and run ranches with the same competence as the men who admire and fear them" (De Miranda N. Coelho 2017: 114).

Filmography

Annie Oakley, director George Stevens, featuring Barbara Stanwyck, Preston Foster, Melvyn Douglas (RKO Radio Pictures, 1935).
Calamity Jane, director David Butler, featuring Doris Day, Howard Keel, Allyn Ann McLerie (Warner Bros., 1953).
Cat Ballou, director Elliot Silverstein, featuring Jane Fonda, Lee Marvin, Michael Callan (Columbia, 1965).
Godless, featuring Jack O'Connell, Michelle Dockery, Scoot McNairy (Netflix, 2017).
The Ballad of Little Jo, director Maggie Greenwald, featuring Suzie Amis, Bo Hopkins, Ian McKellen (Joco and Polygram Filmed Entertainment, 1993).
The Wild Bunch, director Sam Peckinpah, featuring William Holden, Ernest Borgnine, Robert Ryan (Warner Bros., 1969).
True Grit, directors Ethan Coen and Joel Coen, featuring Jeff Bridges, Matt Damon, Hailee Steinfeld (Paramount, 2010).

Bibliography

Benshoff, Harry M. and Griffin, Sean (2009) *America on Film: Representing Race, Class, Gender and Sexuality at the Movies*. Oxford and Chichester: Wiley Blackwell.
Birnbaum, Debra (2017) "'Godless' Team on Making a Western, Feminism and Directing Horses," *Variety*, 16 November 2017 <https://variety.com/2017/tv/news/godless-netflix-jeff-daniels-michelle-dockery-scott-frank-1202617026/> (last accessed 13 October 2018).
Bruzzi, Stella (1997) *Undressing Cinema*. London and New York: Routledge.
Bruzzi, Stella (2013) *Men's Cinema: Masculinity and Mise-en-Scène in Hollywood*. Edinburgh: Edinburgh University Press.
Buscombe, Edward (ed.) (1993) *The BFI Companion to the Western*, 2nd edn. London: BFI.
Buscombe, Edward (1998) "Photographing the Indian," in Edward Buscombe and Roberta E. Pearson (eds), *Back in the Saddle Again*. London: British Film Institute, pp. 29–45.
Buscombe, Edward (2006) "Man to Man," *Sight and Sound*, 16 (1), pp. 34–7.
Calder, Jenni (1974) *There Must Be a Lone Ranger*. London: Hamish Hamilton.
Carter, David (2008) *The Western*. Harpenden: Kamera Books.
Cawelti, John (1970) *The Six-Gun Mystique*. Bowling Green, OH: Bowling Green Popular Press.
Clarke, Roger (2006) "Lonesome Cowboys," *Sight and* Sound, 16 (1), pp. 28–33.
De Miranda N. Coelho, Maria Cecília (2017) "Horses for Ladies, High-Ridin' Women and Whores," in Sue Matheson (ed.), *A Fistful of Icons: Essays on Frontier Fixtures of the American Western*. Jefferson, NC: McFarland, pp. 113–23.
Easthope, Antony (1990) *What a Man's Gotta Do: The Masculine Myth in Popular Culture*. New York and London: Routledge.
Freedman, Carl (2007) "Post-Heterosexuality: John Wayne and the Construction of American Masculinity," *Film International*, 5 (1), pp. 16–31.

Gaines, Jane Marie and Herzog, Charlotte Cornelia (1998) "The Fantasy of Authenticity in Western Costume," in Edward Buscombe and Roberta E. Pearson (eds), *Back in the Saddle Again*. London: British Film Institute, pp. 172–81.
Hintz, Harold (1979) *Horses in the Movies*. South Brunswick, NJ, New York and London: A. S. Barnes.
Hockenhull, Stella (2013) "Horse Power: Equine Alliances in the Western," in Sue Matheson (ed.), *Love in Western Film and Television: Lonely Hearts and Happy Trails*. New York: Palgrave Macmillan, pp. 161–77.
Hockenhull, Stella (2017) "Ride 'Em Cowboy: Equine Representations in the Western," in Sue Matheson (Ed.), *A Fistful of Icons: Essays on Frontier Fixtures of the American Western*. Jefferson, NC: McFarland, pp. 99–112.
Horrocks, Roger (1994) *Masculinity in Crisis: Myths, Fantasies and Realities*. London: Macmillan.
Horrocks, Roger (1995) *Male Myths and Icons: Masculinity in Popular Culture*. London: Macmillan.
Hughes, Howard (2010) *Spaghetti Westerns*. Harpenden: Kamera Books.
Jeffers McDonald, Tamar (2010) *Hollywood Catwalk*. London and New York: I. B. Tauris.
Kitchen-Døderlein, Deborah L. (2017) "Racialized Markers of Gender and Gendered Markers of Race in 1950s Westerns," in Sue Matheson (ed.), *A Fistful of Icons: Essays on Frontier Fixtures of the American Western*. Jefferson, NC: McFarland, pp. 74–85.
Lamont, Victoria (2016) *Westerns: A Women's History*. Lincoln, NE: University of Nebraska Press.
Lusted, David (2003) *The Western*. Harlow: Pearson Longman.
McGillis, Roderick (2009) *He Was Some Kind of a Man: Masculinities in the B Western*. Waterloo, Ont: Wilfrid Laurier University Press.
Matheson, Sue (ed.) (2017) *A Fistful of Icons: Essays on Frontier Fixtures of the American Western*. Jefferson, NC: McFarland.
Mitchell, Lee Clark (1996) *Westerns: Making the Man in Fiction and Film*. Chicago and London: University of Chicago Press.
Modleski, Tania (1999) *Old Wives' Tales: Feminist Re-Visions of Film and Other Fictions*. London and New York: I. B. Tauris.
Nash Smith, Henry (1950) *Virgin Land: The American West as Symbol and Myth*. New York: Vintage Books.
Neale, Steve (1993) "Prologue: Masculinity as Spectacle," in Steve Neale (ed.), *Screening the Male: Exploring Masculinities in Hollywood Cinema*. London and New York: Routledge, pp. 9–20.
Nevins, Jake (2017) "*Godless* Review—Netflix's Wonderfully Wicked Western Fires on All Cylinders," *The Guardian*, 22 November 2017 <https://www.theguardian.com/tv-and-radio/2017/nov/22/godless-review-netflix-wonderfully-wicked-western-fires-on-all-cylinders> (last accessed 13 October 2018).
Peberdy, Donna (2013) *Masculinity and Film Performance*. Basingstoke: Palgrave Macmillan.
Peek, Wendy C. (2003) "The Romance of Competence: Rethinking Masculinity in the Western," *Journal of Popular Film and Television*, 30 (4), pp. 206–19.

Pheasant-Kelly, Frances (2013) "Outlaws, Buddies and Lovers: The Sexual Politics of *Calamity Jane* and *Butch Cassidy and the Sundance Kid*," in Sue Matheson (ed.), *Love in Western Film and Television: Lonely Hearts and Happy* Trails. New York: Palgrave Macmillan, pp. 141–60.

Pheasant-Kelly, Frances (2017) "Outlaws, Buddies and Lovers: The Sexual Signification of the Gun in Western Film," in Sue Matheson (ed.), *A Fistful of Icons: Essays on Frontier Fixtures of the American Western*. Jefferson, NC: McFarland, pp. 124–41.

Saunders, John (2001) *The Western Genre: From Lordsburg to Big Whiskey*. London and New York: Wallflower Press.

Tasker, Yvonne (1993) *Spectacular Bodies: Gender, Genre and the Action Cinema*. London and New York: Routledge.

Thornham, Sue (2012) *What If I Had Been the Hero?* London: Palgrave Macmillan.

Tompkins, Jane (1992) *West of Everything: The Inner Life of Westerns*. Oxford and New York: Oxford University Press.

White, John (2018) *The Contemporary Western: An American Genre Post 9/11*. Edinburgh: Edinburgh University Press.

18. WAGON MISTRESS

Andrew Patrick Nelson

Meek's Cutoff may look like a Western, but Reichardt eschews the conventions of the genre by using long takes, medium and long shots, ambient sound, and much silence. Consequently, her wagon train carries no echoes of a film like John Ford's *Wagon Master* (1950)—no romance, no violence, no rough frontier humor, no simply good or evil characters, and no majestic landscape ... Reichardt has taken all the grandiosity out of the Western.

Leonard Quart, Cineaste, 2011

As scholars increasingly begin to use the massive resources which are in fact available for the study of the American west and its social history, a fair number of myths and theories will have to be re-evaluated. One of these is the tendency to imagine that the frontier, and the west, were inhabited largely if not exclusively by men.

Christianne Fischer, Let Them Speak for Themselves:
Women in the American West, 1977

Judging by the frequency with which the term has been used over the past decade or so, we find ourselves in a veritable golden age of "feminist Westerns." From the Coen Brothers' remake of *True Grit* in 2010, through *The Homesman* (Tommy Lee Jones, 2014), *The Keeping Room* (Daniel Barber, 2014), *Jane Got a Gun* (Gavin O'Connor, 2016), and *Brimstone* (Martin Koolhoven, 2016), to the Netflix series *Godless* (2017), recent Westerns have made clear, concerted efforts to foreground strong women characters—the frequent appearances of whom are all the more striking given, one, how few new Westerns grace our screens nowadays, and two, the genre's reputation as a masculine form.

Observing this trend of Western films focusing on female protagonists, Matthew Carter notes how, with one exception, "female *directors* of Westerns remain largely and lamentably absent" (2018: 38, original emphasis). It is perhaps not surprising, then, that nearly as often as recent Westerns have been described as "feminist" have their feminist credentials been called into question. *Godless* has fared worst in this respect. While the show's promotion emphasized the novel premise of a town populated solely by women after a mining accident kills all of the men—"welcome to no man's land," announced the advertising—critics were quick to point out that the plot in fact centers on a blood feud between two men; that the male characters are active while the female characters, though not passive, are always *reacting* to the actions of men; that most of the cast are men; that the majority of the dialog is spoken by men; and that, in the words of one critic, "[t]he show is filled with unnecessary rapes, voyeuristic violence against women, and frivolous female nudity" (Gutowitz 2017).

To greater and lesser degrees, one could make similar criticisms of the recent Western movies named above, in particular how their central female characters are usually dependent upon and defined by relationships with the various men in their lives. Commenting on the new *True Grit*, Thirza Wakefield fairly sees "the punishment it deals to its teenaged runaway protagonist" as "proof of the impossibility of the self-sufficient female in this setting" (2014). And we might add another criticism to the list, one that links these new works to a longer trend in Western movie-making: a frontier heroine's strength and agency is predicated upon her ability to shoot, ride, and otherwise act like a man.

There is a long history in the Western of what Pam Cook calls "shady ladies": women who "threaten to upset the applecart by challenging men on their own ground; adventurers all, they demand equal status and refuse to take second place, at first, anyway; they wear pants and brandish guns, own land, property and business, demand sexual independence" (2004: 45). Yet even the most subversive of these shady ladies—Joan Crawford in *Johnny Guitar* (Nicholas Ray, 1954) or Barbara Stanwyck in *Forty Guns* (Samuel Fuller, 1957)—end the movie shorn of their masculine trappings and relegated to being the lesser half of the good, heterosexual couple.[1] "[I]f the tomboy has not abandoned her transvestite garb for the hero by the end of the movie," Cook writes, "then she comes to a sticky end" (45). Think of Mercedes McCambridge in *Johnny Guitar*, or Stanwyck in *Maverick Queen* (Joseph Kane, 1954), or Marlene Dietrich in *Rancho Notorious* (Fritz Lang, 1952).

That commercial movies made in the 1950s in the end conform to societal and industrial norms is to be expected, of course, and genre criticism—of a scholarly bent, at least—has by and large avoided reductive interpretations of the role of women in the post-war Western.[2] What an empowered Western femininity that doesn't require wearing pants, carrying a gun, and riding a horse looks like remained an open question in subsequent decades, however.

The 1990s, for example, witnessed some significant shifts in American genre filmmaking, as "many genre movies aimed to open up genres to more progressive representations of race and gender, addressing the growing acceptance of a more liberal political correctness by often deliberately acknowledging and giving voice to groups previously marginalized by mainstream cinema" (Grant 2005: 62). The decade also saw the release of the first sustained cycle of new Western movies since the mid-1970s, spurred on by the critical and commercial success of *Dances with Wolves* (Kevin Costner, 1990), and *Unforgiven* (Clint Eastwood, 1992). In keeping with the larger trend shaping commercial cinema at the time, the 1990s cycle of Westerns notably focused on groups the genre had arguably neglected in the past, like American Indians (*Geronimo: An American Legend* [Walter Hill, 1993] and *Dead Man* [Jim Jarmusch, 1995]), blacks (*Posse* [Mario Van Peebles, 1993]), and especially women (*The Ballad of Little Jo* [Maggie Greenwald, 1993], *Bad Girls* [Jonathan Kaplan, 1995], and *The Quick and the Dead* [Sam Raimi, 1994]). I've argued elsewhere that many of these films, intent on correcting the genre's earlier slights, do so by drawing upon time-honored conventions and narratives of Western heroism in order to elevate their consciously gendered and raced protagonists to the level of myth, with the (surely unintended) consequence of reinforcing many of the values the films initially seemed set on challenging (Nelson 2013: 25–7). This, too, is in keeping with larger trends. As Barry Keith Grant observes, whatever their progressive intentions, many 1990s genre movies simply inserted minorities into roles usually reserved for white men. He writes:

> [I]n merely reversing conventional gender representations, many of these movies fall into the trap of repeating the same dubious values of the patriarchal system they want to critique. Thus, the question of whether female action heroes [of the 1990s and 2000s] are progressive, empowering representations of women or merely contain them within a masculine sensibility has been a matter of considerable debate. (Grant 2005: 64)

While the Western may have prompted this question decades ago—"Is there no place for women on that ritual frontier between civilization and wilderness in any function greater than a prop in the male game of revolt and choice? Can the conventions of the western permit women to be 'westerners' without at the same time destroying the genre?" asked Jacqueline Levitin in 1982 (62)— recent Westerns seem no closer to answering it with any certainty.

Despite serious questions about its feminist credentials, *Godless* was a hit, and many commentators did see its representations of women as empowering, even as the series restaged many of the Western's conventional conflicts and scenarios. In series creator Scott Frank's telling, this was the intention all along. "I really set out to embrace every single western cliché I could think of and that was the fun of it," he told *Deadline Hollywood* in 2018:

> That's why I wanted to write it. I wanted to write about the gunfights. I wanted to write about breaking horses, all of the train robberies, all of the old tropes were really . . . it was really fun for me to try and weave all of it into a new story. That was really it. I knew I was gonna take a lot of old ingredients and then try and locate them in somewhat of a fresh context. (Raymos 2018)

That "fresh context" is the all-woman Old West town, a rare but real phenomenon Frank learned about in the early 2000s while researching what he initially envisioned as an epic feature film. *Time*, and Netflix's marketing strategy, transformed what was intended as a traditional Oedipal drama with an unusual, historically documented backdrop into a "feminist Western." For his part, Frank resists this characterization: "I wasn't interested in making a giant feminist statement. I don't know that I have the right to" (Birnbaum 2017).

If *Godless* is a case of opportunistic marketing creating false expectations, it is also an example of one of the enduring challenges of Western storytelling: balancing myth and history. The Western dramatizes a mythical conflict between civilization and savagery, in which the forces of progress triumph through the exercise of socially sanctioned violence. Generally speaking, the genre's dramatic depictions of this conflict—showdowns at high noon, wagon trains besieged by Indians—are far removed from the historical West, where duels were rare (and often impulsive and chaotic) and pioneers were several hundred times more likely to die from disease than an Indian's arrow. Nevertheless, the Western is constrained by a need to retain a certain historical plausibility. This presents difficulties when it comes to depictions of women. "The genre demands action in order to dramatise the conflict, but in the 19th century women did not, on the whole, go rushing round on horseback shooting at Indians," writes Edward Buscombe; "So all too often women's roles are confined to supporting the menfolk, rather than being more actively engaged" (2011: 40).

The only female-centered Western in recent years to avoid many of the traps detailed above is also the only one directed by a woman: Kelly Reichardt's *Meek's Cutoff* (2010). The film is based on the true story of a wagon train of two hundred families bound for Oregon, who, in the summer of 1845, elected to leave the Oregon Trail and follow a mountain man and guide named Stephen Meek on what he claimed was a quicker, alternative route that avoided the perilous

Blue Mountains, the last mountain range American pioneers needed to cross on the journey west. Far from the shortcut Meek promised, the detour through the desert added forty days and four hundred miles to the original journey and cost the lives of twenty-three people. Reichardt and screenwriter Jonathan Raymond reduce the size of the wagon train down to Meek (Bruce Greenwood) and three families—the Tetherows, Whites, and Gatelys—but the perils the party faces crossing the punishing high desert of Oregon are in no way diminished.

The film opens with the wagon train crossing a river. The men drive the carts, while the women, chest-deep in the water, carry belongings on their heads. The relative tranquility of this scene—this is no raging river—is undercut by the film's first word: LOST. It is not spoken by a character, but carved by one of the pioneers, Thomas Gately (Paul Dano), into a piece of driftwood. We soon learn that what was supposed to be a two-week journey has stretched to five. Has the braggart Meek simply made a mistake he is unwilling to admit to? Has he purposely misled the settlers as part of a conspiracy to stem American emigration? The men of the party are uncertain, but they decide to give Meek more time. The days stretch on, the arid landscape appearing increasingly interminable. The supply of water runs low. Adding to the confusion, an Indian on horseback appears on the horizon, and is eventually captured by Meek and the men. Meek warns that the Indian, a Cayuse, is not to be trusted and should be killed, but the men, hopeful that the Indian can lead them to water, vote to keep him alive. Days pass, with no sign of water. No one in the wagon train, not even Meek, can communicate with the Indian. Is he indeed shepherding them to water? Are his stone carvings signals to his people? Uncertainty reigns, but the party presses on, following their new guide. Calamities continue to befall the group. In a tense moment, after the Tetherow wagon is destroyed descending a steep hill, Meek pulls his pistol on the Indian. Emily Tetherow (Michelle Williams) draws a rifle on Meek. Meek relents. The following day the Indian leads the wagon train to a large tree, but as the pioneers gather around it and yet again debate their next step, he continues on, walking out into the endless desert.

What marks *Meek's Cutoff* as a feminist intervention into the Western is a combination of what we see and how we see it. Rather than simply revising its portrayal of Western women in accordance with contemporary sensibilities—the standard approach for "feminist Westerns"—the film both shows us in detail the "women's work" elided from many Western narratives and aligns our experience of the film's events with those of its three westbound wives. The subject and the approach to filming it were inspired by Reichardt's and Raymond's research into the history of the Oregon Trail and the role that women played in the nation's westward migration. Pioneer diaries proved especially influential. "It's when we began reading the diaries that we realized how little of [the women's] point of view was ever on screen," Reichardt explained to Leonard Quart of *Cineaste*: "The diaries also begin with big ideas and grand dreams

Figure 18.1 Mrs Tetherow (Michelle Williams) takes up arms against Stephen Meek (Bruce Greenwood) in *Meek's Cutoff* (2010).

when they start out, but as they go, the trip turns into a stripped-down, barebones list of chores (e.g. pitching a tent)" (2011: 41). Such observations about the historical writings of westbound women are in line with the work of historians like Christianne Fischer, who notes: "Writings by women are generally close to the basic elements and rituals of life, and only occasionally rise to the general; they present the stuff that daily life is made of. They seem to bring reality within reach and give it such a concrete aspect that one can almost feel it" (1977: 15).

The sensorial dimension of the feminine pioneer experience comes to the fore in *Meek's Cutoff*, which, again, aligns our experience of events with those of the women. Reichardt has explained her use of the more square 1.37:1 aspect ratio, rarely seen in cinema since the advent of widescreen technology in the mid-1950s, as intended to restrict the viewer's perception of the expansive desert in the same way that the bonnets worn by the women limit their peripheral vision.[3] In key moments, the sound design denies us important information: we remain with the women, straining to hear the hushed, and increasingly desperate, conversations of their husbands huddled nearby. If the film is about, in Reichardt's words, "the labor it takes to walk across the country and the chores involved" (quoted in Fusco and Seymore 2017: 63), conveying how such labor *felt* is a priority. A minority of reviewers may have decried *Meek's Cutoff* as "tedious" and "boring," but even they had to concede that this was precisely the point of the movie.

When asked by Quart if she was consciously working against the Western conventions associated with John Ford and Howard Hawks, Reichardt responded by lamenting how "Westerns are so macho and masculine. They are collections of heightened moments." She makes a similar point about the connection between masculinity and action elsewhere. "There are a lot of Westerns that I like, except the macho element gets so tiresome," Reichardt told the *New York Times*, "These constant completely heightened moments, as if that's all a day is: moments of confrontation where people outman themselves. That part of the western is not interesting to me" (Rapold 2011). The reinscription of the dreary, historical experiences of women into an otherwise familiar Western scenario—the wagon train plot—is what produces the de-dramatization.

Timothy Hughes argues that Reichardt's various claims about the Western being a masculine form may be generally correct, but are also representative of a broader, reductivist tendency in revisionist approaches to classical film genres. He writes, "Revisionist Westerns in a sense practice the kind of thinking strenuously avoided in genre criticism, in which the generic tradition is oversimplified and innovations to its assumed formulas and structures are overemphasized" (2016: 142). Putting aside the degree to which genre criticism has, in fact, "strenuously avoided" reductive interpretations of older movies, this is an astute observation about the rhetoric that has accumulated around many of the most critically lauded Westerns of the past forty years or so—a rhetoric that is often initiated by filmmakers and furthered by critics.

Reichardt's interviews about *Meek's Cutoff* are peppered with references to older Westerns. On first pass, these both signal her knowledge of the genre and accentuate what her movie does differently. Consider this widely reproduced quote from *The Guardian*: "I always wondered what, say, John Wayne in *The Searchers* must have looked like to the woman cooking his stew" (Gilbey 2011). This comment succinctly conveys her aim to show the female perspectives and labor occluded from earlier Western movies. I have to wonder, though, *which woman* in *The Searchers* is Reichardt referring to? Which scene does she have in mind? There is no "stew cooking scene," per se, in the movie. Does she mean Carmen, who serves Marty a plate of beans after he and Ethan unexpectedly come upon Mose Harper in Mexico? Or perhaps she means Marty's Indian "wife" Look, whom Ethan sarcastically asks for a cup of coffee? Is she thinking of Mrs Jorgenson, or her daughter Laurie? Or is Reichardt instead making a more general, or generic, point about the role of women in the Western? Absent a follow-up query, it's hard to say. But the suggestion that we come away from

The Searchers not knowing how the many women around him perceive Ethan is certainly debatable. Or consider another example. While nearly every review of and article about *Meek's Cutoff* repeats Reichardt's explanation that the 1.37:1 aspect ratio was intended to approximate the restricted perception of her heroines—thereby denying viewers the sweeping widescreen vistas so associated with the Western—thousands of Westerns, including numerous classics of the genre, were produced prior to the wholesale adoption of widescreen technology by the American film industry in the mid-1950s. Reichardt has acknowledged this connection to the genre's past, telling *Filmmaker Magazine*, "I mean, Anthony Mann used a square in Westerns. I think *Yellow Sky* is a square, the [William] Wellman film" (Ponsoldt 2011). The implication here—surely unintended on Reichardt's part—is that shooting in the square aspect ratio was a choice, which it wasn't. Mann and Wellman (and Ford and Hawks and every other filmmaker) made Westerns in the 1.37:1 aspect ratio until the arrival of CinemaScope and VistaVision, after which they lensed their Westerns in widescreen.

Should we expect directors to have an encyclopedic knowledge of the genres in which they traffic? No, of course not. And any contemporary filmmaker who can reference an excellent but decidedly non-canonical movie like *Yellow Sky* (1947) in the course of an interview has probably seen her share of Westerns. Yet the overall impression, fair or not, is that Reichardt's understanding of the Western—or perhaps *conception* of the Western—is of the type one gains from a basic college film class, centered not only on canonical films, but canonical interpretations of them, emphasizing themes like race and gender. She is certainly not alone in this regard. That the majority of filmmakers today are introduced to the Western genre as a historical, academic subject in the course of their professional training is a context scholarly studies of the genre have yet to acknowledge, let alone grapple with the implications.

In certain respects, film criticism, in the broad sense, is equally if not more at fault. Reading Reichardt's many interviews about *Meek's Cutoff* brought to mind interviews conducted with John Ford in the 1960s. Occasionally, Ford would discuss his Westerns in relation to the great Western artists who preceded him, describing, for example, his attempts to capture "the color and the movement" of Frederic Remington in *She Wore a Yellow Ribbon*, or using a "Charlie Russell motif" in *The Searchers*. Never once was Ford, who knew these artists intimately, and even knew Russell personally, asked a follow-up question.[4] Perhaps this was because interviewers were intimidated being in the presence of Ford. More likely it was because they didn't know what he was talking about, just as it is likely that those charged with questioning Reichardt about her engagement with the Western's history and conventions didn't have the knowledge to probe her about her references and influences—or to even make plausible claims of their own about her movie. For example, Quart's assertion that "her wagon train carries no echoes of a film like John Ford's *Wagon Master* (1950)" is preposterous. If anything, *Meek's Cutoff* explicitly echoes *Wagon Master* in multiple ways, and could even be seen as a dark mirror to Ford's optimistic (uncharacteristically, for this period in his career) vision of westward expansion. The latter concludes with a triumphant river crossing by a wagon train of pious pioneers, while the former, as if in response, shows us the ominous fate that awaits the group on the opposite bank. Yet, so far as I've been able to find, Reichardt was not once asked about *Wagon Master*.[5]

As with Ford and his influences, unasked questions have consequences for our understanding of the Western. At worst, the discourse around a particular contemporary Western can perpetuate stereotypes about older movies and further impoverish the history of the genre. *Meek's Cutoff* was widely described as a "revisionist" Western on the same grounds as nearly every other acclaimed Western since at least the late 1960s, including historical accuracy, the destruction of naive myths, the restoration and elevation of the role of minorities in Western history, and a liberal commentary on contemporary politics. A paragraph from Mark Olsen's review in the *Los Angeles Times* offers a succinct example: "*Meek's Cutoff* is a revisionist western richly layered to consider the emergence of women's role in society, divisions of class and a nascent concern for native peoples as well as a bracing parable of what happens when one enters the desert with an uncertain leader" (Olsen 2011). Nearly the exact same thing was said of *Little Big Man* (1970) over forty years prior. And now, as then, critics often take their interpretive lead from filmmakers. Just as Arthur Penn in the 1970s was quick to speak of *Little Big Man* in relation to Vietnam, so did Reichardt discuss *Meek's Cutoff* with reference to Iraq. "It's an allegory for so much of what's happening right now," she explained to the *National Post*. "When these wagon trains started out they would hire people as pilots, and then they created these laws that had to be followed and hierarchy to enforce it" (Monk 2011: PM6).

In one sense, *Meek's Cutoff* in fact has less to do with the Western than it does with contemporary art cinema. Hughes argues that *Meek's Cutoff* achieves "a new form of genre revisionism, in which previously marginalized perspectives on traditional generic material are revealed primarily through formal strategies imported from outside the genre" (138). These formal strategies are those of the international "slow cinema" associated with filmmakers like Bela Tarr, Albert Serra, and Apichatpong Weerasethakul. Expectedly, however, these strategies are ultimately in the service of ideological critique. In their monograph on Reichardt's films, Katherine Fusco and Nicole Seymore (2017) argue that *Meek's Cutoff*'s slowness subverts the *pacing* of the Western (50), which in turn suggests the "noninevitability of western settlement" (51), decoupling temporal progress from ideas of success and productivity (56). Hence film's emphasis on "stories of those left out, left behind by, or remarked upon in tales of U.S. progress" (57)—that is, on the stories of women.

Meek's Cutoff's altogether uneven engagement with the legacy of women in the Western produces some unintended consequences. Indeed, it seems appropriate to invoke the cliché that those who don't learn from history are doomed to repeat it.

As much as the film prompts the viewer to identify with the women, it ultimately demonstrates that the women are no more reliable than their husbands. The film sees Emily take control of the wagon train, true, but she is just as prone to wishful thinking and speculation as any other member of the party. "He's saying we're close!" she exclaims in response to the mysterious gestures and unintelligible words of the Indian, "He's saying just over the hill! Just over there!" "Some have claimed the film as a feminist intervention," writes critic Susan Morrison, "but other than depicting women's work . . . and having Mrs. Tetherow confront Meek, verbally and in a standoff with a gun, it's worth noting that she herself opts for another male leader. If this is a feminist version, it's a pretty mild one." The film strongly imparts the experience of women, only to demonstrate, emphatically, that the words and actions of women do not alter the course of history—whether that be the history of the West or the Western. "We're all just playing our parts now," observes Meek at the film's conclusion. "This was written long before we got here."

Notes

1. On the play of gender in *Johnny Guitar* and *Forty Guns*, see, respectively, J. Peterson (1996), "The Competing Tunes of Johnny Guitar," and A. P. Nelson (2013), "Only a Woman After All? Gender Dynamics in the Westerns of Barbara Stanwyck."
2. In addition to Cook (1988) and Peterson (1996), see, for example, P. Evans (1996), "*Westward the Women*: Feminising the Wilderness," B. Lucas (1998), "Saloon Girls and Ranchers' Daughters: The Women in the Western," T. J. McDonald (2007), "Carrying Concealed Weapons: Gendered Makeover in *Calamity Jane*," and the essays collected in S. Matheson (2013).
3. Explaining her use of the "square" frame, Reichardt additionally cites her admiration for the compositions of photographer Robert Adams (see, for example, Quart 2011: 41, and Ponsoldt 2011), as well as pre-widescreen Westerns of the late 1940s and early 1950s. The latter influence will be addressed later in this essay.
4. The best scholarly study of the influence of Western art on the films of John Ford remains William Howze's doctoral dissertation *The Influence of Western Painting and Genre Painting on the Films of John Ford* (University of Texas at Austin, 1986). Also see E. Buscombe (1984), "Painting the Legend: Frederic Remington and the Western," *Cinema Journal*, 23 (4), pp. 12–27.
5. Equally surprising is that Reichardt was never asked about William Wellman's *Westward the Women* (1951).

Filmography

Bad Girls, director Jonathan Kaplan, featuring Madeleine Stowe, Mary Stuart Masterson, Andie MacDowell (20th Century Fox, 1994).

Brimstone, director Martin Koolhoven, featuring Guy Pearce, Dakota Fanning, Emilia Jones (N279 Entertainment, 2016).

Dances with Wolves, director Kevin Costner, featuring Kevin Costner, Mary McDonnell, Grahame Greene (Tig Productions, 1990).

Dead Man, director Jim Jarmusch, featuring Johnny Depp, Gary Farmer, Crispin Glover (Pandora Filmproduktion, 1995).

Forty Guns, director Samuel Fuller, featuring Barbara Stanwyck, Barry Sullivan, Dean Jagger (20th Century Fox).

Geronimo: An American Legend, director Walter Hill, featuring Jason Patric, Gene Hackman, Robert Duvall (Columbia, 1993).

Godless, featuring Jack O'Connell, Michelle Dockery, Scoot McNairy (Netflix, 2017).

Jane Got a Gun, director Gavin O'Connor, featuring Natalie Portman, Joel Edgerton, Ewan McGregor (1821 Pictures, 2016).

Johnny Guitar, director Nicholas Ray, featuring Joan Crawford, Sterling Hayden, Mercedes McCambridge (Republic, 1954).

Little Big Man, director Arthur Penn, featuring Dustin Hoffman, Faye Dunaway, Chief Dan George (Cinema Center Films, 1970).

Maverick Queen, director Joseph Kane, featuring Barbara Stanwyck, Barry Sullivan, Scott Brady (Republic, 1954).

Meek's Cutoff, director Kelly Reichardt, featuring Michelle Williams, Bruce Greenwood, Paul Dano (Evenstar Films, 2010).

Posse, director Mario Van Peebles, featuring Mario Van Peebles, Stephen Baldwin, Charles Lane (Polygram Filmed Entertainment, 1993).

Rancho Notorious, director Fritz Lang, featuring Marlene Dietrich, Arthur Kennedy, Mel Ferrer (Fidelity Pictures, 1952).

She Wore a Yellow Ribbon, director John Ford, featuring John Wayne, Joanne Dru, John Agar (Argosy Pictures, 1949).

The Ballad of Little Jo, director Maggie Greenwald, featuring Suzy Amis, Bo Hopkins, Ian McKellen (Joco and Polygram Filmed Entertainment, 1993).

The Homesman, director Tommy Lee Jones, featuring Tommy Lee Jones, Hilary Swank, Grace Gummer (EuropaCorp, 2014).

The Keeping Room, director Daniel Barber, featuring Brit Marling, Hailee Steinfeld, Sam Worthington (Gilbert Films, 2014).

The Quick and the Dead, director Sam Raimi, featuring Sharon Stone, Gene Hackman, Russell Crowe (Tristar, 1994).

The Searchers, director John Ford, featuring John Wayne, Jeffrey Hunter, Vera Miles (C. V. Whitney Pictures, 1956).

True Grit, directors Ethan Coen and Joel Coen, featuring Jeff Bridges, Matt Damon, Hailee Steinfeld (Paramount, 2010).

Unforgiven, director Clint Eastwood, featuring Clint Eastwood, Gene Hackman, Morgan Freeman (Warner Bros., 1992).

Wagon Master, director John Ford, featuring Ben Johnson, Joanne Dru, Harry Carey, Jr (Argosy Pictures, 1950).
Yellow Sky, director William A. Wellman, featuring Gregory Peck, Anne Baxter, Richard Widmark (20th Century Fox, 1948).

Bibliography

Birnbaum, D. (2017) "'Godless' Team on Making a Western, Feminism and Directing Horses," *Daily Variety*, <https://variety.com/2017/tv/news/godless-netflix-jeff-daniels-michelle-dockery-scott-frank-1202617026/> (viewed 30 August 2018).

Buscombe, E. (2011) "Go West, Young Woman," *Sight and Sound*, 21 (5), p. 40.

Carter, M. (2018) "'I've Been Looking for You': Reconfiguring Race, Gender, and the Family through the Female Agency of *The Keeping Room*," *Papers on Language and Literature*, 54 (1), pp. 25–45.

Cook, Pam (2004) *Screening the Past: Memory and Nostalgia in Cinema*. London: Routlege.

Evans, P. (1996) "*Westward the Women*: Feminising the Wilderness," in Ian Cameron and Douglas Pye (eds), *The Book of Westerns*. New York: Continuum, pp. 206–13.

Fusco, K. and Seymour, N. (2017) *Kelly Reichardt*. Urbana, IL: University of Illinois Press.

Fischer, C. (ed.) (1977) *Let Them Speak for Themselves: Women in the American West*. New York: Dutton.

Gilbey, R. (2011) "Kelly Reichardt: how I trekked across Oregon for *Meek's Cutoff* then returned to teaching," *The Guardian* <https://www.theguardian.com/film/2011/apr/09/kelly-reichardt-meeks-cutoff> (viewed 30 August 2018).

Grant, B. K. (2005) "Anti-Oedipus: Feminism, the Western, and *The Ballad of Little Jo*," *CineAction*, 96, pp. 60–9.

Gutowitz, J. (2017) "Women Deserve Better than Netflix's faux-feminist Godless," *Dazed* <https://www.dazeddigital.com/film-tv/article/38199/1/women-deserve-better-than-netflix-s-faux-feminist-godless> (viewed 1 September 2018).

Hughes, T. (2016) "'The Unheightened Moment': Work, Duration, and Women's Point of View in *Meek's Cutoff*," in Lee Broughton (ed.), *Critical Perspectives on the Western: From A Fistful of Dollars to Django Unchained*. Lanham, MD: Rowman & Littlefield, pp. 137–52.

Levitin, J. (1982) "The Western: Any Good Roles for Feminists?" in *Film Reader 5*. Chicago: Northwestern University Press, pp. 95–108.

Lucas, B. (1998) "Saloon Girls and Ranchers' Daughters: The Women in the Western," Jim Kitses and Gregg Rickman (eds), *The Western Reader*. New York: Limelight Editions, pp. 301–20.

McDonald, T. J. (2007) "Carrying Concealed Weapons: Gendered Makeover in *Calamity Jane*," *Journal of Popular Film and Television*, 34 (4), pp. 179–87.

Matheson, S. (ed.) (2013) *Love in Western Film and Television*. New York: Palgrave Macmillan.

Monk, K. (2011) "Meek's Cutoff: The Director," *National Post*, 13 May, PM6.

Morrison, S. (2010) "In Transit: Kelly Reichardt's Meek's Cutoff," *CineAction*, 82–3, pp. 40–4.
Nelson, A. P. (2013a) "Only a Woman After All? Gender Dynamics in the Westerns of Barbara Stanwyck," in Sue Matheson (ed.), *Love in Western Film and Television: Lonely Hearts and Happy Trails*. New York: Palgrave Macmillan, pp. 19–34.
Nelson, A. P. (2013b) "Revisionism 2.0? *Unforgiven* and the Hollywood Western of the 1990s," in Nelson, A. P. (ed.), *Contemporary Westerns: Film and Television since 1990*. Lanham, MD: Rowman & Littlefield, pp. 15–30.
Olsen, M. (2011) "A Starkly Different Western," *Los Angeles Times*, 17 April, D5.
Peterson, J. (1996) "The Competing Tunes of *Johnny Guitar*," *Cinema Journal*, 35 (3), pp. 3–18.
Ponsoldt, J. (2011) "Lost in America: Kelly Reichardt's 'Meek's Cutoff,'" *Filmmaker Magazine* <https://filmmakermagazine.com/35034-lost-in-america-kelly-reichardts-meeks-cutoff/> (viewed 30 August 2018).
Quart, L. (2011) "The Way West: A Feminist Perspective: An Interview with Kelly Reichardt," *Cineaste*, 36 (2), pp. 40–2.
Rapold, N. (2011) "Oregon Frontier, From Under a Bonnet," *New York Times* <https://www.nytimes.com/2011/04/03/movies/meeks-cutoff-from-kelly-reichardt.html> (viewed 30 August 2018).
Raymos, D. (2018) "'Godless': Scott Frank & Steven Soderbergh Talk Western Clichés and Being Labeled a 'Feminist Western,'" *Deadline Hollywood* <https://deadline.com/2018/08/godless-scott-frank-steven-soderbergh-emmys-jeff-daniels-merritt-wever-michelle-dockery-netflix-feminist-western-1202450537/> (viewed 1 September 2018).
Wakefield, T. (2014) "Women's Shadow in the American Western," *Granta*, 128 <https://granta.com/womens-shadow-in-the-american-western/> (viewed 30 August 2018).

PART THREE

FILMOGRAPHY AND BIBLIOGRAPHIES

19. WOMEN IN THE WESTERN FILMOGRAPHY AND BIBLIOGRAPHY

Camille McCutcheon

The following filmography and bibliographies were compiled to demonstrate the diversity of women's roles in the American Western. These compilations complement one another—the filmography is not only supported and furthered by the selected, representative bibliography of resources on women in the Western, it is also sustained by the historical foundation provided by the selective, representative bibliography of resources of women in the nineteenth-century US West. Remarkably, the most challenging aspect of this project turned out to be managing its immense scope. There were so many resources for consideration that they created a dilemma: a whole book could have been fashioned out of them. As a result, the following parameters for academic researchers and members of the general public were established.[1]

Selective, Representative Filmography of Female-Led US Westerns

To be considered for inclusion in this filmography, a film must be included in the American Film Institute (AFI) Catalog of Feature Films and feature female actor(s) in a prominent role or roles. In addition, the principle female actor must receive first or second billing. "Female" includes girls, adolescents, and women. AFI must classify the film in the Western genre, and the film itself must be set in the American West. The Exceptions List contains films in which the principle female actor receives third billing or less. The Exceptions List also includes films classified as musicals or drama. Some films have been remade or are remakes, but due to space considerations, only one version appears in the filmography. The two exceptions to this rule are Cecil B. DeMille's *The Squaw Man*, which was released in 1914 and 1931, and Henry Hathaway's *True Grit* released in 1969 and Ethan and Joel Coen's *True Grit* released in 2010.

1910s

The Broken Doll, director D. W. Griffith, featuring Gladys Egan, Dark Cloud, Jack Pickford, Alfred Paget (Biograph Co., 1910).

A Ranchman's Wooing, director G. M. Anderson, featuring G. M. Anderson, Clara Williams, Gladys Field, William Russell (Essanay Film Mfg Co., 1910).

Red Wing's Constancy, director Fred J. Balshofer, featuring Princess Red Wing, Charles K. French (Bison, 1910).

Western Chivalry, director G. M. Anderson, featuring Clara Williams, William Russell, Shorty Cunningham, Joe Dennis (Essanay Film Mfg Co., 1910).

Salomy Jane, director Lucius Henderson, featuring Beatriz Michelena, House Peters, William Pike, Clara Byers (California Motion Picture Corp., 1914).

Sealed Valley, director Lawrence McGill, featuring Dorothy Donnelly, J. W. Johnson, Rene Ditline (Metro Pictures Corp., 1915).

Jim Grimsby's Boy, director Reginald Barker, featuring Frank Keenan, Enid Markey, Robert McKim, Fanny Midgley (New York Motion Picture Corp.; Kay-Bee, 1916).

The Love Mask, director Frank Reicher, featuring Cleo Ridgley, Wallace Reid, Earle Foxe, Bob Fleming (Jesse L. Lasky Feature Play Co., 1916).

The Quitter, director Charles Horan, featuring Lionel Barrymore, Marguerite Skirvin, Paul Everton, Charles Prince (Rolfe Photoplays, Inc., 1916).

By Right of Possession, director William Wolbert, featuring Mary Anderson, Antonio Moreno, Otto Lederer, Leon Kent (Vitagraph Co. of America, 1917).

Golden Rule Kate, director Reginald Barker, featuring Louise Glaum, William Conklin, Jack Richardson, Mildred Harris (Triangle Film Corp., 1917).

The Kill-Joy, director Fred E. Wright, featuring Mary McAlister, Granville Bates, James F. Fulton, James West (Essanay Film Mfg. Co., 1917).

The Girl Who Wouldn't Quit, director Edgar Jones, featuring Louise Lovely, Henry A. Barrows, Mark Fenton, Charles Hill Mailes (Universal Film Mfg Co., 1918).

The Gun Woman, director Frank Borzage, featuring Texas Guinan, Ed Brady, Francis McDonald, Walter Perkins (Kay-Bee, 1918).

Petticoats and Politics, director Howard Mitchell, featuring Anita King, R. Henry Grey, Gordon Sackville, Charles Dudley (Plaza Pictures, 1918).

Two-Gun Betty, director Howard Hickman, featuring Bessie Barriscale, Lee Shumway, Catherine Van Buren, Helen Hawley (Robert Brunton Productions, 1918).

Unclaimed Goods, director Rollin S. Sturgeon, featuring Vivian Martin, Harrison Ford, Casson Ferguson, George McDaniel (Famous Players-Lasky Corp., 1918).

Wild Honey, director Francis J. Grandon, featuring Doris Kenyon, Frank Mills, Edgar Jones, John Hopkins (De Luxe Pictures, Inc., 1918).

The Arizona Cat Claw, director William Bertram, featuring Edythe Sterling, William Quinn, Gordon Sackville, Leo Maloney (World Film Corp., 1919).

As the Sun Went Down, director E. Mason Hopper, featuring Edith Storey, Lew Cody, Harry S. Northrup, William Brunton (Metro Pictures Corp., 1919).

Nugget Nell, director Elmer Clifton, featuring Dorothy Gish, David Butler, Raymond Cannon, Regina Sarle (The New Art Film Co., 1919).

The She Wolf, director Clifford S. Smith, featuring Texas Guinan, George Chesebro, Ah Wing, Charles Robertson (Frohman Amusement Corp., 1919).

1920s

The Fighting Shepherdess, director Edward José, featuring Anita Stewart, Wallace MacDonald, Noah Beery, Walter Long (Louis B. Mayer Productions; Anita Stewart Productions, Inc., 1920).

The Flame of Hellgate, director George E. Middleton, featuring Beatriz Michelena, Jeff Williams, Albert Morrison, William Pike (Beatriz Michelena Features, 1920).

The Girl Who Dared, director Clifford S. Smith, featuring Edythe Sterling, Jack Carlyle, Steve Clemento, Yakima Canutt (Republic Pictures, 1920).

The Stampede, director Francis Ford, featuring Texas Guinan, Francis Ford, Frederick Moore, Jean Carpenter (Victor Kremer Film Features, 1921).

The Stranger in Canyon Valley, director Clifford S. Smith, featuring Edith Sterling (Arrow Film Corp., 1921).

That Girl Montana, director Robert Thornby, featuring Blanche Sweet, Mahlon Hamilton, Frank Lanning, Edward Peil Sr (Pathé Exchange, Inc., 1921).

The Crimson Challenge, director Paul Powell, featuring Dorothy Dalton, Jack Mower, Frank Campeau, Irene Hunt (Famous Players-Lasky Corp., 1922).

Thorobred, director George Halligan, featuring Helen Gibson, Robert Burns, Otto Nelson, Jack Ganzhorn (Clark-Cornelius Corp., 1922).

Galloping Gallagher, director Albert S. Rogell, featuring Fred Thomson, Hazel Keener, Frank Hagney, Nelson McDowell (Monogram Pictures Corp.; H. J. Productions, 1924).

The Sawdust Trail, director Edward Sedgwick, featuring Hoot Gibson, Josie Sedgwick, David Torrence, Charles K. French (Universal Pictures, 1924).

Daring Days, director John B. O'Brien, featuring Josie Sedgwick, Edward Hearne, Frederick Cole, Zama Zamoria (Universal Pictures Corp., 1925).

Queen of Spades, director Harry Fraser, featuring Gordon Clifford, Charlotte Pierce, Richard R. Neill, Herbert Lindley (Bear Productions, 1925).

West of Broadway, director Robert Thornby, featuring Priscilla Dean, Arnold Gray, Majel Coleman, Walter Long (Metropolitan Pictures Corp. of California, 1926).

1930s

Woman Hungry, director Clarence G. Badger, featuring Sidney Blackmer, Lila Lee, Raymond Hatton, Fred Kohler (First National Pictures, Inc., 1931).

Come on Danger!, director Robert Hill, featuring Tom Keene, Julie Haydon, Roscoe Ates, Robert Ellis (RKO Radio Pictures, Inc., 1932).

Wild Girl, director Raoul Walsh, featuring Charles Farrell, Joan Bennett, Ralph Bellamy, Eugene Pallette (Fox Film Corp., 1932).

The Girl of the Golden West, director Robert Z. Leonard, featuring Jeanette MacDonald, Nelson Eddy, Walter Pidgeon, Leo Carrillo (Metro-Goldwyn-Mayer Corp., 1938).

Destry Rides Again, director George Marshall, featuring Marlene Dietrich, James Stewart, Mischa Auer, Charles Winninger (Universal Pictures Co., 1939).

Ride 'Em Cowgirl, director Samuel Diege, featuring Dorothy Page, Milton Frome, Vince Barnett, Lynn Mayberry (Coronado Films, Inc., 1939).

The Singing Cowgirl, director Samuel Diege, featuring Dorothy Page, Dave O'Brien, Vince Barnett, Dorothy Short (Coronado Films, Inc., 1939).

Water Rustlers, director Samuel Diege, featuring Dorothy Page, Dave O'Brien, Vince Barnett, Stanley Price (Coronado Films, Inc., 1939).

1940s

Arizona, director Wesley Ruggles, featuring Jean Arthur, William Holden, Warren William, Porter Hall (Columbia Pictures Corp., 1940).

Shooting High, director Alfred E. Green, featuring Jane Withers, Gene Autry, Marjorie Weaver, Frank M. Thomas (Twentieth Century-Fox Film Corp., 1940).

Go West, Young Lady, director Frank R. Strayer, featuring Penny Singleton, Glenn Ford, Ann Miller, Charlie Ruggles (Columbia Pictures Corp., 1941).

The Lady from Cheyenne, director Frank Lloyd, featuring Loretta Young, Robert Preston, Edward Arnold, Frank Craven (Universal Pictures Company, Inc.; Frank Lloyd Productions, Inc., 1941).

Jackass Mail, director Norman Z. McLeod, featuring Wallace Beery, Marjorie Main, J. Carrol Naish, Darryl Hickman (Metro-Goldwyn-Mayer Corp., 1942).

The Woman of the Town, director George Archainbaud, featuring Claire Trevor, Albert Dekker, Barry Sullivan, Henry Hull (Harry Sherman Productions, 1943).

Gentle Annie, director Andrew Marton, featuring James Craig, Donna Reed, Marjorie Main, Henry "Harry" Morgan (Metro-Goldwyn-Mayer Corp., 1944).

Moonlight and Cactus, director Edward F. Cline, featuring Patty Andrews, Maxine Andrews, LaVerne Andrews, Leo Carrillo (Universal Pictures Company, Inc., 1944).

Tall in the Saddle, director Edwin L. Marin, featuring John Wayne, Ella Raines, Ward Bond, George Hayes (RKO Radio Pictures, Inc., 1944).

Along Came Jones, director Stuart Heisler, featuring Gary Cooper, Loretta Young, William Demarest, Dan Duryea (International Pictures, Inc.; Cinema Artists Corp., 1945).

Flame of Barbary Coast, director Joseph I. Kane, featuring John Wayne, Ann Dvorak, Joseph Schildkraut, William Frawley (Republic Pictures Corp., 1945).

Frontier Gal, director Charles Lamont, featuring Yvonne De Carlo, Rod Cameron, Andy Devine, Fuzzy Knight (Universal Pictures Company, Inc., 1945).

Under Western Skies, director Jean Yarbrough, featuring Martha O'Driscoll, Noah Beery Jr, Leo Carrillo, Leon Errol (Universal Pictures Company, Inc., 1945).

Bad Bascomb, director S. Sylvan Simon, featuring Wallace Beery, Margaret O'Brien, Marjorie Main, J. Carrol Naish (Metro-Goldwyn-Mayer Corp., 1946).

Renegades, director George Sherman, featuring Evelyn Keyes, Willard Parker, Larry Parks, Edgar Buchanan (Columbia Pictures Corp., 1946).

Singin' in the Corn, director Del Lord, featuring Judy Canova, Allen Jenkins, Guinn "Big Boy" Williams, Alan Bridge (Columbia Pictures Corp., 1946).

Angel and the Badman, director James Edward Grant, featuring John Wayne, Gail Russell, Harry Carey, Bruce Cabot (Patnel Productions, 1947).
Duel in the Sun, director King Vidor, featuring Jennifer Jones, Joseph Cotten, Gregory Peck, Lionel Barrymore (Vanguard Films, Inc., 1947).
Ramrod, director Andre DeToth, featuring Joel McCrea, Veronica Lake, Don DeFore, Donald Crisp (Enterprise Productions, Inc., 1947).
The Sea of Grass, director Elia Kazan, featuring Spencer Tracy, Katharine Hepburn, Robert Walker, Melvyn Douglas (Metro-Goldwyn-Mayer Corp., 1947).
Feudin', Fussin and A-Fightin," director George Sherman, featuring Donald O'Connor, Marjorie Main, Percy Kilbride, Penny Edwards (Universal-International Pictures Co., Inc., 1948).
The Paleface, director Norman Z. McLeod, featuring Bob Hope, Jane Russell, Robert Armstrong, Iris Adrian (Paramount Pictures, Inc., 1948).
Station West, director Sidney Lanfield, featuring Dick Powell, Jane Greer, Agnes Moorehead, Burl Ives (RKO Radio Pictures, Inc., 1948).
The Beautiful Blonde from Bashful Bend, director Preston Sturges, featuring Betty Grable, Cesar Romero, Rudy Vallee, Olga San Juan (Twentieth Century-Fox Film Corp., 1949).
Colorado Territory, director Raoul Walsh, featuring Joel McCrea, Virginia Mayo, Dorothy Malone, Henry Hull (Warner Bros. Pictures, Inc., 1949).
Daughter of the West, director Harold Daniels, featuring Martha Vickers, Philip Reed, Donald Woods, Marion Carney (Martin Mooney Productions, Inc., 1949).
The Gal Who Took the West, director Frederick De Cordova, featuring Yvonne De Carlo, Charles Coburn, Scott Brady, John Russell (Universal-International Pictures Co., Inc., 1949).
Hellfire, director R. G. Springsteen, featuring Wild Bill Elliott, Marie Windsor, Forrest Tucker, Jim Davis (Elliott-McGowan Productions, 1949).
Red Canyon, director George Sherman, featuring Ann Blyth, Howard Duff, George Brent, Edgar Buchanan (Universal-International Pictures Co., Inc., 1949).
Roughshod, director Mark Robson, featuring Robert Sterling, Gloria Grahame, Claude Jarman Jr, John Ireland (RKO Radio Pictures, Inc., 1949).

1950s

Bandit Queen, director William Berke, featuring Barbara Britton, Willard Parker, Philip Reed, Barton MacLane (Lippert Productions, Inc., 1950).
Comanche Territory, director George Sherman, featuring Maureen O'Hara, MacDonald Carey, Will Geer, Charles Drake (Universal-International Pictures Co., Inc., 1950).
The Furies, director Anthony Mann, featuring Barbara Stanwyck, Wendell Corey, Walter Huston, Judith Anderson (Wallis-Hazen, Inc., 1950).
Rio Grande, director John Ford, featuring John Wayne, Maureen O'Hara, Ben Johnson, Claude Jarman Jr (Argosy Pictures Corp., 1950).
A Ticket to Tomahawk, director Richard B. Sale, featuring Dan Dailey, Anne Baxter, Rory Calhoun, Walter Brennan (Twentieth-Century-Fox Film Corp., 1950).
Arizona Manhunt, director Fred C. Brannon, featuring Michael Chapin, Eilene Janssen, James Bell, Lucille Barkley (Republic Pictures Corp.; Valley Vista Productions, 1951).

Belle Le Grand, director Allan Dwan, featuring Vera Hruba Ralston, John Carroll, William Ching, Hope Emerson (Republic Pictures Corp., 1951).

Cattle Queen, director Robert Emmett Tansey, featuring Maria Hart, Drake Smith, William Fawcett, Robert Gardette (Jack Schwarz Productions, Inc.; United International Pictures, 1951).

Frenchie, director Louis King, featuring Joel McCrea, Shelley Winters, Paul Kelly, Elsa Lanchester (Universal-International Pictures Co., Inc., 1951).

The Lady from Texas, director Joseph Pevney, featuring Howard Duff, Mona Freeman, Josephine Hull, Gene Lockhart (Universal-International Pictures Co., Inc., 1951).

The Secret of Convict Lake, director Michael Gordon, featuring Glenn Ford, Gene Tierney, Ethel Barrymore, Zachary Scott (Twentieth Century-Fox Film Corp., 1951).

Silver City, director Byron Haskin, featuring Edmond O'Brien, Yvonne De Carlo, Barry Fitzgerald, Richard Arlen (Paramount Pictures Corp., 1951).

Oklahoma Annie, director R. G. Springsteen, featuring Judy Canova, John Russell, Grant Withers, Roy Barcroft (Republic Pictures Corp., 1952).

Outlaw Women, director Sam Newfield, featuring Marie Windsor, Richard Rober, Carla Balenda, Jackie Coogan (Howco Productions, Inc.; A Ron Ormond Production, 1952).

Rancho Notorious, director Fritz Lang, featuring Marlene Dietrich, Arthur Kennedy, Mel Ferrer, Gloria Henry (Fidelity Pictures, Inc., 1952).

Son of Paleface, director Frank Tashlin, featuring Bob Hope, Jane Russell, Roy Rogers, Trigger (Hope Enterprises, Inc.; Paramount Pictures Corp., 1952).

Westward the Women, director William A. Wellman, featuring Beverly Dennis, Renata Vanni, John McIntire, Julie Bishop (Metro-Goldwyn-Mayer Corp., 1952).

Wild Horse Ambush, director Fred C. Brannon, featuring Michael Chapin, Eilene Janssen, James Bell, Richard Avonde (Republic Pictures Corp.; Valley Vista Productions, 1952).

The Moonlighter, director Roy Rowland, featuring Barbara Stanwyck, Fred MacMurray, Ward Bond, William Ching (Abtcon Pictures, Inc.; J. B. Productions, Inc., 1953).

The Redhead from Wyoming, director Lee Sholem, featuring Maureen O'Hara, Alex Nicol, William Bishop, Robert Strauss (Universal-International Pictures Co., Inc., 1953).

Cattle Queen of Montana, director Allan Dwan, featuring Barbara Stanwyck, Ronald Reagan, Gene Evans, Lance Fuller (Filmcrest Productions, Inc.; RKO Radio Pictures, Inc., 1954).

Johnny Guitar, director Nicholas Ray, featuring Joan Crawford, Sterling Hayden, Mercedes McCambridge, Scott Brady (Republic Pictures Corp., 1954).

Jubilee Trail, director Joseph Inman Kane, featuring Vera Ralston, Joan Leslie, Forrest Tucker, John Russell (Republic Pictures Corp., 1954).

The Outlaw's Daughter, director Wesley Barry, featuring Bill Williams, Kelly Ryan, Jim Davis, George Cleveland (Twentieth Century-Fox Film Corp., 1954).

Passion, director Allan Dwan, featuring Cornel Wilde, Yvonne De Carlo, Raymond Burr, Lon Chaney Jr (Filmcrest Productions, Inc., 1954).

Rails into Laramie, director Jesse Hibbs, featuring John Payne, Mari Blanchard, Dan Duryea, Joyce MacKenzie (Universal-International Pictures Co., Inc., 1954).

Red Garters, director George Marshall, featuring Rosemary Clooney, Jack Carson, Guy Mitchell, Pat Crowley (Paramount Pictures Corp., 1954).

Three Hours to Kill, director Alfred Werker, featuring Dana Andrews, Donna Reed, Dianne Foster, Stephen Elliot (Columbia Pictures Corp., 1954).

Apache Woman, director Roger Corman, featuring Lloyd Bridges, Joan Taylor, Lance Fuller, Morgan Jones (Golden State Productions, 1955).

One Desire, director Jerry Hopper, featuring Anne Baxter, Rock Hudson, Julie Adams, Carl Benton Reid (Universal-International Pictures Co., Inc., 1955).

Strange Lady in Town, director Mervyn LeRoy, featuring Greer Garson, Dana Andrews, Cameron Mitchell, Lois Smith (Warner Bros. Pictures, Inc., 1955).

The Tall Men, director Raoul Walsh, featuring Clark Gable, Jane Russell, Robert Ryan, Cameron Mitchell (Twentieth Century-Fox Film Corp., 1955).

Texas Lady, director Tim Whelan, featuring Claudette Colbert, Barry Sullivan, Ray Collins, James Bell (Holt-Rosen Productions; RKO Radio Pictures, Inc., 1955).

Two-Gun Lady, director Richard H. Bartlett, featuring Peggie Castle, William Talman, Marie Windsor, Earle Lyon (Associated Film Releasing Corp; L & B Productions, 1955).

The Vanishing American, director Joseph I. Kane, featuring Scott Brady, Audrey Totter, Forrest Tucker, Gene Lockhart (Republic Pictures Corp., 1955).

Gunslinger, director Roger Corman, featuring John Ireland, Beverly Garland, Allison Hayes, Martin Kingsley (Roger Corman Productions, 1956).

The King and Four Queens, director Raoul Walsh, featuring Clark Gable, Eleanor Parker, Jean Willes, Barbara Nichols (Russ-Field Corp.; Gabco Productions, Ltd., 1956).

The Maverick Queen, director Joseph I. Kane, featuring Barbara Stanwyck, Barry Sullivan, Scott Brady, Mary Murphy (Republic Pictures Corp., 1956).

The Oklahoma Woman, director Roger Corman, featuring Richard Denning, Peggie Castle, Cathy Downs, Michael Connors (Sunset Productions, 1956).

The White Squaw, director Ray Nazarro, featuring David Brian, May Wynn, William Bishop, Nancy Hale (Columbia Pictures Corp., 1956).

The Buckskin Lady, director Carl K. Hittleman, featuring Patricia Medina, Richard Denning, Gerald Mohr, Henry Hull (Bishop-Hittleman Pictures, Inc., 1957).

The Dalton Girls, director Reginald LeBorg, featuring Merry Anders, Lisa Davis, Penny Edwards, Sue George (Bel-Air Productions, Inc.; Clark Productions, Inc., 1957).

Forty Guns, director Samuel Fuller, featuring Barbara Stanwyck, Barry Sullivan, Dean Jagger, John Ericson (Globe Enterprises, Inc., 1957).

The Guns of Fort Petticoat, director George Marshall, featuring Audie Murphy, Kathryn Grant, Hope Emerson, Jeff Donnell (Brown-Murphy Pictures, Inc., 1957).

Outlaw Queen, director Herbert S. Greene, featuring Harry James, Andrea King, Robert Clarke, Andy Ladas (Ashcroft and Associates, Inc., 1957).

Trooper Hook, director Charles Marquis Warren, featuring Joel McCrea, Barbara Stanwyck, Earl Holliman, Edward Andrews (Fielding Productions, Inc.; Filmaster Productions, Inc., 1957).

The Big Country, director William Wyler, featuring Gregory Peck, Jean Simmons, Carroll Baker, Charlton Heston (Anthony-Worldwide Productions, 1958).

Bullwhip, director Harmon Jones, featuring Guy Madison, Rhonda Fleming, James Griffith, Don Beddoe (Romson Productions, Inc.; William F. Broidy Pictures Corp., 1958).

The Hanging Tree, director Delmer Daves, featuring Gary Cooper, Maria Schell, Karl Malden, George C. Scott (Baroda Productions, Inc., 1959).

1960s

Cimarron, director Anthony Mann, featuring Glenn Ford, Maria Schell, Anne Baxter, Arthur O'Connell (Metro-Goldwyn-Mayer Corp., 1960).

Five Bold Women, director Jorge López-Portillo, featuring Jeff Morrow, Merry Anders, Jim Ross, Guinn "Big Boy" Williams (Jim Ross Productions, Inc., 1960).

Heller in Pink Tights, director George Cukor, featuring Sophia Loren, Anthony Quinn, Margaret O'Brien, Steve Forrest (Ponti-Girosi Productions; Paramount Pictures Corp., 1960).

The Unforgiven, director John Huston, featuring Burt Lancaster, Audrey Hepburn, Audie Murphy, John Saxon (James Productions, Inc.; Hecht-Hill-Lancaster, 1960).

The Deadly Companions, director Sam Peckinpah, featuring Maureen O'Hara, Brian Keith, Steve Cochran, Chill Willis (Carousel Productions, 1961).

McLintock!, director Andrew V. McLaglen, featuring John Wayne, Maureen O'Hara, Patrick Wayne, Stefanie Powers (Batjac Productions, Inc., 1963).

Cat Ballou, director Elliot Silverstein, featuring Jane Fonda, Lee Marvin, Michael Callan, Dwayne Hickman (Harold Hecht Corp., 1965).

The Hallelujah Trail, director John Sturges, featuring Burt Lancaster, Lee Remick, Jim Hutton, Pamela Tiffin (Kappa Corp.; Mirisch Corp., 1965).

A Big Hand for the Little Lady, director Fielder Cook, featuring Henry Fonda, Joanne Woodward, Jason Robards Jr, Paul Ford (Eden Productions, 1966).

The Ballad of Josie, director Andrew V. McLaglen, featuring Doris Day, Peter Graves, George Kennedy, Andy Devine (Universal Pictures, 1968).

1970s

The Cockeyed Cowboys of Calico County, director Tony Leader, featuring Dan Blocker, Nanette Fabray, Jim Backus, Wally Cox (Universal Pictures, 1970).

Soldier Blue, director Ralph Nelson, featuring Candice Bergen, Peter Strauss, Donald Pleasence, Bob Carraway (Katzka-Berne Productions, 1970).

McCabe & Mrs. Miller, director Robert Altman, featuring Warren Beatty, Julie Christie, Rene Auberjonois, William Devane (Lion's Head; David Foster Productions, 1971).

Molly and Lawless John, director Gary Nelson, featuring Vera Miles, Sam Elliott, Clu Gulager, John Anderson (Malibu Productions, Inc., 1973).

Zandy's Bride, director Jan Troell, featuring Gene Hackman, Liv Ullmann, Eileen Heckart, Harry Dean Stanton (Warner Bros., Inc., 1974).

Rooster Cogburn, director Stuart Millar, featuring John Wayne, Katharine Hepburn, Anthony Zerbe, Richard Jordan (Universal Pictures, 1975).

The Duchess and the Dirtwater Fox, director Melvin Frank, featuring George Segal, Goldie Jeanne Hawn, Conrad Janis, Thayer David (Twentieth Century-Fox Film Corporation, 1976).

From Noon Till Three, director Frank D. Gilroy, featuring Charles Bronson, Jill Ireland, Douglas Fowley, Stan Haze (A Frankovich/Self Production, 1976).

Wanda Nevada, director Peter Fonda, featuring Peter Fonda, Brooke Shields, Fiona Lewis, Luke Askew (Paradise Productions, Ltd, 1979).

1980s

Heartland, director Richard Pearce, featuring Rip Torn, Conchata Ferrell, Barry Primus, Lilia Skala (Wilderness Women; Filmhaus, 1981).

Lust in the Dust, director Paul Bartel, featuring Tab Hunter, Divine, Lainie Kazan, Geoffrey Lewis (Fox Run Productions, Inc., 1985).

1990s

The Ballad of Little Jo, director Maggie Greenwald, featuring Suzy Amis, Bo Hopkins, Ian McKellen, David Chung (Manifesto Film Sales; Fine Line Features, 1993).

Bad Girls, director Jonathan Kaplan, featuring Madeleine Stowe, Mary Stuart Masterson, Andie MacDowell, Drew Barrymore (Twentieth Century Fox, 1994).

The Quick and the Dead, director Sam Raimi, featuring Sharon Stone, Gene Hackman, Russell Crowe, Leonardo DiCaprio (TriStar Pictures, 1995).

2000s

Gang of Roses, director Jean Claude LaMarre, featuring Monica Calhoun, Stacey Dash, LisaRaye, Marie Matiko (Warning Films, 2003).

The Missing, director Ron Howard, featuring Tommy Lee Jones, Cate Blanchett, Eric Schweig, Evan Rachel Wood (Revolution Studios; Imagine Entertainment, 2003).

2010s

The Last Rites of Ransom Pride, director Tiller Russell, featuring Lizzy Caplan, Peter Dinklage, Dwight Yoakam, Jason Priestley (Horsethief Pictures, 2010).

The Homesman, director Tommy Lee Jones, featuring Tommy Lee Jones, Hilary Swank, Grace Gummer (EuropaCorp; Ithaca; Javelina Film Company, 2014).

Jane Got a Gun, director Gavin O'Connor, featuring Natalie Portman, Joel Edgerton, Ewan McGregor, Noah Emmerich (1821 Pictures; Boies/Schiller Film Group; Eaves Movie Ranch; Handsomecharlie Films; Relativity Media; Scott Pictures; Straight Up Films; Unanimous Pictures; WeatherVane Productions, 2015).

Woman Walks Ahead, director Susanna White, featuring Jessica Chastain, Louisa Krause, Boots Southerland, Chaske Spencer (Black Bicycle Entertainment; Potboiler Productions; The Bedford Falls Company, 2017).

Historical Figures

Annie Oakley

Annie Get Your Gun, director George Sidney, featuring Betty Hutton, Howard Keel, Louis Calhern, J. Carrol Naish (Metro-Goldwyn-Mayer Corp., 1950).

Annie Oakley, director George Stevens, featuring Barbara Stanwyck, Preston Foster, Melvyn Douglas, Moroni Olsen (RKO Radio Pictures, Inc., 1935).

Belle Starr

Belle Starr, director Irving Cummings, featuring Randolph Scott, Gene Tierney, Dana Andrews, Shepperd Strudwick (Twentieth Century-Fox Film Corp., 1941).

Montana Belle, director Allan Dwan, featuring Jane Russell, George Brent, Scott Brady, Forrest Tucker (Fidelity Pictures, Inc.; Republic Pictures Corp., 1952).

Calamity Jane

Calamity Jane, director David Butler, featuring Doris Day, Howard Keel, Allyn McLerie, Phil Carey (Warner Bros. Pictures, Inc., 1953).

Calamity Jane and Sam Bass, director George Sherman, featuring Yvonne De Carlo, Howard Duff, Dorothy Hart, Willard Parker (Universal-International Pictures Co., Inc., 1949).

The Texan Meets Calamity Jane, director Ande Lamb, featuring Evelyn Ankers, James Ellison, Lee "Lasses" White, Ruth Whitney (Columbia Pictures Corp., 1950).

Rose Dunn

Rose of Cimarron, director Harry Keller, featuring Jack Buetel, Mala Powers, Bill Williams, Jim Davis (Alco Pictures Corp., 1952).

Exceptions List

A Western Maid, director G. M. Anderson, featuring G. M. Anderson, Pete Morrison (Essanay Film Mfg. Co., 1910).

The Ranger's Bride, director G. M. Anderson, featuring Joseph Smith, G. M. Anderson, Fred Ilenstine, Fred Church (Essanay Film Mfg. Co., 1910).

The Squaw Man, director Cecil B. DeMille, featuring Dustin Farnum, Monroe Salisbury, Winifred Kingston, Mrs A. W. Filson (Jesse L. Lasky Feature Play Co., 1914).

Rangeland, director Neal Hart, featuring Ben Corbett, Patrick Megehee, Neal Hart, Max Wesell, William Quinn, Blanche McGarity (William Steiner Productions, 1922).

White Gold, director William K. Howard, featuring Jetta Goudal, Kenneth Thomson, George Bancroft, George Nichols (De Mille Pictures Corp., 1927).

The Squaw Man, director Cecil B. DeMille, featuring Warner Baxter, Lupe Velez, Eleanor Boardman, Charles Bickford (Metro-Goldwyn-Mayer Corp., 1931).

Man from Cheyenne, director Joseph I. Kane, featuring Roy Rogers, George Hayes, Sally Payne, Lynne Carver (Republic Pictures Corp., 1942).

The Old Chisholm Trail, director Elmer Clifton, featuring Johnny Mack Brown, Tex Ritter, Fuzzy Knight, Jennifer Holt (Universal Pictures Company, Inc., 1942).

The Silver Bullet, director Joseph H. Lewis, featuring Johnny Mack Brown, Fuzzy Knight, William Farnum, Jennifer Holt (Universal Pictures Company, Inc., 1942).

The Outlaw, director Howard Hughes, featuring Jack Buetel, Thomas Mitchell, Jane Russell, Walter Huston (Hughes Productions, 1943).

Girl Rush, director Gordon Douglas, featuring Wally Brown, Alan Carney, Frances Langford, Vera Vague (RKO Radio Pictures, Inc., 1944).

Oklahoma Raiders, director Lewis D. Collins, featuring Tex Ritter, Fuzzy Knight, Dennis Moore, Jennifer Holt (Universal Pictures Company, Inc., 1944).

Sunset in Eldorado, director Frank McDonald, featuring Roy Rogers, Trigger, George Hayes, Dale Evans (Republic Pictures Corp., 1945).

The Harvey Girls, director George Sidney, featuring Judy Garland, John Hodiak, Ray Bolger, Angela Lansbury (Metro-Goldwyn-Mayer Corp., 1946).

Home in Oklahoma, director William Witney, featuring Roy Rogers, Trigger, George Hayes, Dale Evans (Republic Pictures Corp., 1946).

Gun Town, director Wallace W. Fox, featuring Kirby Grant, Fuzzy Knight, Lyle Talbot, Claire Carleton (Universal Pictures Company, Inc., 1946).

The Wistful Widow of Wagon Gap, director Charles Barton, featuring Bud Abbott, Lou Costello, Marjorie Main, Audrey Young (Universal-International Pictures Co., Inc., 1947).

Belle Starr's Daughter, director Lesley Selander, featuring George Montgomery, Rod Cameron, Ruth Roman, Wallace Ford (Twentieth Century-Fox Film Corp.; Alson Productions, Inc., 1948).

The Hawk of Powder River, director Ray Taylor, featuring Eddie Dean, White Cloud, Roscoe Ates, Jennifer Holt (Producers Releasing Corp., 1948).

Dakota Lil, director Lesley Selander, featuring George Montgomery, Rod Cameron, Marie Windsor, John Emery (Twentieth Century-Fox Film Corp.; Alson Productions, Inc., 1950).

Devil's Doorway, director Anthony Mann, featuring Robert Taylor, Louis Calhern, Paula Raymond, Marshall Thompson (Metro-Goldwyn-Mayer Corp., 1950).

Valley of Fire, director John English, featuring Gene Autry, Champion, Gail Davis, Russell Hayden (Gene Autry Productions, 1951).

Denver & Rio Grande, director Byron Haskin, featuring Edmond O'Brien, Sterling Hayden, Dean Jagger, Kasey Rogers (Paramount Pictures Corp., 1952).

The Marshal's Daughter, director William Berke, featuring Hoot Gibson, Johnny Mack Brown, Jimmy Wakely, Preston Foster, Buddy Baer, Harry Lauter, Robert Bray, Bob Duncan, Ken Murray, Laurie Anders (Ken Murray Productions, 1953).

Woman They Almost Lynched, director Allan Dwan, featuring John Lund, Brian Donlevy, Audrey Totter, Joan Leslie (Republic Pictures Corp., 1953).

Oklahoma!, director Fred Zinnemann, featuring Gordon MacRae, Gloria Grahame, Gene Nelson, Charlotte Greenwood (Rodgers & Hammerstein Pictures, Inc., 1955).

Tennessee's Partner, director Allan Dwan, featuring John Payne, Ronald Reagan, Rhonda Fleming, Coleen Gray (Filmcrest Productions, Inc., 1955).

Once Upon a Horse . . ., director Hal Kanter, featuring Dan Rowan, Dick Martin, Martha Hyer, Leif Erickson (Universal-International Pictures Co., Inc., 1958).

These Thousand Hills, director Richard O. Fleischer, featuring Don Murray, Richard Egan, Lee Remick, Patricia Owens (Twentieth Century-Fox Film Corp., 1959).

Mail Order Bride, director Burt Kennedy, featuring Buddy Ebsen, Keir Dullea, Lois Nettleton, Warren Oates (Metro-Goldwyn-Mayer, Inc., 1964).

True Grit, director Henry Hathaway, featuring John Wayne, Glen Campbell, Kim Darby, Jeremy Slate (Hal Wallis Productions; Paramount Pictures Corp., 1969).

The Cheyenne Social Club, director Gene Kelly, featuring James Stewart, Henry Fonda, Shirley Jones, Sue Ane Langdon (National General Productions, Inc., 1970).

The Hired Hand, director Peter Fonda, featuring Peter Fonda, Warren Oates, Verna Bloom, Robert Pratt (Pando Company, Inc.; Universal Pictures, 1971).
The Shooting, director Monte Hellman, featuring Warren Oates, Will Hutchins, B. J. Merholz, Millie Perkins (Santa Clara Productions, Inc.; Proteus Films, 1972).
Cattle Annie and Little Britches, director Lamont Johnson, featuring Burt Lancaster, John Savage, Rod Steiger, Diane Lane (Hemdale; Cattle Annie Films Inc.; King-Hitzig Productions, 1981).
True Grit, director Joel Coen, featuring Jeff Bridges, Matt Damon, Josh Brolin, Barry Pepper, Hailee Steinfeld (Mike Zoss Productions; Skydance Productions, 2010).
Sweetwater, director Logan Miller, featuring Ed Harris, Jason Isaacs, January Jones, Eduardo Noriega (Raindance Entertainment; Atlas International; ARC Entertainment; Kickstart Productions; Mythic International Entertainment, 2013).

Select Representative Bibliography of Resources on Women in the Western

Books

Bandy, Mary Lea and Stoehr, Kevin L. (2012) *Ride, Boldly Ride: The Evolution of the American Western*, Berkeley, CA: University of California Press.
Blottner, Gene (2000) *Universal-International Westerns, 1947–1963: The Complete Filmography*. Jefferson, NC: McFarland.
Blottner, Gene (2003) *Universal Sound Westerns, 1929–1946: The Complete Filmography*. Jefferson, NC: McFarland.
Broughton, Lee (ed.) (2016) *Critical Perspectives on the Western: From* A Fistful of Dollars *to* Django Unchained. Lanham, MD: Rowman & Littlefield.
Broughton, Lee (2016) *The Euro-Western: Reframing Gender, Race and the "Other" in Film*. New York: I. B. Tauris.
Buscombe, Edward, and Pearson, Roberta E. (eds) (1998) *Back in the Saddle Again: New Essays on the Western*. London: British Film Institute.
Calder, Jenni (1974) *There Must Be a Lone Ranger: The American West in Film and in Reality*. New York: Taplinger.
Cameron, Ian and Pye, Douglas (eds) (1996) *The Book of Westerns*. New York: Continuum.
Cantarini, Martha Crawford and Spicer, Chrystopher J. (2010) *Fall Girl: My Life as a Western Stunt Double*. Jefferson, NC: McFarland.
Etulain, Richard W. and Riley, Glenda (eds) (2001) *The Hollywood West: Lives of Film Legends Who Shaped It*. Golden, CO: Fulcrum Pub.
Fagen, Herb (1996) *White Hats and Silver Spurs: Interviews with 24 Stars of Film and Television Westerns of the Thirties through the Sixties*. Jefferson, NC: McFarland.
Fitzgerald, Michael G. and Magers, Boyd (2001) *Ladies of the Western: Interviews with Fifty- One More Actresses from the Silent Era to the Television Westerns of the 1950s and 1960s*. Jefferson, NC: McFarland.
George-Warren, Holly (2002) *How Hollywood Invented the Wild West: Featuring the Real West, Campfire Melodies, Matinee Idols, Four Legged Friends, Cowgirls & Lone Guns*. Pleasantville, NY: Reader's Digest.

Gregory, Mollie (2015) *Stuntwomen: The Untold Hollywood Story*, Lexington, KY: University Press of Kentucky.
Holland, Ted (1989) *B Western Actors Encyclopedia: Facts, Photos, and Filmographies for More Than 250 Familiar Faces*. Jefferson, NC: McFarland.
Indick, William (2008) *The Psychology of the Western: How the American Psyche Plays Out on Screen*. Jefferson, NC: McFarland.
Joyner, C. Courtney (2009) *The Westerners: Interviews with Actors, Directors, Writers and Producers*. Jefferson, NC: McFarland.
Katchmer, George A. (2002) *A Biographical Dictionary of Silent Film Western Actors and Actresses*. Jefferson, NC: McFarland.
Kitses, Jim and Rickman, Gregg (eds) (1998) *The Western Reader*. New York: Limelight Editions.
Loy, R. Philip (2001) *Westerns and American Culture, 1930–1955*. Jefferson, NC: McFarland.
Loy, R. Philip (2004) *Westerns in a Changing America, 1955–2000*. Jefferson, NC: McFarland.
Lusted, David (2003) *The Western*. New York: Pearson/Longman.
McDonald, Archie P. (ed.) (1987) *Shooting Stars: Heroes and Heroines of Western Film*. Bloomington, IN: Indiana University Press.
McMahon, Jennifer L. and Csaki, B. Steve (eds) (2010) *The Philosophy of the Western*. Lexington, KY: University Press of Kentucky.
Magers, Boyd and Fitzgerald, Michael G. (1999) *Westerns Women: Interviews with 50 Leading Ladies of Movie and Television Westerns from the 1930s to the 1960s*. Jefferson, NC: McFarland.
Matheson, Sue (ed.) (2013) *Love in Western Film and Television: Lonely Hearts and Happy Trails*. New York: Palgrave Macmillan.
Matheson, Sue (ed.) (2017) *A Fistful of Icons: Essays on Frontier Fixtures of the American Western*. Jefferson, NC: McFarland.
Mitchell, Lee Clark (1996) *Westerns: Making the Man in Fiction and Film*. Chicago: University of Chicago Press.
O'Connor, John E. and Rollins, Peter C. (eds) (2005) *Hollywood's West: The American Frontier in Film, Television, and History*. Lexington, KY: University Press of Kentucky.
Pitts, Michael R. (2009) *Western Film Series of the Sound Era*. Jefferson, NC: McFarland.
Rainey, Buck (1992) *Sweethearts of the Sage: Biographies and Filmographies of 258 Actresses Appearing in Western Movies*. Jefferson, NC: McFarland.
Swann, Thomas Burnett (1977) *The Heroine or the Horse: Leading Ladies in Republic's Films*. South Brunswick, NJ: A. S. Barnes.
Tompkins, Jane P. (1992) *West of Everything: The Inner Life of Westerns*. New York: Oxford University Press.
Tuska, Jon (1985) *The American West in Film: Critical Approaches to the Western*. Westport, CT: Greenwood Press.
Verhoeff, Nanna (2006) *The West in Early Cinema: After the Beginning*. Amsterdam: Amsterdam University Press.
Wildermuth, Mark E. (2018) *Feminism and the Western in Film and Television*. Cham, Switzerland: Palgrave Macmillan.

Yoggy, Gary A. (ed.) (1998) *Back in the Saddle: Essays on Western Film and Television Actors*. Jefferson, NC: McFarland.

Articles

Aleiss, A. (1995) "Native Americans: The Surprising Silents," *Cineaste*, 21 (3), pp. 34–5.

Baglia, J. (2012) "Dueling Dualisms: Are Women in the Western at Home on the Range?" *Cultural Studies/Critical Methodologies*, 12 (6), pp. 491–9.

Buscombe, E. (2011) "Go West, Young Woman," *Sight & Sound*, 21 (5), p. 40.

Cochran, D. (1994) "Violence, Feminism, and the Counterculture in Peter Fonda's *The Hired Hand*," *Film & History*, 24 (3/4), pp. 84–98.

Crissman, J. K., Moran, D. R. and Kandra, K. L. (2012) "Women as the Lead Characters in the B-Western Motion Picture," *Journal of the West*, 51 (2), pp. 60–71.

Dowell, P. (1995) "The Mythology of the Western: Hollywood Perspectives on Race and Gender in the Nineties," *Cineaste*, 21 (1–2), pp. 6–10.

Foote, C. (1983) "Changing Images of Women in the Western Film," *Journal of the West*, 22 (4), pp. 64–71.

Foster, G. (1994) "The Women in *High Noon*: A Metanarrative of Difference," *Film Criticism*, 18–19 (3/1), pp. 72–81.

Foster, G. (1996) "Crossdressing and Disruptions of Identity in *The Dalton Girls*," *Film Criticism*, 20 (3), pp. 24–33.

Graham, D. (1980) "The Women of *High Noon*: A Revisionist View," *Rocky Mountain Review of Language and Literature*, 34 (4), 243–51.

Horak, L. (2013) "Landscape, Vitality, and Desire: Cross-Dressed Frontier Girls in Transitional-Era American Cinema," *Cinema Journal*, 52 (4), pp. 74–98.

Howe, W. (2003) "Professional Women—Women in *The Professionals* (1966)," *Film & History*, 33 (2), pp. 12–18.

Luhr, W. (1995) "The Scarred Woman Behind the Gun: Gender, Face, and History in Recent Westerns," *Bilingual Review*, 20 (1), pp. 37–44.

Modleski, T. (1995–6) "Our Heroes Have Sometimes Been Cowgirls: An Interview with Maggie Greenwald," *Film Quarterly*, 49 (2), pp. 2–11.

Modleski, T. (1997) "A Woman's Gotta Do . . . What a Man's Gotta Do? Cross-Dressing in the Western," *Signs: Journal of Women in Culture & Society*, 22 (3), pp. 519–44.

Movshovitz, H. (1984) "The Still Point: Women in the Westerns of John Ford," *Frontiers: A Journal of Women Studies*, 7 (3), pp. 68–72.

Mukherjee, T. (1996) "Woman in the Patriarchal Unconscious: Western Films of John Ford and Howard Hawks," *Indian Journal of American Studies*, 26 (1), pp. 99–107.

O'Brien, S. R. (1996) "Leaving Behind 'The Chisholm Trail' for *Red River*—Or Refiguring the Female in the Western Film Epic," *Literature/Film Quarterly*, 24 (2), pp. 183–92.

Oshana, M. (1981) "Native American Women in Westerns: Reality and Myth," *Frontiers: A Journal of Women Studies*, 6 (3), pp. 46–50.

Peterson, J. (1996) "The Competing Tunes of *Johnny Guitar*: Liberalism, Sexuality, Masquerade," *Cinema Journal*, 35 (3), pp. 3–18.

Quart, L. (2011) "The Way West: A Feminist Perspective: An Interview with Kelly Reichardt," *Cineaste*, 36 (2), pp. 40–2.

Rich, B. R. (1993) "At Home on the Range," *Sight & Sound*, 3 (11), pp. 18–22.

Schackel, S. (1993) "Barbara Stanwyck: Uncommon Heroine," *California History*, 72 (1), pp. 40–55.
Schwarz, M. T. (2014) "Searching for a Feminist Western: *The Searchers*, *The Hired Hand*, and *The Missing*," *Visual Anthropology*, 27 (1/2), pp. 45–71.
Smith, I. A. (2016) "Westward the Women," *Sight & Sound*, 26 (5), pp. 46–8.
Terry, P. (1994) "A Chinese Woman in the West: *Thousand Pieces of Gold* and the Revision of the Heroic Frontier," *Literature/Film Quarterly*, 22 (4), pp. 222–6.
Wilmington, M. (1974) "Nicolas Ray's *Johnny Guitar*," *Velvet Light Trap: A Critical Journal of Film & Television*, 12, pp. 19–25.

Select Representative Bibliography of Resources on Women in the Nineteenth-Century US West

Books

Westward, Ho!

Armitage, Susan H., and Jameson, Elizabeth (eds) (1987) *The Women's West*. Norman, OK: University of Oklahoma Press.
Billington, Monroe Lee and Hardaway, Roger D. (eds) (1998) *African Americans on the Western Frontier*. Niwot, CO: University Press of Colorado.
Brown, Dee ([1958] 1981) *The Gentle Tamers: Women of the Old Wild West*. Lincoln, NE: University of Nebraska Press.
Butler, Anne M. and Siporin, Ona (1996) *Uncommon Common Women: Ordinary Lives of the West*. Logan, UT: Utah State University Press.
Butruille, Susan G. (1995) *Women Voices from the Western Frontier*. Boise, ID: Tamarack Books.
Cross, Mary Bywater (1996) *Quilts and Women of the Mormon Migrations: Treasures of Transition*. Nashville, TN: Rutledge Hill Press.
Dary, David (2000) *The Santa Fe Trail: Its History, Legends, and Lore*. New York: A. A. Knopf.
De León, Arnoldo (2002) *Racial Frontiers: Africans, Chinese, and Mexicans in Western America, 1848–1890*. Albuquerque, NM: University of New Mexico Press.
Dunlap, Patricia Riley (1995) *Riding Astride: The Frontier in Women's History*. Denver, CO: Arden Press.
Enss, Chris (2006) *How the West Was Worn: Bustles and Buckskins on the Wild Frontier*. Guilford, CT: TwoDot.
Faragher, John Mack (2001) *Women and Men on the Overland Trail*, 2nd edn. New Haven, CT: Yale University Press.
Jeffrey, Julie Roy (1998) *Frontier Women: "Civilizing" the West? 1840–1880*, rev. edn. New York: Hill & Wang.
Johnson, Benjamin Heber (2007) *Making of the American West: People and Perspectives*. Santa Barbara, CA: ABC-CLIO.
Jones, Mary Ellen (1998) *Daily Life on the Nineteenth Century American Frontier*. Westport, CT: Greenwood Press.

Katz, William Loren (1971 [2005]) *The Black West: A Documentary and Pictorial History of the African American Role in the Westward Expansion of the United States.* New York: Harlem Moon/Broadway Books.
Lackmann, Ronald W. (1997) *Women of the Western Frontier in Fact, Fiction, and Film.* Jefferson, NC: McFarland.
Luchetti, Cathy (1993) *Home on the Range: A Culinary History of the American West.* New York: Villard Books.
Luchetti, Cathy (2001) *Children of the West: Family Life on the Frontier.* New York: Norton.
McLynn, Frank (2002) *Wagons West: The Epic Story of America's Overland Trails.* New York: Grove Press.
McManus, Sheila (2011) *Choices and Chances: A History of Women in the U.S. West.* Wheeling, IL: Harlan Davidson.
Marriott, Alice (1953 [1993]) *Hell on Horses and Women.* Norman, OK: University of Oklahoma Press.
Moody, Ralph (1967 [1998]) *Stagecoach West.* Lincoln, NE: University of Nebraska Press.
Moore, Shirley Ann Wilson (2016) *Sweet Freedom's Plains: African Americans on the Overland Trails, 1841–1869.* Norman, OK: University of Oklahoma Press.
Moynihan, Ruth Barnes, Armitage, Susan H., and DiChamp, Christiane Fischer (eds) (1998) *So Much to Be Done: Women Settlers on the Mining and Ranching Frontier,* 2nd edn. Lincoln, NE: University of Nebraska Press.
Paul, Rodman W. (1963 [2001]) *Mining Frontiers of the Far West, 1848–1880,* rev. edn, ed. E. West. Albuquerque, NM: University of New Mexico Press.
Peavy, Linda S. and Smith, Ursula (1996 [1998]) *Pioneer Women: The Lives of Women on the Frontier.* Norman, OK: University of Oklahoma Press.
Peavy, Linda S. and Smith, Ursula (1999) *Frontier Children.* Norman, OK: University of Oklahoma Press.
Ravage, John W. (2008) *Black Pioneers: Images of the Black Experience on the North American Frontier,* 2nd edn. Salt Lake City, UT: University of Utah Press.
Riley, Glenda (ed.) (1982) *Women in the West.* Manhattan, KS: Sunflower University Press.
Riley, Glenda (1992) *A Place to Grow: Women in the American West.* Arlington Heights, IL: Harlan Davidson.
Riley, Glenda (2003) *Taking Land, Breaking Land: Women Colonizing the American West and Kenya, 1840–1940.* Albuquerque, NM: University of New Mexico Press.
Riley, Glenda (2004) *Confronting Race: Women and Indians on the Frontier, 1815–1915.* Albuquerque, NM: University of New Mexico Press.
Schlissel, Lillian, Ruiz, Vicki, and Monk, Janice J. (eds) (1988) *Western Women: Their Land, Their Lives.* Albuquerque, NM: University of New Mexico Press.
Schlissel, Lillian, Gibbens, Byrd, and Hampsten, Elizabeth (1989) *Far from Home: Families of the Westward Journey.* New York: Schocken Books.
Seagraves, Anne (1996) *Daughters of the West.* Hayden, ID: Wesanne Publications.
Smith, Sherry L. (1990) *The View from Officers' Row: Army Perceptions of Western Indians.* Tucson, AZ: University of Arizona Press.

Unruh, John David (1979) *The Plains Across: The Overland Emigrants and the Trans-Mississippi West, 1840–60*. Urbana, IL: University of Illinois Press.

West, Elliott (1989) *Growing Up with the Country: Childhood on the Far Western Frontier*. Albuquerque, NM: University of New Mexico Press.

Woodworth-Ney, Laura (2008) *Women in the American West*. Santa Barbara, CA: ABC-CLIO.

Accounts of Captivity

Carlson, Paul Howard (2010) *Myth, Memory, and Massacre: The Pease River Capture of Cynthia Ann Parker*. Lubbock, TX: Texas Tech University Press.

Exley, Jo Ella Powell (2001) *Frontier Blood: The Saga of the Parker Family*. College Station, TX: Texas A&M University Press.

Frost, John (1854 [1976]) *Heroic Women of the West*. New York: Garland.

Gwynne, S. C. (2010) *Empire of the Summer Moon: Quanah Parker and the Rise and Fall of the Comanches, the Most Powerful Indian Tribe in American History*. New York: Scribner.

Kelly, Fanny (1871 [1990]) *Narrative of My Captivity among the Sioux Indians*, eds C. C. Spence and M. L. Spence. New York: Konecky & Konecky.

Kestler, Frances Roe (comp.) (1990) *The Indian Captivity Narrative: A Woman's View*. New York: Garland.

McGinty, Brian (2005) *The Oatman Massacre: A Tale of Desert Captivity and Survival*. Norman, OK: University of Oklahoma Press.

Meredith, Grace E. and German, Catherine (1927 [1977]) *Girl Captives of the Cheyennes*. New York: Garland.

Mifflin, Margot (2011) *The Blue Tattoo: The Life of Olive Oatman*. Lincoln, NE: University of Nebraska Press.

Ramsay, Jack C. (1990) *Sunshine on the Prairie: The Story of Cynthia Ann Parker*. Austin, TX: Eakin Press.

Stratton, R. B. (1857 [1983]) *Captivity of the Oatman Girls*. Lincoln, NE: University of Nebraska Press.

California

Bagley, Will (2012) *With Golden Visions Bright before Them: Trails to the Mining West, 1849–1852*. Norman, OK: University of Oklahoma Press.

Beebe, Rose Marie and Senkewicz, Robert M. (trans.) (2006 [2015]) *Testimonios: Early California through the Eyes of Women, 1815–1848*. Norman, OK: University of Oklahoma Press.

Benemann, William (ed.) (1999) *A Year of Mud and Gold: San Francisco in Letters and Diaries, 1849–1850*. Lincoln, NE: University of Nebraska Press.

Chartier, JoAnn and Enss, Chris (2000) *With Great Hope: Women of the California Gold Rush*. Helena, MT: TwoDot.

Egli, Ida Rae (ed.) (1997) *No Rooms of Their Own: Women Writers of Early California*, 2nd edn. Berkeley, CA: Heyday Books.

Farnham, Eliza W. (1856 [1972]) *California In-Doors and Out*. Nieuwkoop: De Graaf.

Hays, Lorena L. (1988) *To the Land of Gold and Wickedness: The 1848–59 Diary of Lorena L. Hays*, ed. J. H. Watson. St Louis, MO: Patrice Press.

Hurtado, Albert L. (1988) *Indian Survival on the California Frontier*. New Haven, CT: Yale University Press.

Hurtado, Albert L. (1999) *Intimate Frontiers: Sex, Gender, and Culture in Old California*. Albuquerque, NM: University of New Mexico Press.

Kirby, Georgiana Bruce (1987) *Georgiana: Feminist Reformer of the West: The Journal of Georgiana Bruce Kirby*, eds C. Swift and J. Steen. Santa Cruz, CA: Santa Cruz County Historical Trust.

Langum, David J. (2014) *Quite Contrary: The Litigious Life of Mary Bennett Love*. Lubbock, TX: Texas Tech University Press.

Levy, JoAnn (1992) *They Saw the Elephant: Women in the California Gold Rush*. Norman, OK: University of Oklahoma Press.

Levy, JoAnn (2004) *Unsettling the West: Eliza Farnham and Georgiana Bruce Kirby in Frontier California*. Berkeley, CA: Heyday Books.

McDonnell, Jeanne Farr (2008) *Juana Briones of Nineteenth-Century California*. Tucson, AZ: University of Arizona Press.

Margo, Elisabeth (1955 [1992]) *Women of the Gold Rush*. New York: Indian Head Books.

Megquier, Mary Jane (1994) *Apron Full of Gold: The Letters of Mary Jane Megquier from San Francisco, 1849–1856*, 2nd edn, ed. P. W. Kaufman. Albuquerque, NM: University of New Mexico Press.

Nunis, Doyce B. (1991) *The Bidwell-Bartleson Party: 1841 California Emigrant Adventure: The Documents and Memoirs of the Overland Pioneers*. Santa Cruz, CA: Western Tanager Press.

Royce, Sarah (2009) *Across the Plains: Sarah Royce's Western Narrative*, ed. J. D. Adkison. Tucson, AZ: University of Arizona Press.

Starr, Kevin and Orsi, Richard J. (eds) (2000) *Rooted in Barbarous Soil: People, Culture, and Community in Gold Rush California*. Berkeley, CA: University of California Press.

Willoughby, Robert J. (2003) *The Great Migration to the Gold Fields of California, 1849–1850*. Jefferson, NC: McFarland.

Cowgirls and Women Ranchers

Chrisman, Harry E. (1964 [1998]) *Lost Trails of the Cimarron*, 2nd edn. Norman, OK: University of Oklahoma Press.

Hunter, J. Marvin (ed.) (1963) *The Trail Drivers of Texas*, 2 vols, new edn. New York: Argosy-Antiquarian.

Massey, Sara R. (ed.) (2006) *Texas Women on the Cattle Trails*. College Station, TX: Texas A&M University Press.

McClure, Grace (1985) *The Bassett Women*. Athens, OH: Swallow Press/Ohio University Press.

Miller, Darlis A. (2010) *Open Range: The Life of Agnes Morley Cleaveland*. Norman, OK: University of Oklahoma Press.

Monday, Jane Clements and Vick, Frances Brannen (2007) *Petra's Legacy: The South Texas Ranching Empire of Petra Vela and Mifflin Kenedy*. College Station, TX: Texas A&M University Press.

Randall, Isabelle (1887 [2004]) *A Lady's Ranch Life in Montana*, ed. R. L. Saunders. Norman, OK: University of Oklahoma Press.

Roach, Joyce Gibson (1990) *The Cowgirls*, 2nd edn, rev. and enl. Denton, TX: University of North Texas Press.

Diaries, Journals, Letters, and Other Writings

Archer, Patience Loader (2006) *Recollections of Past Days: The Autobiography of Patience Loader Rozsa Archer*, ed. S. A. Petree. Logan, UT: Utah State University Press.

Bird, Isabella L. (1999) *Isabella Lucy Bird's A Lady's Life in the Rocky Mountains: An Annotated Text*, ed. E. S. Bernard. Norman, OK: University of Oklahoma Press.

Crosby, Caroline Barnes (2005) *No Place to Call Home: The 1807–1857 Life Writings of Caroline Barnes Crosby, Chronicler of Outlying Mormon Communities*, eds E. L. Lyman, S. W. Payne, and S. G. Ellsworth. Logan, UT: Utah State University Press.

Dichamp, Christiane Fischer (ed.) (1977) *Let Them Speak for Themselves: Women in the American West, 1849–1900*. Hamden, CT: Archon Books.

Earp, Josephine Sarah Marcus (1976) *I Married Wyatt Earp: The Recollections of Josephine Sarah Marcus Earp*, ed. G. G. Boyer. Tucson, AZ: University of Arizona Press.

FitzGerald, Emily McCorkle (1962 [1986]) *An Army Doctor's Wife on the Frontier: The Letters of Emily McCorkle FitzGerald from Alaska and the Far West, 1874–1878*, ed. A. Laufe. Lincoln, NE: University of Nebraska Press.

Floyd, Janet (2002) *Writing the Pioneer Woman*. Columbia, MO: University of Missouri Press.

Georgi-Findlay, Brigitte (1996) *The Frontiers of Women's Writing: Women's Narratives and the Rhetoric of Westward Expansion*. Tucson, AZ: University of Arizona Press.

Guerin, Elsa Jane (1968) *Mountain Charley, or, The Adventures of Mrs. E. J. Guerin, Who Was Thirteen Years in Male Attire: An Autobiography Comprising a Period of Thirteen Years Life in the States, California, and Pike's Peak*, new edn. Norman, OK: University of Oklahoma Press.

Hafen, Mary Ann (1938 [1983]) *Recollections of a Handcart Pioneer of 1860: A Woman's Life on the Mormon Frontier*. Lincoln, NE: University of Nebraska Press.

Holmes, Kenneth L. (ed.) (1995–2000) *Covered Wagon Women: Diaries & Letters from the Western Trails*, 11 vols. Lincoln, NE: University of Nebraska Press.

Holmes, Kenneth L. (ed.) (2008) *Best of Covered Wagon Women*, 2 vols. Norman, OK: University of Oklahoma Press.

LaSalle, Michael E. (2011) *Emigrants on the Overland Trail: The Wagon Trains of 1848*. Kirksville, MO: Truman State University Press.

Lawrence, Deborah (2006) *Writing the Trail: Five Women's Frontier Narratives*. Iowa City, IA: University of Iowa Press.

Mathews, M. M. (1880 [1985]) *Ten Years in Nevada: or, Life on the Pacific Coast*. Lincoln, NE: University of Nebraska Press.

Miller, Susan Cummins (ed.) (2000 [2007]) *A Sweet, Separate Intimacy: Women Writers of the American Frontier, 1800–1922*. Lubbock, TX: Texas Tech University Press.

Myres, Sandra L. (1980) *Ho for California! Women's Overland Diaries from the Huntington Library*. San Marino, CA: Huntington Library.

Myres, Sandra L. (1982) *Westering Women and the Frontier Experience, 1800–1915*. Albuquerque, NM: University of New Mexico Press.

Russell, Marion Sloan (1954 [1984]) *Land of Enchantment: Memoirs of Marion Russell along the Santa Fe Trail*. Albuquerque, NM: University of New Mexico Press.

Schlissel, Lillian (1992) *Women's Diaries of the Westward Journey*, exp. edn. New York: Schocken Books.

Sessions, Patty Bartlett (1997) *Mormon Midwife: The 1846–1888 Diaries of Patty Bartlett Sessions*, ed. D. T. Smart. Logan, UT: Utah State University Press.

Snow, Eliza R. (1995) *The Personal Writings of Eliza Roxcy Snow*, ed. M. U. Beecher. Salt Lake City, UT: University of Utah Press.

Strahorn, Carrie Adell (1911 [1988]) *Fifteen Thousand Miles by Stage: A Woman's Unique Experience during Thirty Years of Path Finding and Pioneering from the Missouri to the Pacific and from Alaska to Mexico*, 2 vols Lincoln, NE: University of Nebraska Press.

Winnemucca, Sarah (1883 [1994]) *Life among the Piutes: Their Wrongs and Claims*. Reno, NV: University of Nevada Press.

Great Plains

Alderson, Nannie T. and Huntington Smith, Helena (1942 [1969]) *A Bride Goes West*. Lincoln, NE: University of Nebraska Press.

Bartley, Paula, and Loxton, Cathy (1991) *Plains Women: Women in the American West*. New York: Cambridge University Press.

Broome, Jeff (2009) *Dog Soldier Justice: The Ordeal of Susanna Alderdice in the Kansas Indian War*. Lincoln, NE: University of Nebraska Press.

Carrington, Frances C. (1910 [2004]) *My Army Life and the Fort Phil Kearney Massacre: With an Account of the Celebration of "Wyoming Opened,"* Lincoln, NE: University of Nebraska Press.

Carrington, Margaret Irvin (1868 [1983]) *Absaraka, Home of the Crows: Being the Experience of an Officer's Wife on the Plains*. Lincoln, NE: University of Nebraska Press.

Carter, Sarah (ed.) (2009) *Montana Women Homesteaders: A Field of One's Own*. Helena, MT: Farcountry Press.

Custer, Elizabeth Bacon (1885 [2010]) *Boots and Saddles, or, Life in Dakota with General Custer*. Lincoln: NB: University of Nebraska Press.

Custer, Elizabeth Bacon (1890 [1994] *Following the Guidon*. Lincoln, NE: University of Nebraska Press.

Dick, Everett (1954 [1979)] *The Sod-House Frontier, 1854–1890: A Social History of the Northern Plains from the Creation of Kansas & Nebraska to the Admission of the Dakotas*. Lincoln, NE: University of Nebraska Press.

Ellis, Anne (1929 [1980]) *The Life of an Ordinary Woman*. Lincoln, NE: University of Nebraska Press.

Foote, Cheryl J. (1990) *Women of the New Mexico Frontier, 1846–1912*. Niwot: CO: University Press of Colorado.
French, Emily (1987) *Emily, the Diary of a Hard-Worked Woman*, ed. J. Lecompte. Lincoln, NE: University of Nebraska Press.
Harris, Katherine (1993) *Long Vistas: Women and Families on Colorado Homesteads*. Niwot: CO: University Press of Colorado.
Herndon, Sarah Raymond (1902 [2003]) *Days on the Road: Crossing the Plains in 1865: The Diary of Sarah Raymond Herndon*. Guilford, CT: TwoDot.
Kreck, Dick (2013) *Hell on Wheels: Wicked Towns Along the Union Pacific Railroad*. Golden, CO: Fulcrum.
Lee, Bob (ed.) (1976 [2004]) *Gold, Gals, Guns, Guts: A History of Deadwood, Lead, and Spearfish, 1874–1976*. Pierre, SD: South Dakota State Historical Society Press.
Morgan, Lael (2011) *Wanton West: Madams, Money, Murder, and the Wild Women of Montana's Frontier*. Chicago: Chicago Review Press.
Reese, Linda Williams (1997) *Women of Oklahoma, 1890–1920*. Norman, OK: University of Oklahoma Press.
Reese, Linda Williams (2013) *Trail Sisters: Freedwomen in Indian Territory, 1850–1890*. Lubbock, TX: Texas Tech University Press.
Riley, Glenda (1988) *The Female Frontier: A Comparative View of Women on the Prairie and the Plains*. Lawrence, KS: University Press of Kansas.
Ronan, Mary and Ronan, Margaret (2003) *Girl from the Gulches: The Story of Mary Ronan*, ed. E. Baumler. Helena, MT: Montana Historical Society Press.
Sanford, Mollie Dorsey (1959 [2003]) *Mollie: The Journal of Mollie Dorsey Sanford in Nebraska and Colorado Territories, 1857–1866*. Lincoln, NE: University of Nebraska Press.
Smith, Shannon D. (2008) *Give Me Eighty Men: Women and the Myth of the Fetterman Fight*. Lincoln, NE: University of Nebraska Press.
Stewart, Elinore Pruitt (1914 [1989]) *Letters of a Woman Homesteader*. Lincoln, NE: University of Nebraska Press.
Stewart, Elinore Pruitt (1915 [1979]) *Letters on an Elk Hunt: By a Woman Homesteader*. Lincoln, NE: University of Nebraska Press.
Stewart, Elinore Pruitt (1992) *The Adventures of the Woman Homesteader: The Life and Letters of Elinore Pruitt Stewart*, ed. S. George-Bloomfield. Lincoln, NE: University of Nebraska Press.
Stratton, Joanna L. (1981) *Pioneer Women: Voices from the Kansas Frontier*. New York: Simon & Schuster.

Lives of Women in the West

Aikman, Duncan (1927 [1987]) *Calamity Jane and the Lady Wildcats*. Lincoln, NE: University of Nebraska Press.
Benson, Maxine (1986) *Martha Maxwell, Rocky Mountain Naturalist*. Lincoln, NE: University of Nebraska Press.
Canfield, Gae Whitney (1983) *Sarah Winnemucca of the Northern Paiutes*. Norman, OK: University of Oklahoma Press.

Corbett, Christopher (2010) *The Poker Bride: The First Chinese in the Wild West*. New York: Atlantic Monthly Press.
Etulain, Richard W. (2014) *The Life and Legends of Calamity Jane*. Norman, OK: University of Oklahoma Press.
Etulain, Richard W. (2015) *Calamity Jane: A Reader's Guide*. Norman, OK: University of Oklahoma Press.
Gray, Dorothy (1976 [1998]) *Women of the West*. Lincoln, NE: University of Nebraska Press.
Havighurst, Walter (1954 [1992]) *Annie Oakley of the Wild West*. Lincoln, NE: University of Nebraska Press.
Herr, Pamela (1987) *Jessie Benton Frémont: A Biography*. Norman, OK: University of Oklahoma Press.
Howard, Harold P. (2001) *Sacajawea*. Norman, OK: University of Oklahoma Press.
Jenkins, Malinda and Lilienthal, Jesse (1998 [1933]) *Gambler's Wife: The Life of Malinda Jenkins*. Lincoln, NE: University of Nebraska Press.
Kasper, Shirl (1992) *Annie Oakley*. Norman, OK: University of Oklahoma Press.
Kirschner, Ann (2013) *Lady at the O.K. Corral: The True Story of Josephine Marcus Earp*. New York: Harper.
L'Aloge, Bob and Nelson-L'Aloge, Virginia C. (1995) *Pistols & Petticoats: 13 Female Trailblazers of the Old West*. Los Lunas, NM: Flying Eagle-Thunderhawk Enterprises.
Luchetti, Cathy and Olwell, Carol (1982) *Women of the West*. St George, UT: Antelope Island Press.
McLaird, James D. (2005) *Calamity Jane: The Woman and the Legend*. Norman, OK: University of Oklahoma Press.
McLaird, James D. (2008) *Wild Bill Hickok & Calamity Jane: Deadwood Legends*. Pierre, SD: South Dakota State Historical Society Press.
Monson, Marianne (2016) *Frontier Grit: The Unlikely True Stories of Daring Pioneer Women*. Salt Lake City, UT: Shadow Mountain.
O'Brien, Mary Barmeyer (1997) *Heart of the Trail: The Stories of Eight Wagon Train Women*. Helena, MT: TwoDot.
Peavy, Linda S. and Smith, Ursula (1994) *Women in Waiting in the Westward Movement: Life on the Home Frontier*. Norman, OK: University of Oklahoma Press.
Phillips, Catherine Coffin (1935 [1995]) *Jessie Benton Frémont: A Woman Who Made History*. Lincoln, NE: University of Nebraska Press.
Riley, Glenda (1994) *The Life and Legacy of Annie Oakley*. Norman, OK: University of Oklahoma Press.
Riley, Glenda and Etulain, Richard W. (eds) (1997) *By Grit & Grace: Eleven Women Who Shaped the American West*. Golden, CO: Fulcrum.
Seagraves, Anne (1992) *High-Spirited Women of the West*. Lakeport, CA: Wesanne Publications.
Seagraves, Anne (2002) *Roses of the West*. Hayden, ID: Wesanne Publications.
Sollid, Roberta Beed (1958 [1995]) *Calamity Jane: A Study in Historical Criticism*. Helena, MT: Montana Historical Society Press.
Thrapp, Dan L. (1988–94) *Encyclopedia of Frontier Biography*, 4 vols. Glendale, CA: A. H. Clark.

Turner, Erin H. (ed.) (2016) *Wild West Women: Fifty Lives That Shaped the Frontier.* Guilford, CT: TwoDot.
Underwood, Larry (1991) *Love and Glory: Women of the Old West.* Lincoln, NE: Media.
Underwood, Larry (1997) *Dreams of Glory: Women of the Old West.* Lincoln, NE: Dageforde.
Wagner, Tricia Martineau (2007) *African American Women of the Old West.* Guilford, CT: TwoDot.
Western Writers of America (1980) *The Women Who Made the West.* Garden City, NY: Doubleday.
Zanjani, Sally Springmeyer (2001) *Sarah Winnemucca.* Lincoln, NE: University of Nebraska Press.

Love, Mail Order Brides, Marriage, and Polygamous Women

Chartier, JoAnn and Enss, Chris (2002) *Love Untamed: Romances of the Old West.* Guilford, CT: TwoDot.
Enss, Chris (2005) *Hearts West: True Stories of Mail Order Brides on the Frontier.* Guilford, CT: TwoDot.
Enss, Chris (2013) *Object, Matrimony: The Risky Business of Mail-Order Matchmaking on the Western Frontier.* Guilford, CT: TwoDot.
Enss, Chris (2014) *Love Lessons from the Old West: Wisdom from Wild Women.* Guilford, CT: TwoDot.
Luchetti, Cathy (1996) *'I Do!' Courtship, Love, and Marriage on the American Frontier: A Glimpse at America's Romantic Past through Photographs, Diaries, and Journals, 1715–1915.* New York: Crown Trade Paperbacks.
Morris, Mary Lois Walker (2007) *Before the Manifesto: The Life Writings of Mary Lois Walker Morris*, ed. M. L. Milewski. Logan, UT: Utah State University Press.
Stenhouse, T. B. H., Mrs. (1872 [2008]) *Exposé of Polygamy: A Lady's Life among the Mormons*, ed. L. W. DeSimone. Logan, UT: Utah State University Press.
Ulrich, Laurel Thatcher (2017) *A House Full of Females: Plural Marriage and Women's Rights in Early Mormonism, 1835–1870.* New York: Alfred A. Knopf.
Whitney, Helen Mar (2003) *A Widow's Tale: The 1884–1896 Diary of Helen Mar Kimball Whitney*, ed. C. M. Hatch and T. Compton. Logan, UT: Utah State University Press.
Zug, Marcia A. (2016) *Buying a Bride: An Engaging History of Mail-Order Matches.* New York: New York University Press.

Military Lives

Alexander, Eveline Martin (1977) *Cavalry Wife: The Diary of Eveline M. Alexander, 1866–1867: Being a Record of Her Journey from New York to Fort Smith to Join Her Cavalry-Officer Husband, Andrew J. Alexander, and Her Experiences with Him on Active Duty among the Indian Nations and in Texas, New Mexico, and Colorado*, ed. S. L. Myres. College Station, TX: Texas A&M University Press.
Baldwin, Alice Blackwood (1929 [1975]) *An Army Wife on the Frontier: The Memoirs of Alice Blackwood Baldwin, 1867–1877*, eds R. C. Carriker and E. R. Carriker. Salt Lake City, UT: Tanner Trust Fund, University of Utah Library.

Biddle, Ellen McGowan (1907 [2002]) *Reminiscences of a Soldier's Wife*. Mechanicsburg, PA: Stackpole Books.
Boyd, Orsemus Bronson, Mrs (1894 [1982]) *Cavalry Life in Tent and Field*. Lincoln, NE: University of Nebraska Press.
Campbell, Robin Dell (2005) *Mistresses of the Transient Hearth: American Army Officers' Wives and Material Culture, 1840–1880*. New York: Routledge.
Clarke, Charles Francis and Clarke, Mary (1941 [1997]) *Above A Common Soldier: Frank and Mary Clarke in the American West and Civil War*, 2nd edn, rev. edn. ed. D. A. Miller. Albuquerque, NM: University of New Mexico Press.
Corbusier, Fanny Dunbar (2003) *Fanny Dunbar Corbusier: Recollections of Her Army Life, 1869–1908*, ed. P. Y. Stallard. Norman, OK: University of Oklahoma Press.
Custer, Elizabeth Bacon (1895 [1994]) *Tenting on the Plains, or, General Custer in Kansas and Texas*. Norman, OK: University of Oklahoma Press.
Custer, George A. and Custer, Elizabeth Bacon (1950 [1987]) *The Custer Story: The Life and Intimate Letters of General George A. Custer and His Wife Elizabeth*, ed. M. Merington. Lincoln: NB: University of Nebraska Press.
Eales, Anne Bruner (1996) *Army Wives on the American Frontier: Living by the Bugles*. Boulder, CO: Johnson Books.
Enss, Chris and Chartier, JoAnn (2016) *Soldier, Sister, Spy, Scout: Women Soldiers and Patriots on the Western Frontier*. Guilford, CT: TwoDot.
Fougera, Katherine Gibson (1942 [1986]) *With Custer's Cavalry*. Lincoln, NE: University of Nebraska Press.
Grierson, Alice Kirk (1989) *The Colonel's Lady on the Western Frontier: The Correspondence of Alice Kirk Grierson*, ed. S. A. Leckie. Lincoln, NE: University of Nebraska Press.
Laurence, Mary Leefe (1996) *Daughter of the Regiment: Memoirs of a Childhood in the Frontier Army, 1878–1898*, ed. T. T. Smith. Lincoln, NE: University of Nebraska Press.
Lawrence, Jennifer J. (2016) *Soap Suds Row: The Bold Lives of Army Laundresses, 1802–1876*. Glendo, WY: High Plains Press.
Leckie, Shirley A. (1993) *Elizabeth Bacon Custer and the Marking of a Myth*. Norman, OK: University of Oklahoma Press.
McInnis, Verity (2017) *Women of Empire: Nineteenth-Century Army Officers' Wives in India and the U.S. West*. Norman, OK: University of Oklahoma Press.
Mattes, Merrill J. (1960 [1988]) *Indians, Infants, and Infantry: Andrew and Elizabeth Burt on the Frontier*. Lincoln, NE: University of Nebraska Press.
Nacy, Michele J. (2000) *Members of the Regiment: Army Officers' Wives on the Western Frontier, 1865–1890*. Westport, CT: Greenwood Press.
Poolman, Jeremy (2002) *A Wounded Thing Must Hide: In Search of Libbie Custer*. New York: Bloomsbury.
Roe, Frances Marie Antoinette Mack (1909 [1981]) *Army Letters from an Officer's Wife, 1871–1888*. Lincoln, NE: University of Nebraska Press.
Stallard, Patricia Y. (1978 [1992]) *Glittering Misery: Dependents of the Indian Fighting Army*. Norman, OK: University of Oklahoma Press.
Steinbach, Robert H. (1989) *A Long March: The Lives of Frank and Alice Baldwin*. Austin, TX: University of Texas Press.

Summerhayes, Martha (1911 [1979]) *Vanished Arizona: Recollections of the Army Life of a New England Woman*. Lincoln, NE: University of Nebraska Press.

Tucker, Phillip Thomas (2002) *Cathy Williams: From Slave to Female Buffalo Soldier*. Mechanicsburg, PA: Stackpole Books.

Notorious Ladies and Outlaw Women

Brown, Robert L. (1978) *Saloons of the American West: An Illustrated Chronicle*. Silverton, CO: Sundance Books.

Burke, John (1974 [1989]) *The Legend of Baby Doe: The Life and Times of the Silver Queen of the West*. Lincoln: NB: University of Nebraska Press.

Butler, Anne M. (1997) *Gendered Justice in the American West: Women Prisoners in Men's Penitentiaries*. Urbana, IL: University of Illinois Press.

Drago, Gail (1996) *Etta Place: Her Life and Times with Butch Cassidy and the Sundance Kid*. Plano, TX: Republic of Texas Press.

Drago, Harry Sinclair (1969) *Notorious Ladies of the Frontier*. New York: Dodd, Mead & Co.

Enss, Chris (2015) *Wicked Women: Notorious, Mischievous, and Wayward Ladies from the Old West*. Guilford, CT: TwoDot.

Etulain, Richard W. and Riley, Glenda (eds) (1999) *With Badges & Bullets: Lawmen & Outlaws in the Old West*. Golden, CO: Fulcrum.

Hufsmith, George W. (1993) *The Wyoming Lynching of Cattle Kate, 1889*. Glendo, WY: High Plains Press.

Martin, Cy (1974) *Whiskey and Wild Women: An Amusing Account of the Saloons and Bawds of the Old West*. New York: Hart.

Rascoe, Burton (2004) *Belle Starr: "The Bandit Queen."* Lincoln, NE: University of Nebraska Press.

Riley, Glenda, and Etulain, Richard W. (eds) (2003) *Wild Women of the Old West*. Golden, CO: Fulcrum.

Rutter, Michael (2003) *Wild Bunch Women*. Guilford, CT: TwoDot.

Rutter, Michael (2008) *Bedside Book of Bad Girls: Outlaw Women of the American West*. Helena, MT: Farcountry Press.

Shirley, Glenn (1982) *Belle Starr and Her Times: The Literature, the Facts, and the Legends*. Norman, OK: University of Oklahoma Press.

Steele, Phillip W. (1989) *Starr Tracks: Belle and Pearl Starr*. Gretna, LA: Pelican.

Oregon and the Oregon Trail

Bagley, Will (2010) *So Rugged and Mountainous: Blazing the Oregon and California Trails, 1812–1848*. Norman, OK: University of Oklahoma Press.

Brown, Daniel James (2009) *The Indifferent Stars Above: The Harrowing Saga of a Donner Party Bride*. New York: William Morrow.

Butruille, Susan G. (1993) *Women's Voices from the Oregon Trail: The Times That Tried Women's Souls, and a Guide to Women's History along the Oregon Trail*. Boise, ID: Tamarack Books.

Cross, Mary Bywater (1993) *Treasures in the Trunk: Quilts of the Oregon Trail*. Nashville, TN: Rutledge Hill Press.

Dary, David (2004) *The Oregon Trail: An American Saga*. New York: Alfred A. Knopf.

Drury, Clifford Merrill (ed.) (1963–6) *First White Women Over the Rockies: Diaries, Letters, and Biographical Sketches of the Six Women of the Oregon Mission Who Made the Overland Journey in 1836 and 1838*, 3 vols. Glendale, CA: A. H. Clark.

Fulton, Arabella, Greenberg, Judith E., and McKeever, Helen Carey (1995) *A Pioneer Woman's Memoir: Based on the Journal of Arabella Clemens Fulton*. New York: F. Watts.

Jeffrey, Julie Roy (1991) *Converting the West: A Biography of Narcissa Whitman*. Norman, OK: University of Oklahoma Press.

Masterson, Martha Gay (1990) *One Woman's West: Recollections of the Oregon Trail and Settling the Northwest Country*, new exp. 2nd edn, ed. L. Barton. Eugene, OR: Spencer Butte Press.

Prescott, Cynthia Culver (2007) *Gender and Generation on the Far Western Frontier*. Tucson, AZ: University of Arizona Press.

Smith, Sarah Gilbert White and Smith, Asa Bowen (1966 [1999]) *The Mountains We Have Crossed: Diaries and Letters of the Oregon Mission, 1838*. Lincoln, NE: University of Nebraska Press.

Walker, Mary Richardson and Eells, Myra Fairbanks (1963 [1998]) *On to Oregon: The Diaries of Mary Walker and Myra Eells*. Lincoln, NE: University of Nebraska Press.

Whitman, Narcissa Prentiss and Hart Spalding, Eliza (1963 [1997]) *Where Wagons Could Go: Narcissa Whitman and Eliza Spalding*. Lincoln, NE: University of Nebraska Press.

Youst, Lionel (1997) *She's Tricky like Coyote: Annie Miner Peterson, an Oregon Coast Indian Woman*. Norman, OK: University of Oklahoma Press.

Prostitutes and Lady Gamblers

Agnew, Jeremy (2008) *Brides of the Multitude: Prostitution in the Old West*. Lake City, CO: Western Reflections.

Butler, Anne M. (1985) *Daughters of Joy, Sisters of Misery: Prostitutes in the American West, 1865–90*. Urbana, IL: University of Illinois Press.

Collins, Jan MacKell (2009) *Red Light Women of the Rocky Mountains*. Albuquerque, NM: University of New Mexico Press.

Cook, Mary J. Straw (2007) *Doña Tules: Santa Fe's Courtesan and Gambler*, Albuquerque, NM: University of New Mexico Press.

Devereaux, Jan (2009) *Pistols, Petticoats, & Poker: The Real Lottie Denos—No Lies or Alibis*. Silver City, NM: High-Lonesome Books.

Enss, Chris (2007) *The Lady Was a Gambler: True Stories of Notorious Cardsharps of the Old West*. Guilford, CT: Globe Pequot.

Hunter, J. Marvin (1959) *The Story of Lottie Deno, Her Life and Times*. Bandera, TX: 4 Hunters.

Miller, Ronald Dean (1964) *Shady Ladies of the West*. Los Angeles, CA: Westernlore Press.

Monahan, Sherry (2005) *The Wicked West: Boozers, Cruisers, Gamblers, and More*. Tucson, AZ: Rio Nuevo Publishers.

Oharazeki, Kazuhiro (2016) *Japanese Prostitutes in the North American West, 1887–1920*. Seattle, WA: University of Washington Press.
Rose, Cynthia (1994) *Lottie Deno: Gambling Queen of Hearts*. Santa Fe, NM: Clear Light.
Rutter, Michael (2005) *Upstairs Girls: Prostitution in the American West*. Helena, MT: Farcountry Press.
Seagraves, Anne (1994) *Soiled Doves: Prostitution in the Early West*. Hayden, ID: Wesanne.
Simmons, Alexy (1989) *Red Light Ladies: Settlement Patterns and Material Culture on the Mining Frontier*. Corvallis, OR: Department of Anthropology, Oregon State University.
Washburn, Josie (1909 [1997]) *The Underworld Sewer: A Prostitute Reflects on Life in the Trade, 1871–1909*. Lincoln, NE: University of Nebraska Press.

Texas

Blevins, Don (2001) *From Angels to Hellcats: Legendary Texas Women, 1836 to 1880*. Missoula, MT: Mountain Press.
Blücher, Maria Augusta von (2002) *Maria von Blücher's Corpus Christi: Letters from the South Texas Frontier, 1849–1879*, ed. B. S. Cheeseman. College Station, TX: Texas A&M University Press.
Burnett, Georgellen (1990) *We Just Toughed It Out: Women in the Llano Estacado*. El Paso, TX: Texas Western Press.
Caughfield, Adrienne (2005) *True Women & Westward Expansion*. College Station, TX: Texas A&M University Press.
Coleman, Ann Raney Thomas (1971) *Victorian Lady on the Texas Frontier: The Journal of Ann Raney Coleman*, ed. C. R. King. Norman, OK: University of Oklahoma Press.
Cummins, Light Townsend (2009) *Emily Austin of Texas, 1795–1851*. Fort Worth, TX: TCU Press.
Embree, Henrietta Baker and Embree, Tennessee Keys (2008) *Tandem Lives: The Frontier Texas Diaries of Henrietta Baker Embree and Tennessee Keys Embree, 1856–1884*, ed. A. L. Wink. Knoxville, TN: University of Tennessee Press.
Exley, Jo Ella Powell (1985) *Texas Tears and Texas Sunshine: Voices of Frontier Women*. College Station, TX: Texas A&M University Press.
Gould, Florence C. and Pando, Patricia N. (1991) *Claiming Their Land: Women Homesteaders in Texas*. El Paso, TX: Texas Western Press.
King, C. Richard (1981) *The Lady Cannoneer: A Biography of Angelina Belle Peyton Eberly, Heroine of the Texas Archives War*. Burnet, TX: Eakin Press.
Maverick, Mary Adams and Maverick, Madison, Geo (1921 [1989]) *Memoirs of Mary A. Maverick*, ed. R. M. Green. Lincoln, NE: University of Nebraska Press.
Pickrell, Annie Doom (1929 [1991]) *Pioneer Women in Texas*. Austin, TX: State House Press.
Ramsay, Jack C. (2001) *Texas Sinners and Revolutionaries: Jane Long and Her Fellow Conspirators*. Plano, TX: Republic of Texas Press.
Russell, Charles H. (2006) *Undaunted: A Norwegian Woman in Frontier Texas*. College Station: TX: Texas A&M University Press.

Scheer, Mary L. (2012) *Women and the Texas Revolution*. Denton, TX: University of North Texas Press.

Wooster, Robert (1987) *Soldiers, Sutlers, and Settlers: Garrison Life on the Texas Frontier*. College Station, TX: Texas A&M University Press.

Woman Suffrage

Beeton, Beverly (1986) *Women Vote in the West: The Woman Suffrage Movement, 1869–1896*. New York: Garland.

Grimes, Alan Pendleton (1967) *The Puritan Ethic and Woman Suffrage*. New York: Oxford University Press.

Mead, Rebecca J. (2004) *How the Vote Was Won: Woman Suffrage in the Western United States, 1868–1914*. New York: New York University Press.

VanBurkleo, Sandra F. (2015) *Gender Remade: Citizenship, Suffrage, and Public Power in the New Northwest, 1879–1912*. New York: Cambridge University Press.

Women Entertainers

Agnew, Jeremy (2011) *Entertainment in the Old West: Theater, Music, Circuses, Medicine Shows, Prizefighting and Other Popular Amusements*. Jefferson, NC: McFarland.

Bricklin, Julia (2017) *America's Best Female Sharpshooter: The Rise and Fall of Lillian Frances Smith*. Norman, OK: University of Oklahoma Press.

Chartier, JoAnn and Enss, Chris (2003) *Gilded Girls: Women Entertainers of the Old West*. Guilford, CT: TwoDot.

Enss, Chris (2006) *Buffalo Gals: Women of Buffalo Bill's Wild West Show*. Guilford, CT: TwoDot.

Enss, Chris (2016) *Entertaining Women: Actresses, Dancers, and Singers in the Old West*. Guilford, CT: TwoDot.

Seagraves, Anne (1991) *Women Who Charmed the West*. Lakeport, CA: Wesanne.

Women's Occupations

Carter, Jennie (2007) *Jennie Carter: A Black Journalist of the Early West*, ed. E. Gardner. Jackson, MS: University Press of Mississippi.

Chaput, Donald (1995) *Nellie Cashman and the North American Mining Frontier*. Tucson, AZ: Westernlore Press.

Crawford, Isabel (1915 [1998]) *Kiowa: A Woman Missionary in Indian Territory*. Lincoln, NE: University of Nebraska Press.

Dary, David (2008) *Frontier Medicine: From the Atlantic to the Pacific, 1492–1941*. New York: Alfred A. Knopf.

Eastman, Elaine Goodale (1978 [2004]) *Sister to the Sioux: The Memoirs of Elaine Goodale Eastman, 1885–91*, ed. K. Graber. Lincoln, NE: University of Nebraska Press.

Enss, Chris (2006) *The Doctor Wore Petticoats: Women Physicians of the Old West*. Guilford, CT: TwoDot.

Enss, Chris (2008) *A Beautiful Mine: Women Prospectors of the Old West*. Guilford, CT: TwoDot.

Enss, Chris (2008) *Frontier Teachers: Stories of Heroic Women of the Old West*. Guilford, CT: TwoDot.

Fletcher, Alice C. (2013) *Life among the Indians: First Fieldwork among the Sioux and Omahas*, eds J. C. Scherer and R. J. DeMallie. Lincoln, NE: University of Nebraska Press.
Fletcher, Alice C. (2016) *Dividing the Reservation: Alice C. Fletcher's Nez Perce Allotment Diaries and Letters 1889–1892*, ed. N. Tonkovich. Pullman, WA: Washington State University Press.
Foote, Mary Hallock (1972) *A Victorian Gentlewoman in the Far West: The Reminiscences of Mary Hallock Foote*, ed. R. W. Paul. San Marino, CA: Huntington Library.
Gay, E. Jane (1981) *With the Nez Perces: Alice Fletcher in the Field, 1889–92*, eds F. E. Hoxie and J. T. Mark. Lincoln, NE: University of Nebraska Press.
Illing, Thora Kerr (2016) *Gold Rush Queen: The Extraordinary Life of Nellie Cashman*. Victoria, BC: TouchWood Editions.
Kaufman, Polly Welts (1984) *Women Teachers on the Frontier*. New Haven, CT: Yale University Press.
Kinkead, Joyce A. (1996) *A Schoolmarm All My Life: Personal Narratives from Frontier Utah*. Salt Lake City, UT: Signature Books.
Ledbetter, Suzann (1993) *Nellie Cashman, Prospector and Trailblazer*. El Paso, TX: Texas Western Press, University of Texas at El Paso.
Luchetti, Cathy (1989) *Under God's Spell: Frontier Evangelists, 1772–1915*. San Diego, CA: Harcourt Brace Jovanovich.
Mark, Joan T. (1988) *A Stranger in Her Native Land: Alice Fletcher and the American Indians*. Lincoln, NE: University of Nebraska Press.
Miller, Darlis A. (2002) *Mary Hallock Foote: Author-Illustrator of the American West*. Norman, OK: University of Oklahoma Press.
Morris, Juddi (1994) *The Harvey Girls: The Women Who Civilized the West*. New York: Walker.
Poling-Kempes, Lesley (1989) *The Harvey Girls: Women Who Opened the West*. New York: Paragon House.
Rehwinkel, Bessie Lee Efner and Rehwinkel, Alfred Martin (1963) *Dr Bessie; The Life Story and Romance of a Pioneer Lady Doctor on Our Western and the Canadian Frontier*. St Louis, MO: Concordia.
Rowland, Mary Canaga (1994) *As Long as Life: The Memoirs of a Frontier Woman Doctor, Mary Canaga Rowland, 1873–1966*, ed. F. A. Loomis. Seattle, WA: Storm Peak Press.
Sargent, Theodore D. (2005) *The Life of Elaine Goodale Eastman*. Lincoln, NE: University of Nebraska Press.
Skinner, H. L. (2001) *Eye of the Blackbird: A Story of Gold in the American West*. Boulder, CO: Johnson Books.
Steele, Volney (2005) *Bleed, Blister, and Purge: A History of Medicine on the American Frontier*. Missoula, MT: Mountain Press.
Webb, Bernice Larson (1987) *Lady Doctor on a Homestead: The Thomas County Years, 1879–1890, of Mary Amelia Hay (1832–1907)*. Colby, KS: H. F. Davis Memorial Library, Colby Community College.
Zanjani, Sally Springmeyer (1997) *A Mine of Her Own: Women Prospectors in the American West, 1850–1950*. Lincoln, NE: University of Nebraska Press.

Journal Articles

Andreadis, H. (1989) "True Womanhood Revisited: Women's Private Writing in Nineteenth-Century Texas," *Journal of the Southwest*, 31 (2), pp. 179–204.

Baker, A. P. (2005) "Daughters of Mars: Army Officers' Wives and Military Culture on the American Frontier," *The Historian*, 67 (1), pp. 20–42.

Bledsoe, L. J. (1984) "Adventuresome Women on the Oregon Trail: 1840–1867," *Frontiers: A Journal of Women Studies*, 7 (3), pp. 22–9.

Boag, P. (2005) "Go West Young Man, Go East Young Woman: Searching for the Trans in Western Gender History," *Western Historical Quarterly*, 36 (4), pp. 477–97.

Brackman, B. (1992) "Quiltmaking on the Overland Trails," *Uncoverings*, 13, pp. 45–60.

Butler, A. M. (2005) "There Are Exceptions to Every Rule: Adjusting the Boundaries—Catholic Sisters and the American West," *American Catholic Studies*, 116 (3), pp. 1–22.

Cahill, C. D. (2008) "'You Think It Strange That I Can Love an Indian': Native Men, White Women, and Marriage in the Indian Service," *Frontiers: A Journal of Women Studies*, 29 (2/3), pp. 106–45.

Carter, T. (2000) "Living the Principle: Mormon Polygamous Housing in Nineteenth-Century Utah," *Winterthur Portfolio*, 35 (4), pp. 223–51.

Cesar, D. T. and Smith, J. K. (2007) "The Image of Women Teachers in Indian Territory in the Nineteenth Century," *American Educational History Journal*, 34 (1), pp. 39–54.

Chalmers, C. (1999) "Françoise, Lucienne, Rosalie: French Women-Adventurers in the Early Days of the California Gold Rush," *California History*, 78 (3), pp. 138–45, 147–53.

Cloud, B. (1993) "Images of Women in the Mining-Camp Press," *Nevada Historical Society Quarterly*, 36 (3), pp. 194–207.

Cole, J. K. (1990) "A Wide Field for Usefulness: Women's Civil Status and the Evolution of Women's Suffrage on the Montana Frontier, 1864–1914," *American Journal of Legal History*, 34 (3), pp. 262–94.

Compton, T. M. (2013) "Challenging Imperial Expectations: Black and White Female Homesteaders in Kansas," *Great Plains Quarterly*, 33 (1), pp. 49–61.

Conlin, J. R. (1985) "Eating on the Rush: Organizing Meals on the Overland Trail," *California History*, 64 (3), pp. 218–25.

Cope, M. (1998) "She Hath Done What She Could: Community, Citizenship, and Place among Women in Late Nineteenth-Century Colorado," *Historical Geography*, 26, pp. 45–64.

Downs, F. (1986) "'Tryels and Trubbles': Women in Early Nineteenth-Century Texas," *The Southwestern Historical Quarterly*, 90 (1), pp. 35–56.

English, L. (2002) "Revealing Accounts: Women's Lives and General Stores," *The Historian*, 64 (3/4), pp. 567–85.

Godfrey, A. M. (2006) "'The Queen of Inventions': The Sewing Machine Comes to Utah," *Journal of Mormon History*, 32 (3), pp. 82–103.

Goetz, H. K. (1983) "Kate's Quarter Section: A Woman in the Cherokee Strip," *Chronicles of Oklahoma*, 61 (3), pp. 246–67.

Hall, P. (1991) "Diaries and Journals: Telling the Tales of Western Movement," *Gilcrease Magazine of American History & Art*, 13 (3), pp. 18–27.

Hallgarth, S. A. (1989) "Women Settlers on the Frontier: Unwed, Unreluctant, Unrepentant," *Women's Studies Quarterly*, 17 (3/4), pp. 23–34.

Helvenston, S. I. (1986) "Ornament or Instrument?: Proper Roles for Women on the Kansas Frontier," *Kansas Quarterly*, 18 (3), pp. 35–49.

Hoffert, S. D. (1991) "Childbearing on the Trans-Mississippi Frontier, 1830–1900," *Western Historical Quarterly*, 22 (3), pp. 272–88.

James, R. M. (1993) "Women of the Mining West: Virginia City Revisited," *Nevada Historical Society Quarterly*, 36 (3), pp. 153–77.

Jeffrey, J. R. (1988) "'There is Some Splendid Scenery': Women's Responses to the Great Plains Landscape," *Great Plains Quarterly*, 8 (2), pp. 69–78.

Johnson, K. A. (2006) "Undaunted Courage and Faith: The Lives of Three Black Women in the West and Hawaii in the Early 19th Century," *Journal of African American History*, 91 (1), pp. 4–22.

Lindgren, H. E. (1989) "Ethnic Women Homesteading on the Plains of North Dakota," *Great Plains Quarterly*, 9 (3), pp. 157–73.

Montrie, C. (2005) "'Men Alone Cannot Settle a Country': Domesticating Nature in the Kansas-Nebraska Grasslands," *Great Plains Quarterly*, 25 (4), pp. 245–58.

Murphy, M. (1984) "The Private Lives of Public Women: Prostitution in Butte, Montana, 1878–1917," *Frontiers: A Journal of Women Studies*, 7 (3), pp. 30–5.

Osselaer, H. (2014) "On the Wrong Side of Allen Street: The Businesswomen of Tombstone, 1878–1884," *Journal of Arizona History*, 55 (2), pp. 145–66.

Palmquist, P. E. (1992) "Pioneer Women Photographers in Nineteenth-Century California," *California History*, 71 (1), pp. 110–27.

Prescott, C. C. (2007) "'Why She Didn't Marry Him': Love, Power, and Marital Choice on the Far Western Frontier," *Western Historical Quarterly*, 38 (1), pp. 25–45.

Riley, G. (1986) "Women on the Panama Trail to California, 1849–1869," *Pacific Historical Review*, 55 (4), pp. 531–48.

Riley, G. (1993) "Frederick Jackson Turner Overlooked the Ladies," *Journal of the Early Republic*, 13 (2), pp. 216–30.

Riley, G. (1998) "Sesquicentennial Reflections: A Comparative View of Mormon and Gentile Women on the Westward Trail," *Journal of Mormon History*, 24 (1), pp. 28–53.

Schrems, S. H. (1987) "Teaching School on the Western Frontier: Acceptable Occupation for Nineteenth Century Women," *Montana: The Magazine of Western History*, 37 (3), pp. 54–63.

Stuntz, J. A. (2008) "West Texas Women in Ranching: Myth and Reality," *West Texas Historical Association Yearbook*, 84, pp. 49–57.

Taniguchi, N. J. (2000) "Weaving a Different World: Women and the California Gold Rush," *California History*, 79 (2), pp. 141–68.

Underwood, J. O. (1985) "Western Women and True Womanhood: Culture and Symbol in History and Literature," *Great Plains Quarterly*, 5 (2), pp. 93–106.

Voeller, C. R. (2006) "'I Have Not Told Half We Suffered': Overland Trail Women's Narratives and the Genre of Suppressed Textual Mourning," *Legacy*, 23 (2), pp. 148–62.

Watson, J. H. (1995) "'Cult of Domesticity' Versus 'Real Womanhood' on the Overland Trails," *Californians*, 12 (2), pp. 25–33.

Wilson, K. (2006) "Substance Versus Superficiality: Women's Prescribed Roles in Early Territorial Utah, 1850–70," *Journal of Mormon History*, 32 (2), pp. 139–72.

NOTE

1. The filmography and bibliographies detailed here are dedicated to the memory of my cat, Lamentations, who passed away before the completion of this project. He was a faithful viewer of many of the Westerns listed in the filmography and closely supervised me as I compiled the bibliographies.

CONTRIBUTORS

David Blanke is the Paul and Mary Haas Professor of History at Texas A&M University-Corpus Christi. He teaches undergraduate and graduate courses in US history, the Gilded Age and Progressive Era, and US Modern Popular Culture. Dr Blanke has published five scholarly books, dozens of articles and reviews, and has been featured on programs aired on the History Channel, the BBC, and C-SPAN. His research examines the role of culture in modern American life, including consumerism, automobiles, and commercial film. His latest study examines the noted film careers of Cecil B. DeMille and John Ford.

Maria Cecília de Miranda Nogueira Coelho is Associate Professor of Philosophy at the Universidade Federal de Minas Gerais, Brazil. She spent a year as a Visiting Researcher at Brown University (as part of her PhD in Classics at the Universidade de São Paulo on Euripides' Helen), has a master's in Philosophy and degrees in Philosophy and Mathematics. She was a Visiting Professor at King's College, Universidad de Cádiz and Poznań University, and is former president of Sociedade Brasileira de Retórica and Associação Lationo-Americana de Retórica. She has published papers on Greek Tragedy, Gorgias, Plato and Classics in Cinema, and is the editor of *Retórica, Persuasão e Emoções* (2018). She also co-edited *Cinema: Lanterna Mágica da História e da Mitologia* (2009), *Ensaios sobre Literatura, Teatro e Cinema* (2013), and *Retórica e Análise do Discurso em diálogo* (forthcoming 2020).

CONTRIBUTORS

Stella Hockenhull is an Honorary Research Fellow at the University of Wolverhampton. She has built up a strong research profile in British cinema and has published extensively in this area, producing a large body of work which includes three monographs and a number of articles. Her interest in British cinema extends to women in the British film industry, in particular the role of women, the division of labor, and the gender politics within contemporary British cinema. She has also published widely on the Western genre although, more recently, her research has branched out into the field of animals in film. She currently supervises five PhD students, is editing a Tim Burton volume, and co-writing a book on animal stardom.

Martin Holtz taught American literature and film until recently at Greifswald University. His dissertation *American Cinema in Transition: The Western in New Hollywood and Hollywood Now* was published in 2011. His most recent book *Constructions of Agency in American Literature on the War of Independence: War as Action 1775–1860* was published in 2019.

David Huxley is the editor of the *Journal of Graphic Novels and Comics* (Routledge). He was a senior lecturer at Manchester Metropolitan University until 2017. He has written widely on comics, including works on various artists, underground and horror comics, superheroes, and also popular film. He has also drawn and written for a range of British comics. His most recent publication is *Lone Heroes and the Myth of the American West in Comic Books 1945–1962* (Palgrave Macmillan, 2018).

J Paul Johnson is Professor of English and Film Studies and former chairperson of the Department of Mass Communication at Winona State University in Minnesota. He currently teaches a range of Film Studies courses in genre, theory, curation, and adaptation, and his current conference presentations and publications focus on the intersections of these with intertextuality and audience response in films like *Logan*, *American Sniper* and *The Quick and the Dead*. His article on the adaptation of *Blue Is the Warmest Color* appeared in the Winter 2018 issue of *Literature/Film Quarterly*.

Camille McCutcheon holds the rank of Librarian and serves as the Assistant Dean and Coordinator of Collection Management at the University of South Carolina Upstate Library. She earned her BA from Columbia College (Columbia, SC) and a Joint Master's Degree in English and Library and Information Science from the University of South Carolina. She has published articles in *CHOICE: Current Reviews for Academic Libraries*, *Against the Grain*, and *Research Strategies*, and is the author of two chapters for the annual reference book *Magazines* *for Libraries*. Her research interests include children's and adolescent literature, film history, and film star biographies.

Kelly MacPhail teaches English, Philosophy, and Religious Studies as an Assistant Professor at the University of Minnesota Duluth. His interdisciplinary research focuses on Transatlantic literary modernism, environmental criticism, and belief studies. He has published on subjects as diverse as modernist poetry, Puritan sermons, *film noir*, animal domestication, nautical fiction, and the Western.

Sue Matheson is Chair of English at the University College of the North in Manitoba, Canada. Her interests in film, culture, and literature may be found in more than sixty articles published in a wide range of books and scholarly journals. The Western is one of her specializations. She is the editor of *Love in Western Film and Television: Happy Hearts and Lonely Trails* (Palgrave 2013) and the author of *The Westerns and War Films of John Ford* (Rowman & Littlefield 2016).

Cynthia J. Miller is a cultural anthropologist specializing in visual media. She teaches in the Institute for Liberal Arts at Emerson College, and is the editor or co-editor of seventeen scholarly volumes, including *International Westerns: Relocating the Frontier* (2013) and the forthcoming *Dark Forces at Work: Essays on Social Dynamics and Cinematic Horrors* (2019). Cynthia is the recipient of the Peter C. Rollins prize for a book-length work in popular culture, and the James Welsh prize for lifetime achievement in adaptation studies. She serves on the editorial board of the *Journal of Popular Television*, and also edits the Film and History book series for the Rowman & Littlefield publishing group.

Christopher Minz has an MA in Cinema Studies from New York University and is currently a PhD Candidate at Georgia State University. His research focuses are genre (especially the Western and James Bond films), formal aesthetics, masculinity studies, and psychoanalysis in relation to geopolitics. He has presented papers at SCMS, Film & History, and the International Melodrama Conference on topics ranging from Melodrama and Horror in *The Shining*, Calm and Chaos in *The Thin Red Line*, and traumatic ellipses in Budd Boetticher's Westerns. His published works focus mostly on the American Western. He has taught a range of courses at Georgia State University, among them courses on Eastern European Cinema, Film Aesthetics, and a survey of the American Western.

Erin Lee Mock is Associate Professor and Director of the Program in Film Studies at the University of West Georgia. Her articles have appeared in *Camera*

Obscura, Quarterly Review of Film and Video, Journal of Popular Culture, Film and History, Love in Western Film and Television, and elsewhere. Her current manuscript considers the role of popular culture in facilitating the reintegration of veterans in the post-World War II United States.

Andrew Patrick Nelson is Chair of the Department of Film and Media Arts at the University of Utah. He is author of *Still in the Saddle: The Hollywood Western, 1969–1980* and co-editor of *The Films of Delmer Daves*.

Frances Pheasant-Kelly is MA Film and Screen Course Leader and Reader in Screen Studies at the University of Wolverhampton, UK. Her research centres on American film, including fantasy and science fiction, terrorism and post-9/11 cinema, space, science, and abjection. She is the author of numerous publications including two monographs, *Abject Spaces in American Cinema: Institutions, Identity and Psychoanalysis in Film* (I. B. Tauris 2013) and *Fantasy Film Post 9/11* (Palgrave 2013), and the co-editor of *Spaces of the Cinematic Home: Behind the Screen Door* (Routledge 2015). She is currently working on a third monograph entitled *The Bodily Turn in Film and Television* and a co-edited collection (with Stella Hockenhull) titled *Tim Burton's Bodies*.

Vincent Piturro is Associate Professor of Film and Media Studies at Metropolitan State University of Denver and holds a PhD in Comparative Literature. His areas of study include Westerns, science fiction, documentaries, Italian cinema, vampire films, and international cinema. Publications include a book chapter on *The Ballad of Little Jo* in the edited collection *Love in Western Film and Television*, an international journal article on documentary film rhetoric, a book chapter on gays in Westerns in the edited volume *The New Western*, and a book chapter on Jim Jarmusch's *Only Lovers Left Alive*.

Robert Spindler is a postdoctoral researcher and lecturer at the Department of American Studies at the University of Innsbruck, and is currently involved in the research project SLAVES, funded by the Austrian Federal Ministry of Education, Science and Research (BMBWF). His main research interests are medievalism, Barbary captivity narratives, and the Western film. He is currently completing a monograph on Barbary captivity narratives in early modern Germany. His recent publications include the articles "An Early Schelmenroman: The Picaresque Elements in the German Barbary Captivity Narrative *Verzeichnis der Reise* (1558) by Balthasar Sturmer" (*Germanisch-Romanische Monatsschrift* 69.1) and "Benevolent Masters, Despicable *Renegados*: Relativizing Portrayals of Muslims in British Barbary Captivity Narratives, 1595–1739" (forthcoming in *Anglistik: International Journal of English Studies*).

Gaylyn Studlar is David May Distinguished University Professor in the Humanities at Washington University in St Louis, where she has directed the Program in Film & Media Studies for the last decade. She has published widely on issues of gender and sexuality in American film. Her publications on the Western include *Have Gun Will Travel* (2015, Wayne State University Press), and the co-edited volume, *John Ford Made Westerns: Filming the Legend in the Sound Era* (2001, Indiana University Press). Recently, she provided commentary for the Kino-Lorber Blu-ray release of *Duel in the Sun*.

Martin M. Winkler is University Professor and Professor of Classics at George Mason University. His books on antiquity and cinema are *The Roman Salute: Cinema, History, Ideology* (2009), *Cinema and Classical Texts: Apollo's New Light* (2009), *Classical Literature on Screen: Affinities of Imagination* (2017), and *Ovid on Screen: A Montage of Attractions* (2019). He has also edited seven essay collections on the subject. He is the author of over a hundred articles, book chapters, reviews, etc., including a fistful on Westerns.

Paul Zinder is Senior Lecturer in Film Production at the University of Gloucestershire. He is co-editor of the collection *The Multiple Worlds of* Fringe: *Essays on the J. J. Abrams Science Fiction Series* (2014), and his writing on genre and cult television appears in the volumes Justified *and Philosophy* (2015), *Contemporary Westerns: Film and Television since 1990* (2013), *The Last Western:* Deadwood *and the End of American Empire* (2012), *Investigating* Veronica Mars: *Essays on the Teen Detective Series* (2011), and *Investigating* Alias: *Secrets and Spies* (2007). He is also an award-winning filmmaker whose work can be seen at <www.paulzinder.com>.

INDEX

3:10 to Yuma (2007), 161, 233
9/11, 122, 125, 126, 134, 162, 168, 169, 223, 224, 225, 226, 227, 228, 229, 231, 235, 237, 239n, 283n
40-Horse Hawkins, 19

A Fistful of Dollars, 182, 183n, 204
A Girl of the West, 8
A Man Called Horse, 160, 163, 168
A Romance of the Redwoods, 46, 47, 49, 56, 57
A Ticket to Tomahawk, 6
Abbie Irving, 38–9
abduction, 127, 129, 131, 141, 145, 152, 154, 155n
adult Western, 77, 84
Aegisthus, 101n, 102n
Aeschylus, 96, 97, 98, 100, 101n, 102n
Agamemnon, 91, 94, 98, 101n
Agamemnon, 96, 101n
agency 15, 21, 38, 50, 52, 53, 55, 57, 111, 127, 181, 182, 183, 238n, 244, 245, 251, 252n, 288
"Alive Day," 252n
Altman, Robert, 201
angel, 22, 31, 34, 182
Annie Get Your Gun, 156n
Annie Oakley, 276
anti-hero, 243, 252n
Antigone, 196
Apocalypse Now, 166

Appaloosa, 161
Arizona, 78
Arthur, Jean, 52, 53, 260
Assassination of Jesse James by the Coward Robert Ford, The, 161
assimilation, 50, 53, 141, 142, 150, 176, 248
Audition, 182
avenger, 91, 168, 188, 194, 207, 212, 224, 225, 229, 230, 232, 233, 234, 237–8

baby, 34, 39, 51, 55, 68, 98, 102n, 147, 148, 150, 154, 179, 192, 195
Baby Face, 95
Bad Girls, 289
Badman's Territory, 214n
Ball of Fire, 95
Ballad of Little Joe, The, 69, 125, 183, 188, 194, 195, 196, 260, 276, 283n, 289
bandidas, 231, 232, 233
Bandidas, 225, 229–33, 237, 238n, 239n
bandit, 17, 29, 107, 202, 203, 230, 231; see also outlaw
Bargain, The, 29
Beautiful Blonde from Bashful Bend, The, 6
Belle Starr, 18, 124, 201, 202–4, 207–12, 214n
"Belle Starr," 202, 214n
Belle Starr, 78, 197n, 204
Belle Starr Story, The, 39, 197n, 202, 204, 205, 206, 207–13

341

Big Country, The, 76, 95
Big Trail, The, 31, 261
Big Valley, The, 85n
Black Market Rustlers, 6
Bless the Beasts and Children, 258
"Bloody Harlan," 248, 252n, 253n
Boetticher, Budd, 61, 110, 111, 112, 118n
Borges, J. L., 195, 197–8
Bravados, The, 5, 188, 190, 192, 196
Brimstone, 288
Brokeback Mountain, 161, 183
Broken Arrow, 126, 160, 168
Broken Trail, 5, 174, 177–80, 181
Bronco Billy's Narrow Escape, 18
brother, 29, 46, 48, 81, 83, 91, 93, 97, 98, 142, 148, 149, 150, 151, 167, 190, 193, 195, 198, 208, 250, 271, 272, 276, 278, 282
    brother-in-law, 95, 196
Buccaneer, The, 46
Bucking Broadway, 29, 31
Buffalo Bill, 52, 56, 62, 202, 205, 276
Buffalo Bill, Hero of the Far West, 205
Bullets Don't Argue/Pistols Don't Argue/Guns Don't Argue, 205
"Burned," 252n
butch, 20, 108, 113, 115, 116, 118n
butchness, 108, 112, 114

Calamity Jane, 18, 52, 55, 56, 124, 125, 129, 201, 203, 205
Calamity Jane, 39, 68, 156n, 276
Calamity Jane and Sam Bass, 68
California, 13, 16, 20, 178, 234, 260, 272
Call of the North, The, 46
Campaigning with Custer, 20
Captain Courtesy, 20
captivity, 142, 197n, 225
    narrative, 141, 207
"Cash Game," 253n
Cat Ballou, 39, 156n, 201, 215, 283n
Cattle Kate *see* Watson, Ella
Cattle Queen of Montana, The, 39
Celluloid Indian Maiden, 160, 167, 169n
Cemetery Without Crosses, 188, 194, 196
Charge at Feather River, The, 155n
Chato's Land, 207
Cheyenne Social Club, The, 6
Cimarron, 31, 64
civilization, 28, 36, 50, 67, 83, 121, 122, 162, 163, 164, 193, 227, 228, 233, 235, 237, 261, 280, 283, 289, 290
classic Western, 32, 92, 111, 121, 122, 124, 161, 164, 165, 167, 169, 177, 179, 180, 181, 182, 183, 201, 244, 247, 248, 249, 251, 253n, 260, 272, 294

Clytemnestra, 91, 94, 95, 96, 97, 98, 99, 100, 102n
Cockeyed Cowboys of Calico County, The, 6
Coen, 236, 258, 287, 304
Colorado, 16, 261
Comanche Station, 194
comedy, 21, 98, 144, 204, 213, 233, 259
community, 37, 142, 143, 148, 151, 154, 163, 164, 181, 189, 210, 224, 230 246, 264, 273
conduct, 27, 39, 233, 236, 237, 244
conformity, 50, 52, 53, 111, 112
conquest, 15, 146, 163, 195, 214n
contamination, 33, 142, 145, 146, 150
Corman, Roger, 108, 114
Costner, Kevin, 161, 170n, 224
courage, 12, 22, 193, 195, 272
Court-Martial, 201
Covered Wagon, The, 30, 39n
cowboy, 14, 18, 20, 27, 28, 29, 30, 62, 63, 78, 85n, 167, 179, 244, 246, 248, 250, 251, 252n, 253n, 272, 273, 275, 276, 277, 281, 282
    hero, 277
    rhetoric, 125
Crawford, Joan, 77, 112, 113, 118n, 124, 156n, 165, 260, 288
crime, 13, 49, 51, 65, 115, 161, 162, 167, 188, 196n, 203, 245, 246
Crime and Punishment, 73
Cruze, James, 30, 40n
Cuddy, Mary Bee, 258, 259–62, 263, 264, 265–7
Curtiz, Michael, 31, 37, 39, 40n

Dabney, Lucy, 189
Dakota Lil, 68
Dallas, 32–3, 34, 35–6
Dances with Wolves, 161, 167, 170n, 289
Dangerous Nan McGrew, 20
daughter, 8n, 11, 14, 18, 22, 29, 34, 53, 76, 77, 80, 81, 91, 92, 94, 95, 96, 98, 99, 100, 127, 128, 146, 165, 167, 168, 169n, 178, 188, 194, 196n, 207, 225, 226, 227, 230, 248, 251, 252n, 253n, 293
Dead Man, 289
Decision at Sundown, 111, 112, 118n
deconstruction, 162, 225, 244
DeMille, Cecil, 8n, 31, 45–59, 59n, 64
Depression, 31, 47, 58
desire, 27, 36, 39, 72, 75, 76, 81, 82, 84, 85n, 99, 114, 117–18n, 124, 127, 147, 151, 162, 176, 190, 192, 208, 223, 260, 264, 283, 283n
    sexual, 151, 190
Destry Rides Again, 31, 36–7, 39, 40
Dietrich, Marlene, 36, 288

Dime novel, 13, 62, 188, 201, 203
display
  body, 130
  homoerotic, 118
  masculine, 27
  phallic, 109
  sexual, 80
Django Unchained, 233
Dodge City, 31, 37–9, 40n
domesticity, 50, 51, 52, 54, 61, 75, 84, 128, 224, 248, 260, 282
Dragon Seed, 175
Duel in the Sun, 76–84, 78, 92, 188, 190, 195
Dumb and Dumber To, 258

East, 15, 16, 17, 30, 39, 50, 51, 52, 53, 54, 55, 56, 58, 63, 64, 65, 92, 125, 178, 179, 195, 258, 261
Easterner, 14, 51
Eastwood, Clint, 193, 197, 259
El Dorado, 7
Electra, 91, 92, 94, 95, 97, 98, 99, 100, 101n, 102n, 103n
  complex, 92, 101n
  Western, 103n
Electra, 92, 95, 100, 102n
Electra (1962), 91, 99
epic, 30, 31, 37, 40n, 45, 76, 92, 95, 101n, 188, 191, 195, 196, 197n, 290
Euripides, 91, 95, 97, 98, 99, 101n, 102n
exceptionalism, 59, 121
expansion
  American, 66
  character, 11, 12
  gender, 17
  Western, 30, 58, 175, 179, 180, 183, 261, 295
expansionism, 30

Face to Face, 208
family, 8n, 28, 29, 34, 39, 51, 52, 68, 76, 77, 78, 82 83, 84, 85n, 87, 94, 96, 99, 126, 127, 128, 129, 142, 143, 144, 147, 148, 149, 150, 156n, 164, 180, 190, 197n, 203, 212, 225, 226, 227, 228, 229, 237, 243, 247, 248, 251, 271, 273, 283
  Asian, 180
  on the land, 28, 76, 77, 79, 82, 83, 84, 85n
  life, 39, 75
  oedipalized, 82
"Fate's Right Hand," 253n
femininity, 28, 39, 111, 114, 117, 122, 213, 214, 237, 276, 277, 282, 289
feminism, 7, 58, 85n, 125, 206, 214n, 224
  second-wave, 206, 214n
feminist Western, 127, 257, 260, 272, 287, 290, 291
femme fatale, 95, 115, 247, 251, 252n, 253n

Feudin', Fussin and A-Fightin, 6
Fleming, Victor, 64, 204
For a Few Dollars More, 188, 193, 196, 207, 208
"For Blood of Money," 253n
Ford, John, 20, 30, 31, 32, 35, 37, 53, 56, 83, 86n, 109, 110, 118n, 142, 143, 145, 146, 153, 154, 162, 170n, 189, 191, 196n, 197n, 212, 225, 287, 293, 294–5
Forgotten Pistolero, The, 96, 98–9
Fort Apache, 126
Forty Guns, 39, 73n, 82, 85n, 197n, 260, 288, 296n
freedom, 17, 36, 52, 54, 57, 58, 72, 77, 75, 130, 159, 161, 177, 208, 251, 252n, 277, 278, 281
  individual, 58
  sexual, 54
  social, 208
Frenchy, 36–7
frontier, 11, 12, 13, 14, 15, 16, 17, 19, 21, 22, 27, 36, 47, 49, 50, 52, 54, 55, 56, 57, 58, 75, 121, 122, 123, 124, 126, 127, 128, 134, 162, 163, 179, 223, 224, 227, 228, 248, 251, 259, 260, 261, 262, 264, 268, 287, 289
  justice, 52
  melodrama, 30
  rhetoric, 223
  society, 39
  thesis *see* Turner, Frederick Jackson
  town, 38, 49
"Fugitive Number One," 253n
Fuller, Sam, 85, 260
Furies, The, 39, 76, 82, 84, 85, 92–4, 96, 100, 102n, 103n, 156n

Gang of Roses, 7
Gangsters of the Frontier, 6
gender 12, 14, 17, 20, 27, 28, 32, 35, 38, 39, 46, 48, 50, 51, 52, 53, 56, 57, 58, 59, 78, 80, 84, 108, 110, 111, 112, 113, 114, 115, 116, 122, 125, 127, 131, 134, 142, 152, 159, 165, 166, 187, 205, 208, 212, 213, 224, 225, 229, 232, 234, 238, 244, 251, 268, 271, 283n, 244, 251, 259, 260, 268, 271, 279, 283n, 289, 294, 296n
  coding, 28, 38, 122
  cross-gender, 224
  expectations, 260
  gendered myth, 13
  ideals, 32
  politics, 127, 131, 134, 238
  relations, 39
  roles, 12, 14, 17, 27, 111, 113, 114, 116, 165, 205, 208, 213
  typing, 43

Geronimo: An American Legend, 289
Gilkeson, Magdalena, 127, 128–9, 130–1, 132–3, 134
girl, 13, 14, 17, 18, 19, 22, 34, 55, 56, 63, 65, 68, 78, 80, 98, 114, 123, 124, 127, 129, 130–2, 133, 134, 142, 144, 148, 152, 168, 178–9, 180, 181, 183, 188, 189, 192, 195, 204, 210, 225, 226, 227, 228, 234, 238, 262, 266, 303
   Asian, 177, 178–9, 180, 181
   bad girls, 17, 22, 124
   cowgirl, 17, 18, 20, 21, 78, 114
   saloon, 29, 31, 32, 36, 37, 108, 109, 110, 111, 112, 113, 114, 115, 118n
   working, 112
Girl from Montana, The, 14
Girl of the Golden West, The, 14, 46, 49
Go West Young Woman, 20
Godless, 272–83, 288, 290
Gone with the Wind, 79, 204
good-bad girl, 34, 39
Great Man's Lady, The, 78
gun, 13, 14, 17, 20, 38, 39, 51, 52, 65, 67, 69, 84, 109, 112, 113, 114, 115, 116, 126, 156n, 193, 210, 212, 236, 238, 267, 272, 273, 274, 275, 276, 288, 289, 290, 296
Gunless, 174, 180
gunslinger, 11, 55, 180, 182
Gunslinger, 108, 114–17, 118n

Hallelujah Trail, The, 6
Hang 'em High, 5, 188, 194, 196
Hannie Caulder, 39, 197, 118n
hate, 69, 83, 91, 94, 95, 153
Hateful Eight, The, 233
Hathaway, Henry, 7, 260, 304
Hawks, Howard, 39, 95, 118n, 293
Hazards of Helen The, 20
Helen of Troy, 198n
Hell Bent, 29
Heller in Pink Tights, 6
hero, 14, 19, 22, 28, 29, 39, 45, 53, 57, 58, 62, 67, 72, 76, 77, 78, 83, 95, 98, 107, 108, 109, 112, 116, 117, 121–2, 124, 125, 134, 142, 143, 149, 150, 152, 163, 164, 165, 170n, 192, 194, 197n, 202, , 208, 224, 227, 231, 236, 238n, 245, 253n, 272, 273, 276, 277, 278, 279, 281, 288
   female, 15, 289
   Greek, 91, 187
heroine, 13, 14, 15, 18, 19, 28, 30, 31, 32, 34, 36, 37, 38, 39, 61, 62, 68, 69, 77, 78, 80, 84, 95, 111, 116, 163, 201, 205, 211, 224, 225, 229, 232, 237, 283, 294
   action, 224
   Stanwyck's, 124
   strength and agency, 288

heroism, 11, 28, 39, 125, 164, 193, 213, 289
High Noon, 56, 59, 260
His Hour of Manhood, 28
Holmes, Helen, 11, 12, 19, 20
home, 15, 18, 28, 29, 30, 31, 33, 34, 38, 39, 49, 50, 52, 54, 55, 57, 61, 76, 83, 84, 92, 125, 130, 142, 143, 146, 193, 194, 195, 214n, 225, 229, 234, 245, 260, 267, 268, 279, 283
   home-front, 78, 224
   homestead, 16, 17, 57, 125, 130, 131, 152, 210, 211, 225, 230, 231, 236, 259, 261, 264, 273, 274, 279
   soil, 125
Homesman, The, 233, 257–68, 287
homoeroticism, 116, 118n
honor, 188, 190, 192, 193, 194, 202, 209
House of Atreus, 101n
Huston, John, 142

"I of the Storm, The," 252n
I Spit on Your Grave, 206
I Walk Alone, 101n
I Want Him Dead, 208
Ichi the Killer, 182
icon, 114, 224
iconography, 116, 161, 162, 244, 259, 272, 282
ideal, 16, 31, 32, 46, 54, 56, 59, 82, 83, 174, 206, 213, 231, 252n, 281
   feminine, 29
   feminist, 38
   New Woman, 27
identity, 11, 13, 15, 27, 28, 30, 49, 50, 83, 96, 110, 113, 114, 115, 117–18n, 124, 142, 147–9, 150, 153–4, 160, 205, 279
Idiot, The, 94
I'll Be Seeing You, 82
Imitation of Life, 84
incest, 150, 151, 203
Indian, 8n, 17, 48, 49, 52, 53, 54, 56, 59, 65, 80, 81, 122, 124, 126, 129, 130, 131, 133, 144, 147, 148, 151, 152, 154, 155, 156n, 159, 160, 161, 162–3, 166, 167, 168, 169, 170n, 177, 193, 197n, 203, 206, 207, 208, 214n, 225, 226, 227, 228, 229, 238n, 262, 274, 289, 290, 291, 293, 296
   American Indian Movement, 15
   Indianness, 150
   reservation, 81, 161, 162, 163, 166, 177
   Territory, 34
   uprising, 49
   see also Native American
individualism, 52, 54, 272
innocence, 80, 224, 234, 235, 236
insanity, 262, 266

Iron Horse, The, 30, 31, 53, 109, 110, 112, 117
Iron Trail, The, 20

Jane Got a Gun, 126, 238n, 283n
Jeffords, Vance, 84, 85, 92, 93, 94, 95, 101n
Jeremiah Johnson, 160, 163, 168
Jesse James, 31
Johnny Guitar, 39, 61, 100, 108, 112, 113, 114, 115, 116, 117, 124, 156n, 165, 260, 288, 296n
Jones, Buck, 18
Jones, Del, 18
Jones, Jennifer, 76, 79, 81, 190
Jones, Tommy Lee, 126, 127, 257, 258, 259, 264, 266, 267
Jorgenson, Debbie, 85–6n, 142, 143, 144, 145, 146–7, 148, 149, 150, 151, 154, 155n, 156n, 190, 191, 229
Jorgenson, Lucy, 146, 147, 156n, 191
Jorgenson, Mrs, 293
journey, 15, 16, 33, 34, 50, 68, 179, 180, 257, 258, 259, 260, 261, 262, 264, 266, 268, 291
justice, 19, 31, 49, 52, 56, 63, 143, 148, 231, 233, 234, 235, 237, 245, 249

Kane, Amy Fowler, 260
Kansas, 30, 153, 155n, 261
Keeping Room, The, 287
Kennedy, Burt, 118n
King and Four Queens, The, 6
King Lear, 94

Lady Eve, The, 95
land, 16, 17, 28, 63, 76, 77, 80, 102n, 112, 115, 167, 177, 180, 187, 196, 230, 243, 246, 247, 252n, 259, 280, 281, 282, 288
rush, 80
Laskey, Jr., Jesse L., 40n
Last House on the Left, 206, 214n
Last of the Mohicans, The, 155n
law, 29, 33, 38, 63, 65, 67, 69, 116, 164, 174, 178, 203, 207, 223, 226, 227, 230, 234, 235, 236, 238, 245, 246, 248, 273, 295
lawbreaking, 72
lawyer, 38, 80, 81
lawkeeping, 64
miscegenation, 176
Leone, Sergio, 183n, 211
Libation Bearers, The, 97, 100, 101n, 102
liberty, 16, 231, 273, 277, 280, 281
Little Big Man, 155n, 163, 295
Lizards, The, 213
Lone Hand, The, 19
Lone Ranger, 258

love, 13, 28, 29, 30, 37, 48, 49, 51, 52, 53, 62, 68, 77, 78, 79, 80, 81, 92, 94, 95, 97, 109, 124, 143, 147, 165, 168, 176, 194, 195, 197n, 202, 208, 210, 211, 212, 248, 250, 264, 276
interest, 49, 52, 61, 62, 63, 73n, 82, 165, 168, 202, 231, 273
lover, 13, 14, 29, 36, 37, 52, 79, 80, 95, 96, 97, 99, 111, 116, 190, 208, 225, 226, 247, 250, 271, 279, 282
melodramatic, 30
romantic, 28, 149
triangle, 30, 53, 92, 282
Love Letters, 78
Lust in the Dust, 6
lynching, 18, 51, 63, 154, 214n
death-by-lynching, 264

McCabe and Mrs Miller, 174, 177, 181, 201
madness, 97, 261, 262, 263, 267
Mallory, Lucy, 33–5
Man from Laramie, The, 103n
Man of the West, 191, 195
Man Who Loved Cat Dancing , The, 207
manliness, 28, 39, 131, 272, 273, 277
Mann, Anthony, 27, 92, 94, 99, 100, 102n, 156n, 192, 294
marriage, 18, 28, 29, 30, 34, 37, 39, 45, 76, 79, 97, 102n, 143, 144, 150, 151, 165, 169n, 182, 248, 249, 261
interracial, 159, 168
proposal of, 193, 261, 247, 264, 266
Marshall, George, 19, 31, 36, 40n
masculinity, 27, 108–9, 110–17, 117n, 118n, 121, 122, 127, 166, 207, 238, 259, 273, 274, 275, 277, 278, 281, 293
Maté, Rudolph, 95
matriarch, 66, 76, 181, 243, 246
matrimony, 39, 77
Maverick, 6, 214
Maverick Queen, The, 39, 288
Meek's Cutoff, 126, 161, 287–96
melodrama, 13, 17, 21, 27, 28, 30, 32, 33, 34, 35, 36, 37, 46, 47, 52, 57, 58, 76, 78, 79, 82, 83, 84
Metamorphoses, 98, 188, 196n
Mexico, 36, 80, 98, 227, 230, 231, 232, 233, 238–9n, 293
Middle East, 223, 230, 231, 238n
migration, 16, 291
Mildred Pierce, 112
Millay, Tess, 39
miscegenation, 124, 132, 142, 146, 150, 151, 153, 154, 156n
laws, 176
Missing, The, 122, 126, 127–34, 155n, 162, 225, 229, 237

345

INDEX

Monaghan, Josephine 183, 195, 197
Montana, 178, 261
Montana Belle, 204
"Moonshine War, The," 252n
morality, 45, 109, 118n, 233, 237
Morocco, 40n
mother, 28, 34, 50, 52, 62, 72, 77, 79, 80, 83, 91, 94, 95, 96, 97, 98, 99, 100, 123, 124, 130, 133, 146, 147, 154, 156n, 167, 179, 181, 182, 191, 203, 212, 214n, 224, 226, 229, 243, 245, 247, 250, 251, 260, 262, 263, 278, 282
    grandmother, 66, 191, 247, 278
    mother's bedroom, 84, 93
    mother-in-law, 167, 274
    motherhood, 226, 247, 249, 251, 262
    surrogate, 246, 247, 251, 252n
Mrs Miniver, 78
Ms .45, 206
My Darling Clementine, 212, 224, 248

Native American, 48, 49, 51, 52, 53, 56, 122, 123, 126, 128, 129, 130, 131, 132, 134, 141, 143, 145, 147, 150, 151, 153, 154, 155, 156n, 159, 160, 161, 163, 164, 165, 166, 167, 168, 169, 170n, 177, 178, 189, 191, 207, 214n, 226, 244, 271, 277; *see also* Indian
Nebraska, 259, 261, 265, 267
neo-Western, 160, 161, 162, 168
New Mexico, 127, 265
New Woman, 15, 27, 38, 40n, 47
    journalist, 32, 38, 39
    postmistress, 53, 55
No Country for Old Men, 233, 236, 259
noir, 13, 77, 92, 93, 95, 101n, 115, 244, 245, 247, 249, 251, 252n, 253n
North West Mounted Police, 46
Northwest Passage, 155n
Now, Voyager, 78
Nscho-Tschi, 169–70n

Oakley, Annie, 13, 18, 62, 67, 124, 201
oedipal complex, 80, 86n, 124, 239n, 290
Oedipus Western, 103n
Oklahoma, 19, 64, 145
Oklahoma Annie, 6
Old Wives for New, 48
Once Upon a Time in the West, 208, 214n, 244, 260
Open Range, 224, 283n
Orestes, 91, 96, 97, 98, 100, 101n, 102n
Oriental, 125
Other, 45, 49, 112, 160, 231, 238n
    Othered, 152
    Otherness, 176
    social Othering, 32

outlaw, 13, 22, 30, 49, 51, 65, 69, 107, 113, 121, 124, 162, 163, 164, 169, 190, 192, 193, 201, 203, 246, 253n, 271, 272
    gang, 67, 191, 272
    see also bandit
"Outlaw," 253n
Outlaw, The, 9

Pale Face, The, 6
Panic Room, 224
Parker, Cynthia Ann, 8n, 141, 155n
parody, 98, 113, 182
pathos, 28, 29, 32, 34, 35, 37, 39, 51, 162, 166, 224
patriarchy, 37, 48, 76, 238
Pearl Harbor, 238
Peckinpah, Sam, 197n, 283n
Penn, Arthur, 295
"Perilous Passage," 214
phallic symbol, 113, 272, 273, 274
phallus, 108, 109, 112, 113, 114, 116, 117, 117–18n, 118n
Philomela, 188, 196
pioneer, 15, 16, 17, 30, 66, 75, 123, 124, 258, 259, 260, 262, 263, 266, 267, 268, 290, 291, 295
Plainsman, The, 52, 53–5, 56
Pocahontas, 141, 156n, 169n
Posse, 161, 289
Posse from Hell, 197n
Postman Always Rings Twice, The, 101n
power, 22, 29, 35, 38, 55, 59, 69, 72, 76, 78, 124, 128, 130, 142, 146, 150, 181, 187, 196n, 198n, 215n, 230, 232, 235, 236, 244, 245, 247, 249, 250, 252n, 260, 273, 277, 279
    girl power, 238
    Red Power Movement, 214
    seductive powers, 110
Procne, 196
Professionals, The, 7
progress, 45, 53, 261, 267, 290, 295, 296
"Promise, The," 253
property, 16, 76, 131, 187, 192, 196n, 274, 288
Proposition, The, 170, 233
Prospectors: A Romance of the Gold Fields, The, 14
prostitute, 31, 32, 33, 34, 109, 111, 112, 115, 123, 176, 177, 179, 182, 276, 279
    madam, 22, 115, 178, 176, 179
    soiled dove, 11, 22, 31, 37, 124
    whore, 32, 110, 124, 173, 181, 182, 195, 238, 249, 271
psychological Western, 201, 153
purity, 132, 142, 150, 156n
    sexual, 33, 35
Pursued, 76, 83, 84, 92

346

quest, 58, 111, 124, 226, 227, 236, 253n, 260
Quick and the Dead, The, 116, 161, 289

racism, 143, 144, 145, 147, 153, 154, 174, 175, 180, 190, 191, 225, 227
Raiders of Sunset Pass, 6
Ramrod, 73n, 76, 77
Ranch Girls on a Rampage, 20
Rancho Notorious, 36, 288
Rango, 7
rape, 118n, 122, 125, 131, 132, 146, 151, 152, 156n, 182, 187, 188–9, 190, 191–2, 193, 194, 195–6, 197n, 198n, 202, 205, 206, 207, 208, 211, 212, 214n, 215n, 224, 263, 271, 280
   revenge, 195, 196, 202, 206, 207, 211, 212
Rawhide, 73n
Ray, Nicholas, 61, 84, 108, 112, 156n, 260
Rebel without a Cause, 4
Red River, 39, 101n, 118n, 261
Reel Injun, 170n
Reichardt, Kelly, 287, 291, 292, 293, 294, 295, 296n
repression, 32, 50, 83
revision/ism, 11, 32, 107, 116, 122, 124, 126, 160, 161, 162, 163, 165, 168, 169, 183, 201, 224, 244, 249, 251, 257, 258, 260, 293, 295
Riddle Rider, The, 12, 19
Ride the High Country, 197n
Rider, The, 161
romantic, 11, 18, 20, 28, 29, 30, 31, 34, 36, 37, 38, 52, 78, 115, 116, 149, 150, 151, 165, 193, 210, 211, 212, 259, 266, 283
Roosevelt, Franklin D., 164
Roosevelt, Theodore, 62
Rose of Cimarron, 61, 67–8, 72
Rose of the Rancho, The, 46
Ross, Mattie, 28, 127, 234–5, 236, 237, 239n
Rowdy Ann, 12, 20
Rowlandson, Mary, 141
Russell, Jane, 204
Ruth of the Range, 20

Sacajawea, 170n
savagery, 28, 32, 121, 122, 163, 227
Sea of Grass, The, 76
Searchers, The, 56, 59, 83, 142–7, 148, 150, 153, 154, 155, 162, 170n, 188, 191, 193, 195, 197n, 225, 229, 244, 293, 294
Selznick, David O., 79, 80, 82, 84
Seraphim Falls, 161, 233
Sergeant Rutledge, 189–90, 196
serial, 12, 13, 15, 18, 19, 20, 31, 145, 243, 271, 272, 274, 278, 280, 282, 283
settlement, 225, 261, 268, 281, 295
sex slave, 179, 181, 183

sexism, 48, 58, 59, 251
sexuality, 30, 48, 82, 84, 114, 190, 197n, 215n, 249
Shane, 212, 224, 252n, 260
She Wore a Yellow Ribbon, 294
Sheridan, Phil, 155–6n
Sheridan, Taylor, 160
Shootist, The, 258
silence, 191, 194, 196n
   silenced, 191, 258, 263, 264, 265, 267, 268
silent Westerns, 9–22, 28, 40n, 67, 68, 124
Silverstein, Elliott, 160, 201
Since You Went Away, 78, 82
slapstick, 20, 153
Soldier Blue, 155n
Some Came Running, 84
Song of Bernadette, The, 79
Sophocles, 92, 97, 99, 100, 101n, 102n
"Sounding," 253n
South Dakota, 177, 261
Spaghetti Western, 101n, 182, 201, 202, 204–5, 206, 207, 208, 211, 212, 213, 214n
Spellbound, 82
Squaw Man, The, 46–8, 50, 51, 304
Stagecoach, 17, 31–6, 40n, 179, 261
Stalking Moon, The, 155n, 193, 194
Stanwyck, Barbara, 53, 55, 76, 77, 85, 85n, 92, 95, 96, 100, 124, 156n, 193, 197n, 260, 276, 288, 296n
stereotype, 34, 39, 62, 77, 112, 115, 123, 124, 125, 126, 143, 147, 148, 175, 176, 177, 183, 207, 224, 230, 244, 272, 283, 295
Stevens, George, 212
Straight Shooting, 29, 31
Straw Dogs, 197n
stuntwomen, 11–22
Sudden Impact, 197
suffering, 28, 29, 30, 31, 35, 39, 82, 151, 230, 237, 264
suffrage, 15, 21
suicide, 49, 52, 151, 167, 179, 193, 195, 208, 233, 247, 265, 266, 268
Sukiyaki Western Django, 174, 182
Sum of All Fears The, 238n
Sundown Valley, 6
Sunset Limited, The, 58
Support Your Local Sheriff, 6
Sweetwater, 237

terror, 17, 227
Texas, 8n, 17, 79, 80, 141, 142, 147, 155n, 232, 235
Texas, Adios, 98
They Died With Their Boots On, 6
They Live by Night, 101n
They Rode West, 155n
"Thick as Mud," 253n

This Time Let's Talk About Men, 213
Three Burials of Melquiades Estrada, The, 61, 258
Thunderball, 99
Titus, 188, 191
Titus Andronicus, 18
Toll of the Sea, The, 175
tomboyism, 114
tragedy, 95, 96, 97, 99, 100, 117, 100n, 190, 195, 196, 196n, 226
  Shakespearean, 188
Trail of the Lonesome Mine, 20
Trail of the Lonesome Pine, The, 46
Train Robbers, The, 7
"Trash and the Snake, The," 252n
trauma, 82, 86n, 115, 146, 147, 165, 191, 194, 202, 208, 210, 212
Trooper Hook, 155n, 193
True Grit (1969), 28
True Grit (2010), 28, 126, 127, 225, 233–7, 258, 283n, 287
Turner, Frederick Jackson, 162, 188
Two Rode Together, 197

Übermensch, 57
Unconquered, 46
Unforgiven, 181, 289
Unforgiven, The, 142, 144, 147–55, 155n
Union Pacific, 31, 40n, 46, 53, 54, 56, 78
Utah, 16, 189

vamp, 175, 252n
Vanishing Rider, The, 12
vice, 31, 32, 51, 56
victim, 22, 32, 36, 53, 56, 82, 122, 124, 125, 126, 127, 131, 134, 147, 160, 164, 165, 167, 189, 190, 196, 198n, 202, 205, 207, 208, 211, 212, 214n, 215n, 224, 228, 230, 236, 237, 239, 250, 261, 262, 268, 274, 280
Vienna, 112–13, 114, 115, 165
violence, 36, 37, 45, 51, 56, 58, 63, 66, 69, 76, 77, 78, 83, 84, 93, 94, 98, 102n, 109, 111, 116, 147, 153, 156n, 164, 179, 180, 187, 195, 197n, 202, 208, 210, 212, 213, 224, 225, 227, 233, 237, 238n, 249, 272, 273, 287, 288, 290
Violent Men, The, 76, 82, 95, 96, 98, 99
Virgin Spring, The, 214n
Virginian, The (1902), 62–3
Virginian, The (1903), 61–2
Virginian, The (1914), 64

Virginian, The (1929), 65–6
Virginian, The (1946), 66
Virginian, The (1965), 66–7
virtue, 28, 32, 99, 112
von Sternberg, Josef, 36, 37, 40n
vote, 16, 28, 291

Wagon Master, 287, 295
Walsh, Raoul, 31, 261
war
  range, 29, 77, 252n
  War on Terror, 169, 223, 229, 230, 237, 238n, 239n
  World War I, 15
  World War II, 47, 75, 76, 78, 84, 169, 174, 181, 195
Waterhole #3, 6
Watson, Ella, 17
Wayne, John, 28, 52, 83, 142, 143, 170n, 191, 229, 293
Wellman, William A., 262, 294, 296n
Wertmüller, Lena, 202, 208, 209, 211, 212, 213, 215n
westering, 54, 122, 123, 124, 127, 133, 134, 187
Westerner, The, 101n
Westward the Women, 101n, 125, 126, 260, 262, 296n
Westworld, 59
What Happened to Mary, 12
wife, 29, 31, 32, 33, 34, 36, 37, 39, 48, 49, 57, 63, 81, 83, 85n, 91, 95, 96, 97, 98, 99, 111, 116, 123, 124, 128, 146, 147, 154, 156n, 165, 167, 181, 190, 191, 192, 193, 194, 195, 205, 207, 210, 214n, 262, 263, 267, 293
Wild and Western, 20
Wild Horse Rustlers, 6
wilderness, 28, 54, 57, 142, 164, 180, 233, 235, 236, 261, 276, 277, 282, 283, 289
Wind River, 159–69, 170n
Wister, Owen, 46, 49, 61, 62, 63, 64, 224
Woman Walks Ahead, 161
World of Suzie Wong, The, 176
Wyler, William, 95
Wyoming, 16, 63, 67, 161, 163, 166, 178, 179, 180, 183, 261

Yellow Sky, 294
Yojimbo 174, 181, 182, 183

Zero Dark Thirty, 238n

EU representative:
Easy Access System Europe
Mustamäe tee 50, 10621 Tallinn, Estonia
Gpsr.requests@easproject.com